Hoosier Spies
and Horse Marines

Hoosier Spies and Horse Marines

A History of the Third Indiana Cavalry, East Wing

James A. Goecker

McFarland & Company, Inc., Publishers
Jefferson, North Carolina

Maps by Edward Alexander.

LIBRARY OF CONGRESS CATALOGUING-IN-PUBLICATION DATA

Names: Goecker, James A., author.
Title: Hoosier spies and horse marines : a history of the Third Indiana Cavalry, East Wing / James A. Goecker.
Other titles: History of the Third Indiana Cavalry, East Wing
Description: Jefferson, North Carolina : McFarland & Company, Inc., Publishers, 2023 | Includes bibliographical references and index.
Identifiers: LCCN 2023032581 | ISBN 9781476692586 (paperback : acid free paper) ∞
ISBN 9781476650432 (ebook)
Subjects: LCSH: United States. Army. Indiana Cavalry Regiment, 3rd (1861–1865) | United States—History—Civil War, 1861–1865—Regimental histories—Indiana. | United States—History—Civil War, 1861–1865—Campaigns.
Classification: LCC E506.6 3d .G64 2023 | DDC 973.7/472—dc23/eng/20230725
LC record available at https://lccn.loc.gov/2023032581

BRITISH LIBRARY CATALOGUING DATA ARE AVAILABLE

ISBN (print) 978-1-4766-9258-6
ISBN (ebook) 978-1-4766-5043-2

© 2023 James A. Goecker. All rights reserved

No part of this book may be reproduced or transmitted in any form or by any means, electronic or mechanical, including photocopying or recording, or by any information storage and retrieval system, without permission in writing from the publisher.

Front cover image: Often identified as being taken in Petersburg in November 1864, this group photograph of the Re-Organized 3rd Indiana Cavalry is more likely to have been taken earlier (Library of Congress)

Printed in the United States of America

*McFarland & Company, Inc., Publishers
Box 611, Jefferson, North Carolina 28640
www.mcfarlandpub.com*

To the memory of my grandmother, Alma Thoele, who, through her countless family stories, gifted me the love of history.

And to my best friend who spent innumerable hours listening, editing, traveling, encouraging, and generally putting up with me. Without you, this book would never have been written.

To my wife Deb, I love you and thank you.

Acknowledgments

When research and writing are spread over 22 years and into retirement, some of the early memories of the quest can fade. There were many people who assisted and encouraged me along the way and I know I will leave out some of those worthy of inclusion. To them, I sincerely apologize.

There are, however, many whom I do remember and know. To the following, a huge thank you for the book would surely not have been written without their help and support. My thanks go to Edward Alexander, whose maps bring alive the long journey of the East Wing; Amy Harshbarger, reference librarian at Rose-Hulman Institute of Technology who patiently worked with me with my many interlibrary loan requests; Olga Tsapina who provided extensive research assistance in the Joseph Hooker Papers at Huntington Library; Bryce Suderow for his research expertise in the National Archives; Michael Winey at the United States Army Military History Institute for his assistance in reviewing the photographic collection of the Institute; Erin Foley of the Circus World Museum who shared postwar information about the fascinating life of George Middleton; Gary Powell for his discovery of John Irby in the Bureau of Military Information; Virginia Matthews for sharing James Matthews' diary; Eloise Chestnut for sharing her unpublished book of William Patton's Civil War service; Dan Goris who allowed me access to Thomas Day's letters; the research staffs of the Indiana State Library, Indiana Historical Society, National Archives, Library of Congress, Hanover College Archives, Jefferson County Historical Society, Virginia Military Institute, and Virginia Historical Society who all provided valuable and needed support for this effort. Finally, Eric Wittenberg, a Civil War cavalry historian extraordinaire whose arc of contact with this book spans 20 years, thank you.

Table of Contents

Acknowledgments	vi
Preface	1
Prelude to War	3
1. April 1861–October 14, 1861	5
2. October 15, 1861–May 25, 1862	13
3. May 26, 1862–August 8, 1862	25
4. August 13, 1862–September 13, 1862	33
5. September 14, 1862–April 30, 1863	44
6. May 1, 1863–May 25, 1863	58
7. May 26, 1863–June 29, 1863	67
8. June 30, 1863–July 1, 1863	77
9. July 2, 1863–September 9, 1863	86
10. September 23, 1863–February 27, 1864	97
11. February 28, 1864–May 6, 1864	107
12. May 7, 1864–June 15, 1864	118
13. June 16, 1864–July 12, 1864	129
14. July 13, 1864–September 25, 1864	139
15. September 26, 1864–December 31, 1864	151
16. January 1, 1865–April 7, 1865	161
17. April 8, 1865–Postwar	175
Appendix: Casualty List for Gettysburg	187
Regimental Roster: Original and Re-Organized	189
Chapter Notes	261
Bibliography	275
Index	279

Preface

In late 2000, my wife was working diligently on her family tree. She had identified a great-great-great grandfather who would have been in his twenties during the 1860s. My lifelong interest in the Civil War made it easy to quickly volunteer my help to determine any Civil War service. Within days, I found him in Company G, Third Indiana Cavalry. As a descendant of Germans who did not participate in the war, I was thrilled to finally have a personal connection. As I began to explore the unit's war history, I became intrigued that the regiment was, in essence, two autonomous units connected by name only. The East Wing served with the Army of the Potomac in the eastern theater, and the West Wing served in the western theater. For a time there was even a third "wing" that remained in Indiana for 18 months before joining the West Wing in Tennessee. At some point in 2001, I cavalierly told my wife, "I'm going to write a regimental history of the Third Indiana Cavalry." Little did I know about the long journey ahead.

A few years later I undertook an executive role at my college and the time demands led to sporadic work on research and writing sandwiched between long periods of inactivity. The manuscript slowly evolved so that by 2012 the history of the East Wing was nearing completion.

In late 2012, ransomware infected my files—research, manuscript, rosters—and everything was lost. And there everything stood until 2018. While cleaning 25 years of old files on my work computer, I found a copy of the East Wing manuscript circa 2011. Energized, I dove back into the project, but realized that the book could only cover the East Wing. Hence, my wife's ancestor—the impetus of this book—has ironically been left out.

Approximately 750 men served in the Third Indiana Cavalry, East Wing. Their story has been poorly served by a 1906 history written by the former adjutant of the wing. The research time he spent reviewing the 128 volumes of the recently published Official Record of the Rebellion is impressive, but very little personal narrative—the "what"—was included.

Those who fought the Civil War were a literate generation. Letters home provide surprising insight to their beliefs, opinions, and world views. At the same time, formal education could be sporadic, creating inventive spelling and grammar decisions. All quotes in the book contain the original spelling, punctuation and sentence syntax of the original source. Only a few have been edited for clarity. In so doing, I hope the reader will gain a flavor of the times and a more intimate view of these men in a way a sanitized version would never be able to convey.

Certain period cavalry terms may also need some explanation. While the designation of companies as troops and privates as troopers was official terminology, the men and reports never used those words. Also, "orderly sergeants" were the senior non-commissioned officer in a company, akin to a first sergeant. The rank of orderly sergeant is used as the term in use at that time. "Squadrons" were unique to the cavalry and referred to a formation of two companies. Finally, while this is a history of the East Wing, I have referred to the wing as simply the 3rd Indiana Cavalry throughout the book, only designating the "wings" of the regiment when needed for clarity.

Many consider the East Wing to be among the elite cavalry units in the Army of the Potomac. I agree. What they accomplished as a demi-regiment was amazing. I let the reader to determine if I have done them justice.

Prelude to War

It was late April 1861 and General Winfield Scott was worried. Scott commanded the United States Army and saw rebellion sweeping across the Southern states. His 16,000-man army was scattered over the continent and he had few men near at hand to deal with the crisis. Scott had joined the army in 1808 and had been commanding general since 1841, but nothing had prepared him for the task he currently faced. At 75 years of age, overweight and afflicted with gout, the general faced the greatest challenge of his long career.

The president had called for 75,000 men to volunteer for three months, and many thousands more had responded throughout the North. Begrudgingly, Scott would have to rely upon volunteers for infantry. The performance of volunteers 13 years ago in Mexico had been spotty, at best. He did know one thing—there was no way volunteer cavalry could be raised, equipped, and trained in time to be of any use. No one expected the rebellion to last very long. Besides, the terrain of most of the expected field of operations was unsuited to the maneuvering of large bodies of mounted troops. Also, Scott knew firsthand how expensive cavalry was to raise and maintain.

He had fought hard in appropriation hearings over the past 20 years and knew by heart the cost of every single piece of horse equipment. Saddle: $18.18, curry comb and brush: $1.61—in fact, the total cost to simply equip a cavalryman with the tools of his trade was $28.08.[1] Then there was the cost of arming a man. New-fangled revolvers were nearly $15.00. Finally, there was the expense of the horses. In total, it would cost at least $500,000 to outfit one regiment of cavalry.

Conventional wisdom said that it took a minimum of one year and as many as three years to train men to be a proper cavalryman. No one expected the rebellion to last three months, let alone three years. Better to leave the army's needs for a mounted arm to the five regiments of dragoons and cavalry—about 4,000 troops—scattered across the continent.[2] Granted, the five regiments had suffered numerous resignations from Southern-born officers, but the bulk of the force was still in place. He just needed to get them to Washington.[3]

A few months later, the disaster at Bull Run changed everything. With only seven companies of U.S. cavalry in the capital, Union general Irwin McDowell had virtually no horsemen available to match the Confederate mounted troops. Tales of the fearful Rebel "Black Horse Troop" sabering panic-stricken Northern troops as they ran from the battlefield were rampant. Lincoln and the nation's leadership now realized that the war would be a long and difficult struggle and began to make plans for a grueling conflict. Scott with his disdainful attitude toward volunteers was on the way out. Replacing him would be 34-year-old, forward-thinking George McClellan. Men for every branch were now needed, including cavalry. The call went out to all of the Northern states—send men.

Chapter 1

April 1861–October 14, 1861

After the battle at Manassas, the plea for men was met by an overwhelming patriotic wave of volunteers. Thousands of men rallied into local encampments in hopes of formal enlistment. Across the state of Indiana, companies were being raised by enterprising men who clamored for Governor Oliver Hazard Morton to accept them into service. For the men of what would become the 3rd Indiana Cavalry, June 10, 1861, was a momentous day. General Order No. 1 was issued: "The regiment of cavalry authorized by special order no. 1, issued June 10th, 1861, for the organization of a regiment of cavalry in the counties bordering on the Ohio River, will be organized for the United States service for three years, unless sooner discharged, and that order is modified accordingly."[1]

For young men in these counties, a grand adventure beckoned. They would be the first Hoosier horsemen, the first of an eventual 13 regiments of cavalry raised from Indiana.[2]

All across the southern rim of the state, men flocked to recruiting meetings. In Vevay, down in Switzerland County, Scott Carter was busy organizing a company as early as May.[3] Carter was 14 when the family moved to Indiana and at the age of 21 began the study of law under the tutelage of noted Hoosier attorney Joseph Eggleston. During the Mexican War he had fought at Buena Vista as a captain of the Third Indiana Infantry.[4]

Carter's company filled so quickly that a second company was being raised. Local businessman and former comrade of Scott Carter during the Mexican War, Theophilus Danglade led this effort.[5] Up river in Aurora, Daniel Keister raised a company from men hailing from Dearborn and Ohio counties.[6] Down in the prosperous river town of Madison, wharf boat owner and merchant William McClure was calling together a company of men.[7] In Corydon, local dentist James D. Irwin was recruiting.[8] And up in Fayette County, a county NOT bordering the Ohio River, Patrick Carland had gotten organized even earlier. The Methodist minister tendered the services of a company of men to the state on April 27.[9]

This enlistment fervor may have been driven by an unusual clause in Special Order No. 1. The proviso stated that each non-commissioned officer and private "shall furnish his own horse and horse equipage and shall receive 40 cents per day for their use and risk."[10] In essence, this doubled the $13.00 monthly pay of a private.

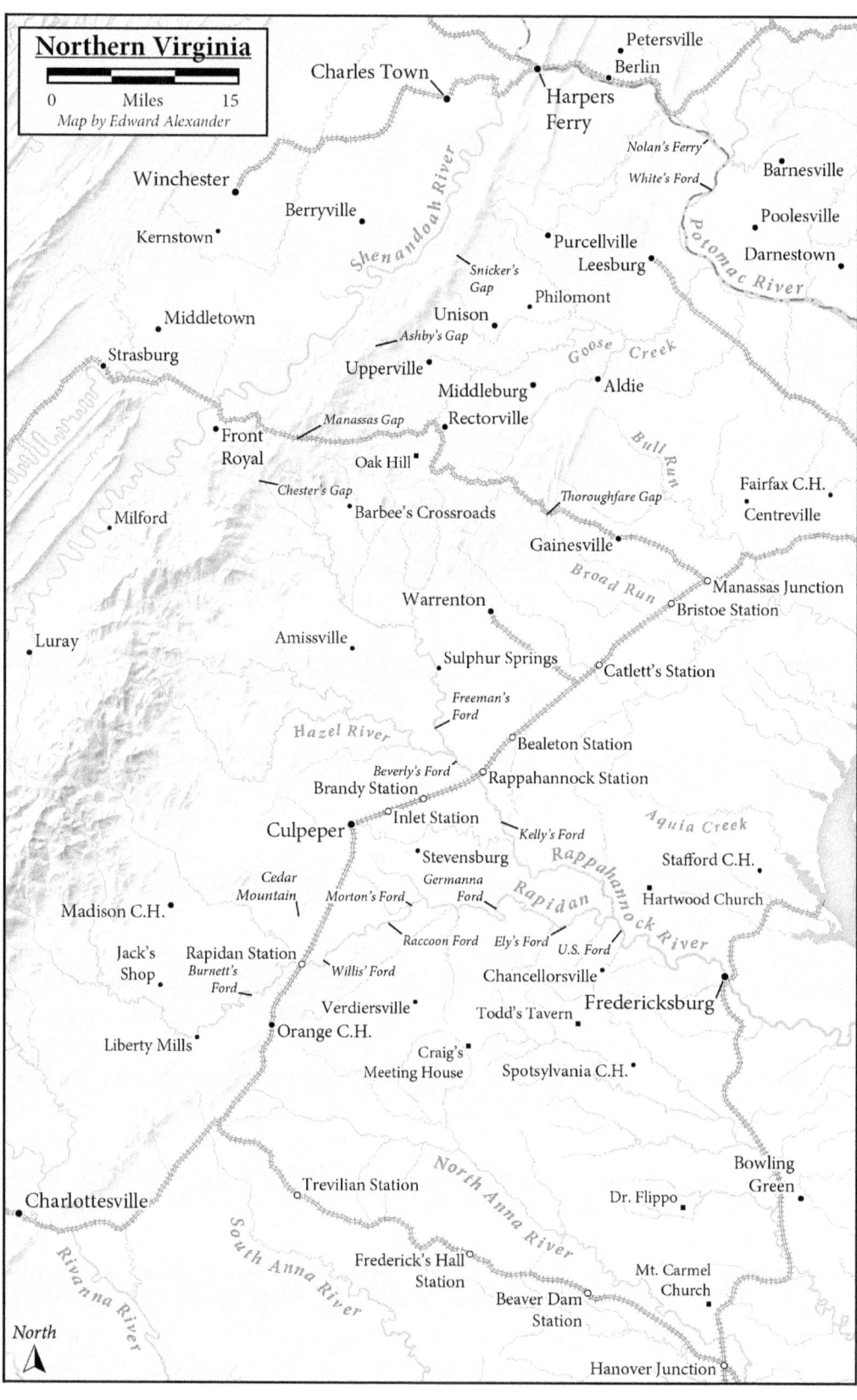

Men desperate to join the new unit searched high and low for a suitable mount and appropriate equipment. A burgeoning business of "renting" horses to those who enlisted sprang up. "Forty cents a day for the use of a horse will soon pay for the animal, one hundred and forty-six dollars for the services of a horse for twelve months pays handsomely for the investment and risk," opined one local newspaper, blithely ignoring the possibility of the loss of the animal in battle or to sickness.[11]

In addition to the Special Order release was the announcement of Conrad Baker as colonel of the newly named 1st Indiana Cavalry. He immediately proceeded to Evansville on the southwest corner of the state to organize the companies rendezvousing there. Scott Carter was named lieutenant colonel and was ordered to Madison, there to organize the companies that would comprise the other half of the regiment. Turning command of his company over to Jacob Buchanan, Carter hurried south and to his new duties.[12]

By August 1, five companies were in Madison with the sixth company, Carland's from Fayette County, arriving later that month.[13] As the companies moved toward the rendezvous at Madison, the men enjoyed a leisurely march from their homes. Not yet exposed to the hardships of war and the long service awaiting them, they reveled in the glow of patriotism. People all along their march plied the men with pies and cakes and corn for their horses. It was a heady time to be a soldier, especially a cavalryman. Upon reaching Madison, restaurants, bars, and hotels were thrown open to them.[14]

Carter began drilling his new recruits as best he could. Without weapons, equipment, or trained cadre he faced a daunting task. His infantry experiences from nearly two decades ago did little to prepare him for the organizing and training of his novice horsemen and their mounts. He needed help whipping the raw recruits into shape.

Help arrived in the form of diminutive Major George H. Chapman. Barely 5'4" tall and wearing glasses, Chapman looked more like a school teacher than a major of cavalry. His looks, however, belied his military background. Born in Massachusetts in 1832, his family moved to Indiana where he was appointed to the U.S. Naval Academy at the age of fifteen. After graduation, he served three years at sea, including time on the venerable USS *Ironsides*, even managing to be knocked overboard from its deck.[15] Returning to Indiana, he pursued the family business, running newspapers in Indianapolis and Terre Haute. Eventually, he turned to the study of law and was admitted to the bar in 1857. Within a year, he had secured a clerkship in the United States House of Representatives.[16]

The month of August continued at a breakneck pace. Uniforms arrived, giving the men a martial air despite having no idea what they were to do. Officers were elected and regimental structure began to take shape. Not surprisingly, the organizers of each company were elected captains by their respective men. On August 22, 1861, the men were mustered into federal service for the length of three years.[17]

Still short of horse equipment, men became anxious for service. Many of the men had little more than a halter to control their horses. In addition, the men had no weapons. But the war waited for no one, and orders arrived for the men in Madison. The eight companies in Evansville were ordered to St. Louis while the six companies in Madison were ordered to Washington, D.C. On August 24, 1861, the men and horses were loaded onto four steamers for the long trip to Washington, D.C.

The boats chugged up the Ohio River to Vevay were the steamers stopped, affording some of the men one last visit home. The men were welcomed with pies, hams, and food of all types. Re-boarding, the men continued up river where they were cheered at every stop and town along the way. As they traveled east, the river slowly dropped. An unusually

Small in stature at only 5'4", George Chapman was the one constant in the lives of the Third Indiana Cavalry, whether leading the regiment or the brigade. Shown here in the uniform of a colonel, Chapman developed into a very competent leader of cavalry, being brevetted major general by the end of the war (Library of Congress).

dry summer had left the Ohio River at near record lows and by the time the steamers reached the Virginia/Pennsylvania border, the boats ran aground. The men and horses disembarked at Wheeling, Virginia, and began riding the 60 miles to Pittsburgh.[18]

The internecine nature of war was brought close to home soon after they disembarked. The novice soldiers saw 42 Rebel prisoners recently captured in actions in western Virginia. They were shocked to see Thomas B. McGregor of Bennington, Indiana, among the captives. McGregor was an acquaintance of several men, and his presence as an enemy suddenly made the war very personal.[19] Most of the men had joined the cavalry for the pay, adventure, and the desire to serve their country. Few joined because of their expertise with horses. Despite the requirement that all men provide their own horse and horse equipment, many of the men were without saddles or bridles. After a few hours of riding bareback, the men soon found out that toughening one's "seat" was going to be a very painful experience. The more resourceful begged feed bags from farmers along the way and stuffed them with straw to fashion a rudimentary saddle to ease their suffering. Stolen clotheslines served as stirrups. Others shared rides with friends who had equipment, splitting time between saddle and bareback.[20]

The men's pain and suffering finally ended as they arrived in Pittsburgh and boarded trains. As they travelled east food, drink, and cheering greeted them at communities across Pennsylvania and Maryland. At Cockeysville, Maryland, the men were loudly cheered by the 20th Indiana Infantry showing "they are still in possession of genuine Hoosier lungs."[21]

Interspersed throughout the trip were discussions of an ecclesiastic nature. Captain Patrick Carland, recent Methodist minister, enjoyed the repartee of theological discussion. His orderly sergeant, Robert K. Jones, was a fiery Universalist preacher. Between the two of them, there was no lack of debate. Jones, being the more aggressive of the two, harangued the men with sermons about spiritual redemption.[22]

The exigencies of war dictated that the last 40 miles of their journey be made in cars most recently used to transport hogs. Dirty, smelly, sore, and excited, the men arrived in Washington on September 6. They found a city transformed into a giant army camp. "To see the earth dotted over with tents, and hill and valley chequered with long trains of army wagons, does not remind the rural Hoosier of anything he has seen," commented an awed soldier.[23]

Gone were the carefree camps enjoyed by troops before Bull Run. All was now military discipline. How severe that could be was quickly demonstrated when three men were arrested for taking fence posts for their fire on the first night in the city. Ordered to the War Department for disciplining, the men—Will Sharp, Jonathan Dailey, and Corporal George Armstrong—were fortunate to receive only a severe reprimand and were ordered back to the regiment.[24]

The political nature of the city also became evident when the Honorable William Dunn, U.S. Congressman for many of the men, showed up to welcome them. Ever the politician, Dunn used his congressional franking privilege to postmark letters home for his constituents.[25]

The deluge of men arriving in the capital had left the supplying of the troops haphazard, at best. Two days after reaching the capital, some of the companies received saddles, bridles, and halters. The supply problems did not matter to Lieutenant Colonel Carter. He wrote to Governor Morton complaining that he was still without the standard issue McClellan saddles for two of his companies and, instead, had been provided "saddles, which I am satisfied, will ruin horses." Reminding the governor that the men had provided their own mounts, he implored Morton to try and procure proper saddles for the men.[26]

As the men settled into camp just north of the Capitol building, they also

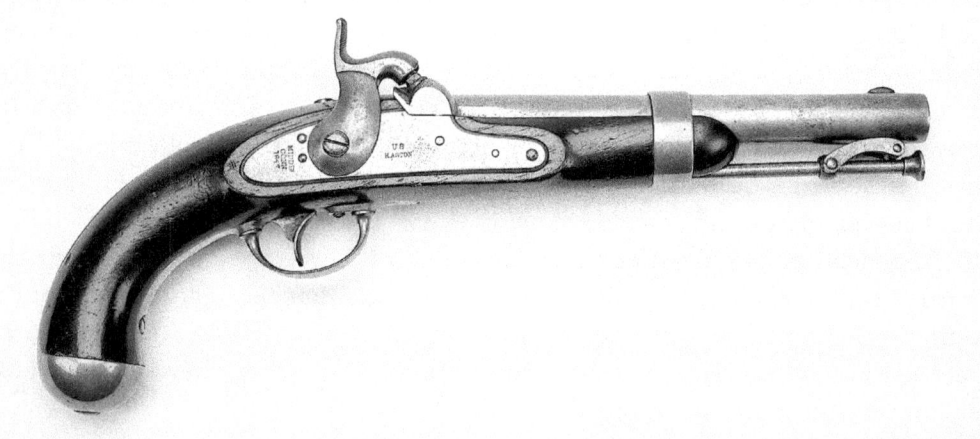

The men of the regiment were bitterly disappointed to be issued these smoothbore, muzzle-loading, single shot pistols as their first firearms; they were relics from the Mexican War (NRA Firearms Museum).

received a sobering dose of reality. A young man in Jacob Buchanan's company had fallen ill during the trip and had been left in Baltimore. On September 9, he died of typhoid fever. James M. Wright thus became the first from the Hoosier regiment to give the ultimate sacrifice for the Union cause.[27]

The men's spirits were lifted the next day with the arrival of weapons. They were excited to finally receive those nice Colt Navy revolvers promised to them back in Indiana. The depths of their disappointment can only be imagined when they were issued the Model 1842 Dragoon Pistol instead. This outdated Mexican War relic was sometimes called a horse pistol. It was a single shot, muzzleloading, .54 caliber smoothbore pistol of dubious accuracy. One man described it in a letter home as a "one single barreled, six pound weight, knocks-down-at-both-ends, kill-all-together, ounce ball, horse pistol."[28] Others took an equally dim view of the weapon. "In practicing marksmanship, it was never wise to choose for a mark anything smaller than a good size barn, and if right-handed, when you aimed at one end you would hit the other or miss the mark entirely."[29] In addition, 10 carbines of similar vintage were issued to each company. Essentially, 10 men in each company would have one shot at about 150 yards while each man would have one shot at a much shorter range. When the enemy got within handshaking distance, they would resort to their sabers. Needless to say, the men were not comforted by their weaponry.

The men had to make do. Army life now commenced in earnest, and the companies began to learn the intricate gyrations of cavalry tactics. Men unaccustomed to the saddle found that being a cavalryman was hard work. Not only did the novice horseman have to learn his trade, but he was also responsible for his horse. Feeding and watering the horses occurred twice daily, and each man was expected to care for his mount before he cared for himself. There was a right way to picket the horse, the right way to saddle the horse and the right way to ride the horse. All had to be learned—and the expectation of providing for their horses before their own needs had to be absorbed.

Drill at squad, company, squadron, and regimental levels were repeated over and over to ensure instant response to orders. From column into line, and line into column, the men learned the maneuvers of mounted warfare. In combat, quick execution of an order could well mean the difference between life and death. As the novice horsemen learned the intricacies and nuances of cavalry, amusing and unexpected things were bound to happen. Many a drill dissolved into a milling mass of men and horses as they tried to move from column to line to company to squadron fronts. Drill ended abruptly one day when an orderly sergeant ordered the men to "follow me when I jump that ditch right there." Applying spurs to his mount, the horse balked and the man landed head first in the middle of the ditch with canteen, haversack, pistol, and saber flying in as many different directions. Not wanting to literally obey the order of "follow me," the men turned around and trotted back to camp.[30]

Officers had the same difficulties in adjusting to army life. They were responsible for the men and their horses. In addition, they had to learn to be leaders of men. Sometimes, this created confusion on all parts. During a drill early in their time in Washington, Lieutenant Colonel Carter gave the command to a captain to separate his company into two columns and to deploy right and left. The captain knew what the maneuver required but could not remember the proper orders to give to accomplish the task. In desperation, he yelled, "Attention! One half get on one side and the other half on the other side, and scatter out like yesterday!"[31]

By the first of October, the men had been mostly outfitted, partially armed, and had begun rudimentary drill and training. Now all they needed was a purpose. The first order received was a common one for cavalry in the early part of the war. Twelve men and a sergeant were ordered to General Daniel Sickles' brigade headquarters to serve as orderlies. A similar detail was sent to General Cowdin's brigade. Having just received their new sabers the day before, the men couldn't wait to show them off. Competition was keen to be chosen as one of the 26 men. One man, so overwhelmed at not being selected for this duty, broke down and cried for being left out.[32]

The men did have their disappointment abated somewhat by their first ever review. Parading with thousands of other cavalrymen on October 7, the men put on a fine martial show. "I was dressed out in full uniform Red belt, Sword, Spurs, & Complete and was mounted on a Splendid Black horse," boasted First Lieutenant William Patton.[33] On the 13th, another 12 men and sergeant were ordered to General Joseph Hooker's division headquarters. Two days later, the rest of the regiment followed and were formally assigned to duty with Hooker in eastern Maryland.[34]

Since its formation, the 1st Indiana Cavalry was an organizational mess. With fourteen companies, it was too large. Eight companies in St. Louis and six in Washington made normal operations impossible. Governor Morton solved this nightmare by re-organizing the two wings. On October 21, the six eastern companies were given a new identity. Given Indiana's practice of designating regiments with ordinal numbers as well as their designation numbers, the new regiment was declared the 45th Regiment of Indiana Volunteers, 3rd Indiana Cavalry.[35] Scott Carter was promoted to colonel.[36] Other staff included Major George Chapman and Surgeon Elias W.H. Beck. The positions of lieutenant colonel, adjutant, quartermaster, and commissary were left unfilled. The companies and their officers:

	Captain	*1st Lieutenant*	*2nd Lieutenant*
Company A	Jacob Buchanan	William Patton	Robert P. Porter
Company B	James D. Irvin	Benjamin Q.A. Gresham	Marshall Lahue
Company C	Theophilus Danglade	Charles Lemmon[37]	Paul Clark
Company D	Daniel B. Keister	Matthew Mason	Henry Wright
Company E	William S. McClure	George H. Thompson	Abner Shannon
Company F	Patrick Carland	Oliver M. Powers	Thomas Moffitt

Mustered in for the first time as the Forty-Fifth Regiment of Indiana Volunteers, Third Indiana Cavalry on November 1, 1861, there were 579 men in its ranks.[38]

The Third Indiana Cavalry was now a reality. Born and bred in Indiana, trained in Washington and assigned duty in Maryland, the Hoosiers of the 3rd Indiana were about to place their imprint on the terrible national drama unfolding.

Chapter 2

October 15, 1861–May 25, 1862

Eastern Maryland was a hotbed of secessionist sentiment and support and served as a conduit for supplies and information between Virginia and Baltimore. For the past several months, a network of mail carriers, supply runners, and spies had been established throughout the area. Hooker was ordered to stop the trade as well as help hold Maryland for the Union in the upcoming elections. Upon breaking camp in the capital on October 15, the 3rd Indiana crossed the Potomac River in a driving rain. Arriving at Hooker's headquarters, the regiment was administratively assigned to Cowdin's brigade. Regimental headquarters was established at Budd's Ferry, about 25 miles southeast of Washington on the Potomac River.

To achieve the first part of his orders, Hooker decided he needed a larger presence further south and east along the Potomac River to intercept traffic from Virginia. He assigned the 3rd Indiana Cavalry this task. Companies A, C, and D were to patrol the area running from Budd's Ferry to Port Tobacco on the south central shore of eastern Maryland peninsula. Major Chapman took companies B, E, and F into St. Mary's and Charles counties, establishing his headquarters at Leonardtown. His position placed him 30 miles southeast of Port Tobacco and about 20 miles northwest of Point Lookout at the junction of the Chesapeake Bay and the Potomac.[1]

This 50-mile stretch of shoreline was slashed with small creeks and inlets where small boats from Virginia could land and remain hidden after the six-mile crossing of the Potomac River. Chapman established outposts at Point Lookout, Chaptico Creek, Millstone Landing, and Allen's Fresh. The men's duties would now include the roles of border patrol, policemen, and counterinsurgency spies.

Shortly after establishing themselves in their new billets, the men were joined by a small group of civilians working for a Major E.J. Allen. The men soon realized that the major was Allen Pinkerton and the civilians were "Pinkerton Men." Hired by Major General George McClellan to provide military intelligence, Pinkerton's men were far more adept at ferreting out malfeasance on the railroads, their former trade, than assessing an enemy's military strengths. Given their pre-war modus operandi, it was not surprising that Pinkerton set his men to investigating the civilians living in the area. The men of the Third were often ordered to accompany these erstwhile military intelligence officers in arresting suspected disloyal Marylanders.[2]

Perhaps more important to the national government was the desire to keep

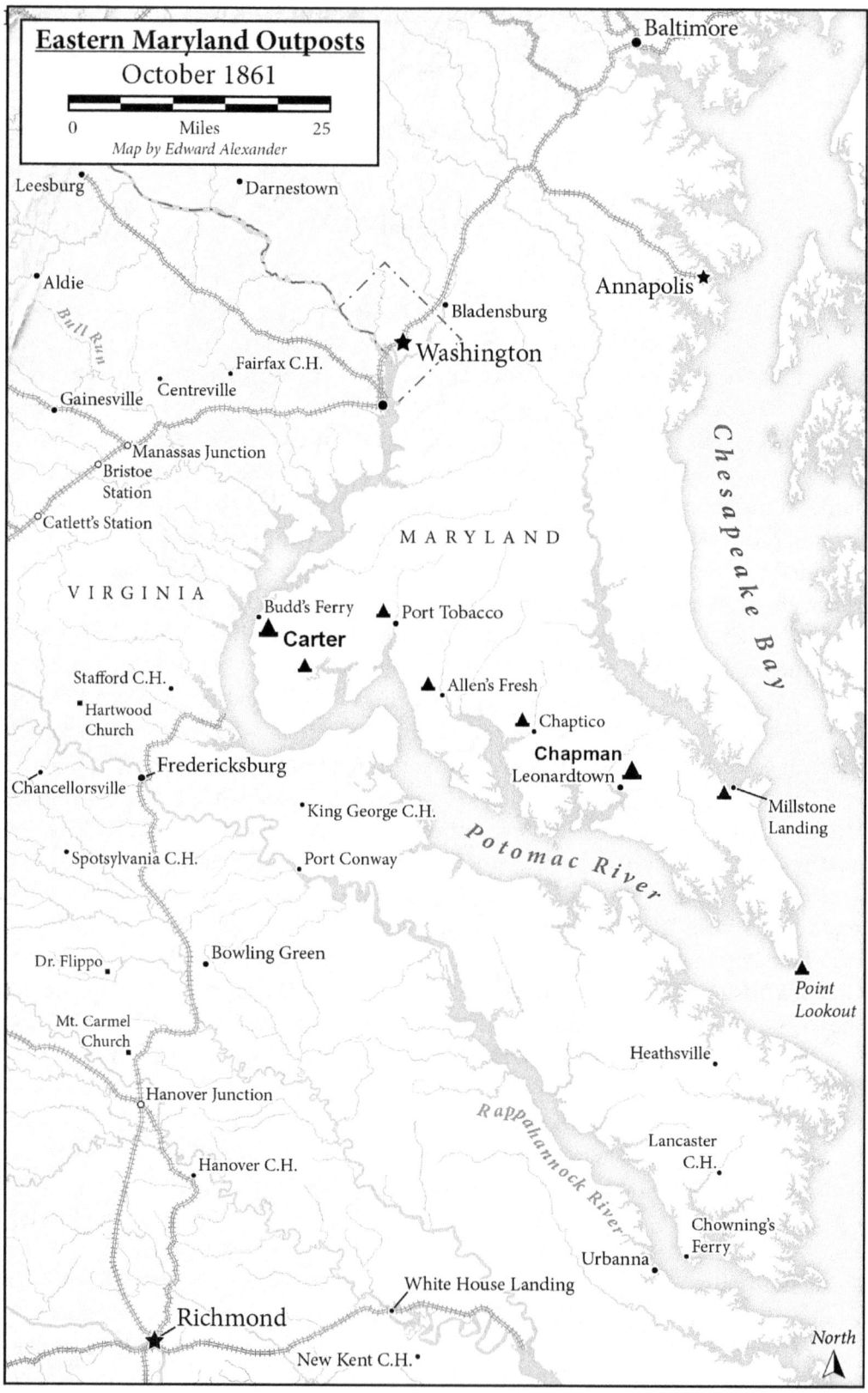

slaveholding Maryland in the Union. It was essential that a pro–Union slate be elected, and federal troops were to be used to "protect" the polling places. Hooker went so far as to order Major Chapman to arrest a secessionist candidate for the legislature and hold him until after the election.[3] The Third Indiana men were sent to numerous polling places on election day and voting went off without a hitch. Needless to say, their presence assured a preponderance of pro–Union votes.[4]

During this same time, the regiment also had immediate organizational issues pending. Indiana governor Morton made the unusual decision to allow the captains to select the lieutenant colonel. Soon, letters were flowing back to Indiana from every captain in the regiment petitioning for the position. Eventually, and no doubt with the influence of his old friend Colonel Carter, Captain Jacob Buchanan of Company A was promoted to lieutenant colonel with rank dating from November 8, 1861.[5] Soon thereafter, First Lieutenant William Patton was appointed captain of Company A with Second Lieutenant Robert Porter promoted to first lieutenant. Charles W. Lee, a private of the company, was promoted to second lieutenant.[6] This unusual ascension to commissioned officer from private was due to the still prevalent practice of letting the men elect their own officers. Colonel Carter realized the folly of this arrangement and opined later: "eight men in ten will vote for the man that will insure them the easiest going time. Whatever democracy may be in Civil affairs, it is the Curse of the army."[7]

Carter continued to be concerned about the paucity of equipment for the regiment, particularly the lack of adequate and modern firearms. One single shot pistol and saber per man and a smattering of antiquated carbines hardly presented a formidable military force. Late in October he traveled to Washington to meet with Governor Morton who was visiting from Indiana. He was relieved and heartened to learn that Morton would be traveling to Philadelphia to try and find revolvers for the regiment.[8]

As the men settled into their new routine, they were again graced with the presence of another "military

Indiana governor Oliver Perry Morton wielded extraordinary power during the war. Convinced there was a real threat of insurrection due to the amount of Southern sympathy in the state, he would stymie efforts by both the East and West wings to obtain the services of companies L and M for more than a year (Library of Congress).

intelligence officer." Captain Lafayette C. Baker of the "United States Secret Service"[9] had already made a name for himself identifying and rooting out spies, both real and imagined. Sure that he could help end the treachery he had heard of in eastern Maryland, he had convinced the government he could do so much more proficiently than Pinkerton. Baker arrived in Budd's Ferry on November 18, and Company D was put at his disposal. Baker was soon busy making arrests. "We captured four mounted traitors and one rebel spie [sic]" he bragged to General Hooker just 10 days after his arrival.[10] Sixteen men accompanied Baker and his prisoners to Baltimore to deliver the suspects to authorities. Baker remained while the men returned to the Potomac shoreline.

Despite the questionable help from Washington, the men began to make their own impact on the illicit trade route between eastern Maryland and Virginia. Captured individuals were sent to Major Chapman who interrogated the suspects. Located fifty miles from divisional headquarters, the major played both judge and jury in matters concerning river crossings. The results of his decisions determined whether an individual was forwarded to headquarters or released. Throughout the winter, a steady stream of suspects were sent north to Hooker's headquarters for the general's judgement.[11] Hooker, for his part, was well pleased with the performance of the regiment. In a letter to the Indiana adjutant general, Hooker stated, "The 3rd Indiana Cavalry has been on the wing almost all the time since they joined me singly and in bodies, and I have yet to learn of their first irregularity."[12]

As the weather shifted from the cool of autumn to the cold of winter, the men of the 3rd Indiana continued their patrols and began to feel the effects of active campaigning in a hostile land. At the end of the supply line, the men and horses were often short of forage, food, and other supplies. The men did not receive overcoats until December 5.[13] Men became ill from exposure and unsanitary conditions. "During the month of November, there were one hundred and thirty-nine cases treated, ten of which were typhoid fever, fifteen of ague, the balance diarrhea, flux, colds, etc." reported a military agent from Indiana. Despite this, he pronounced the health of the regiment as "pretty fair," all things considered.[14]

But within dry reports was human tragedy. Benjamin Boyd and William Winchell died on November 30. Winchell's death was even more difficult for the men to accept. While in the supposed safe care of the hospital, he was inadvertently given a double dose of morphine, hastening his demise.[15] Injuries were also bound to happen. David Dyer of Company A had the misfortune to fall off of his horse and break his leg. In 1861, this was considered a disabling injury, and he was discharged and sent home.[16]

Finding ways to deal with the monotony of their duty also weighed heavily on the men. One enterprising soldier turned to horse trading. After three trades, he ended up with his original mount. In the process, he made $20.00 plus acquired a Colt revolver worth $15.00. "Trading horses is certainly an easier way of making money than soldiering for it," he remarked to the folks back home.[17] Others turned to horticulture. To the Hoosiers from the Midwest, the coastal area offered a variety of plant life not seen back home. One young man sent some seeds to his wife. In his fractured English he described the plant from which they came. "You will find inclosed some seeds that came off of a evergreen tree. I want you to plant them. I think They will gro in that country. It is a butiful tree and bears a red berey. The name is holley."[18]

While death or injury were the only way home for the enlisted men, officers had the luxury of resigning their commissions when they decided they had had enough. Captain Theophilus Danglade of Company C found adjusting to army life more difficult than he imagined and resigned on December 15 and returned home to Vevay. First Lieutenant Charles Lemmon was promoted to captain, and regular promotion moved Second Lieutenant Paul Clark to first lieutenant. Orderly Sergeant Ephraim Martin received the commission for second lieutenant.[19]

Patrolling continued and bore fruit. On December 15, a four-man patrol of Company E spotted a sailing vessel near Spencer's Landing in one of the inlets of the Potomac River. Guy Nichols, Oscar Trigg, Jack Hoagland, and Ham Stapp found a small boat and started paddling out toward the vessel. Men on the suspected contraband boat saw them coming and panicked, jumping ship and swimming to the shore where they disappeared into the neighboring countryside.

The cavalrymen pulled alongside the abandoned boat and were in a quandary. They had captured the "Victory of Baltimore," a sloop that required sailing ability to move her. Unfortunately, none of the men had sailing experience save maybe a flatboat on the Ohio River. Fortunately, a passing U.S. Navy ship was hailed, and the sailors helped the men bring the boat back to camp.[20]

Major Chapman must have felt nostalgic upon seeing the sloop. Ever the navy midshipman of his youth, he estimated the boat size to be 40 ton and laden with military and commercial goods. Cargo included 86,000 percussion caps, 87 dozen "fancy" military buttons and 43 pounds of flax thread. In an obvious reference to his poorly armed men, Chapman mentioned "the caps are suitable for Colt's revolvers. I regret that my men are not so armed."[21]

General Hooker was delighted with the capture and forwarded a report to the Army of the Potomac headquarters: "The intelligence, energy and good conduct displayed by Major Chapman and his command in the service in which they are engaged merit and will receive my commendation ... the conduct of the enlisted men is as exemplary in the absence of authority as it is when present. It seems that no example, no temptation can lead them astray."[22] Hooker was soon referring to the 3rd Indiana as his "horse marines."

Hooker seemed to have special fondness for these tough and sometimes unruly Westerners. A postwar reminiscence related how a 3rd Indiana cavalryman delivered an order from Hooker to an officer of another regiment. The officer refused to accept the message until the Hoosier dismounted and saluted. Disgusted by this seemingly unnecessary piece of military mumbo jumbo, the soldier simply rode his horse to the officer's tent and threw the paper through the flaps. The officer, fuming with anger, went to General Hooker and demanded the man be arrested. Replied Hooker, "well, the next time that happens, you pull off your coat and offer to lick him. If he doesn't fight you, he's the only man in the company who won't."[23]

Late in December, an old acquaintance reappeared at Millstone Landing, Chapman's new headquarters. Lafayette Baker was back and had brought reinforcements in the form of six policemen and 13 members of Pennsylvania cavalry. Within two weeks he wore out his welcome, and an exasperated Chapman wrote to Hooker complaining of Baker's high handed tactics and the policemen's depredations on the local community. Union men in the area, whom Chapman had assiduously cultivated as sources of information, were arrested by Baker with no provocation. Others were taken to Baltimore for further questioning. Baker had intimated that Chapman's course of action had thus far left a lot to be desired. The angry major reported to Hooker that Chapman's success thus far "certainly equaled that which attended Mr. Baker. I hope, however, that no justification of myself or the course I have pursued in St. Mary's county will be necessary with the General." Mercifully, Baker left on the 29th, never again to bother Chapman.[24]

Elected second lieutenant of Company C upon muster, Paul Clark was promoted to first lieutenant in December 1861. Questioning the regiment's readiness for real combat, Clark resigned in June 1862. In December 1863, he was commissioned as first lieutenant of Company D, 10th Indiana Cavalry. Several of his former enlisted comrades of the 3rd Indiana were commissioned in the 10th Indiana, including two company commanders (U.S. Army Heritage and Education Center).

While this activity seemed to be making a difference, not all of the men were impressed with their service record or

The men received these peculiar Savage .36 caliber revolvers, an ugly example of Yankee ingenuity, to replace their outdated horse pistols only to have them replaced by the lighter and more reliable Colt revolver a few months later (NRA Firearms Museum).

military conduct so far. Newly-promoted First Lieutenant Paul Clark of Company C remarked in a letter to his hometown paper "we are not very well disciplined yet from the fact that we have been used as pickets and messengers a great portion of the time. We ought to have been taking lessons in discipline, consequently many of our men are not familiar with many of the different modes of drilling."[25] As 1861 drew to a close, time would tell if Clark's apprehensions were justified.

While Chapman's detachments were busy chasing boats and arresting suspicious characters, Colonel Carter was busy with three important issues; decent weapons for the men, the consolidation of the 10 companies of the regiment under his command, and the recruitment to bring all companies to a strength of 97 men. He had mixed success.

His earlier trip to see Governor Morton in Washington had paid dividends as shipments of revolvers started to arrive. When the crates were opened, however, the men found themselves armed with the unusual .36 caliber Savage six-shot revolver. More than a foot long and possessing a unique cocking trigger separate from the firing trigger, this ugly duckling quickly found a home with the troops. On January 4, the men gladly exchanged the old horse pistols for the new arms. "There is many a skinned nose and blackened cheek that rejoiced to think they would never have to sight on them again," remarked a relieved Flavius Bellamy. The next day, Bellamy took a little target practice and found he could come within four inches of center at 116 yards with the new pistol.[26] The new weapons came a little too late for Private James S. Miller in Company A. While holstering his horse pistol a week before, the weapon accidentally went off and resulted in a nasty leg wound.[27]

Recruiting trips back to Indiana had increased the regimental roll by about 20 men. One man, however, didn't make it to Maryland. Eli Bowman died in Aurora before the detachment boarded the boat.[28] By the end of the winter, subsequent trips would fill all companies to their authorized strength.

On the matter of consolidating the regiment, Carter had no luck. Despite writing Governor Morton, General Hooker, General McClellan, and his senators over the winter, Carter was never able to pry the companies out of Indiana or later when they had moved Kentucky. The exigencies of war simply kept the transfer of four companies of cavalry from one theater to another. For the remainder of the war, the six companies with the Army of the Potomac would serve as the East Wing, Third Indiana Cavalry. In all subsequent duty, the six companies would be expected to do the service of a full regiment. Their truncated size soon earned the regiment a new nickname: The Little Third.[29]

As mentioned, their constant patrolling along the banks of the Potomac kept a steady stream of suspected Confederate sympathizers flowing to division headquarters throughout the winter. Chapman's initial interviews, however, did keep a few from the long trip north. One young man was arrested and brought before the major. The father, Joseph Millburn, was considered by Chapman to be a Union man. The major had ordered the arrest of young Millburn when it was learned he had crossed the Potomac. The boy admitted the crossing three times since the war began, transporting nine men to Virginia. Apparently, the arrest and the father's wrath created a sense of contrition in the young man. "I don't think young Millburn will be found crossing the river soon again or that he will act disloyally toward the government" Chapman reported to Hooker. The chastised young man was released.

R. Jackson Redmond was brought before him, and Chapman decreed him "ignorant and poor and hardly worth feeding as a prisoner" and released him. One William Norris had been arrested for crossing the Potomac three times, but "Norris is poor, ignorant, worthless and a cripple—very repentant—and I released him upon taking the oath of allegiance." Apparently being poor and ignorant were among the prerequisites for being considered harmless to the Union cause by Chapman.

Others apprehended during the winter months were Federal deserters. The problem worsened as winter deepened and the men's martial ardor had been tempered by the cold winds of winter and the long separation from loved ones. Men from the Excelsior Brigade of Joseph Sickles were the most numerous and were typically returned to their unit.[30]

Military discipline also suffered. Captain Patrick Carland decided he needed a break from the monotony of camp life and went to visit regimental headquarters at Budd's Ferry. Unfortunately, he had not asked permission from Major Chapman to make such a visit. Chapman reported this breach of military etiquette to division headquarters but requested leniency and a little help from General Hooker. "I do not desire to make any formal charges in the matter but I am sure if the General would impress him with a proper sense of responsibilities and proprieties of his position, it would be of advantage to him and his company."[31] Carland wasn't the only officer to find trouble. Placing shoulder straps on the western men did not automatically imbue them with the manners of a gentleman. First Lieutenant Robert Porter of Company A was one such individual.

Budd's Ferry served as headquarters for Hooker's Division as well as the Third

Indiana. It was also a popular landing site for the many Navy ships plying the Potomac River. The inevitable friction between seaman and landlubber often occurred. In mid-January, Lieutenant Porter and a sailor from one of the clippers "had a difficulty" whereupon Porter shot the sailor in the face. Amazingly, no charges were filed.[32]

As the captures of the Third Indiana grew, Major Chapman catalogued the contraband and sent an accounting to General Hooker. Large amounts of silk and sewing equipment as well as tapelines, rulers, and auger bits were listed. The major only requested to retain one item from the list; one case of amputating instruments as there was only one in the entire regiment, and none with his detachment.[33]

The winter months brought winds off of the Atlantic and down the river. Resupply was made more difficult by the poor conditions of the roads. The isolation intensified their desire for letters from home. William Patton gave his address to family and stated, "the above address is best ... they know where 'Hooker's Division' is, and 'Hooker's Division' will be where the 3rd Indiana Cavl will be and there they will know where the Co. is."[34]

For some the isolation and nasty weather was too much. The company guard of Company D was called out one day when gunfire was heard in camp. One of the men had been frustrated in his attempts to catch his horse. Exasperated, the soldier pulled out his revolver and shot the animal. In the belief that the man was mentally deranged, he was placed under arrest.[35]

Over in Company B, Private Ed Kelso went on a drunk and tried to stab some of the guard sent to arrest him. Captain Carland sought to end the stalemate by striking Kelso several times on the head with the flat of his saber. Kelso's hangover the next morning was no doubt exacerbated by the fact that Carland's saber tip had inflicted a severe cut as well as welts to Kelso's throbbing head.[36]

Such problems were expected among bored young men miles away from home. Not anticipated nor covered in the manuals was the question of runaway slaves. The Emancipation Proclamation was still nearly a year away. For many of the Hoosier horsemen, they felt legally bound to return "contraband." John B. Abrell of Washington City had stayed with the men of Company F for some time. Abrell's owner complained and Captain Carland arrested the slave and placed him in the local jail. The local press opined that the captain had done the right thing. "So far, the negroes in this county has shown little disposition to desert their masters, and, we are satisfied, the very prompt and commendable conduct of Capt. Carlin [sic], in the above case, will save both our citizens and the military much trouble upon this subject."[37]

A Mrs. Thomas complained about a young slave boy who had attached himself to the regiment. He had been useful in grooming horses and was even sent to Budd's Ferry with a company wagon for provisions. Chapman ordered the boy returned to the Thomas family and ordered all detachments to not harbor runaway slaves. So far, this was a war to save the Union, not end slavery.[38]

Finally, spring began to warm the eastern shores of Maryland and spirits brightened. Warm weather meant the resumption of campaigning and General George McClellan had decided to approach Richmond by sea. For the 3rd Indiana, it was hoped that their exile along the Potomac would end, and they would rejoin the Army of the Potomac. Those hopes were crushed in March as no orders came to join in on the campaign. For days on end, boats and ships sailed down the Potomac River. As they passed the outposts of the Third Indiana, the men were forcibly reminded that they were destined to remain in the backwaters of the war. In early April, this feeling was compounded when the entire Hooker Division was ordered to Virginia—minus the 3rd Indiana. In the meantime, Benjamin Miller, blacksmith for Company A was discharged and started home. On the way, he sold his horse for $150.[39]

The lack of movement made Colonel Carter furious and he was heard to refer to his regiment as Maryland Home Guards. The men began to also disparage themselves. Mistakenly believing that Governor Morton exerted influence over their military assignment, the men began to grumble. "Our boys remain here [Maryland] and the boys say that Gov. Morton has transferred us to the Governor of Maryland to act as a home guard. So much for Gov. Morton.... It does not set well on our stomachs; send us anywhere, for God knows we don't want to stay here any longer."[40] The war was getting nearer, however. Daniel Funk of Company B had the distinction of being the first member of the regiment to be wounded. While on picket on April 9, Funk was wounded and had his pinky finger on his left hand amputated.[41]

With the war still viewed as a short term affair, everyone wanted to be part of the campaign. When the Indiana members of the House of Representatives heard of this situation, they acted. With so few Hoosiers in the Army of the Potomac, the state congressional delegation was sensitive to any real or imagined slight to their western men in an eastern army. The congressmen and senators penned a letter to Major General McClellan decrying this omission and requested the Third be immediately ordered to the Peninsula. Unmoved by the political pressure brought to bear on behalf of 500 men in an army of 120,000, there is no record that McClellan responded to the demand.[42]

Frustrated and convinced that they were being left out of the culminating fight of the war, tempers were short. "What is all this coming to? Are we to be kept here any great while longer—hope not" lamented Major Chapman in his diary.[43] While officers might confide in their diaries, enlisted men let their frustration out in unhealthy ways. In Company A, Benjamin Workman and J.R. Reed got into an argument. The two squared off with Workman the decidedly larger of the two. To equalize the fight, Reed grabbed a camp axe and struck Workman in the head, fracturing his skull. Reed was immediately placed under arrest.[44]

Softening the disappointment and anger over being left behind was the presence of several officers' wives. "The officers who have wives live in little log huts about 200 yards from camp. Their Village I have named Womansville and it goes by that name.

They have a fine time of it. Each family has two or three contraband negroes to wait on them."[45]

Duty still had to be performed, and the men continued their patrols. The smugglers continued to refine their tactics, and the men had to constantly counter these efforts. Chapman tried disguising some of his men as civilians to see if they could make contact with the smugglers. In April, a squad of men from Company A was sent to investigate several freshly dug graves in a nearby cemetery. Their search turned up 400 blankets, several guns, and "two dead Negroes."[46]

On May 10, the regiment was suddenly ordered to Washington. There, they were to assume provost duty in the streets of the capital city. Any movement closer to the war was welcomed by the men, and they happily bade east Maryland a not so fond farewell. Making matters, even better, recruits arrived from Indiana, bringing all six companies back up to a strength of 97 men.[47] The move only took two days, but one man was left behind at the hospital at Budd's Ferry. David McNeal died of illness on May 17.[48]

The men assumed their provost guard duties and found them more boring than Maryland. "'Post,' or as the boys term it, 'compost' guards are stationed on Pennsylvania Avenue at every cross street, for the purpose of 'stopping fast riding or driving, and also to see that not more than two rode in the driver's seat of government ambulances.' This is so that sick or wounded soldiers riding therein can have plenty of air and that their progress be not impeded by too much weight … [the duty entails] sitting erect in the saddle, with sabre drawn four hours per day," harrumphed one private.[49] Adding insult to injury, duty was doubled for some men. Mumps had afflicted many in the camp, and the healthy had to pull extra duty to cover the regiment's responsibilities.[50]

Yet there was time to see the sights of Washington when off duty. Samuel Gilpin took advantage of his time in the capital to visit the attractions. He recorded visits to the Capitol, Patent Office, and the Smithsonian Institution where he saw the bones of a mastodon and a stuffed gorilla.[51]

Provost duty was more than standing at street intersections. On May 13, Company A was ordered to report immediately to General Abner Doubleday. Through heavy rain, the company plodded toward the general's headquarters where Captain Patton was escorted in to see the General. There, he was ordered to one of the forts surrounding Washington to deal with a potential mutiny. It seemed that an artillery company stationed at the fort had refused to accept the muskets issued to them because of their inferior manufacture. Patton was ordered to "compel" the company to accept the weapons or bring them in as prisoners. Fortunately, by the time they arrived, the rebellious artillerymen had decided to accept the muskets and conflict was averted.[52]

"Compost" duty was mercifully short. As McClellan's fortunes stalled on the Peninsula, Confederate forces under General Stonewall Jackson had been unleashed in the Shenandoah Valley to attract forces away from McClellan and threaten

Washington. On May 25, the men of the Third hooked their sabers to their belts, checked their revolvers, tightened their horses' cinch belts, rolled their bedrolls, tied them to the back of the saddles, and nervously trotted across the Potomac into Virginia. Now ordered to the west, their hopes and desires had come true. They were now in the seat of war and would soon "see the elephant."

Chapter 3

May 26, 1862–August 8, 1862

By the summer of 1862, Northern Virginia had already seen its share of the war. The Manassas campaign the previous summer and the long period of inactivity and fortification following had already denuded the landscape. Entire forests had disappeared to provide fuel for the army's campfires. For the apprehensive Hoosiers, the landscape was as foreign as the surface of the moon. As they rode further west, the countryside became more pastoral and unblemished, almost peaceful. Little could they have known that over the course of the next three years, they would become intimately familiar with its rolling countryside and Blue Ridge mountains.

With every sense stretched, the Third Indiana trotted west to join Brigadier General Jonathan Geary's infantry brigade at Broad Run. The first day out was a long ride as they passed through Fairfax Courthouse and bivouacked at Gainesville. The next morning, after passing through Thoroughfare Gap and across Broad Run, they continued west until joining Geary at Front Royal.[1]

The men had barely reached Geary's brigade when the general ordered a retreat to Manassas Junction with the Third arriving there on the 28th. Now acting as "real" cavalry, the men were afforded no rest and immediately sent on patrols to the west and north. By the 30th, they had reached out to Upperville, and scouts were posted at Ashby's Gap. Now ordered back toward the Shenandoah Valley through Ashby's Gap, Colonel Carter continued aggressive screening movements, with scouting parties reaching within six miles of Winchester and 12 miles from Front Royal. He reported the presence of a few cannon and 400–600 Confederate cavalry.[2]

The rapid movement of the regiment made resupply virtually impossible. The men reverted to foraging upon the inhabitants of the area. Wrote one Hoosier, "We now subsist and forage upon the country through which we pass. The latter is excellent, from the fact of this being a splendid pasture land and no stock to graze it."[3]

General Geary, in a panic over the supposed advance of Jackson's Confederate forces, ordered a retreat. Included in the order was the burning of all supplies not easily transported. New to this type of war, the Third felt humiliated by the order. Colonel Carter was heard to say that his regiment "Won't fall back if the whole Rebel army comes till I've looked 'em in the eye!"[4] Despite not seeing the Confederates, the sullen Hoosiers retreated back to Ashby's Gap on May 30. There they were to guard against the phantom Rebel army from using the Gap to move east toward Washington.

Finally able to catch some rest, the men reflected on their first exposure to active campaigning. Overall, they felt good about themselves. They even took time to relax and enjoy their surroundings. Near Oak Hill and the residence of Louis Marshall, the men commandeered a piano for their own amusement. As one played, others "tripped the light fantastic toe in the mazy evolutions of the old Virginia Reel, with fair partners who wore cavalry spurs on their boots."[5]

The men also took stock of their leaders. Carter was generally considered a good commander, who was in his best humor when there was a chance of a fight. Captain Carland saw Carter as a "no feather bed soldier" due to his ability to sleep soundly on a fence rail in the rain. Whether this talent would be useful in combat was yet to be seen.[6]

On June 5, companies A and D were sent out by General Geary to the estate of Green Carroll, a soldier in the Confederate army. Apparently their orders did not discourage vandalism. "When he returns he'll find considerable work to do on his house & grounds, the horses ruined the gardens & fruit trees. He ought to have better breed than to be a Secech or an FFV."[7]

Carter's unique ability of sleeping on rails was given ample opportunity to be displayed for the early days of June 1862 were rainy ones. Despite the weather, scouting parties covered an area that included Front Royal, Warrenton, Barbee's Crossroads, and Salem. On June 13, the men were all ordered south to Luray where a general order was issued "requiring semi-weekly inspection of all arms, horse equipment, cooking utensils, blankets, uniforms, underwear, etc. and further provides that each man's feet must be washed at least twice every week!"[8] Apparently this new fascination with cleanliness did little to help the military situation. Within a week, they were back north of Front Royal.

The rapid movement up and down the Valley was due to Stonewall Jackson and his "foot cavalry."[9] Jackson had defeated General James Shields' forces at Port Republic, and Shields was in full retreat when the Hoosiers arrived in Luray. Barely dismounting, the men were ordered to form a rearguard for Geary's division. The army retreated down the valley to Winchester, nearly 80 miles north of Port Republic. The men were immediately placed on patrol duty to the east and captured a handful of Rebels near Berryville.[10] While in Winchester they learned of a shakeup in the Union army command. Tired of McClellan's slowness on the Peninsula and worried by Jackson's successes in the Shenandoah Valley, Lincoln ordered the creation of the Army of the Virginia under General John Pope. This new creation absorbed all forces operating in Northern Virginia, including the 3rd Indiana.

On June 20, the regiment was ordered to Manassas Junction only to be detoured to Bristoe Station, four miles south of Manassas. This movement, undertaken in sweltering heat, covered 50 miles over three days. Arriving at Bristoe Station, rumors were rife that they were headed to the Peninsula to join McClellan's army, Indeed, by the 29th all of the infantry around the station had left, leaving only the Third and a battalion of artillery in camp.[11]

Chapter 3. May 26, 1862–August 8, 1862

The next two weeks of relative quiet allowed Colonel Carter to catch up on some paperwork. Of critical importance was the replacement of several officers who had departed. Active campaigning had begun weeding out the weak and infirmed and those lacking the stomach for the realities of service. Captain Daniel Keister of Company D resigned his commission on July 1. Likewise, Captain Patrick Carland in Company F had found the hard campaigning too much and turned in his resignation on June 29 on the pretext of an ill child back home in Indiana.[12] Back on May 21, Captain James D. Irvin had resigned from Company B due to a crippling case of rheumatism. Company C's first lieutenant Paul Clark had tendered his resignation on June 21,[13] and First Lieutenant George H. Thompson of Company E had assumed the duties of adjutant. Finally, Lieutenant Colonel Buchanan was again absent due to illness. All told, the regiment was missing five of its 18 line officers. Given that there was only one major, Buchanan's absence also put a big strain on the field officers, as well.[14]

On July 2, Carter and Chapman drafted a letter to Governor Morton concerning these vacancies. First Lieutenant Matthew Mason was recommended to the captaincy of Company D. First Lieutenant Benjamin Q.A. Gresham was likewise recommended to be promoted captain of Company B. In an unusual break from protocol, they recommended Second Lieutenant Thomas Moffitt for the captaincy of Company F, bypassing First Lieutenant Oliver Powers.[15] Upon hearing of the slight, Powers resigned his commission later in the month.[16]

Things got complicated when the recently resigned Captain James Irwin of Company B asked to be reinstated. Apparently, his rest and visit at home appeared to improve his rheumatism so much that he petitioned the governor on June 19 to re-instate him. This news was unwelcomed back in Virginia. Carter, Buchanan (who had rejoined the regiment), and Chapman wrote to Adjutant General of Indiana Lazarus Noble imploring him not to accommodate Irwin: "Capt. Irwin is a gentleman of moral worth and of courage we have no doubt. But he is wholly unfit for the command of a Company." Swayed by the regimental officers, Irwin's commission was not re-issued.[17]

In the same letter, the three officers asked that Sergeant D.R. Spencer be commissioned second lieutenant of Company D jumping over both the orderly sergeant and quartermaster sergeant of the company. In addition, the resignation of Second Lieutenant Ephraim Martin of Company C had not been accepted "and will not be." In fact, the trio asked that Martin be promoted to first lieutenant.[18]

A couple of days later, Major George Chapman sent his own letter to the governor asking for the colonelcy of one of the regiments about to be raised. In a follow up letter, the ambitious Chapman explained his frustration with his current situation. His sentiments could have been voiced by every cavalryman in the Army of the Potomac. "I frankly confess that I am anxious for a change. Anxious to get out of this regiment, if I can do so with honor, and anxious to get out of this arm of the service…. Placed as I am there is no probability of any opportunity occurring for distinction, nor of winning one's promotion by hard blows. So far, we have been Kept in the background and the prospect before us promises nothing better."[19] Chapman's frustrations were shared by many of the officers. Surgeon Elias Beck wrote home: "Well—all of our officers are Mad—half of them talk of resigning—they think we are of no consequence—won't get any fighting & all want, they scarcely know what."[20]

Unsurprisingly, the letters from Carter, Buchanan, and Chapman were not the only ones mailed to Indianapolis. News of the requests by the regiment's leadership for promotions created a blizzard of petitions and letters to the governor and the adjutant general. Second Lieutenant Henry F. Wright of Company D was especially busy. A petition from 37 citizens of Aurora was sent recommending his promotion to captain. Twelve members of Company D wrote in favor of Wright "instead of the person named in the recommendation of Colonel Scott Carter."[21] Wright was unsuccessful in his bid for the captaincy but was promoted to first lieutenant.[22]

Spiritualist and doctor Elias Beck joined the army for the pay. Brother-in-law to Union general Robert Milroy, he was an acerbic writer with a tendency to tell the bitter truth (U.S. Army Heritage and Education Center).

Mexican War service was presented as a reason to promote Private Charles N. White to second lieutenant of Company C. He also called on his hometown for support. A letter sent from Madison pointed out that part of Company C was raised in Jefferson County, and none of the officers, commissioned or non-commissioned, were citizens of the county. No doubt this glaring injustice had been pointed out to the good citizens by none other than Charles N. White.[23]

Fortunately for the governor and adjutant general, the flurry of paper coming from the 3rd Indiana ended on July 8 as the regiment received orders to report to General Rufus King at Fredericksburg. The regiment covered the 35 miles quickly, arriving the next day. Upon reaching the venerable and historic city, the men set up camp on the north shore of the Rappahannock River. One member of the regiment decided to take in the sights. He was distressed to find the tombstone of Mary Washington, mother of the first president, in disrepair. "Stones and hatchets in the hands of reckless boys have nicked and defaced it much, while those silly fools who love to see their names in public places have added to the uncomely appearance by scratching their initials here and there with pencil and knife."[24]

In the comparative safety of camp one did not expect death, but even routine duty could bring tragic results. Private Charles Butcher of Company C rode his horse bareback to the river for a drink of water. Unexpectedly, the current pulled Butcher from his mount, and he disappeared into the waters of the Rappahannock. Only nineteen at the time, the dutiful brother had left an unfinished letter to his sister in his tent.[25]

Butcher's death was the first in the regiment while in the field and a precursor of the coming months. Armed only with revolvers and sabers with a handful of carbines, none had been fired in anger. Saber drill was non-existent. While they had been in the army for almost a year, the men still possessed few of the skills of a seasoned cavalryman. They had learned to take care of their horses and themselves. Some of the ineffective officers and men had been winnowed out, and better leaders had moved up. They could not, however, consider themselves veterans until they had "seen the elephant." Only then would they understand what they needed to yet learn. Whether they would fulfill General Scott's early war assessment that volunteer cavalry would never be able to become effective cavalrymen was about to be tested. The last week of July would begin their new school of instruction.

July 23, 1862, would be the baptism of fire for the Third Indiana Cavalry, East Wing. Companies A and B, led by Major Chapman, joined two companies of the Harris Light Cavalry (2nd New York Cavalry) for a scout to the North Anna River. Commanded by Colonel Judson Kilpatrick from the New York regiment, the column followed the Richmond and Potomac Railroad to the Carmel Church vicinity. Reports had claimed that the Rebels had a camp nearby. When the men arrived at daybreak, no camp was found, but a local woman informed Kilpatrick that the Confederates came to the church every day at 7:00 a.m. Kilpatrick hurriedly set up an ambush. The men were barely in place when a small patrol of Confederate cavalry rode into view. Badly outnumbered, the rebels exchanged shots with the Union horsemen and turned south. Chapman led the two Hoosier companies in pursuit, chasing their enemy five miles to the banks of the North Anna River. There, Kilpatrick caught up with Chapman with the rest of the column. Across the river was an enemy camp of approximately 75 men.[26]

Kilpatrick ordered an immediate attack. Splashing across the river, the New Yorkers and Hoosiers drove the Confederates away and burned the camp, including seven railroad cars filled with corn. Returning to the northern shore of the river, the men took positions around the Carmel church and took an accounting of the day.[27] One rebel had been killed at the church, and two others had been captured in the fighting around the Confederate camp. In addition, 21 horses had been captured. Only James Quinn of Company A had been hit with a wounded leg.[28] The men broke camp and marched back to Fredericksburg, arriving there at 11:00 p.m.

Two days later, another squadron of the regiment would receive its baptism of fire. Companies C and D under the command of Captain Charles Lemmon were ordered to the headquarters of General John Gibbon's brigade of King's Division. There, the cavalrymen joined a battery of artillery and 60 riflemen of the 2nd U.S. Sharpshooters who would accompany Gibbon's brigade. They were to make a scout to Orange Courthouse to ascertain enemy dispositions to the west of Fredericksburg.

Gibbon, a native North Carolinian, was a West Point graduate with 15 years of pre-war experience in the Regular Army artillery. His brigade included four regiments of infantry from Wisconsin and Indiana. He led the column at a brisk pace, but temperatures in the mid-nineties began to take a toll on the infantry. About 5:00 p.m., the column halted to allow the men to rest and give stragglers a chance to catch up. At daybreak the next morning, the command resumed its march to the Courthouse. About five miles from their objective, Gibbon halted the column. He then proceeded forward with Lemmon's squadron and one regiment of infantry, the riflemen, and two pieces of artillery.

As they approached the courthouse, rebel pickets were encountered and driven west. About one and a half miles from the structure, Gibbon decided that he had determined the makeup of the opposing force and turned to rejoin the rest of the command. As his small force retreated, Rebel forces pursued them. Covering the infantry, Captain Lemmon skillfully managed the rearguard action so that no one was lost in the retrograde movement. The Confederates broke off contact when the detachment reached the rest of the column. After a short march, the force went into camp for the night before returning to Fredericksburg on the morning of the 27th.[29] Captain Lemmon had done well in his first combat leadership role. He was singled out by Gibbon in the general's report as having done a skillful job on the scout. This was high praise from an old Regular.

The third squadron of the Third Indiana had not been idle during this period. Thirty men of Company F, led by First Lieutenant Oliver Powers, were ordered on a scout to Bowling Green on July 21. Returning the next day, they were shocked to find out that another scouting party from Company F, led by Second Lieutenant Thomas Moffitt, had ventured too far and had been captured out on the Telegraph Road toward Richmond. Moffitt had left with about 20 men on the 22nd on the mission. Stopping for a break, Moffitt had taken six men with him two miles further up the road to the home of Dr. Flippo and demanded that a meal be provided. Leaving no guard outside, the men sat down to eat. Within an hour, the house was surrounded by a Rebel force of approximately 100 men. In the ensuing firefight, Moffitt and his men were captured after purportedly firing all six rounds from their revolvers. Sergeant William Gwinn had been wounded in the thigh and was paroled and left with Dr. Flippo. The others—Moffitt, Orderly Sergeant Lewis C. Wilson, Sergeant Patrick Nolan, privates George Bailey, George Swift, and Benjamin Loder—were hustled off to Richmond as prisoners of war.[30]

Having already been slighted for promotion and now confronted with running the company single-handed, First Lieutenant Oliver Powers resigned his commission on the 28th. The company would now be commanded by a sergeant with no commissioned officers in camp.[31] Powers' resignation and Moffitt's incautious behavior and capture put Colonel Carter in a difficult situation. No enlisted men seemed up to the task of command, and there were no other officers in Company F. Carter decided to ask Governor Morton to promote Moffitt to captain, contingent upon Moffitt's exchange. Carter wanted to know more about what happened out on the Telegraph Road.[32]

Colonel Carter was in a foul mood. In addition to command problems in Company F, he continued to be plagued by the officer vacancies mentioned earlier. On top of this, he was trying to instill some military discipline in his men. Recently, some men had stolen some boards from a local citizen, and Carter decided to make examples of them. On July 31, the thieves were ordered to carry large rocks around the camp as punishment as well as a warning to the rest of the regiment. One man refused to pick up a rock, and Carter flew into a rage. Turning to the officer of the day, Captain William McClure of Company E, the colonel ordered him to shoot the recalcitrant soldier. Shocked, McClure refused the order. Carter promptly placed the captain under arrest.[33]

During a recent reorganization of the cavalry, the regiment was assigned to Farnsworth's 2nd Brigade of the Cavalry Division. This new alignment meant the army was slowly moving toward a consolidation of the mounted arm into its own corps. The old way of parceling out cavalry to individual infantry divisions was slowly going away. While the regiment was still understrength from men on detached duty to various headquarters, the new command structure would see more frequent movements of two or more regiments at a time. The Third Indiana's first such movement occurred in their baptism of fire as a whole unit.

Having been under fire as squadrons, the entire regiment would take part in the next action. On August 5, the men were ordered to join Gibbon and his brigade for an expedition to the Virginia Central Railroad, there to destroy track. The Harris Light Cavalry and a section of artillery rounded out the scouting party.

The column moved out early in the morning and once again and temperatures approaching 100 degrees prostrated the infantry. After a march of 15 miles, the Third Indiana crossed the Matla River and was attacked. Rebel artillery opened up, and Confederate cavalry were seen sending forces to both flanks. This precipitated a "hasty" retreat back across the river. The race was a near thing. William Burns of Company E was wounded and five men were captured—Stephen C. Lee of Company E, Hugh Stevenson and Ed Kelso of Company C, and brothers Samuel and William Shepard of Company D.[34] Lee's capture was unfortunate in that it may have been caused by one of his own officers. Lt. Robert Porter had killed two rebels in the skirmish by the river when Lee came out of the woods, minus his uniform coat and cap. "Lt. Porter, thinking he was one of the enemy, fired at him and shot his horse from under him and young Lee was taken prisoner."[35]

Gibbon sent the artillery forward, and after it fired a few rounds, the rebels retired back across the river. Having been discovered, Gibbon settled in for the night. The next morning, he received word that General Hatch was approaching with a reserve force. Upon his arrival, Hatch established a position on the banks of the river while Gibbon's men crossed over to continue their mission.

After marching seven miles, word was received that rebel cavalry under Jeb Stuart was moving up the Bowling Green road and threatened to cut them off. With the heat of the day already effecting the infantry, Gibbon decided he had to retrace his steps and rejoin Hatch to meet this new threat.[36] As the Hoosiers began their retreat, they passed by Dr. Flippo's residence and retrieved William Gwinn, the man wounded a week before when Moffitt and the others were captured.[37]

Approaching Hatch's position, artillery fire could be heard further north beyond Hatch. This became concerning when word was received that Stuart had attacked Hatch's supply train and threatened to cut the men off from Fredericksburg. Included in this message was the news that Marmaduke Green of Company D had been killed carrying a message from Gibbon to Hatch.[38]

Carter was ordered to bring his men forward. Armed only with revolvers and sabers, the regiment was ordered to outflank the Rebel position and drive off the Confederate artillery.[39] The order "Draw sabers!" rang out, and the men wound their sword knots tight around their wrists in preparation for the attack. They now would face the vaunted Confederate cavalry of J.E.B. Stuart in open combat. The order "Charge!" was given, and the men shot forward toward the enemy.

Companies A, B, and C were arrayed in the first line with companies D, E, and F in the second wave. Charging up a hill at the enemy battery, the first line sent the artillery's cavalry support flying. The second wave followed and drove the Confederates for two miles toward Bowling Green. Simultaneously, the Union infantry had recaptured the supply train, and the way was open once again to Fredericksburg.[40] As the Hoosiers reassembled they took stock of the costs of the attack. Only two men had been wounded, Benjamin Cole of Company A and John Kincaid of Company E.[41] Unfortunately, two others had been captured, Hugh Stevenson of Company B and James McConnell of Company D.[42]

The column pushed forward and arrived in Fredericksburg on August 8 where the men learned of the death from typhoid fever of the orderly sergeant of Company E the night before.[43] The men of the 3rd Indiana unsaddled their horses and had time to digest their latest experience. They had been under rifle and artillery fire, seen comrades killed, wounded, and captured. They had been chased by the enemy and, in turn, chased the Confederates. Overall, they felt good about their latest scrape with Stuart's horsemen. Charles N. White reported to the folks back in Jefferson County, "Things begin to look different from what they did down in Maryland. We are not the home guard now; we are the advance guard."[44]

Chapter 4

August 13, 1862–September 13, 1862

Being the advance guard was precisely what was on Major George Chapman's mind when he wrote to the Indiana adjutant general on August 13. The officer shortage was no longer a nuisance. In light of active campaigning, it was becoming critical. "Is there anything to prevent the commissioning of the officers required to fill vacancies in this regiment immediately?" he implored Noble. Only one of the six companies had its full complement of officers. Company F had none on duty as Moffitt, the only officer left, was still a prisoner of war. "From this you will perceive the urgent necessity there is for filling the vacancies, especially when I inform you in addition that we are doing Constant duty requiring Commissioned officers & those we have perform double duty," explained Chapman.[1]

Carter was also busy writing letters. He had seen very clearly over the past several weeks the absurdity of his men being armed only with revolvers, and faulty ones at that. The Savages were not up to the demands of field operations and required constant care. More importantly, when they were not in proper repair, they could be dangerous. This was unfortunately demonstrated when James Sturman of Company A had his pistol fire prematurely, shooting himself in the knee. The wound was so severe, it required the amputation of the leg.[2]

Carter had also put in a requisition for carbines to arm the entire regiment. One of the men put it well in a letter to home: "The Rebels shoot at us with their rifles and shotguns, carbines and long single barreled pistols, and then run before we get in range of them with our revolvers." While stopping short of yearning for their own former "long single barreled pistols," he presented a persuasive argument for better arms.[3]

On August 10, Carter saw results from some of his pleas. New Colt Navy revolvers were received to replace the old Savages. Of the same .36 caliber as their former sidearm, the Colts were much easier to maintain and kept in better working condition than the ugly duckling Savages. They were also lighter, weighing nearly a pound less.[4] Also, some carbines were coming to the regiment. While not enough to arm the entire regiment, it was a start. Presumably the Burnside carbines Carter had asked for, the regiment was beginning to acquire the firepower necessary to fight their enemy. Weighing seven pounds and measuring about 40 inches long, the .54 caliber breechloading Burnside would become a familiar weapon to the men of the Third.[5]

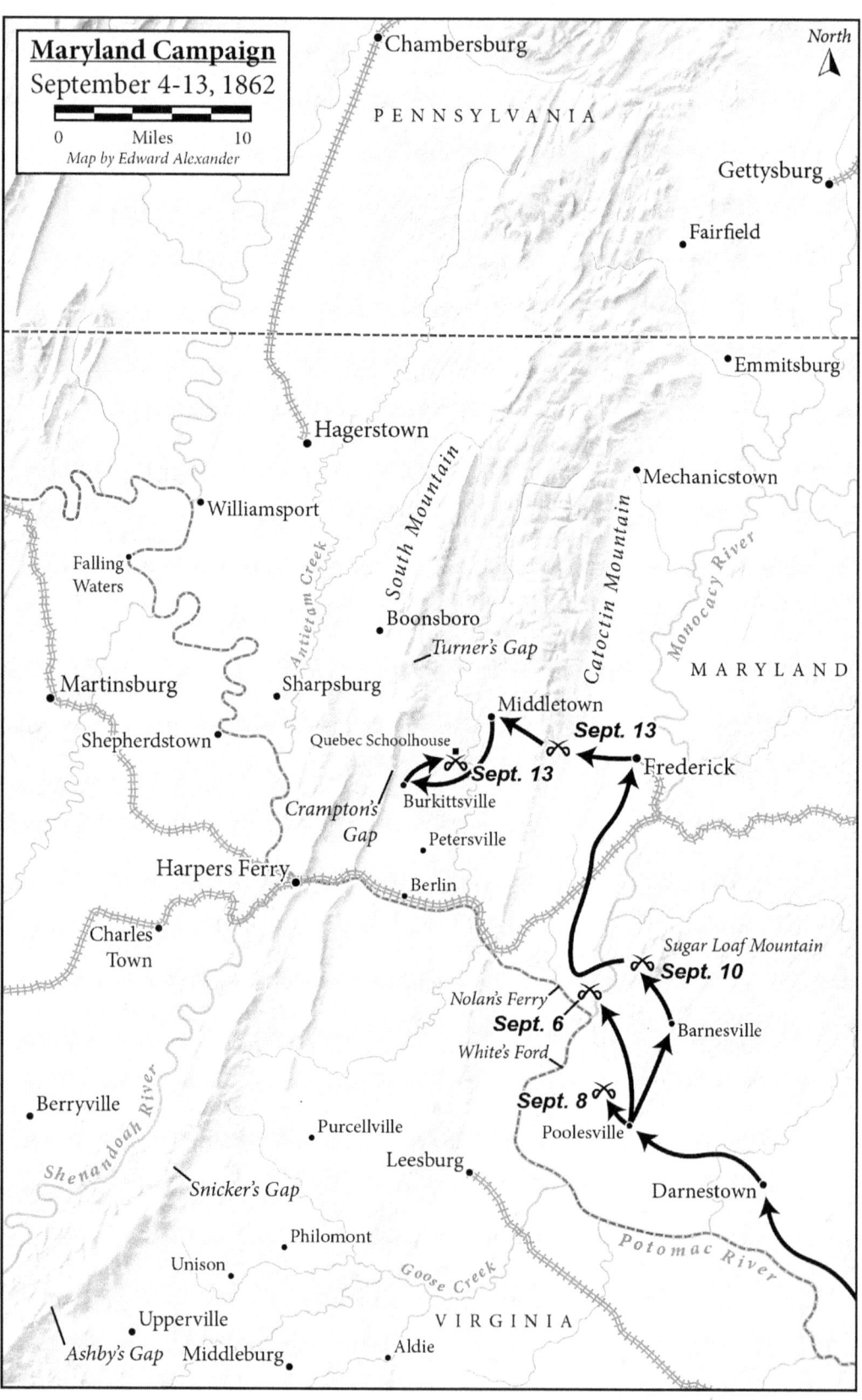

Chapter 4. August 13, 1862–September 13, 1862

The same day as the Colts' arrival, Captain Lemmon took a force of 80 men back down the Bowling Green road along with six companies of infantry and two artillery pieces. After a scout of about 10 miles, the men returned to camp with two prisoners, 30 horses, cattle, and mules.[6] On the 15th, Lemmon and Company C were called upon to accompany Gibbon's brigade on another scout toward Culpeper Courthouse. After returning to Fredericksburg, the company was detached for temporary duty as escort for Division commander General Rufus King. While there, the men were heartened to learn that the enlisted men captured with Lieutenant Moffitt had returned to camp after being exchanged.

Captain Charles Lemmon had made quite an impression on General John Gibbon. In an unusual gesture, a letter signed by all four regimental commanders in Gibbon's brigade, was sent to Governor Morton commending Lemmon as an excellent officer. On the outside of the letter Gibbon wrote: "I have had occasion on two different expeditions lately to notice the conduct of Capt. Lemmon and take great pleasure in recommending him to the favorable notice of the Gov. of Indiana. It is doing the country a wrong to keep such men in subordinate positions and Capt. L should be the head of a regt." Given his own history of being overlooked because of his Southern heritage, Gibbon must have felt strongly that Lemmon deserved better. A cover letter stated that the enclosed letter was sent on the commanders' own volition and without Lemmon's knowledge. Also endorsing this extraordinary recommendation was Gibbon's division commander, Brigadier General Rufus King. "I regard Capt. Lemmon as one of the best Cavalry officers I have met within the service."[7]

On the 25th, Lieutenant Moffitt returned to the regiment from his captivity and Company F finally had a commissioned officer in camp. Colonel Carter interviewed the lieutenant as to the circumstances of his capture and was satisfied. That same day, Major Chapman wrote Indiana adjutant general Laz Noble asking for the promotion of Moffitt to captain.[8]

The men were now on picket duty and guarding the Army of the Potomac ammunition trains in and around Fredericksburg. Danger lurked even in mundane duty as Henry Burtnister of Company B was wounded in the leg while serving as an orderly for an infantry brigade.[9] It was here where they heard of the debacle at Second Manassas. Pope's defeat precipitated rapid troop movements. All troops in and around Fredericksburg were ordered to immediately march to the capital. All supplies not able to be carried were to be destroyed. Marching in the rain, the 3rd Indiana left Fredericksburg with the sound of explosions and roaring flames filling their ears. Arriving at Acquia Creek, the men and horses started boarding the steamer *George Waters* for the short river trip up to Washington. In the process of boarding, one of the horses fell into the river. Several men worked to save the animal, and the mount was brought back to shore. Major General Ambrose Burnside, fellow Hoosier and commander of the IX Corps, helped in the rescue. Upon getting the horse back safely to dry land, Burnside took a flask from his pocket and gave the shivering animal a good pull from his own private stock.[10]

Lee's movement north meant work for the Union cavalry. Trying to determine Lee's plan of invasion, a cavalry screen was ordered to be placed north of Washington. As the men of the 3rd rested in their old campgrounds on September 4, orders were received to proceed to Darnestown, 15 miles northwest of the city. Throughout the day and into the night, the men and horses plodded steadily toward the small Maryland village, arriving early the next day. No rest was coming, however as they were ordered several miles beyond. Word had been received that Rebel forces were crossing the Potomac further up the river near Poolesville. Companies E and F were sent to investigate.[11]

Both men and horses were weary and hungry as they moved north. After a march of nine miles, the squadron reached Poolesville and pushed out toward the Potomac at Nolan's Ferry. As they approached this purported Confederate crossing site, shots were fired as the men ran into enemy pickets. Satisfied that the rebels were in the vicinity, the two companies returned to Darnestown, reaching their camp at 9:00 p.m. "Tired, worn out and almost sick," is how one horseman described the condition of the squadron.[12] Rest would have to wait, however, as the two companies were again ordered to ride back toward Poolesville. Throughout the night, the men chased and were chased by the Rebel cavalry, skirmishing and fighting. They were not relieved until 10:00 a.m. by the rest of the regiment some miles short of Poolesville.[13]

Col. Scott Carter was unhappy with the past few days' events. Poor communication was compounded when an apparent misunderstanding with General

An arrogant self-promoter who was not above working behind his superiors' backs, Alfred Pleasanton was commander of the 1st Division when the Cavalry Corps was formed in the winter of 1862–63. He would later be promoted to the command of the Cavalry Corps only to be unceremoniously transferred to Missouri after he testified against his commander, General George Meade, during Congressional hearings (Library of Congress).

Chapter 4. August 13, 1862–September 13, 1862

Alfred Pleasanton, cavalry division commander, and Carter occurred. Carter was placed under arrest, and Lieutenant Colonel Jacob Buchanan took command of the regiment.[14]

Poolesville had become a prime locale of interest for the Union command, or so it seemed to Colonel John Farnsworth, commander of the 8th Illinois Cavalry. On September 7 and on his own initiative, Farnsworth took Chapman and companies A, B, C, and D along with four of his own companies for a quick look at this seemingly important village. The column rode into town from the southeast and were able to nab two Confederate pickets as they tried to run northwest. Returning to camp in Darnestown, Farnsworth was praised by Pleasanton for going "on their own hook" and checking out the hamlet.[15]

McClellan, in his inimitable slow, cautious way, was still seeking information as to the whereabouts of Lee's army. For the third time in as many days, the men were ordered to Poolesville. This time, the full complement of the 3rd Indiana and the 8th Illinois would be going. Accompanying them were two guns from Company M, 2nd U.S. Artillery. Given their previous visits, little contact with the enemy was expected. After an uneventful ride, the two regiments moved through the town, with the 3rd Indiana going to the northwest and the 8th Illinois southwest to Nolan's Ferry. Unknown to the Union horsemen, two guns of Chew's Battery of Confederate artillery were posted about a mile north of Poolesville. Supporting them were the 7th and 12th Virginia Cavalry. Chew's guns opened up on the Hoosiers as they came into view.

The two Union artillery pieces came into battery about a half mile from the Rebel position. Slipping to the east, Buchanan moved the regiment into a flanking position. He then ordered companies C, D, E, and F to the north to cut off the enemy's retreat to Barnesville. Turning to Captain William Patton of Company A, the lieutenant colonel asked for a detail of a sergeant and 10 fighting men to lead a charge on the opposing artillery. Captain Patton straightened his back and responded, "Colonel, my men are all fighting men!" and the detail was quickly assembled.[16]

Buchanan formed companies A and B under the command of Major Chapman and ordered the charge, slamming into the right flank of the 12th Virginia. At the same time, the four companies to the north came down the Barnesville road hoping to hem in the Confederates and force them toward the river and the waiting 8th Illinois. The 7th Virginia, seeing the threat, whirled about to meet this attack. The smaller 12th Virginia twisted to meet Chapman's one squadron charge. Seeing their peril, Chew's rebel artillerymen tried to limber up as fast as possible. Horsemen, blue and gray, were soon whirling around the guns, slashing at each other and firing pistols. Horses slammed into each other as the Hoosier attack hit the Confederate troops. Men began to fall, and the clang of swords added to the cacophony of battle.

In typical cavalry battle style, the Hoosiers withdrew a short distance to regroup for another try. The attack by the northern squadrons of the 3rd Indiana had split around the artillery position, opening a way out for the Confederates. During the short respite, Chew's men were able to withdraw the guns and begin their retreat to Barnesville. As Buchanan tried to re-organize his men, the 8th Illinois came up and took up the pursuit, a task they finally broke off at dusk.

The quick, vicious action had cost the little regiment dearly. Killed in Chapman's charge on the enemy's right flank was Sergeant David Fallis. Henry Banta, the sergeant who led the 10 "fighting men" in the charge, was bleeding from nine different saber wounds.[17] Others wounded were John Eblin, Frederick Kassebaum, Sergeant Rudolph Lamson, William Stevens, Fletcher Wood and Benjamin Workman, all from Company A.[18] Not found in the official records was the wounding of Captain Henry Wright's servant boy. Hit in the shoulder, he was reported to have returned to camp whistling "The Star Spangled Banner."[19]

The only casualty from the attack along the Barnesville road was William Kennedy of Company C. Kennedy had ridden ahead of the charge and nearly paid dearly for his impetuosity. "Kennedy run at least 3 lengths of his horse ahead of anyone and after emptying his pistol & gun, cut for their flag. 4 men protected it & he would have had it in one minute more but one bullet cut his sword hand just above the thumb, another thru his cartredge Box, another thru his Holster & another thru his left hand. They cut down his sword and it dropped and wound in [the] Bridle and he wheeled out."[20]

Rebel losses were reported to be 16 killed and wounded. As often happened after a fight, a flag of truce was displayed and the Confederates were allowed to gather their dead and wounded. All firing ceased, and the men from both sides mingled and talked. Rebels confided that they were all that was left of Ashby's cavalry and were made up of the first families of Virginia and owned their horses. The Hoosiers quickly responded that they too owned their horses and were first families of Indiana. As the work ended, so did the comradery. Both sides returned to their prospective positions, once again enemies.[21]

McClellan was so enamored by the little affair that he sent a special telegram to Washington telling of the Union cavalry success at Poolesville.[22] The regiment had little time to bask in the glow of their achievements, however. Lee's army was somewhere to the north, and McClellan still needed to know where. That meant probing the Confederate picket line and that meant work for the cavalry.

After caring for the wounded and burying the dead, the men were ordered to continue their scout north the next day. Early contact developed into a daylong push north, capturing 30 to 40 of their adversaries. Among the prisoners was one of particular curiosity to the Hoosiers—a rebel lieutenant who hailed from Indiana.[23] By late afternoon, they approached a prominence known locally as Sugar Loaf Mountain. Anyone on its summit had a complete view of the surrounding countryside. The men knew that the morning would bring an order to attack the mountain.

They were not disappointed. Word arrived early on September 10 to clear out the rebel forces on Sugar Loaf Mountain. Dismounting, the men began the steep ascent, sometimes resorting to hands and knees to make any headway. Unable to reach the summit, the men were able to capture several Confederates with their flag. Deep purple with a rattlesnake in the cross of the black panel, it was purported to belong to a company of Turner Ashby's regiment.[24]

The next morning, September 11, infantry support moved up and took over the assault of Sugar Loaf Mountain. The Confederate forces obliged the foot soldiers by abandoning their position as the massed infantry began their assault. Meanwhile, the 3rd Indiana had moved to the west around Sugar Loaf and traveled to Nolan's Ferry. Companies C and F were sent to ford the river. Once across the men could see long lines of wagons guarded by cavalry on the Virginia side. All were waiting to cross into Maryland.[25]

The pursuit of Lee was undertaken with McClellan's trademark caution. Since leaving Poolesville on September 9, the 3rd Indiana had only moved 10 miles. On the 12th, the men doubled this distance when ordered to Frederick, arriving around 5:00 p.m. to a heroes' welcome. "Men, women and children seemed wild with joy, clapping their hands waving handkerchiefs, and greeting the Union soldiers with every demonstration of enthusiasm. We felt as though we were once again in a land unpolluted by the footprints of traitors," wrote one man.[26] Sam Gilpin in Company C was nearly speechless. "I cannot describe the reception. We passed down the illuminated streets forgetting in the middle of all of the flag waving, singing, shouting, joy and wildness that there was work yet to do."[27]

Work was indeed to be done, and the 3rd Indiana could expect its share of it in the days to come. The men not already equipped with carbines finally received them while in Frederick. There was no time to train the men in their operation, however.[28] Unbeknownst to the cavalrymen, a fellow Hoosier of the 27th Indiana Infantry had discovered a copy of Lee's invasion orders in an old campsite. The orders revealed that Lee's army had taken several routes north and was scattered. If the Union army moved quickly, it had a chance to defeat the Confederates.

Fearing a trap, McClellan waited almost an entire day before ordering his army in pursuit of Lee. By that time, the 3rd Indiana, 8th Illinois and 1st Massachusetts were already on the move down the National Road to the northwest of Frederick. About four miles out from the city they were fired upon by Confederate artillery posted on the ridge of Catoctin Mountain. The fire was inaccurate and allowed the men to count off by fours and dismount on the right of the road. Major Chapman, in command due to Lieutenant Colonel Buchanan's on again, off again illness, ordered two squadrons to proceed as skirmishers up the mountain to flank the rebel artillery position.[29] Resorting to hands and knees once again, the 3rd Indiana pressed the Confederate support—the 1st North Carolina Cavalry—back. The Carolinians were no doubt nervous for they could see the entire Army of the Potomac in the valley below.

Thick undergrowth on the mountain reduced the fighting to sporadic, almost one-on-one combat. An old stone fence ran along the mountain. Oliver Trester of Company D thought it would make good cover as he inched up the mountain. As fellow company members watched, he heaved himself over the seemingly abandoned fence—right on top of two rebs. The North Carolinians killed Trester and ran as quickly as they could away from the advancing Hoosiers.[30] James Quinn of Company A was also wounded in the wild mountainside.[31]

The outnumbered Confederates were flanked and scurried down the other side of the mountain ridge into the village of Middletown. As the pursuing Union cavalrymen crested the ridge the picturesque Middletown Valley spread out below. The horse holders brought the horses up, and the men mounted to continue their pursuit of the retreating enemy. Two artillery pieces came into line and began throwing shells at the fast disappearing Confederates. The Hoosiers and their companions of the 8th Illinois charged down the mountain into the village of Middletown. Too late to capture more than a few stragglers, they were astonished to receive a second rousing welcome from townspeople in as many days as jubilant Middletown residents greeted the men with cool pitchers of water and loaves of warm bread.[32]

By now, it was midafternoon and the rebel forces were getting away. Told that a Confederate wagon train had left town headed south toward Burkittsville and Crampton's Gap, Captain Medill of the 8th Illinois was ordered to take a squadron from the 8th plus companies E and F of the 3rd and pursue the wagon train. In all, the Union column numbered about 230. Moving out toward Burkittsville, the men were in no hurry. They had been in the saddle since early morning and had been fighting off and on all day. The mid–September sun was beginning to dip lower into the western sky, and the eastern slope of South Mountain was already in shadows.

After a pursuit of a mile and a half, Rebel cavalry and artillery were seen at the base of South Mountain. Beyond them, the wagon train could be seen wending its way toward the Gap. For the next half hour the men watched the wagons slowly climb the slope. Medill decided that they had done everything they could and ordered a return to Middletown via a rocky ravine road. The sunken path was flanked on both sides by an old post and picket fence with the Quebec Schoolhouse to the north.

Many remembered the ride back to camp as almost peaceful. The tranquility was enhanced by the children peering out of the schoolhouse windows of the schoolhouse at the passing column.[33] Given the long day the men had experienced, this short cut would get the men to camp sooner for a well-earned rest.[34] Little did the men realize that they were about to engage in one of the nastiest scrapes the 3rd Indiana would ever endure.

When the men descended into the valley earlier that day, its floor looked smooth and undulating. In reality, it was cut by deep ravines and hidden folds that could offer concealment for men and horses. In one such fold was Cobb's Legion of Confederate cavalry. They had watched the Hoosiers and Illinoisians ride by earlier and knew they would have to return to their camp in Middletown. The Georgians of Cobb's Legion waited patiently for the time to spring their trap. They found the perfect opportunity when the returning Union cavalry filed into the narrow road, the

Illinoisians leading with the 3rd Indiana's Company F trailing Company E at the rear of the column. Just as Company F entered the defile, a single shot cracked from the vicinity of the schoolhouse, and a nearby hickory tree's bark was peeled white by the bullet. Two men at the front of the column pulled down a section of the fence and started toward the schoolhouse. They never made it. Halfway there, Cobb's 300 strong Legion erupted out of a nearby ravine, and all hell broke loose.[35]

The thunder of horse hooves, men screaming, and the flash of sabers in the dying sunlight all accentuated the shock attack on the strung out column. Confined by fences in a narrow space with little room to maneuver, the Hoosiers and Illinoisians were trapped. A ragged volley of carbine fire was sent toward the charging horde as Union men and horses milled about in the tight confines of the roadbed. The Confederates came swinging their sabers and firing their pistols over and through the fence as Union officers screamed out orders, trying to assemble some type of defense. In the churning maelstrom of the sunken road, casualties quickly mounted.

Company F was in the most exposed position. In addition to the attack along the fence line, the rebels had curled around the rear of the column, blocking escape in that direction. Corporal Harvey Williamson of Company F went down, his head horribly mangled by a saber blow. Ed Schievelbein twisted to avoid a sword swinging Rebel but took a blow to the head, nonetheless. John Grubb and Jon Childs suffered the same fate as did Peter Welch, his wound coming with a blow to the jaw. William Hinds took a bullet in the back. James Quinn had a bullet shatter his hip. Less severely injured, but down and bleeding, were Thomas Little and Jim Norman.[36]

Trapped and dazed, the men fought back as best they could. One man in Company F was in shock from the ferocity of the attack. Unhorsed and cornered by a couple of saber wielding Confederates, he warded off their blows with his carbine which was soon hacked along its entire length. A stutterer, the man shouted, "Wh-wh-wh-what in the h-h-hell do you mean?" Fortunately, Sergeant James Mount "knew what they meant" and went to the man's assistance.[37] Soon after the rescue, Mount took a bullet in the lung and slumped to the rocky roadbed.[38]

All up and down the column the story was the same. Up in Company E, John Weible called out to his friend Sam Gilpin, "Sam, I've caught one." He had been shot through the body. John Wildman was struck on the back and fell to the ground. Henry Papst took a bullet in the leg, and Smyrna Seever dropped from his saddle, severely wounded. Also severely wounded was Joseph Jones. Thomas Day had his horse killed in the first volley, and as he scrambled to get away from his dead mount, was nearly trampled by other frantic horses. As he tried to climb the fence and escape, a Confederate cut him on the hip, dropping him back into the road.[39]

The Union men frantically looked for a way to respond to the attack. Some men were able to knock down sections of the old fence and attacked the flank of the rebels. In one such opening Sergeant Joseph Lewis of Company E squared off with a Rebel sergeant. Both fired their revolvers at the same time, and both fell dead, Lewis on top of the Confederate, both with bullets in the heart.[40] The flanking attacks convinced the rebels that it was time to leave. Retreating to the northwest, they were gone as quickly as they had come. The remaining Union cavalrymen pulled back toward Middletown, expecting another attack.

Tom Day was left alone in the slaughterhouse of the road. All around him were friends and acquaintances, hurt or dead, some moaning and others silent. Wounded horses screamed in pain. Hearing approaching hoof beats, Day grabbed a small Confederate Maynard carbine, scooped up some loose cartridges from the road, and jumped into some bushes. In a panic, he tried to load the carbine only to discover the bullets were a different caliber than the Maynard. Fortunately, he did not need them. Peering out of the bushes, he saw two Confederate officers and Johnny Smith of the 8th Illinois under a flag of truce. Smith and the rebel officers agreed to allow each side to keep their wounded and all equipment originally belonging to them. When Day stepped out of his hiding place, one of the officers recognized the Confederate issued Maynard and relieved him of the carbine.[41]

Another member of the 8th Illinois joined Day and Smith, and the three Union men tried to provide comfort to the injured. Finding Sergeant Williamson, Day carefully placed a cap under the sergeant's horribly mutilated head and wiped the bloody froth from the sergeant's lips before giving him a sip of water. "He kept throwing up his breast and Smith said to me, 'open his shirt, he knows you and has something he wants you to get.' I did so and found a belt with over $400 in it, (which I gave to his officers to send to his friends) then he sank contented."[42]

Realizing there would be no second attack, the Union cavalry returned to collect the dead and wounded and gather the equipment scattered about. The wounded were taken to a Lutheran church in Middletown where the pews and aisles became stained with their blood. Early the next morning, Williamson and Seever died of their wounds, bringing the butcher's total to three dead and 11 wounded for the Third Indiana. The 8th Illinois suffered one killed and eight wounded. The little fracas near the Quebec Schoolhouse had lasted only a few minutes, but it had been terribly deadly.[43]

But after the initial shock, the western soldiers gave nearly as good as they got. In Wade Hampton's after action report, he listed the Cobb's Legion casualties as four killed and nine wounded. He also reported that the 1st North Carolina had lost nine men wounded that morning on Catoctin Mountain.[44]

While companies E and F were fighting for their lives south of town, the rest of the regiment had continued up the National Road toward Turner's Gap, trying to find the Confederate position. Now late in the day, they were met by enemy picket fire from the mountain shadows. They fired blindly into the sun before breaking off the action and retreating back to Middletown. Unfortunately, it did not end quickly enough for Leander Harris of Company C. He was shot through the body and took a second bullet through his left arm. He was carried back to the makeshift hospital in the church.[45] It had been a harrowing day for the men of the 3rd Indiana. Casualties for the day now totaled four killed and 14 wounded. In additional three were assumed captured. Over the past week, a total of 27 men had been killed or wounded bringing the casualty total to 46 since the beginning of the year.[46]

The Middletown Valley nestled between Catoctin Mountain and South Mountain was one of the most beautiful vistas the men had ever seen.[47] Yet that image would also have attached with it the horrible memory of Catoctin Mountain and Quebec Schoolhouse. With the army moving up behind and around them, the morrow promised to be another busy day.

Chapter 5

September 14, 1862–April 30, 1863

September 14, the men of the Third Indiana were detailed to provide support for Union artillery and took a spectator's seat for the battle of South Mountain. This was the first large scale engagement they had witnessed, and the men took a keen interest in all of the activities. Late in the day, McClellan asked for a brigade of "iron" to make the final assault to Crampton's Gap. The Hoosiers witnessed that attack by their old friends of Gibbon's brigade who were forever after known as the "Iron Brigade."

The next day, the cavalry was again called upon to provide the vanguard of the army. As the men passed over the battlefield of the day before, they witnessed the debris and destruction left behind. "The principle feature of the morning was the dead, dying, wounded, prisoners, stragglers, skirmishers, abandoned artillery, dust and excitement," succinctly wrote Sam Gilpin.[1] The army slowly advanced until the next morning. Lee's Army of Northern Virginia had been found.

Arrayed before the men were gray infantry in positions around the small town of Sharpsburg. The meandering Antietam Creek separated the two armies. McClellan came up and realized he would have to attack. Throughout the evening, he planned a grand attack, a disjointed and poorly executed affair that would result in the loss of more American lives in one day than any other in the history of the republic before or since.

The cavalry's role in this bloodbath was fairly passive. Positioned in reserve near the center of the Union line, the men were called upon to clear the opposite shore of Antietam Creek of rebel sharpshooters. Charging across Middle Bridge, they chased the pesky Confederates away, the only casualty being the ear of John Kernan's horse.[2] Artillery soon followed them and went into action in support of infantry attacking a sunken farm road about a mile away. The ferocious fighting there would result in the renaming of the road as "Bloody Lane." Partially protected by a low ridge, the Hoosiers were still subjected to counter battery fire. During the afternoon, Second Lieutenant Charles Lee and Henry Cotton, both of Company A, were wounded by flying shrapnel.[3]

The long day of carnage came to a close, and the next morning a squadron of the 3rd Indiana got the opportunity to survey the grisly aftermath of war close up. Companies E and F were ordered out to reconnoiter the enemy position. First riding to the left flank and then cutting across the face of the Union army to the right flank, the men surveyed the enemy positions. Remarkably, they were not fired upon during the entire traverse of the battlefield. It was as if neither army wanted to resume the butchery of the day before.[4]

Lee began his retreat across the Potomac the next day, September 19. Once again leading the advance, the Hoosiers were ordered to follow the enemy and report back. Along the way, they picked up Confederate stragglers and some wounded. As they approached the Potomac, they came under artillery fire from across the river. One six-pound cannonball knocked Flavius Bellamy's hat from his head before the regiment could scamper out of range.[5] Over the next several days, McClellan was content to let Lee retreat unmolested back to Virginia. Occasional cavalry scouts were sent across the river to probe the Confederate forces with excursions to Sheperdstown and Martinsburg.[6]

Still encamped on the battlefield, the men were subjected to all of the sights and smells of the carnage of the 17th. Dead men and horses were still scattered over the countryside along with guns, boxes, cooking utensils, unused rations, books, canteens, haversacks, tents, blankets, letters—in other words, all of the possible accoutrements of an army in the field. They also witnessed the morbid curiosity of mankind. "Hundreds of visitors are yet daily passing over the ground, gathering relics and closely observing various marks of destruction."[7]

Amid all of this, the men received word that there was to be a review. Grumbling, the men cleaned their weapons, groomed their horses, and mended their worn uniforms as best they could. On October 3, they filed out to the Hagerstown Pike to an area near the Dunker Church, the site of horrendous fighting only two weeks prior. As they waited, they witnessed a sight that would be repeated countless times over the next several weeks. Only twenty five yards from where they waited, the men watched the disinterment of a New York soldier. Standing to the side were two weeping women—the man's sister and his fiancée. The women, upon hearing of his death, had traveled to Maryland to retrieve his body. With the assistance of the soldier's comrades, his grave was discovered, and he was about to begin the long trip back to New York for reburial.[8]

After several hours of waiting, the command was heard—"Attention! Draw sabers!" as the tall form of the President of the United States could be seen coming past the ranks. The men now realized why there had been such a hubbub. Accompanying the six foot six inch Abraham Lincoln was the five foot eight inch General George McClellan. To one Hoosier, the president "seemed more haggard and care-worn than ever before, showing plainly that recently he has suffered much mental anxiety." Sam Gilpin saw him in a different light. "Old Abe is as _ugly_ as ever," he wrote.[9]

With the review over, the men reverted to the routine of drill and camp duties. For the next several days their time was taken up with saber, carbine, company, squadron and regimental drill. The weather was beginning to have a fall-like edge to it as the evenings turned colder. On the 10th, the men were amused by the arrival of a new regiment to the camp. Now old veterans of 14 months of service, they were dismissive of the new men. "We laughed at them so much. How enthusiastic these new comers are and how unacquainted with soldier life. They will learn," wrote one bemused Hoosier.[10] The routine of camp was shattered on October 11 as word was received that Stuart's cavalry had crossed the Potomac and was headed for Pennsylvania.[11]

Stuart had won fame by riding around the Union army on the Peninsula. Showing little respect for the Union cavalry as he had months before, he now embarked on a raid into Pennsylvania before riding completely around McClellan's army, returning to Virginia via Maryland. Waking to a cold blustery rain, the men of the Third were ordered to saddle up and move westward to Williamsport, ostensibly to chase Stuart. Joining them were the 8th Illinois, 8th New York, 8th Pennsylvania, and Pennington's Battery of horse artillery. When they reached Hagerstown, however, their orders were abruptly changed, and they were ordered east. Picking up speed, the men completed their 20-mile march, reaching Mechanicstown by 9:00 p.m. The men dropped to the ground without unsaddling their horses and fell asleep. Roused at 1:00 a.m., the column was ordered to Frederick, 15 miles to the south.

Stuart was moving faster than the Union command could determine. He had begun his return through Maryland and was reported to be threatening the supply base at Frederick. Arriving in Frederick, the Union cavalrymen found that Stuart had already passed through and was headed west to Virginia. As quickly as their jaded horses would carry them, the men were ordered another 16 miles to the familiar Nolan's Ferry, one of the few Potomac crossing points available to the raiders. Arriving at Nolan's Ferry, the men could see about 500 Rebel cavalry dressed in blue uniforms and overcoats they had captured in Chambersburg, Pennsylvania.[12] Realizing that some of the raiders were still on the Maryland side of the Potomac, the men held out the hope that they could prevent Stuart's force from crossing over to the safety of Virginia.

The grueling march over the past few days had taken its toll on Union horses and men. Horses simply wore out, and their riders were forced to give up the chase. The 3rd Indiana and 8th Illinois had been able to keep some semblance of unit integrity and fanned out into skirmish order and began to advance on the blue-clad Rebels. Two artillery pieces that had been able to keep up with the pursuit went into action. But as the men advanced, they were chagrined to find out that the raiders had slipped across the Potomac at White's Ford, three miles south of Nolan's Ferry. The only satisfaction the men had for their efforts was the recapture of 50 cattle that had refused to cross the river.[13] Ordered to make camp, the regiment collapsed.

The march of 70 miles in 24 hours had been grueling. Barely 200 men and horses had been able to keep up. To make matters worse, it began to rain. Bone tired, frustrated and now soaked, the men pulled saddles from their horses' backs and squatted in the mud for a meal of wormy hardtack. Many looked back on that night as the worst of their service.¹⁴ That night, they cursed the army, Stuart, the rain and mud as they sat in misery on the shore of the Potomac.

General Pleasanton showed his appreciation of their efforts with more duty on October 14. Asserting the 3rd Indiana's horses were in the best condition of his command, he ordered the regiment to Petersville, a 10-mile ride north of Nolan's Ferry. His estimation of the regiment's strength of 350 was wildly exaggerated.¹⁵ By now, only 150 men and horses were able to be mounted. Painfully, the men swung into saddle and slowly rode up the Catoctin Mountain to Petersville. Two days later, the men were ordered to the old government armory town of Harpers Ferry arriving there on the 16th. The men were sent a further four miles west to Charles Town where pickets were sent out, and the men and horses tried to regain a little strength from their recent ordeals.

For the next few weeks, the men rested and picketed the surrounding area. Stragglers from the previous week's trials began to return to camp. On October 21, the cavalry division was reorganized with the 3rd Indiana now brigaded with the 6th U.S., 8th Pennsylvania, 8th Illinois and 8th New York. Five days later, the men recrossed the Potomac with their new brigade comrades to the Maryland side. The men were surprised to see a familiar face when they set up camp—Colonel Scott Carter. Carter had been under arrest since early September. While the exact cause of the arrest is unclear, Carter had been waiting patiently in Washington for a court of inquiry to clear his name and reputation. Pleasanton, who had ordered the arrest, had put off bringing official charges against Carter for so long that the colonel was now entitled to be released from arrest. Carter, his sense of honor wounded, insisted upon the court of inquiry. Pleasanton refused, and there the matter stood.¹⁶

Flavius Bellamy was a devoted letter writer and a shrewd observer of all around him (U.S. Army Heritage and Education Center).

This state of affairs was beginning to have a negative effect on the regiment. Lieutenant Colonel Buchanan had been in bad health throughout the late summer and fall and had been in the field intermittently. Finally, on October 24, he resigned his commission and went home.[17] About this same time, Assistant Surgeon Luther Brusie turned in his resignation, as well. The little regiment of six companies, until Carter was free to return to duty, was now led by one lone major.[18]

Now in command, Major Chapman wrote to the governor about officer vacancies and his claim to be promoted to lieutenant colonel. Four days later, he wrote Adjutant General Noble about the officer vacancies, as well. After reiterating the recommendations that had been made several times previously, he turned to another situation. Since his recommendation of First Lieutenant Matthew Mason of Company D, a great deal had happened. Mason was on sick leave to nurse an injury fairly common in the cavalry—a crushed testicle. Meanwhile, Second Lieutenant Wright had held a grudge against Mason, and they had been quarreling ever since. Chapman confided that, in truth, neither man was fit for company command. He could not recommend the orderly sergeant for promotion to the commissioned ranks for the man "is a constitutional grumbler—the worst sort of man for a Company officer." Chapman pithily concluded that "Company D has been in a bad fix for some time."[19]

Other men were cranking up the papermill to send in their own claims for promotion. It was a foregone conclusion that Chapman would be promoted to lieutenant colonel, which left the majorship open. David McClure of Company E wrote his father concerning his brother William, captain of Company E. He expected his brother to petition the governor for the promotion, and he was correct.[20] McClure not only asked for the promotion, but he also received it, dating from October 25, 1862.[21]

Jacob Greiner had his eye on the commissary position which had never been appointed. In a letter to his father, he included a petition signed by all but three officers of the regiment. The old man dutifully hand delivered the petition to Adjutant General Noble. Either the officers' signatures or an old man's personal appeal did the trick, for Greiner was appointed to the post on November 1.[22]

Chapman's promotion became official on October 25 but was met with mixed emotions in some quarters. He had been in nominal command for several months, and his leadership in the fighting of the past few weeks was seen positively. For others, however, their concerns were not his leadership but rather his drinking.

Several men had mentioned his fondness for liquor in letters home. David McClure, not yet aware of Chapman's promotion, expressed his opinion. "I hope that Chapman may not get anything as he is a disgrace to the Regt—gets drunk when on duty and the like of that. He is Brave But who wants a man that gets drunk when in Command for Lieut. Col.?"[23] That Chapman liked his liquor there was little doubt. Several of his own diary entries referred to drinking parties. Gilpin told of a party in Chapman's tent the evening of the grand review at Antietam where all in attendance got properly pickled.[24] First Lieutenant Henry Wright wrote in a letter months later referring to an episode a few days before the grand review. Supposedly, Chapman got so drunk he lay on the ground vomiting. Wright did admit, however, that he was not an eyewitness but had heard of the incident later.[25]

Chapter 5. September 14, 1862–April 30, 1863

Others may have been put off by his non-martial appearance. Barely five foot six inches, the officer with his round glasses hardly looked like a warrior. In an era where a man's looks often determined what people thought of him, his clerk-like countenance did little to inspire confidence. Flavius Bellamy sniffed in a letter to his family, "Major Chapman now has command of the Regt. I expect he will get the position of Lt. Col. Though he is a little bespectacled upstart, and petty tyrant and no one likes him."[26] Not all of the men saw him that way, however. Captain William McClure commented that Chapman, since taking command, had handled the regiment "splendidly."[27]

Despite what may have been personal flaws, Chapman was the one constant in the leadership of the regiment since its formation. Oftentimes, he would be the only staff officer on duty. His independent command in eastern Maryland had shown him to be a resourceful and competent officer. In addition, his formal training at the Naval Academy and service during his youth had instilled in him the belief that discipline was essential in a military unit. Whether a tyrant, drunk, bespectacled upstart or all of the above, Chapman had been more responsible for the development of the 3rd Indiana Cavalry into a cohesive fighting body than any other man. Given the uncertain situation with Colonel Carter, he was now given the opportunity to lead the regiment outright.[28]

On October 27, the relative quiet was broken as the regiment was ordered to Purcellville, Virginia, a small town 12 miles south of Harpers Ferry. While passing through Snicker's Gap, they came under artillery fire. Eli Powell of Company D was wounded in the foot by grapeshot that passed through three horses before striking Powell.[29] Three days after their arrival, they were ordered seven miles further south to near Philomont where on November 1 they found a rebel force. Near the hamlet of Unison, west of Philomont, the men skirmished with rebel cavalry. During the melee, John Williams of Company C was wounded.[30] On November 2, a squadron was ordered to clear a patch of woods of rebels so that artillery might pass. Dismounting, the men moved to the attack. "We double-quicked across the fields and raising a yell charged into the woods, making the grey coats light out. A 'carbine charge' would have amused infantry."[31] By November 4, the Union cavalry had pushed the enemy forces 20 miles south. The men now found themselves in the vicinity of their June duties. They spent the evening at the Marshall farm where they had appropriated a piano for some impromptu dancing many weeks ago.[32]

The weather turned decidedly colder over the next few days with temperatures dropping near freezing. Despite the lack of overcoats and gloves, the men were ordered further south, where they were attacked at Barbee's Crossroads.[33] Pleasanton was in command and spread out the brigade, with the 3rd Indiana kept in the center as support for the artillery. As he rebels came on, Pleasanton was seen striding about, his nervousness betrayed by the incessant hitting of his leg with a little cowhide whip he always carried. Becoming more agitated, he urged the gunners with shouts of "give 'em hell!" When he was remonstrated by a nearby chaplain that such language might not bring divine support, Pleasanton was reported to reply, "When the 3rd Indiana is back of my guns I don't have to depend on any other support. I can always depend on those Hoosiers!"[34] Depend on them he did, for later in the fight he ordered the regiment to the right to help the 8th New York turn the Rebel line. During the fighting, Augustine Bardwell caught a bullet and limped back to the surgeon.[35]

After pushing the Confederates back from Barbee's Crossroads, the Union horsemen were ordered south another 11 miles and skirmished near Amissville. Snow began to fall as an early winter storm moved across the area. Reaching Amissville, the men went in search of shelter from the cold. A recent outbreak of sickness in the area was discovered when they found tents in a room marked "small pox." Since all of the men had been exposed to the disease, they confiscated the shelters and settled down for the night. A punster in one squad remarked "the cold was not so intense in tents."[36]

For the next week, the men performed picket duty. To unsettle the Union cavalry, Confederate troops made unexpected attacks on the picket outposts. To make matters worse, it began to rain even as the temperatures slowly rose. It rained for a week, making the men and horses miserable. In the middle of the monsoon like weather, the men were ordered east 12 miles to Warrenton and, four days later on November 18, they moved further southeast to Bealeton Station. Three days later they started for Fredericksburg to join the bulk of the Army of the Potomac, arriving on November 23.[37]

While the regiment was maneuvering across Virginia, General McClellan was replaced as commander of the Army of the Potomac with General Ambrose Burnside. An unimaginative leader, Burnside conceived a winter campaign to capture Fredericksburg and open the way to Richmond. For the next 10 days, the regiment served as pickets on the right of the army at U.S. Ford. The only noteworthy occurrence during this deployment was the capture of 32 boxes of chewing tobacco by the 8th Pennsylvania. The Keystoners magnanimously shared the booty with the rest of the brigade and "the strapped and hungry tobacco chewers are now in one of the liveliest moods of rejoicing. I have not seen so many smiling Hoosiers in a long time as last night, when the distributions of the weed took place in the regiment."[38]

With the battle of Fredericksburg eminent, the regiment was ordered back to the town and were assigned the familiar role of support for the artillery. Ten men were detailed to the Signal Corps to patrol the telegraph wire between army headquarters and corps commander Sumner's camp. On December 13, Burnside turned the Army of the Potomac loose on Marye's Heights, and thousands were slaughtered. Six days later, the 3rd Indiana resumed their picket on the right near U.S. Ford.[39]

The men now settled into the routine of picket duty and camp life. Huts were built to ward off the winter chill and to give some sense of permanency. A warm hut was nice to return to after a stint on the picket line. Picket duty consisted of three day rotations when the men left the main camp and moved to positions along the

Rappahannock River to watch the enemy. The pickets next to the river served two hour shifts with four hours off. Regulations required that the men be mounted and facing the enemy. Many days and nights, however, the men had to dismount and move about to keep from freezing. A picket reserve of a handful of men was established about half a mile behind the river. At the reserve, fires were allowed, but the men had to be armed and horses saddled at all times in case of attack.[40]

To alleviate the danger of freezing while on picket duty temporary truces with their opposite number across the river were negotiated. Just as cold and miserable as the Hoosiers, these truces allowed conversation between the two shores and even the occasional fire for warmth. Trading of coffee for tobacco and newspapers also occurred. Done strictly on their own volition, the truces typically were arranged without officers' knowledge.[41]

For much of December and into January, the 3rd Indiana picketed across from Hampton's Legion and their erstwhile friends from Middletown—the Georgia boys of Cobb's Legion. "Spent a few hours pleasantly chatting with the boys of the 1st S.C. Cav. Reg.—Hampton's Legion and Cobb's Legion on picket opposite. The stream is but a few yards wide. It seemed strange to be chatting so pleasantly with those we have been fighting so often," remarked one Hoosier.[42]

Given the conditions, it was hard to feel sorry for themselves as the Confederates across the river often stood guard barefoot or shod only in rags.[43] Orders received on January 19 moved the regiment from the far right of the army to the extreme left flank. Headquartered 12 miles downriver from Fredericksburg at King George's Courthouse, the men took up a picket line stretching all the way to Port Conway, eight miles further east.

Even with local truces, picket duty was dangerous. Like the Hoosiers, Confederate cavalrymen owned their horses. When a Union horseman lost his mount, he could draw a government issue horse. When a rebel cavalryman's horse broken down or was killed, however, it was his responsibility to acquire a new one. The most obvious source was the Union pickets across the river. Many pickets were attacked for no other reason than to capture their horse.

Different from the unmounted Confederate but no less dangerous was the bushwhacker. This all-encompassing term referred to civilians or deserters who took potshots at their enemy when given the chance. Skulkers and deserters particularly had ceased all military affiliation, reported to no one, and were driven only by the booty they might acquire. When these desperate men were met, no mercy was offered or asked. In a fight with a three-man picket of Company F, a bushwhacker was killed. "The dead rebel, after being stripped of a splendid pair of navy revolvers and his shotgun, was unceremoniously tumbled into a shallow grave. Such a funeral one is seldom to witness. Unsympathizing weather-beaten soldiers assembled around the mangled corpse of a bushwhacker amid the lonely wilds of a Virginia forest, giving their respective opinions of his merits in no flattering language is a strange scene in which to mingle."[44]

Even though the 3rd Indiana was only six companies strong, it was expected to perform the duty and cover an equal to that of an entire regiment of 12 companies.[45] What this meant for the men and horses was double the time on picket compared to the rest of the cavalry division. It was a true credit to the men of the 3rd Indiana that they were able to keep their mounts in reasonably good shape throughout the winter while pulling double picket duty. The men took care of their mounts for two interrelated reasons: the men owned the horses, and as long as the horse was serviceable, they continued to receive the 40 cents per day for their use. If the horse was lost or incapacitated, the man lost his extra pay and was provided a "Government" horse, usually of dubious quality. Supplying the army with mounts was a notoriously lucrative business. Unscrupulous dealers passed off substandard mounts to inept government agents. By the time the horse arrived at the front and was placed into service, it was rendered worthless after just a few days.[46]

It was inevitable that the cold, heavy duty and monotony brought trouble. Among the officers, the friction centered around First Lieutenant Henry Wright and Lieutenant Colonel Chapman. Wright had borne a grudge ever since Chapman had recommended Mason for the captaincy of Company D. This animosity manifested itself with squabbling with Mason at every opportunity. Chapman, disgusted with the whole situation, chewed Wright out and insisted that the matter be dropped. Wright, offended by the rebuke, insisted that Chapman apologize. Annoyed, Chapman refused. Wright preferred charges against Chapman the next day.[47]

Among the enlisted men, things took a similar turn. During the month of January, three men—John Caughlin, Charles Cartwright, and William Oldham—faced court martials for disobedience of orders and conduct detrimental to good order. Caughlin was especially singled out for telling his orderly sergeant to "kiss my ass" when he was not clearly heard to be present at roll call. All were fined $5 for the next six months with Caughlin's "kiss" costing him his corporal stripes, as well.[48]

The dangers of picket duty and the grinding monotony of duty also dulled men's senses, and accidents occurred. On December 13, John Sauvine of Company A accidentally fired his carbine, killing Barney Burns of the same company.[49] In February, the aforementioned surly Charles Cartwright of Company B was shot in the hand, and in March, Benjamin Abden of Company D was accidentally wounded in the foot by the discharge of his own revolver.[50]

Sometimes "accidents" occurred on purpose. An officer of the 8th New York had accompanied a squad of the 3rd on picket and spent most of the time berating the men for their unsoldierly ways. He suggested that their picket work was so poor, he could enter their lines without being halted. A few nights later, either as a test or simply trying to find his way to camp, this same officer was halted by the same squad at their picket post. When the officer refused to dismount and be identified, he was fired upon and hit in the hand. The officer found out the hard way that Hoosiers did not take kindly to criticism.[51]

The tedium and danger was occasionally broken up by the unusual. Young men on their own are known to pull pranks, and these Hoosiers were no different. Several civilian families lived near the Union pickets. Love had blossomed between a local boy named Watson and a young belle named Dulcebella Watts. Sergeant Samuel Gilpin had convinced the couple that, as ranking entity in the area, he had the power to perform marriages. In grandiose and florid language and flowing script, Gilpin created a marriage license and arranged a time for the ceremony. Just as the wedding was about to begin, Lieutenant Abner Shannon of Gilpin's company came out to visit the pickets. Learning of the upcoming nuptials, Shannon pulled rank and took over the ceremony, solemnly pronouncing the couple man and wife. No one knows whether the couple lived to a ripe old age blissfully ignorant of their unwedded state or whether they visited the local parson, just to be sure.[52]

The local population also enchanted the Hoosiers. Samuel Heath of Company C found his true love in King George's County. On February 22, he married Miss Mary Staples. Not trusting the ecclesiastical claims of Sergeant Gilpin or Lieutenant Shannon, the couple was married by the Rev. William Ingley.[53]

As the winter lengthened, the regiment began to see the results of Carter's, Buchanan's and Chapman's incessant pleas for promotions. Captain Mason's rupture had worsened to the point that he resigned his commission.[54] First Lieutenant Henry Wright was finally promoted to the coveted captaincy and command of the troubled Company D. John D.R. Spencer was promoted to First Lieutenant and James A. Kelsey was commissioned second lieutenant. In Company E, First Lieutenant George Thompson had been serving as adjutant but moved back to the company as its new captain when William McClure assumed his new rank as Major. Abner Shannon was promoted to first lieutenant, and George Gilchrist, orderly sergeant of the company, was promoted to second lieutenant. Finally, in Company F, Sergeant Lewis C. Wilson was jumped to first lieutenant, and Orderly Sergeant William Cotton received his commission as second lieutenant.[55] With Thompson's elevation to company command, a new adjutant was needed. Chapman and McClure recommended Gamaliel Taylor for the position along with the equivalent rank of lieutenant, and on December 27 he received his appointment. Finally, the arrival of James Knight as assistant surgeon was a welcomed addition.[56]

With the officer complement approaching normal, Chapman turned to another matter—the availability of companies L and M. In accordance with new regulations that cavalry regiments have 12 companies, L and M had been recruited back in Indiana but were being held there by the governor for use as provost marshals and support for the administration. Captain William Patton was back in Indiana on recruiting duty and visited the governor. He also ran into Oliver Powers, late of Company E and now captain of Company L. He warned Chapman that he would have to move quickly if he wanted companies L and M sent to him. "If you want them, get an order from Halleck for them to report to Pleasonton in Virginia. Loose no time or you will loose them," he urged.[57]

Perhaps in an effort to pressure Governor Morton to release the companies to him, Chapman sent an officer to Washington to be sure proper equipment would be available for the men when they arrived and assured the governor that all was ready.[58] Over the next several months, Chapman would try at least four times to convince the governor to send the men to Virginia but was never able to get the companies released.

On January 25, a change of command and organizational philosophy occurred. Ambrose Burnside was replaced as the commander of the Army of the Potomac by Joseph Hooker, their old division commander in Maryland. To the men of the 3rd Indiana, this change bode well for the army. One Hoosier wrote, "We look upon our present commander as one capable of performing the difficult task before him. The men have confidence in him and will stand by him to the last."[59]

With the defeat at Fredericksburg, the army's morale was at an all-time low. Hooker immediately began the reorganization of the Army of the Potomac in general and the cavalry in particular. Hooker had seen the cavalry's effectiveness squandered by parceling out the regiments piecemeal and relegating the mounted arm to little more than message bearers and bodyguards for generals. While he was credited with the saying "Who ever saw a dead cavalryman?," Hooker wanted to create a mounted arm equal to its adversary. He envisioned all of the cavalry organized into one Corps under one commander with equal footing with other corps commanders.

On February 5, General Order Number 6 created the Cavalry Corps of the Army of the Potomac with General George Stoneman as commander.[60] Stoneman was a regular army officer with pre-war experience in the dragoons. Like many general officers, he had his quirks. Initially, he considered outfitting his new command in bright red

Joseph Hooker reinvigorated the Army of the Potomac in the winter of 1862–63. He also established the Cavalry Corps and the Bureau of Military Information. His loss of nerve at Chancellorsville a few months later sealed his fate as commander of the Army of the Potomac (Library of Congress).

Chapter 5. September 14, 1862–April 30, 1863 55

Scouts of the Bureau of Military Information. Three men, Milton Cline (seated in center with his son to his right), Daniel Cole (seated on right), and Daniel Plew (on ground far left) were among the 18 original scouts assigned to the Bureau. Eventually, three others were assigned, John Irby (seated on left), John Hatten (not pictured), and William Jones (not pictured). Cline was named the chief of Scouts and here wears the uniform of a captain. General George Meade requested Cline's promotion to captain after Gettysburg, but it was never approved. Cline is often misidentified as Robert Klein, lieutenant colonel commanding the 3rd Indiana Cavalry, West Wing (Library of Congress).

jackets and caps with pea green trousers. Fortunately, this idea was never adopted. More importantly, he had medical issues. Stoneman suffered from an excruciating case of hemorrhoids that left him incapable of riding a horse for more than a couple of hours.[61]

Hooker also ordered the creation of the Bureau of Military Information. This group would be responsible for the collection and analysis of all information collected by the army. Scout reports, cavalry reports, captured Confederate newspapers, conversations with runaway slaves, interviews with deserters, and captured Rebel soldiers—all would be collected by the Bureau. Given their service in Maryland, it seemed reasonable that members of the 3rd Indiana would be included in the new unit. Sure enough, Sergeant Milton Cline, Daniel Cole, and Daniel Plew were detached to join the new organization.[62]

Within days the new Cavalry Corps was organized into three divisions with the 3rd Indiana assigned to the 1st Division, 1st Brigade, Cavalry Corps of the Army of the Potomac. Joining them in the brigade were their old comrades the 8th Illinois and the 8th New York.[63] Commanding the brigade was Colonel Benjamin F. "Grimes" Davis. A Mississippian by birth and an 1854 U.S. Military Academy graduate, Davis rejected his Southern roots and pledged his allegiance to the North.

Having served in the Dragoons out west before the war, he expected much from his new command and was a strict disciplinarian who expected more "spit and polish" than the Hoosiers were accustomed to.[64] General Alfred Pleasanton commanded the division.

One final piece of unfinished business had to be resolved before the 3rd Indiana began campaigning in the spring of 1863. Colonel Scott Carter, still under arrest and unable to command, had stayed with the regiment throughout the month of December despite his peculiar situation. In January, his decision cost him his health, and he was forwarded to a hospital in Washington. By late February, he had had enough. Pleasanton finally released him from arrest on the 25th, and two weeks later Carter resigned his commission.[65]

Chapman now realized that he would be promoted to colonel and took advantage of the situation to contact Adjutant General Noble once again. His enthusiasm was in marked contrast to some of his early missives to Indianapolis. "This command is now in good condition, notwithstanding the hard labor it has to perform and the winter's exposure of the horses. There are few, if any, regiments of cavalry in the service that have worn as well as this," he enthused.[66]

In the same letter, he informed Noble of Captain Henry Wright's resignation. After so much time and effort to achieve the coveted captaincy, Wright must have been disheartened by Carter's own resignation. As long as Carter was around, there was the chance that Chapman would have to yield command. Wright reasoned that, with Carter gone, Chapman would be free to exact revenge for the charges Wright had brought against him back in December. Using the illness of a child back in Indiana as an excuse, Wright threw in the towel.

Wright may have been right. In the letter to Noble, Chapman made a special point of defining the three types of discharge one could receive; honorable, neutral, and dishonorable. Wright's was a neutral discharge. In other words, his resignation was not seen as an honorable disassociation from the army. It meant simply that the man had resigned.[67] In later correspondence Chapman revealed that Wright had submitted his resignation before, only to withdraw it later. Wright had also claimed an injustice done him by Major McClure while Chapman was away from camp. Chapman assessed the captain this way: "He seems to imagine that he was made a mark by each succeeding commander of the regiment. This resulted from a disposition of the man himself and not because he had any good cause for it."[68]

Other 3rd Indiana men were active during a time of overall inactivity. While spring campaigning had yet to start, on February 25, Sergeant Milton Cline over in the Bureau of Military Information undertook a scout that covered 250 miles over 10 days. Passing himself off as a partisan ranger, he fell in with a group of confederate cavalry and accompanied them on a long traverse of the entire Confederate line and winter camps. Upon his return, he reported upon 24 Confederate camps, 12 locations of artillery batteries, 23 fortifications, and five ambulance and wagon parks. As Cline returned, Sergeant Daniel Cole, another 3rd Indiana scout, was sent out to collect more information.⁶⁹

And so, the Hoosiers of the 3rd Indiana emerged from their second winter of war a hardened combat unit. They had fought frequently and well. While the strenuous duty of the winter had not helped their physical condition, they had fared better than most units. They now had officers who had been tested in battle and in camp and the men had confidence in their leadership. The regimental staff had been expanded to meet the critical supply and administrative needs of the regiment. In a show of unit pride, Chapman wrote Tiffany's in New York about a regiment flag, something the unit had never had.⁷⁰

One of the Bureau of Military Information's original scouts, Daniel Cole represented the resourcefulness and ingenuity that defined the Army of the Potomac's scouts (U.S. Army Heritage and Education Center).

The overall command structure of the Union cavalry had evolved to the point where, for the first time, the mounted arm would be able to put into the field a unified force of equal or greater strength than their Confederate foes. Hooker's reforms had transformed the Army of the Potomac to a confident army ready to bring the war to an end. As the Hoosiers finished the first 18 months of their three year enlistment, they and the army were ready. All hoped the spring of 1863 would bring an end to the war.

Chapter 6

March 1, 1863–May 25, 1863

The 3rd Indiana was ready for the campaign season of 1863. It had its full complement of officers and staff. The officer corps of the East Wing had shed ineffective officers and was now made up of proven leaders as follows:

Regimental Staff

Colonel:	George Chapman[1]
Major:	William S. McClure
Major:	Charles Lemmon
Adjutant:	Gamaliel Taylor
Commissary:	John Greiner
Quartermaster:	John Patton
Surgeon:	Elias Beck
Asst. Surgeon:	James H. Knight

	Captain	*1st Lieutenant*	*2nd Lieutenant*
Company A	William Patton	Robert P. Porter	Charles W. Lee
Company B	Benjamin Q.A. Gresham	Marshall Lahue	Dennis Davis
Company C	Ephraim H. Martin	Ira B. Tinker	Isaac Gilbert[2]
Company D	John D.R. Spencer	James A. Kelsey	James Calhoun
Company E	George Thompson	Abner L. Shannon	George M. Gilchrist
Company F	Thomas W. Moffitt	Lewis C. Wilson	William Cotton

Of the 18 company officers, 12 had started their army careers as enlisted personnel. The returns for the regiment showed 420 men present for duty. In comparison, the November 1862 muster rolls showed 385 men present and on duty.[3] Ninety-four men had been discharged or resigned since leaving Madison, and 28 had paid the ultimate price. These losses were approximately offset, however, by the recruitment of 120 men.[4]

Hooker's reorganization had also accrued to the strength of the regiment and the cavalry corps as a whole. In his reshaping of the mounted arm, he ordered that only the equivalent of two squadrons per division (approximately 200 men) would

Chapter 6. March 1, 1863–May 25, 1863

be detached as orderlies and messengers. For the 3rd Indiana, this meant an additional 37 men present with the regiment in April than in November.[5]

Chapman was itching to prove himself now that he was a full colonel. Not able to sit still, he found a reason to visit division headquarters and took the opportunity to size up Alfred Pleasanton. While the Major General had been in nominal command of the cavalry for several months, his formal appointment as their division commander placed him in a different relationship than before. What Chapman found did not impress him. "Pleasanton is a man who has the air of wisdom without the substance," sniffed Chapman.[6] Surgeon Elias Beck held a similar opinion of their division commander. "Poor pusillanimous Pleasanton wants to Command the Cavalry Corps—to have Stoneman's place–& he is about as fit for it as any 2d Lieutenant in the Command."[7]

Also, the men were still getting used to their new brigade commander, Colonel Benjamin "Grimes" Davis. "Being of the regular army, and of a peculiar disposition, he gives us West Point in a variety of forms. Perhaps he is capable, and perhaps he is not; but we are volunteers and scorn style. This is saying what we think of him [Davis]," grumbled one Hoosier.[8] Another man offered this opinion of Davis' West Point ways with his fractured spelling: "We were out on a grand inspection today and I tell you it is intolerable … to a hole brigad of calvalry all well dressed with Boots blacked so nice but isent very pleasant to us set primp up on a horse for three or four hours in the sun."[9]

As March turned to April, the regiment was back in its position along the Rappahannock River on the army's far right. A surprise snow storm had dumped several inches of snow, adding to their discomfort. Danger was still nearby as Fuel Alley of Company C was wounded on picket on April 5.[10] The men sensed something was in the air, and anticipated action. Adding to the sense of urgency was a grand review attended by President Lincoln on April 10. As the president passed by the 3rd Indiana, Hooker made a point of introducing Chapman to him. As they continued on the review, Hooker casually asked Chapman to report to army headquarters the next day.[11] Due to their service together in Maryland, Hooker knew Chapman to be a reliable officer who provided sound intelligence—a quality that Hooker appreciated. Upon reporting to army headquarters, Chapman was asked by Hooker about the nature of the terrain on the opposite side of the Rappahannock. After giving his report, Chapman was courteously dismissed, still not knowing the purpose of the interview.[12]

Hooker's intentions started to become clearer when the regiment and the rest of the 1st Brigade were ordered to Freeman's Ford on April 14 where they found the entire division consolidating for a raid into Confederate territory. The 1st Brigade was to cross the Rappahannock River and march southeast along the southern bank and flank Confederates guarding Beverly's Ford, clearing the way for the rest of the cavalry corps to cross.[13] The corps would then move through the countryside destroying supplies and railroads. It was anticipated that Lee would have to send elements of his army in pursuit, allowing Hooker to attack the depleted Confederates.

While waiting for orders to move out, Samuel Puckett was shot accidentally by his own pistol. He lingered for weeks before succumbing to the effects of his wound on July 9.[14] On April 15, it began to rain. As the men moved to their position at Freeman's Ford, the rain continued to pelt down. As they crossed the river, the Rebel pickets of the 9th Virginia Cavalry were surprised and sent flying before the 1st Brigade. And, it continued to rain. The men turned south toward Beverly's Ford and reached the Hazel River, normally a little tributary. The small river had risen rapidly, and the men crossed in water lapping at their saddle blankets.[15]

And, it rained. The Rappahannock River was swelling at an alarming rate, rising seven feet in just a few hours. Realizing the main body of the Cavalry Corps would not be able to cross, Stoneman sent word to Davis to retreat back across the river before the river rose too high and made escape impossible.

The retreat placed the men in an awkward and dangerous position. Having driven their adversaries all day, they were ordered to backtrack through the mud and rain. The Confederate cavalry, sensing a change in the dynamics of the fight, quickly reverted to the offensive in an attempt to cut them off from the ford. Now bringing up the rear of the column, companies E and F fought to hold off the rebels so that the rest of the command could make its escape.

Assisting the squadron were two companies of the 8th New York. Formed on the right flank of the Hoosiers, the New Yorkers suddenly withdrew, leaving the 3rd Indiana men exposed. The squadron had to retreat by the flank until only a small group led by Lieutenant Abner Shannon remained. "The little band of twenty or thirty looked small beside the column that we saw coming down the road with the reb flag flying and sabers drawn," wrote Sam Gilpin.[16] After offering token resistance, the little group was flanked on both ends, and the Hoosiers bolted to the ford, all semblance of military order and discipline gone. This was a race for survival.

Sergeant Willis H. "Ham" Stapp of Company E turned to see a saber wielding Confederate charging down on him. Swinging his horse to the side, he narrowly dodged the saber stroke as the Reb rode by. Cocking his pistol, he waited for the grayback to return. At five yards, Stapp pulled the trigger only to hear the cap snap. The rain had ruined the powder in the revolver. Now defenseless, he again avoided the saber stroke. Seeing Stapp's dilemma, a sergeant from Company F fired at the rebel horseman, scaring Stapp's mount. "He jumped into a mud hole about four feet deep and threw me.... I was pulled out of the mud with a pistol to my head and told to surrender," Stapp reported. Disgusted, wet, and covered in mud, the sergeant was able to throw his pistol away before giving up a saber he had captured earlier in the day.[17]

All around Stapp similar scenarios were being played out. While some of the men made it into and across the river, others were surrounded and captured. Private Isaac Higgins of Company F was one of the fortunate ones to escape. A rebel rode up next to him and seized Higgins' reins. Unbeknownst to the Confederate, Higgins had his pistol under his rain coat. Pulling the weapon out while his captor was distracted, he shot the man and whirled toward the river and swam himself and his horse to safety.[18]

Aiding those who were trying to escape were their friends who had already crossed. Many of the men dismounted and took up firing positions along the banks to cover those still crossing. Their fire deterred the pursuing Confederates from entering the river after the fugitives and doubtlessly saved others from capture.[19]

By the time the fiasco in the rain ended, 20 men of the 3rd Indiana had been captured, including First Lieutenant Shannon and five non-commissioned officers of Company E.[20] Now prisoners, the men were made to slog through the mud and muck. Tired, wet, and dejected, the men straightened a bit when one of their captors asked about their unit. Lieutenant Shannon proudly replied, "Third Indiana." Upon hearing this, the little column was halted and horses brought up for the Hoosiers to ride out of respect for their fighting reputation.[21]

Abner Shannon served quietly and faithfully for more than three years with the regiment. Elected second lieutenant of Company E, he was promoted to first lieutenant in July 1862. Wounded once and captured twice, he was in a Confederate prison camp when his enlistment ended. Released from prison, he was honorably discharged on March 12, 1865 (U.S. Army Heritage and Education Center).

Returning across the river to attempt a rescue of their men was out of the question. The rising river made it impossible to cross. While their captured comrades rode south, the surviving members of the regiment were trying to make sense of the day. In Company E, the men tried to understand the folly that allowed 12 of their men to be taken prisoner. Likewise, Company F mourned the loss of eight of its men. The day had started with such promise and had ended so badly. In all, 26 men had been killed, wounded, and captured.[22] Huddled around smoky little fires built of wet wood, they listened to the raindrops hiss into the embers. As the rain continued to fall, the men and horses settled in for a miserable night, wondering what tomorrow would bring.

Tomorrow brought more rain. The next several days were spent in frequent moves in an effort to confuse their enemy across the river. Davis was ordered to take his brigade far out to the east where the 3rd Indiana brought in several prisoners before returning to camp. On the 20th, the river had receded enough to allow another crossing. Gallopers began making the rounds of the divisions and brigades, but just as they began to mount up, it began to rain and continued all night. The assault would have to be postponed again. The men and horses had exhausted their rations and forage, and were sent back toward the Orange & Alexandria Railroad for resupply.[23] Returning to their camps, the men hunkered down to three more days of unrelenting, unabating rain. Around them 8,000 horsemen sat in the same stupor and discomfort. The high hopes of the 15th had long washed away in the torrent.

By April 28, the rain had stopped, and the river had subsided to levels that made a crossing practicable. Orders again went out, and the men again packed their belongings, and again cleaned their weapons. And, again, it began to rain. Fortunately, the rain was of shorter duration and did not affect the Rappahannock's depth as drastically as the previous rains. The order to commence operations on April 29 remained in effect.

The next morning, splashing through puddles and mud, the 3rd Indiana recrossed the Rappahannock, this time at Kelly's Ford. Temporarily attached to Averell's 2nd Division, the 3rd Indiana and its brigade struck out to the west to disrupt the Orange & Alexandria Railroad. Stoneman and the rest of the Cavalry Corps proceeded south to threaten other railroads supplying Lee's army. Averell was to rejoin the Cavalry Corps north of Richmond at the North Anna River. Sam Gilpin tersely wrote in his diary, "Crossed forward in line. Went to sleep in the rain. Advanced—got shelled—halted sometime in the night and spent the remainder of it in line in rain and mud and Morpheus' arms." It is telling that the weary sergeant was able to sleep mounted, seemingly oblivious to the rain.[24]

The next day, April 30, the men rode west as fast as conditions allowed to a sleepy little railroad town called Brandy Station. There they turned and followed the Orange & Alexandria Railroad southwest through Culpeper Court House, arriving at Cedar Mountain around 4:00 p.m. Having ridden all day in the driving rain, the men had skirmished along the Rapidan River and at Cedar Mountain. Tired and miserable, their discomfort was made complete as they rode across part of the Cedar Mountain battlefield. Grim reminders of the battle were strewn about. Wild hogs had uprooted the graves and human bones and skulls were scattered about. That night, the regiment camped in a swamp, with water standing over their shoe tops and the horses' fetlocks. The 20-mile ride and the misery of the night was described as the hardest they had ever seen.[25]

The next morning, May 1, finally brought relief from the weather. Described as a "very beautiful May day," the regiment's spirits improved and brightened their outlook on the whole operation. The column rode the short distance to Rapidan Station and there ran into enemy resistance. Confederates in well prepared rifle pits overlooked and completely commanded the Rapidan River crossings. As the troops fanned out along the river seeking other crossing points, Captain Gresham was seriously wounded in the thigh and abdomen and was hurried off to a makeshift hospital in the rear.[26]

Reaching Stoneman north of Richmond was impossible without crossing the Rapidan. Cannon fire could be heard east of their position and word was received that Hooker had attacked Lee at Chancellorsville, 20 miles away. Early on May 2, the column moved off to the east, now with the intention of rejoining Hooker at Chancellorsville. "Many horses played out," summarized one man. Slogging through the sticky mud on top of the previous days' exertions had proven too much for some of the tired mounts. To keep up, men abandoned their tired horses and stumbled through the mud and muck carrying their saddles and bridles in hopes of acquiring a serviceable mount along the way. As the column strung out and moved forward, the rumble of cannon fire grew louder as they approached Ely's Ford just above Chancellorsville.[27] Crossing the Rapidan on the 3rd, the regiment laid in support to the north and rear of Hooker's army. Fighting could be heard in the "Wilderness" around Chancellorsville, but the day passed quietly for the Hoosiers. Other than cannonading further south at Fredericksburg, the men passed May 4 in like fashion.

While the men rested and the horses recovered, the men were able to witness firsthand the polyglot collection of men who inevitably collected in the rear. Walking wounded, messengers galloping to and from different commands, supply wagons and profane teamsters all had legitimate claim to being there. Others, less so. The skulkers and cowards looking for any opportunity to avoid fighting. Panicked men who had been in the thick of the fighting, but overwhelmed by fear, ran rearward as fast as the legs could carry them. Thieves in soldier blue were looking for the chance to snap up anything of value. This unsavory mix of men also brewed up rampant rumors of impending disaster. From the wounded, the men heard of the ferocity of the fighting. From the panic-stricken and riffraff, one heard of superior forces overwhelming them and that the enemy was liable to arrive at any moment. One Hoosier rightly surmised that one could trust nothing except what one saw with his own eyes. Having been exposed to the backwash of a battle, they were all anxious to be away and in the lead once more.[28]

Hooker's promising attack on Lee had devolved into another defeat and retreat for the Army of the Potomac. About midnight of the 4th, the 3rd Indiana and its comrades mounted up and crossed the Rappahannock River at U.S. Ford and went into camp and picket duty around Harwood Church. By the 6th, they had moved to their familiar picket posts at Bealeton Station near Ely's Ford. Back at the site of the ill-fated crossing on April 15, it began to rain. Rationless, their horses almost ridden to the breaking point, and once again soaked to the skin, the men settled into their old camps and tried to make sense of the past three weeks.[29]

They had lost 20 men by capture. Others had been wounded, including a company commander. Horses were completely worn out by relentless duty. Several men were still missing. The grand raid conceived on April 15 of 8,000 Union cavalrymen ascending on the Confederate army's rear and flank to cripple the enemy's supply line had turned into a fragmented effort. Starting on April 30, 3500 horsemen of the 2nd Division plus Davis' brigade marched 50 miles over two days through mud and rain only to have little to show for their efforts. Stoneman's column of 5,500 men had been equally ineffective.

Fortunately, the regiment was able to rest over the next several days. Horses grazed on new growth grass, and missing men came into camp. The weather cleared, and spring could be definitely felt in the air. Still, with thousands of men and horses in the vicinity, the smells of the season were of a different variety. "Spring fever to be with us at last but it brings no sweet smells of flowers and growing shrubs in this locality, but increases and intensifies the stinks which gather around an army in camp," wrote Colonel Chapman.[30]

The quiet ended on May 18 for companies A and B. Ordered on a scout beyond Stafford Court House, the men spent the next two days patrolling the area. Returning two days later, they brought a man with them who carried $3,600 in bills and $3,300 in bonds. Hearing three different stories as to why he was in the area and why he carried so much money, Captain William Patton brought the man into camp.[31] As the scouting party entered the camp, companies E and F were ordered to army headquarters where they were briefed on a secret mission.

A captured issue of the *Richmond Whig* newspaper had caught the attention of the Bureau of Military Intelligence.[32] Mentioned in the paper was a group of passengers leaving for Urbanna near the mouth of the Rappahannock River. The town was 70 miles from Fredericksburg, and it was believed that the carriages had already departed Richmond. George Thompson was ordered to intercept the carriages and capture the occupants. Ordered to Acquia Creek where his company would board the river steamers *Tallaca* and *Manhattan*, Thompson was to command the expedition and had been provided a cryptic order which he shared with the captains of the riverboats.[33] The navy men were to "be subject to, and in every way obey the orders of Captain George H. Thompson, commanding the squadron." Accompanying the squadron would be a young staff officer attached to Pleasanton's staff—Lieutenant George A. Custer, West Point class of 1860 and an officer in the 5th U.S. Cavalry.[34]

Their destination was a region known as the Northern Neck, a peninsula formed by the Potomac River to the north and the Rappahannock River to the south. From there, the men were to cross the Rappahannock. The Northern Neck was a fertile but strategically unimportant part of the region though both armies took advantage of its relatively untapped resources. In fact, the 8th Illinois was currently in the area. On the 27th, the Illinoisians returned with 500 horses and mules along with hundreds of slaves anxious to be free.[35]

The squadron's target was human, however, not equine. Proceeding down the Potomac, the men could look to the left and identify their posts from the winter of 1861–62: Budd's Ferry, the Nimenjoy River inlet, Port Tobacco. Despite the recent rains, the steamers grounded several times in shallow waters, but the next day the ride became much choppier as the Potomac emptied into the much larger Chesapeake Bay. At noon on the 22nd, the boats eased into the Virginia shore at Little Wicomico River and disembarked the 100 men and horses. A sparsely inhabited area, it was agreed that the steamers would wait here until the raiders' return.

Riding hard throughout the afternoon, the men passed through Heathsville and Lancaster Court House before reaching Chowning's Ferry—an astounding 37-mile ride. Enroute, they met parties of the 8th Illinois on the aforementioned horse raid "leaving them as much in wonder as ourselves concerning our destination."[36] Reaching a point across from Urbanna late in the day, Thompson decided the hour was too late to cross the four-mile-wide Rappahannock River.[37] The next morning the men scrounged up two boats in such poor condition that time had to be taken to repair them. Finally ready, Thompson led one boat of 10 men while Lieutenant Shannon—fresh from his time in a Rebel prison—and 10 men boarded the other. Lieutenant Custer joined Shannon's party. The rest of the squadron secured the launch site. Midway across the river, a small sailboat with several people aboard was seen coming north from the southern shore. Bending their backs into their oars, Shannon's boat veered to the west to try and overtake the vessel.

The riverbanks of the Rappahannock at this point were very shallow and did not drop off into the river channel until several hundred yards from shore. This geography proved to be the sailboat's downfall. After being chased for over a mile, the fugitive vessel turned south. Three hundred yards from the shore, the boat went aground. Three of the men panicked and jumped out of the boat and slogged through the knee high mud toward shore. As the tired men of Shannon's boat pulled along the seemingly abandoned sailing vessel, they were surprised to find six people—a man, his wife, and four children—still aboard. Thinking they might be part of the group they were sent to intercept, Shannon placed three men in the sailboat with instructions to return to their launch site at Chowning's Ferry. Turning back north, Shannon, Custer, and the rest of the men rowed toward Urbanna and a rendezvous with Captain Thompson. Along the way, they spied a large plantation house and a man walking in a gray uniform. Taking four men, Custer went to investigate.

As the men warily approached the house, they could see the man now sitting on the porch with his back to the river. The squad quickly surrounded the man, and Custer declared him his prisoner. Surveying the five weapons leveled at him, the man responded, "I suppose so."[38] Home on recruitment duty, Captain William Hardy of the Confederate artillery had been a student at Virginia Military Institute before the war and had been brushing up on his Shakespeare when captured.[39] Escorting their captive to the river, the men rowed to Urbanna and rejoined Thompson's boat. To their chagrin, they learned that they had arrived too late to intercept their prey.

Destroying all the boats they could find, the men also burned the bridge south of Urbanna to slow any pursuit. They again boarded and rowed across the river to join the rest of the squadron. Upon arrival, Thompson found the men left on the northern bank had not been idle; three men had wandered into their encampment and now sat under guard. Not wanting to give the surrounding countryside time to organize a pursuit, a carriage was found for the comfort of the women and children, and the men mounted and moved out.

Riding throughout the night of the 22nd, they rested a few hours in the morning and arrived at the transports around noon on the 23rd. A relieved group of tired cavalrymen, aka "horse marines," were happy to board the boats and steam north. By noon of May 25, they were back at Acquia Creek.[40] The squadron brought back five men, a woman and four children plus 15 horses. Lieutenant Custer loved horses and knew good horseflesh. He discreetly took two, one to give to his commanding officer, General Pleasanton, and the other he kept for himself. A black stallion, Custer named the horse Roanoke and rode him throughout the rest of the war.[41]

Chapter 7

May 26, 1863–June 29, 1863

Once again reunited, the 3rd Indiana settled back into the routine of camp life, going so far as to build overhangs of cedar boughs and pine branches for protection from the sun. Brigade review was ordered for May 31 and the men went to mending, cleaning, etc. While annoying, reviews seemed to always precede action.[1] The review also gave their new division commander a chance to meet his men.

Hooker had been extremely disappointed in the Cavalry Corps performance prior to Chancellorsville. When Stoneman asked to travel to Washington for treatment of his hemorrhoids, Hooker quickly approved. Stoneman hadn't reached the capital city before Hooker appointed Pleasanton as his replacement.[2]

The big change for the men of the 1st Division was Pleasanton's promotion creating the need for a new 1st Division commander. Pleasanton named as his successor Brigadier General John Buford, a 37-year-old Regular Army veteran. Kentucky bred and West Point educated, Buford would appeal to the western soldiers as no other general officer had. Not one for "style," he was often seen dressed for battle in an old blue hunting shirt with his corduroy pant legs stuffed into the tops of his common boots. A small black felt hat usually rounded out his ensemble.[3] A dragoon by experience, he believed that cavalry had

A West Point graduate and Regular Army officer, John Buford was indifferent to "West Point" ways, which endeared him to the western cavalrymen who served under him. During the grueling campaigning following Gettysburg, he contracted typhoid and died on December 16, 1863 (Library of Congress).

to be a hybrid horseman and infantryman. In other words, capable of hard hitting saber attacks as well as sustained dismounted action. In essence, he expected his men to be both cavalry and infantry. But all of this was in the future; the men would have an opportunity to size up their new commander soon enough.

May 29 brought changes within the regiment. William Patton was promoted to Major, joining William McClure and Charles Lemmon. For the first time, the command had three majors. Patton's promotion allowed the advancement of Second Lieutenant Charles W. Lee to captain, bypassing First Lieutenant Robert P. Porter. According to Chapman, "[Porter] had for months rendered no service of any moment, and it is simply out of regard for his personal feelings that I have not preferred charges against him. If it is necessary to do this in order to defeat his promotion, I shall be compelled to do so."[4] Benjamin F. Gilbert was promoted from orderly sergeant to second lieutenant.[5]

Orders came on June 6 to move out. Chapman was ill in Washington, so the senior major of the regiment—William McClure—led the command out of camp. With no baggage and four days of rations and forage, the regiment marched toward Beverly's Ford, just seven miles from Kelly's Ford, the site of the debacle of April 14.

The plan was for the Cavalry Corps to move south, cross the Rappahannock River at three different crossings, unite at Brandy Station, and attack Jeb Stuart's Confederate cavalry at Culpeper. The only problem with this plan was that Stuart was not at Culpeper; he and his entire division were camped at Brandy Station, three miles to the east of Culpeper. His command was making preparation for Lee's second invasion of the north. Flush from his victory at Chancellorsville, Lee planned to race down the Shenandoah Valley to Pennsylvania. Stuart's job was to shield Lee's forces from prying Union cavalry as he raced north. If successful, Lee would have a considerable head start over Hooker.

J.E.B. Stuart loved the pomp and circumstance of war. Two elaborate reviews were held in early June, churning up the review site with tens of thousands of hooves. On June 8, a third review rode across the landscape, this time under the approving eye of General Robert E. Lee himself. As so often was the case, reviews preceded action. Stuart expected to begin his move north the next morning.

As the Confederate cavalry paraded a few miles away, the Union cavalrymen arrived at their assigned fords. On June 8, the 3rd Indiana and the rest of the 1st Division gathered at Beverly Ford, closest to Brandy Station. Arriving around midnight and camping only a mile from the Ford, the men were cautioned about talking and no fires were allowed. Pickets across the river must not know of their arrival. Standing by their horses, the men spoke in low murmurs and chewed on cold hardtack. At 2:00 a.m., the order was quietly passed to mount, and the column started for the river. Up ahead near the river crossing, their new commander Buford sat his horse calmly puffing on his pipe. Reaching the river in columns of four, staff officers whispered, "Draw sabers." Davis' brigade would lead the attack with the 3rd Indiana behind the 8th New York and 8th Illinois. They were to cross the three foot deep

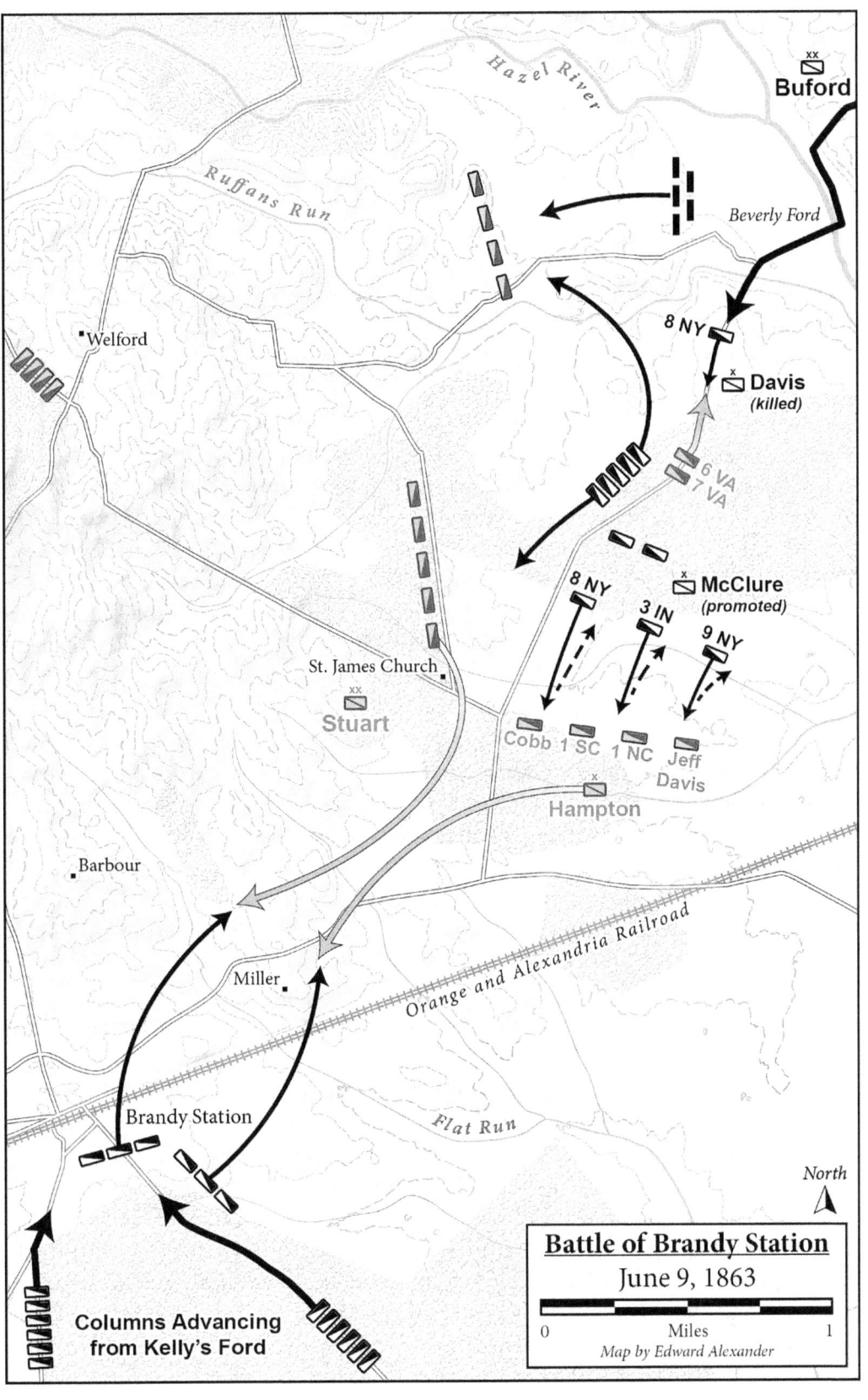

river as rapidly as possible and push the pickets back at least a mile to allow the rest of the command to cross and deploy. As the lead men entered the river, a shot rang out. The battle of Brandy Station, the largest cavalry battle in the history of the Western Hemisphere, had begun.

The lead regiments chased the pickets away from the crossing, and the 3rd Indiana entered the ford. Emerging on the other side, they were ordered to the left to widen the arc of protection and to keep an eye on the sleepy little town of Brandy Station. Another column of the Union advance was crossing at Kelly's Ford and would be coming for the planned rendezvous at Brandy Station through the town. As the regiment fanned out, they spied a familiar figure. Newly promoted captain George Custer had accompanied the column. Ahead and to their right, "Grimes" Davis led the rest of the brigade toward a local promontory called Fleetwood Hill. More of a ridge than a knoll, it also hosted Jeb Stuart's headquarters that morning.

Frantic Rebel pickets pounded up the hill to the nearest camp to report the arrival of Union cavalry by the thousands. Davis and his men followed closely behind. Davis in particular had his "blood up." Outdistancing his men, he realized that intelligence reports had been wrong. Instead of bare ground ahead, he saw thousands of Confederate cavalrymen scrambling to get dressed, catch and saddle their mounts and counterattack his men—not necessarily in that order. Some of these half-dressed, half-awake but all fight rebels met Davis. Surrounded and cut off from his command, Davis was killed in the first clash of the day.

The 8th New York, their beloved former colonel killed and increasing numbers of Rebels joining the fight, was thrown into confusion and began a disorderly retreat. The 8th Illinois and the 3rd Indiana covered their withdrawal. Confusion reigned as staff officers rode around trying to determine who was the next senior officer in the brigade. Major William McClure was that man. A dapper gentleman of thirty-five with a neat goatee adorning his chin, the major turned command of the regiment over to Charles Lemmon and assumed command of the brigade. From temporary command of six companies and 350 men, McClure was now in command of parts of five regiments with a total strength of 1600 in the largest cavalry battle of the war.[6]

McClure ordered a squadron of the 9th New York to the left to defend against a flanking attack, adding a squadron under Major Lemmon to this position. Major William Patton with a squadron of the 3rd Indiana were deployed as skirmishers. The attack by the 6th and 7th Virginia which had claimed Colonel Davis' life had lost its momentum, and the brigade was able to follow the retreating Virginians. Arrayed ahead of them, however, was Hampton's Brigade of Confederate cavalry—Cobb's Legion, 1st South Carolina, 1st North Carolina, and the Jeff Davis Legion. Pressured by this new threat, it was now the blue-clad horsemen's turn to fall back. Regrouping, McClure ordered the brigade south once again. As they approached their previous starting point, they saw Hampton's men turn toward Fleetwood Hill. Company F of the 3rd Indiana charged the fleeing enemy and brought in a handful of prisoners.[7]

Now 9:30 a.m., a stalemate fell across the battlefield. A heavy line of Rebel artillery had been massed around St. James Church on the brigade's right. As the line stabilized, a section of artillery arrived and began counterbattery fire. The exhausted horsemen dismounted and sank to the ground to support the artillery. On the other side of Fleetwood Hill, fighting could be heard as the 2nd Division arrived and now made their attack on the Confederate position. Over the next several hours, the artillery duel produced casualties. In Company B, Benjamin F. Jenkins was dead. Lt. Marshal Lahue had been hit in the right side, and Eugene Page took a bullet in the thigh, as had David Shewmaker. Company E had Samuel Bain and Solon Tilford down. John Walters of Company A was in an ambulance taking the jolting ride across the river with a wound in his neck. Also wounded in Company A was William Kirkpatrick. Company E counted Samuel Bain and Solon Tilford among the casualties.[8] Adjutant Gamaliel Taylor got shot in the leg but had a curious reaction to the wound. "It's a daisy, I wouldn't take $100 for it. It is good for a 60 day furlough. I'll go home and see my girl!"[9]

William McClure began the war as captain of Company E. The dapper, well-groomed gentleman was promoted to major at the end of October 1862. With Chapman's bouncing between regimental and brigade command, he often found himself in charge of the regiment (U.S. Army Heritage and Education Center).

Finally, around 3:00 p.m., the men were ordered to retire to Beverly Ford and recross. With no sleep the night before and under fire all day, they were barely able to mount. They rode to their previous night's bivouac and collapsed. The next morning, they moved further north, eventually reaching Catlett's Station. There, General Pleasanton showed his pride in their performance by ordering a review on the 11th.[10] That same day, Colonel Chapman returned from sick leave and took command of the brigade only to relinquish it two days later to the senior colonel in the brigade, William Gamble of the 8th Illinois.

The men of the 3rd Indiana were pleased to have a "western" man as their commander. A native of Ireland, Gamble had served in the dragoons in the British army before immigrating to the United States. He joined the American army and rose to the rank of sergeant major of the 1st U.S. Dragoons before leaving the service in

1843. Moving to Chicago, Gamble had pursued a career as a civil engineer before re-entering the army as colonel of the 8th Illinois.[11] For the next few days, the men rested and assessed the recent battle. Many of them now realized that Stuart's men were not invincible. "We, as cavalry, understand what we are able to accomplish and only ask Stuart to meet us in a cavalry fight on the Manassas Plains," boasted one Hoosier.[12]

Despite the disquieting attack by the aggressive Union cavalry, Lee was ready to begin his invasion. Slipping his army west through gaps in the Blue Ridge Mountains, Lee disappeared into the Shenandoah Valley. Stuart's bloodied cavalry moved into position to protect these same gaps from Union reconnaissance. Surprised and embarrassed by the attack and near defeat at Brandy Station, Stuart was anxious for his next confrontation with the suddenly more active Union cavalry. In the Union camps, it was whispered that the enemy was moving and that meant the cavalry would be sent out to find him. On June 15, the rumors were confirmed as the men marched to Bristoe Station near Manassas. All the next day was spent in the eerie vicinity of the two battles that had been fought there in 1861 and 1862. The men were confident, however, that 1863 would be different. "No more Bull Runs for we are too sharp for them," boasted one Hoosier.[13]

By the 17th, Union scouts on the prowl in the Loudon Valley between the Bull Run and Blue Ridge Mountains reported contact with Stuart's forces. Ever mindful of protecting Washington, Hooker moved the army north. The cavalry fanned out west trying to find a gap in Stuart's protective shield and discover the whereabouts of Lee's army. The 3rd Indiana and the rest of the 1st Division were sent west in the heat and dust toward Snicker's Gap and reached Aldie after the 2nd Division had had a sharp fight with Stuart's men. The next morning, the men could see many of the dead men and horses dotting the fields. Looking down into the valley below, the Hoosiers had a ringside seat as skirmishing continued below.[14]

As dawn broke on the 19th, the men and horses were subjected to a drenching rain, turning the roads into muddy messes. Continuing west, they could hear gunfire as the 2nd Division pushed Stuart's men back toward the Blue Ridge Mountains. Orders were received to turn north as the 1st Division tried to flank the stubborn Rebels at the little village of Middleburg. Unknown to Buford, Stuart had extended his line much further north than reported. A mile and half past Middleburg, Buford turned the division west only to run into the Confederate line. Frustrated in the attempt to flank the rebels, the men dismounted and contented themselves with long range sniping before returning to Middleburg for the evening.

During this action, the men were surprised to see Captain George Custer once again accompanying the regiment. During the afternoon, Custer and a group of Hoosiers detected a line of men behind a stone wall to their front. Not knowing if they were friend or foe, Custer kept prodding the men to move closer. As the men inched nearer, it was determined that the "foe" behind the wall were Union. Custer, well known to the men from the Northern Neck expedition and Brandy Station, was good-naturedly chided by the men for risking his life and their own. When asked what he meant to do if the men protected by the stone wall had been Confederates, Custer confidently replied, "I meant to demand their surrender."[15]

The rain began as they entered Middleburg and continued throughout the night.[16] Army headquarters still needed to know Lee's whereabouts, and the cavalry was ordered to resume their probing of Stuart's protective shield on June 21. The 2nd Division was to take the advance down the National Road toward Upperville with Buford's division retracing their steps north and west of Middleburg to the right.

Sunday morning, June 21, after another night of rain, held promise for a beautiful summer day. As they packed and saddled their horses, rations arrived, but the urgency of movement precluded the distribution of the food. Hungry and still damp, the men of 3rd Indiana swung into saddle for what promised to be a long, hard day.[17] The column moved down the Ashby Gap turnpike to Middleburg and turned north on Pot House Road. As the column turned west, the regiment was thrown out ahead as skirmishers.

Arriving at Goose Creek, Buford followed the stream, looking for an opportunity to strike Stuart's line.[18] Suddenly shots rang out as the skirmishers found Stuart's picket line. Manned by the 12th Virginia, they were soon sent flying west when dismounted men of the 3rd Indiana flanked the rebel post. Remounting, the men rode toward the little hamlet of Millville.

To the south, they could hear fighting between the 2nd Division and Rebel cavalry. From some of the higher hills, they could actually see the Union cavalry in action.[19] If the 1st Division could push south and join the 2nd Division, Buford could cut off a portion of the Rebel forces and be able to push the remaining Confederates through the Ashby's Gap. From there, the Union horsemen would be able to see into the Valley and determine Lee's location. Continuing to follow Goose Creek, the skirmishers in the lead started to receive fire as they moved toward Upperville. Intermittently, over the next two hours, the men would be attacked, and the column would shake out into line. As the shooting ended, the skirmishers would start forward while the brigade re-mounted, re-formed into column, and continued the march. This classic delaying action by the Confederates was designed to buy time to consolidate their forces and thwart the effort to cut them off.

These stops and starts were necessary as Gamble never knew when he might meet the main Rebel force. The brigade that day only numbered about 900 men consisting of the 8th Illinois, two squadrons of the 12th Illinois and the three squadrons of the 3rd Indiana.[20] The 8th New York was detached and accompanied a battery of artillery at the end of the column. The terrain also played into the slowness of the march and the effectiveness of the Confederate tactics. Rolling hills cut by creeks met them as they moved forward. Nearly every road was also bordered by the ubiquitous stone fences, making movement off of the roads difficult.

Finally reaching Millville, Buford realized that the fighting to the south had already passed Rectorville, his original destination. If the original plan was followed,

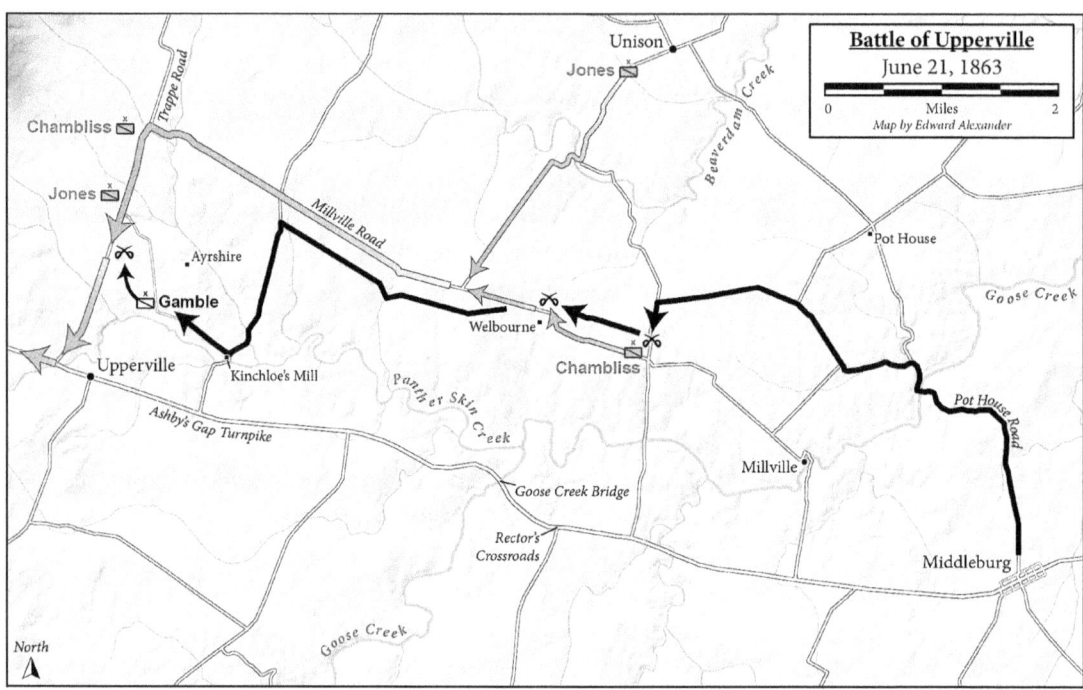

his division would come in behind the 2nd Division and be of no use. Though only a mile and a half from his comrades, Buford turned the column around and returned to the Upperville Road, turned west once more and again attempted to turn Stuart's flank and cut off a part of the Confederate force. Marching west, the men could actually see enemy wagons and men marching from their right to the south. Seeing that their path placed the Union cavalry on a shorter, inside track to Ashby's Gap, Gamble's men accelerated their march in an effort to cut off the Confederates and play havoc on Stuart's left flank.[21]

The road being used by the Confederates was known as Trappe Road. Running north and south, it joined the Ashby Gap Turnpike just below the Gap. An open field swept downhill to the east where an old sunken road angled northwest, meeting Trapp Road north of the scurrying Rebel troops. Stone walls bordered both sides of Trapp Road and the sunken road.[22]

The troops that had been discovered were the Confederate brigades of Chambliss and Jones. They were well aware of the nearby Union horsemen and were moving at the gallop to get to Ashby Gap ahead of their pursuers. The skirmishers of the 3rd Indiana dismounted and took up a position behind the stone fence bordering the sunken road. The rest of the regiment formed into line of battle with the rest of the brigade. Ahead, Chew's Confederate artillery could be seen going into battery in a bid to slow the Union forces and allow their comrades to escape. Supporting the battery were the 10th Virginia and 2nd North Carolina, but their position was in the open field with their backs to the stone wall bordering Trappe Road. Gamble saw an opportunity to strike the two regiments out in the open. Chew had positioned his artillery so as to take the charging Federal troops in flank.[23]

Gamble started the brigade up the hill, and the 3rd Indiana skirmishers rose up from behind their stone wall at the sunken road and delivered a devastating volley to the Rebels. The brigade charged up to a few rods from the guns, driving the 10th Virginia and 2nd North Carolina away. Just as they gathered for the final push to the guns, Confederate reinforcements from the 12th Virginia were seen entering the field from Trappe Road through a break in the stone wall. Other men could be seen frantically clawing at the rocks in an effort to open additional holes. Only able currently to enter the field two at a time, the initial attack by the Virginians had little chance of success. The Hoosiers behind the wall at the sunken road peppered the attackers, and the counterattack ended before it really started. One rebel later wrote, "it was the hardest fight that I ever saw it looked awful."[24] The 6th and 11th Virginia forced their way through the stone wall at Trappe Road as additional gaps were being made. Other men dismounted behind the Trappe Road's stone fence and tried to counter the fire by the Hoosiers across the field in the sunken road. About this time, Chew's battery began to fire. The Virginians attacked, slammed into Gamble's reforming Union horsemen, and the melee began with saber and pistol liberally applied.

Classic cavalry combat commenced with charge, regroup, countercharge, regroup, charge. Gamble's westerners absorbed the attack and then retreated a short distance to regroup and delivered their own assault. Sabers flashed, horses reared, pistols fired and men and horses were wounded and died. Sergeant Dave Haskell of Company A went down with a wound to the thigh. Matthias Miller was hit in both shoulder and side. In Company C, Orderly Sergeant Charley Johnson reeled in his saddle, his thigh broken by a bullet. Meanwhile, Sergeant William Peters cradled a wounded shoulder.[25] The ebb and flow of the battle continued for half an hour, including an attack on the sunken road by a squadron of Confederate cavalry that was severely punished by the hidden Hoosiers.[26]

Finally an attack by the 7th, 9th, and 11th Virginia pushed Gamble's attackers downhill to the cover of the sunken road and the dismounted men of the 3rd Indiana. As the Virginians' attack neared the wall, a mounted squadron of the 3rd Indiana slammed into their flank and sent the Southerners reeling back up the hill. Between the mounted attack and carbine fire from the sunken road, the Virginians left 27 dead in the small field.[27] William Hyden of Company F returned from this flank attack with a carbine bullet in his foot.[28]

As the fighting swept up and down the hill, the Hoosier carbineers behind the wall laid such a fire upon Chew's battery that the battery horses were unable to be brought forward. Feeling the pressure of the Union attack, the Confederate artillery resorted to retreat by recoil. Slowly, the pieces moved backward where the men hitched up the guns and move to a small knoll on the other side of Trappe Road.[29] Their fire allowed the rest of the column to escape.

The Union men and horses were exhausted. As Devin's brigade came up to continue the pursuit, the 3rd Indiana and Gamble's brigade looked around the battlefield and tried to understand its meaning. The Confederate cavalrymen and their wagons had successfully thwarted the attempt to cut them off from the rebel lines. In the process, a bitter, savage fight had taken place, and there were signs of the carnage scattered all over the little field between the sunken road and Trappe Road. For some of the men, their trials were only beginning. First Lieutenant William W. Long of Company C was beginning his long trip to prison, having been captured in the afternoon's melees.[30] Surgeon Beck took one look at Charley Johnson's badly wounded and broken thigh and decided the leg had to be amputated immediately. Beck found a suitable location nearby, and Johnson endured the procedure literally "on the field."[31]

The men made camp on the battlefield just north of Upperville. Still without food, the men tried to ignore their grumbling stomachs. The next day they buried 30 Confederate dead and many more horses and marched back to Aldie. There, they were able to eat and horses were shod in preparation for the continued pursuit of Lee.[32] They looked back on their performance at Trappe Road with satisfaction. Having fought all or parts of six regiments of Confederate cavalry plus a five gun battery, Gamble's abbreviated brigade of two regiment strength reported 44 casualties. The 3rd Indiana had had five men wounded and lost 17 horses. Buford had witnessed the fighting and proclaimed, "I'll be damned, if I can't whip a little corner of Hell with the First Brigade!"[33]

Meanwhile, Sergeant Cline had conducted another of his deep scouts into the Confederate lines. On June 17, he and a small band of scouts started a five day trip that pinpointed the Confederate army and units as it moved down the Valley. His value as a scout was emphasized when one of the Bureau officers asked specifically for Cline. From Frederick, Maryland, he pleaded, "If my mission here is of importance, for Gods sake send me one man who wont run when there is no one after him and is not frightened when he sees a greyback."[34] Within a few days, Cline was on his way to Frederick.

Leaving Aldie on June 26, the 3rd Indiana and their comrades of the 1st Brigade, 1st Division of the Cavalry Corps of the Army of the Potomac crossed the Potomac River at Leesburg and moved north. Four days later, they would enter a small Pennsylvania town named Gettysburg.

Chapter 8

June 30, 1863–July 1, 1863

The regiment entering Gettysburg on June 30, 1863, barely resembled the ragtag recruits that left Madison in September 1861. Now nearing the two year mark of their three year enlistment, the regiment mustered 392 enlisted men and 17 officers with 34 men and officers on detached duty, in rebel prisons, or on sick leave. Fifty of the men were reported sick but serving with their companies. Present for duty were 327 battle toughened and campaign-hardened men and officers.[1] Armed primarily with the .52 caliber breech loading Gallager carbine, a handful still had Sharps carbines, and a few carried the .50 caliber Smith carbine.[2] Most of the men had traded their .36 caliber Navy Colt revolvers for the newer, more powerful .44 Army Colts.[3] In addition, many of the men carried a second revolver—picked up on the battlefield or purchased with their own money—in a saddle holster. All carried sabers.

The regiment and companies were led, for the most part, by tested and capable officers. The officer corps was again depleted due to resignations, capture and illness. Only nine company officers were on duty on June 30 out of its complement of 18. Three companies had only one officer present—Company B was commanded by Second Lieutenant Dennis Davis, Company C was led by Captain Ephraim H. Martin, and Company D was commanded by First Lieutenant John D.R. Spencer. Offsetting this shortage of field officers was a field staff of majors Charles Lemmon, William McClure, and William Patton. All of the majors had been company officers and knew their business.[4] Colonel George Chapman, their short, bespectacled leader, had grown in the estimation of the men. He may have been a drinker, but he was also a fighter who looked after his men. For the first time in the war, the colonel would also command a force nearly equal to a full regiment. Four companies of the 12th Illinois were temporarily assigned to his leadership.

They entered Pennsylvania under another new commanding General. Lincoln, having lost faith in Joe Hooker, replaced him with George Meade on June 27. The Third's long association with Hooker had made him a favorite with the regiment. From the early days in eastern Maryland to his ascendancy to command of the Army of the Potomac, the men had considered Hooker a good leader and had faith in his abilities. While respectful of Meade, they would always remember Hooker with a fondness based on familiarity.

On June 30, the men crossed the Mason-Dixon Line into Pennsylvania. After encountering rebel forces at Fairfield, the division recrossed into Maryland and moved southeast to Emmitsburg before re-entering Pennsylvania once again and marched to Gettysburg. The proximity of the enemy was confirmed when the advance guard led by Corporal Henry Sparks captured several Rebel stragglers as the blue-clad horsemen galloped into town.[5]

Lee's army had scattered out across the countryside of Pennsylvania. As the Army of the Potomac approached from their screening position around Washington, Lee ordered the consolidation of his force at Gettysburg because of the town's network of roads. He respected George Meade enough that the consolidation of his forces was mandatory. The town has been described as a hub of a wheel with roads radiating out in all directions. This made it an ideal site for the Confederate army to gather. Lee, however, envisioned doing battle elsewhere and ordered that no general engagement be attempted until the entire army was in place.

Buford was also formulating a plan that, hopefully, would thwart Lee's intentions. Recognizing the strategic significance of the town and its network of roads, Buford sent scouts to the north and west to locate the enemy. Once the Confederates were located, Buford planned to use the rolling hills and ridges of the surrounding countryside to slow the Rebels while the rest of the army arrived to support them. Most important to his plan was McPherson's Ridge to the northwest of Gettysburg.

The division rode through town and encamped on the ridge. The 3rd Indiana was positioned on the north side of the Chambersburg Pike and north of an unfinished railroad cut. The four companies of the 12th Illinois settled in on the Hoosiers' left flank between the Pike and the railroad cut. The command was on the right flank of Gamble's brigade. Devin's brigade extended the line further north on the 3rd's right. Scattered out across the face of Gamble's brigade were the six guns of Calef's battery of horse artillery. Four guns sat astride the Chambersburg Pike in front of the western men of the 12th Illinois and 3rd Indiana.[6] Pickets were sent out about one mile down the Chambersburg Pike to Herr's Ridge and the next ridge, Knoxlyn Ridge, another half mile beyond Herr's. The valley that separated McPherson's and Herr's Ridges was cut by a small stream called Willoughby's Run. Behind and to the left of their position rose Seminary Ridge, so named for a Lutheran seminary located there. Buford established his headquarters on this ridge.

Settling into camp, a few lucky Hoosiers had been invited to dinner by some grateful citizens of Gettysburg and after an attempt to clean up, rode back into town for a sumptuous meal. Food and drink were placed before them in quantities they had not seen in many months. For the men, it was the first time they had sat down with a family for a meal since leaving Indiana. Sated, the men rode back to camp with invitations to return for breakfast.[7] As the men settled down for the night, they knew that a fight was in the offing.[8] Enough reports of Confederates approaching had given the men a good idea of what they faced.

Out beyond the pickets, Lee and his Army of Northern Virginia anticipated an early start. Henry Heth's Confederate division was preparing to march to Gettysburg to meet other elements of the army. Unaware of Union horsemen in the vicinity, Heth did not expect to find much resistance in town. They had passed through the hamlet scarcely 36 hours before, and there was no evidence of Union troops. To his knowledge, only home guard and small squads of cavalry were present.

This lack of awareness by the Confederates was due, in part, to the Union cavalry. J.E.B. Stuart had been surprised at Brandy Station three weeks before and had been embarrassed. In addition, the tough delaying actions at Aldie, Middleburg, and Upperville had been wearing on him and his command. He longed for the opportunity to recover some of the luster to his reputation. He had proposed to Lee a raid to cut in behind the Union army, head northeast, swing around to the west and re-join Lee after another circumnavigation of the Union army. Lee agreed though it left his army nearly blind, and Stuart was many miles away trying to find his way back to the Confederate invaders as the army stumbled along blissfully unaware of the proximity of Union troops.

Dawn, July 1, sunlight slowly spread across the Pennsylvania countryside. Union pickets out on Knoxlyn Ridge were tired and looking forward to the upcoming change of pickets. Major William McClure led the sleepy relief for the 3rd Indiana. As he crossed Willoughby's Run, he was hailed by Major Charles Lemmon, the commander of the overnight pickets. Lemmon had just come in from the picket line on Knoxlyn Ridge and was leaning against a large tree along the stream. There in the fog and semi-light of early morning, Lemmon offered McClure a drink from his flask and a grim premonition. "Major, drink with me; it will be the last one we will ever take

Charles Lemmon became a highly competent cavalry officer after being elected first lieutenant of Company C. Promoted to captain in December 1861, he impressed officers of the future "Iron Brigade" with his professionalism and skill. Promoted to Major in March 1863, he would have undoubtedly led the regiment except for his untimely death at Gettysburg (Indiana State Library).

together as I will be a dead man before night." His fellow major tried to encourage the gloomy Lemmon, but was unable to raise the man's spirits.[9]

Others were stirring back in camp. Thomas Day of Company E was thinking of another good meal. One of the fortunate men who had eaten in town the night before, he had been invited back for breakfast, and he was up early for a return visit with the generous family. With only a halter, he led his horse down to Willoughby's Run for a drink of water around 7:00 a.m. His finicky horse refused to drink from the stream so Day walked up the hill to Herr's Ridge were he found a watering trough in a farm lot that was acceptable to his mount. As he watched the sunrise from behind a nearby ridge, he heard shots fired to his right and saw Rebel skirmishers advancing. Scrambling onto his horse bareback, Day galloped back to camp to raise the alarm.[10]

General Buford had been receiving reports about approaching enemy infantry and scanned the hills. Sensing that these troops represented the main body of Lee's forces, he sent gallopers to various army corps headquarters to the south, urging them to hurry north. Down in the camps, bugles were blowing "saddle and mount!" Men scrambled to get dressed and saddle their horses. Company E was sent toward the sound of rifle and carbine fire with orders to delay the advancing Rebels for as long as possible. "Startled ... by the report of the pickets that the rebs were advancing in force up the Chambersburg Road. Saddled in a hurry—and advanced towards the hills" reported one man.[11] Skirmishers raced forward to join the pickets, and soon, a large part of the regiment was actively fighting out on Knoxlyn Ridge. Edward C. Reid joined Lemmon's skirmishers only to be driven back. "Moved back and forth over the field between Getsbg and the Seminary avoiding exposure to shell with difficulty," he recorded that night.[12] All across McPherson's Ridge the scene repeated from regiment to regiment as the entire division jumped into action.[13]

The swarm of carbineers slowed Heth's advance to a crawl. Surprised by the intensity and volume of fire he faced, Heth realized these were Army of the Potomac soldiers, not home guard. Now more cautious and uncertain, he ordered his artillery to unlimber and fire on the pesky skirmishers. He then ordered his division to deploy into battle line, a maneuver that took nearly 90 minutes. By doing so, he was bringing on the major engagement Lee had specifically ordered not to occur. Moving forward slowly, his line pushed the Union horsemen back toward Herr's Ridge. Grudgingly, the cavalrymen gave ground to the overwhelming advance. Among the Hoosiers, all types of ruses were used to slow the advancing Rebels. Company E's Matthew Glauber, born in Germany and still possessing a strong Germanic accent, yelled at the top of his lungs. "Scharge! Scharge the b_____!" The men responded to the impetuous Glauber and his profane order and drove a part of the Confederate line back a short distance.[14]

Such heroics, however, could only provide temporary relief for the outnumbered cavalrymen. Pushed over Herr's Ridge, the men scampered down the hill and into the trees bordering Willoughby's Run. Here, the men's carbines continued a steady fire as the Confederate line crested ridge. Now only a mile from McPherson's Ridge, Heth's division presented a formidable adversary. Flanking Buford's command on both ends of his short line, the blue-clad horsemen were outnumbered more than 3 to 1. For the first time in the war, the 3rd Indiana would have to fight dismounted against veteran infantry to buy time. If they held long enough, elements of the Army of the Potomac would arrive and secure the position. If they didn't, they would have to mount and ride for their lives.

Casualties began to mount. Sergeant James Boyd was hit in the side and sent to the rear. William Park was hit in the chest, and bright red blood frothed from the wound. Others were hit as the men broke from Willoughby's Run and ran up the north face of McPherson's Ridge to the main line. Now about 9:00 a.m., the men settled into their position in support of Calef's spread out battery. A total of 15 Confederate cannons were soon arrayed along Herr's Ridge and were shelling Calef and the Union horsemen of the 1st Division. With four of Calef's guns on their side of the Chambersburg Pike, the 3rd Indiana received more than their share of artillery fire. Barely a mile away, the Confederate artillery belched their lethal charges at them as Heth's infantry continued to deploy for battle.

Now subjected to the worst cannonade they had or would ever experience, shells shrieked over and into the dismounted men. Horses, though further back and partially protected by the back side of the ridge, were also hit. Jesse Smith of Company E was struck by a shell, gouging a path through his body.[15] Captain Ephraim Martin of Company C was hit in the shoulder and headed back toward town and aid.[16] Other men were wounded including Benjamin Sellers who was hit by shell fragments in the side and leg.[17]

About 9:30 a.m., the gray line began to advance on the thin line of cavalrymen. Some of the brigade began to waver, but the men of the 3rd Indiana continued their steady fire at the oncoming mass.[18] Succumbing to overpowering numbers, the Union line retreated across the shallow swale of McPherson's Ridge past Calef's frantic artillerymen trying to withdraw their guns, and re-formed on the east crest of the Ridge. In minutes, maybe less, the long Rebel line would re-appear before them, and there would be little the men could do but fire, run and mount, and ride for their lives. Throwing glances over their left shoulders, they held out hope that succor was on the way. Mercifully, blue infantrymen could be seen coming at the quick march down from the town toward the waiting horsemen. The I Corps had arrived. By 10:00 a.m., Cutler's brigade began arriving at the 3rd Indiana's position. To their left, their old comrades of the Iron Brigade replaced the 8th Illinois just as the gray-clad Confederates crested McPherson's Ridge. Grateful Hoosiers ran back to their horses and swung into saddle for the ride back to town. They had held.

Some, emboldened by the arrival of reinforcements, exchanged their carbines for longer ranged rifles and joined the Iron Brigade in their fight.[19] Matthew Glauber, his Teutonic blood still boiling from the morning's fight, was one of these men. He was joined by Will Rea of Company E, but they had a different motive in mind.

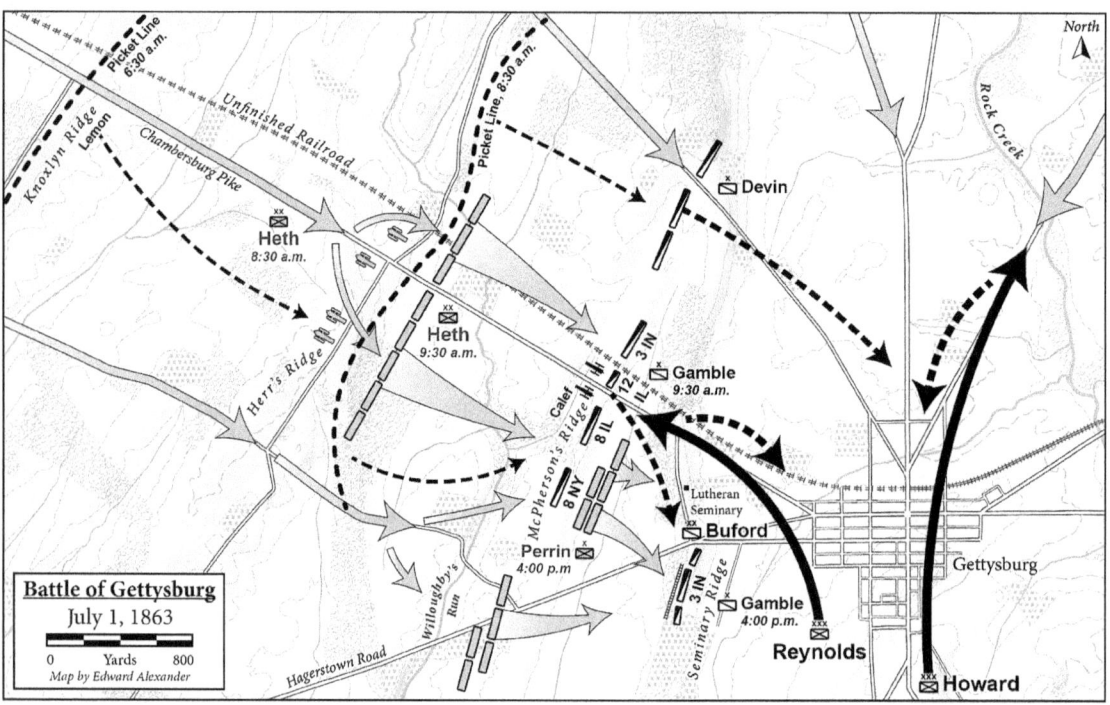

Glauber had his eye on an artillery horse left at Calef's position, his own horse having been killed. Rea had designs on an officer's saddle and pistols located on a dead horse in advance of their position. As the Union infantrymen surged past them, they moved forward to claim their prizes.[20]

Not all of the men survived whole. Having been under fire for nearly three hours, the mental strain was too much for one man. Louis Tufts of Company D was a sensitive young man who regularly corresponded with the folks back home through letters to the newspaper under the pseudonym Americus. In the maelstrom of battle, Tufts had seen his best friend Jesse Smith torn apart by an artillery shell and killed. The dazed Tufts was riding back toward town when he saw the body of General Reynolds, commander of the I Corps, carried by. There in the surreal and smoke covered field, young Tufts went mad.[21]

The regiment withdrew a short distance toward Gettysburg. Though still under artillery fire, the men could watch the ebb and flow of the fighting as it played out below them. Wadsworth's Division had brought the Confederate attack to a standstill. To the left of their old position, the Iron Brigade was fighting, and over to their right, in an unfinished railroad cut, rebel forces were trapped and forced to surrender.

Around noon, the regiment was ordered to the southwest of town and into the broad fields that lay between Seminary and Cemetery Ridge.[22] As they rode through town, they were shocked to hear female voices singing. Students from the local women's college had climbed to the roof of a nearby building and were serenading the passing soldiers with their rendition of "Rally 'Round the Flag, Boys."[23]

The morning's fight had been a near thing for the Union, but timely arrival of reinforcements brightened the outlook. The cavalrymen could take pride in their morning's work. They had slowed the Confederate advance, exacted a toll on the enemy, and held out until reinforcements stopped the Confederate advance cold. Unfortunately, the rebel troops were now arriving faster than the Union reinforcements.

The Union XI Corps had been deployed to the north of Gettysburg, but arriving Confederate columns routed the blue clad infantrymen, and they were streaming into town toward a new Union line on Cemetery Ridge. Meanwhile, the Iron Brigade and their comrades of the I Corps, after their initial success, were being pushed back toward town and would soon be flanked on their right by the forces pursuing the XI Corps. Coming down the Hagerstown Road, another column of Rebels threatened the I Corps' left flank. If successful, this column could "roll up" the I Corps as well as cut off the fugitives from the XI Corps. Literally thousands of Union soldiers could be captured or lost.

Around 3:30 p.m., Gamble's brigade was ordered to move to Seminary Ridge. There they were to take a position on the exposed Union left flank and to hold the advancing Confederates long enough to allow the escape of I and XI Corps troops. The brigade, now shrunk to about 1000 men, due to the 8th Illinois being detached to another part of the battlefield, hurried to their new position. The brigade now consisted of the six companies of the 3rd Indiana, four companies of the 12th Illinois, and the 8th New York. After the horse holders were subtracted, Gamble would initially have fewer than 700 men to face this threat. The men dismounted and formed a line along a low stone fence just a few hundred yards south of the Lutheran Seminary. Tree lined on both sides, the wall provided good cover. They crouched in its protection and waited for the oncoming Rebel attack. Some of the horse holders remained mounted so that they could add their fire over the heads of the dismounted troops.[24]

The men were barely in position when they saw the red battle flags of the advancing Confederates moving obliquely from their left to their right. The attacking Rebs were Perrin's brigade of South Carolinians. Taking aim, the 3rd Indiana and their comrades fired into the right flank of the attackers and slowed the attack. The 12th and 13th South Carolina angled to their right and made for the stone wall. The range shortened as the horsemen used both carbine and revolver. Under the intense fire from the cavalrymen, the South Carolinians were taking casualties, and the first line fell back in confusion onto the second line. Adding to the Confederate troubles was Calef's battery. Unlimbering nearby, the battery, short on ammunition, fired slowly but effectively in support of the little band of horsemen.[25]

Perrin now had to divert his entire brigade's attack from its original course and deal with the pesky Union cavalrymen. As the infantry moved toward the stone wall, Hoosiers began to fall. Augustus Wright slumped quietly to the ground, dead. John Weaver went down in a heap, his knee shattered by a Minié ball.[26] Sergeant Samuel

Lamb, temporarily in command of Company C due to Captain Martin's wounding earlier, crumpled to the earth with his head horribly wounded.[27] Several others were hit, and Major Charles Lemmon had his premonition fulfilled as he was mortally wounded in the head.[28]

For thirty precious minutes, the men slugged it out with the Confederate infantry and diverted their attack. The South Carolinians were right up to the wall "within less than 10 paces" and threatened to engulf the blue-clad horsemen.[29] Another attacking force was threatening their left flank. That evening, another recalled, "At last, our whole left wing was routed. We held it for a time against a whole rebel brigade of infantry—but at last were forced to fall back."[30] Ordered to mount, the men ran back to the waiting horses. Captain George Thompson of Company E had a few anxious moments when his horse broke free and ran off in the confusion. Only the quick reaction and running catch of the mount by Private John Wildman saved the officer from capture.[31] Riding away from the wall, they traveled toward Cemetery Ridge. They had done their duty well; while many members of the I and XI Corps would be captured in the streets of Gettysburg, many more were saved by the delaying fight along the stone wall.

Their day was still not over. Around 4:15 p.m., Buford was implored to provide reinforcement to the collapsing Union line further out on Seminary Ridge. Ordered out into the open ground in front of Cemetery Hill as a demonstration of power, Buford's small, tired division checked the enemy advance. This second appearance on the Confederate right once again stalled an enemy attack and prevented the capture of retreating, routed Union soldiers through the streets of Gettysburg.

Now in the early evening, the men were ordered to the south down the Emmitsburg Road. There, the men settled into camp near a peach orchard located at the foot of two hills known locally as Little and Big Round Top. In the sparse shade and near some odd rock formations known as Devil's Den, they found little protection from the hot July sun setting in the west. The tepid waters of Plum Run offered little comfort to the men or their mounts. "Slim fare and slight cover" was Chapman's succinct description of their bivouac.[32]

As they picketed the army's far right flank, the exhausted men were finally able to absorb the long, costly day. Major Lemmon was horribly wounded and not expected to live. Isaac Vibbert, Augustus Wright, and Jesse Smith were known to be dead. Louis Tufts had gone mad. Twenty-three others were wounded while others were missing and presumed captured. (See Appendix for complete casualty list.)[33] Company C was under the command of a sergeant. Over in the 12th Illinois, Chapman counted an additional 20 casualties. The combined 10 companies had over half of the casualties suffered by the 1st Brigade.

The Hoosiers had seen more war that day than they witnessed in their entire 22 months of service. Under fire by as many as 15 pieces of artillery in the morning and facing enemy infantry in overwhelming numbers on two different occasions, the men had reason to be proud. They had fought hard and had fought well. They had proven worthy of Buford's ideal of a dragoon. Buford recognized this in his report: "A heavy task was before us; we were equal to it, and shall all remember with pride that at Gettysburg we did our country much service."[34] The men knew they had accomplished a great deal. The regiment had "fought like wildcats all day," remembered one proud Hoosier.[35]

Chapter 9

July 2, 1863–September 9, 1863

The next morning opened with the promise of more hot weather and more hot fighting. Throughout the night, both armies were reinforced and their lines extended. Buford's pickets had heard movement off to the west and knew that Rebel forces were occupying the length of Seminary Ridge. The men braced for another day of fighting, but fortunately, the morning passed quietly. Colonel Chapman was relieved. "The morning has been comparatively quiet, a little work between skirmishers & an occasional shot from the artillery is all," is how he described it.[1] But, the men and horses were worn out. Physically exhausted by the events of July 1, they had been in the saddle almost continuously since the beginning of May. Simple things like clothing and horseshoes were in dire need of replacement and repair. "We are after supplies for men & horses, both having been on short allowance for four days," reported Colonel Chapman.[2] After sporadic fire along the picket line all morning, at noon, they welcomed orders to saddle up and head south. They were to travel to Taneytown, Maryland, there to rest and re-fit.

By July 3, now at Westminster, the men had set up camp and begun the time consuming but essential task of shoeing the horses. Foraging upon the surrounding countryside was necessary as they had yet to be supplied with food or forage. Some lucky few were fed by local farmers. Sam Gilpin of Company E had a "sumptuous" dinner at one such farmhouse.[3] While engaging in horseshoeing and food, the men could hear faint cannonading to the north. Unknown to them at the time, Lee was throwing 15,000 men against the center of the Union line in what became known as Pickett's Charge.[4]

On the 4th of July, the men celebrated Independence Day in a pouring rain and learned of Pickett's defeat the previous day as they moved toward Frederick. Long lines of Confederate prisoners were seen filing past on their way to Washington and prisoner of war camps. Although the battle of Gettysburg was over, there was still work to be done. Lee was retreating back to Virginia, and it was the cavalry's job to keep him from using the Potomac River crossings. If successful, they would deny Lee the opportunity to escape and trap the Confederate army on the north side of the river. If they were successful, it could mean an end to the war.

Plodding through the driving rain, horses began to break down and be abandoned. Tired out, the column was forced to camp five miles short of Frederick. On

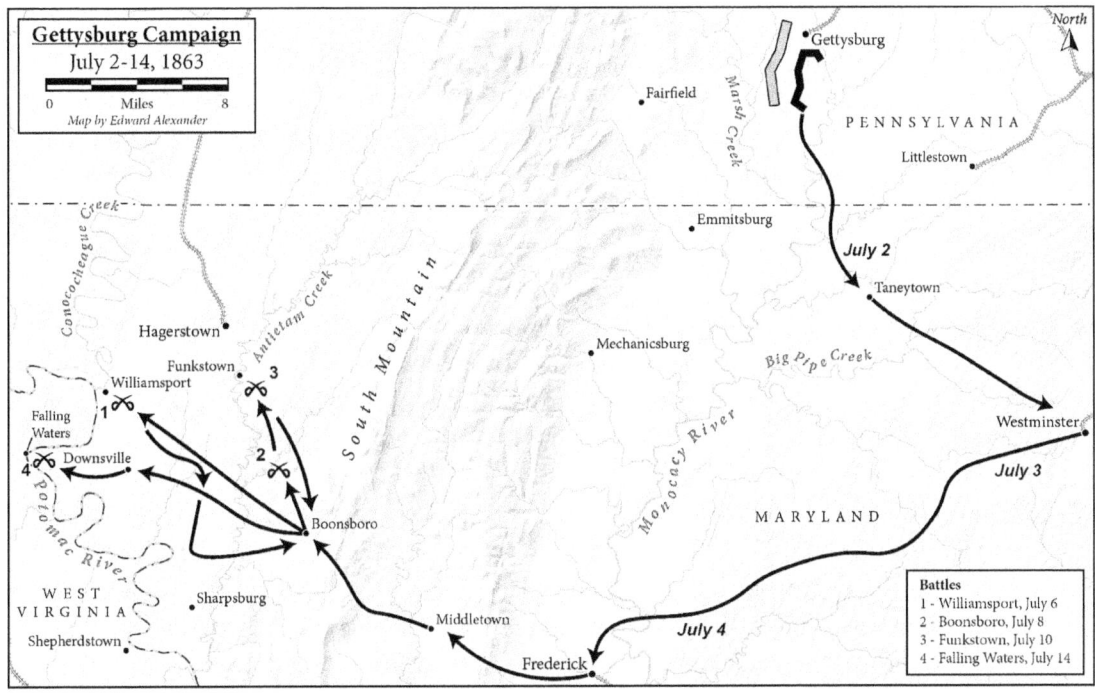

July 5, they were once again surprised to hear singing as local girls sang patriotic tunes as the passed through the town. A loyalist farmer opened his barns, and the grateful men and horses were able to eat heartily.[5] Now moving west they were on familiar ground; Middletown, South Mountain, Boonesborough. They were headed to Williamsport on the Potomac with the 3rd Indiana in the lead.[6]

There was a ford at Williamsport, but recent rains had made it impassable. If the men could reach the ford, they would be able to deny the retreating Confederate army a vital crossing. Hold it long enough, and the Union infantry could fall on its enemy's rear. The cavalry just had to reach Williamsport and block the Rebels. Unfortunately, there were already Confederate forces at the river. A motley mix of cavalrymen, teamsters, quartermasters, wagoners, commissaries and wounded soldiers from Gettysburg were guarding the crossing for Lee's approaching army. While slim on infantry, the force had a considerable amount of artillery mounted and well sighted. It was this improvised line the 3rd Indiana and the rest of the 1st Division approached.[7]

On the 6th, about six miles east of Williamsport. the Confederate picket line was met on the campus of a local boarding school. Gunfire crackled as the Union force pushed in the pickets and rode toward Williamsport. A spirited skirmish developed as the men approached the town. In an attempt to flank the Confederate position, the 3rd Indiana was moved to the extreme left of the Union line and had small success with the capture of seven wagons.[8] Confederate cavalry appeared opposite Gamble's brigade, and the 3rd Indiana were subjected to localized cavalry charges on their front. The liberal use of artillery and the reinforcement of the Rebel position slowed the Union attack to a crawl. By 3:00 p.m., some Union infantry arrived to relieve the cavalry. The men rode eight miles and crossed Antietam Creek before camping near the Antietam battlefield. They had fought long and well that day, but the desperate Confederates were fighting for their lives. One Hoosier thought they had been fighting 15,000 Rebs.[9] The same man found a newspaper that opined that Lee's army was in full retreat, and its capture all but certain. "I don't see it," he said ruefully.[10]

The next morning, the men again rode toward Boonesborough but were ordered to dismount and form a line on a ridge about one and a half miles northwest of the village. This change from an offensive to defensive stance was precipitated by the arrival of Jeb Stuart's Confederate cavalry division. Stuart's mission was to protect the river crossing for Lee's army. At sunup on July 8, he attacked the Union line and soon had it under considerable pressure. The 3rd Indiana was positioned to the horse artillery's right flank, and their situation soon became uncomfortable. Rebel artillery to their right on a commanding hill was firing down on them. Sam Gilpin of Company C had a shell explode directly under his horse, throwing man and beast into the air. Miraculously, neither was badly injured, but Gilpin reported seeing "constellations that the astronomy makes no mention of," from a bump on the head.[11] Pollard Brown over in Company F was hit in the head by a spent bullet, cutting his ear and giving him a headache.[12]

In addition to the artillery fire, Confederate troops could be seen working their way around their flank, and it would be a matter of minutes before the men would be forced back to a more defensible position. Timely arrival of reinforcements on their left eased the pressure, and the 3rd Indiana was able to stay.

Stuart's gray-and-butternut-clad horsemen had succeeded in pushing the Union cavalry back. Now he began his own retreat toward Hagerstown. Emboldened, the dismounted Union cavalry began to chase after the mounted Confederates. Skirmishers were shocked to see their 37-year-old division commander John Buford himself "shaking his fat sides" alongside his men. Now nearly 5:00 p.m., the pursuit was called off, and the winded Buford complimented the Hoosiers and Illinoisians of Gamble's brigade. "These boys beat anything in the world in a foot skirmish," boasted a winded Buford.[13]

Ordered back to Boonesborough, the men were nearly played out. Company C had only 18 men able to report for duty on July 8. Company E had 20 men. Worn out and unshod horses accounted for the majority of men unable to mount for duty.[14] The six companies of the regiment numbered a total of 158 mounted and ready for duty.[15] Still, Lee was on the north bank of the Potomac by high water, and hard work was required. On the 9th, forward elements of Meade's infantry arrived and probing attacks were made to determine the Confederate positions. Falling back to lines along the river near Williamsport, the Rebel position was a strong one with natural and manmade strength. While the army now had the Confederates trapped against

Chapter 9. July 2, 1863–September 9, 1863

the river, the strength of the position gave Meade pause as he contemplated the best way to attack Lee.

The 3rd Indiana and the 1st Division had been moved to the left flank of the Union army and pushed out toward Funkstown, pushing rebel videttes all the way to Antietam Creek. The apparent unwillingness of the gray-clad horsemen to give battle soon became apparent as Confederate infantry splashed across the creek and took up positions. Dismounting, the 3rd Indiana took its position in the center of the 1st Brigade's line. For the next several hours, they kept up a steady fire with their Gallager and Smith carbines. On the firing line, the regiment's luck ran out. Since the terrible fighting on July 1, 10 days ago, they had avoided casualties. But here near Antietam Creek, Josiah Daily of Company A was hit in the knee and went down.[16] Walter Kennedy of Company F was also dangerously wounded.[17] After several hours and nearly out of ammunition, Buford's command was replaced by infantry in late afternoon.

Leaving the line, the men were ordered to Middletown. Arriving there, they men collapsed. Horses were unsaddled for the first time in a week, and the regiment drew rations and forage. Tired and worn out, the strain of the past 14 days was beginning to show. One Hoosier was heard crying in the darkness one night as he gave into emotional catharsis for relief.[18]

Little duty was asked of the men for the next three days other than moving nearer Downsville on the southern edge of Lee's army. There, they monitored the Confederate lines and the level of the Potomac River. Floodwaters were receding, and everyone knew Meade would have to attack soon or see the Lee's army escape over the river to the safety of Virginia. Given the success at Gettysburg, the men still believed that one more climatic battle could end the war. "We expect every moment an engagement…. The troops are eager for it."[19]

Lee began laying a pontoon bridge at appropriately named Falling Waters on the evening of July 13. Shortly thereafter, his men began the tedious task of crossing the still raging river. Early the next morning, Union pickets reported the disappearance of the enemy. This could mean only one thing; the river had dropped enough to be crossed. Buford's men mounted and started in pursuit. If they hurried and were lucky, they might still be able to cut off a portion of Lee's army.

As Buford entered the abandoned Confederate lines, troops could be seen crossing on pontoons. To their right, Kilpatrick's division of Union cavalry was also hurrying after the retreating rebels. If the two divisions coordinated their attacks, a portion of the waiting enemy army could still be cut off and captured. Buford contacted Kilpatrick suggesting that Buford cut in behind the rebels, and Kilpatrick could then push the enemy toward the waiting troops of the 1st Division. Instead, Kilpatrick rashly ordered an immediate mounted attack. The men of the 3rd Indiana remembered Kilpatrick from their initiation to warfare back in the spring of 1862. Promoted to Brigadier General only three weeks earlier, he had already made one mistake by ordering a mounted attack on the Confederate right after the failure of Pickett's Charge on the afternoon of July 3. The attack had been cut to shreds. The coming charge threatened another catastrophe.

As horrified Hoosiers watched, Kilpatrick ordered an unsupported charge and was stopped cold by the Confederate rearguard. Many of the men would have agreed with brigade commander William Gamble's assessment of the attack. "Any competent cavalry officer could foretell the result" of the ill-starred charge.[20] The last of the Rebel troops broke for the river and the pontoon bridge. Hurrying his troops forward, Buford tried to salvage some success from the mess. In the ensuing firefight, Joseph Hall of Company F was hit in the thigh.[21] The men had to be content with cutting off and capturing 500 men of the rearguard—a considerably smaller number than if Kilpatrick had waited just 10 minutes before making his attack. Galloping toward the river, the men knew they could still capture the intact bridge, and Meade's army could continue its pursuit of Lee. As they approached the river, the pontoon bridge was cut loose from the opposite shore.

The Gettysburg campaign was over. With the Rebel army back safe in Virginia, the war would continue. There was still one more chance for the Union to snatch victory from the jaws of disappointment. If the Union cavalry could get across the river and cut into the Shenandoah Valley ahead of Lee's slow moving ambulances, infantry, and artillery, there might be a chance to stop them long enough for the Army of the Potomac to trap the Confederates for another decisive battle. The 3rd Indiana still had lots of campaigning ahead.

On July 16, the regiment had moved to Berlin by way of Petersville.[22] For the next couple of days the men and horses rested. Now located near a pontoon bridge at Berlin, the regiment was joined by a small contingent of men recently exchanged from the debacle on April 15 at Kelly's Ford.[23] These small additions were welcome. Since the commencement of campaigning in April, the regiment had lost over 90 men killed, wounded, captured, or died of disease. The effective strength of the regiment had been severely affected by the loss of horses. All were tired and nerves were stretched thin. Adding to their mental strain was knowing that their homes had been invaded by Confederates.

Confederate general John Morgan had crossed the Ohio River and invaded Indiana. He had been reported to have crossed near Louisville and travelled northeast, across the heart of the 3rd Indiana's recruiting area. The men were rightfully anxious for news from home and the events there. Mail and newspapers were eagerly sought to learn the latest of the raid.

On the 18th, their short rest was over, and the regiment crossed the Potomac, encamping "somewhere in Loudon County" that evening.[24] The next day, the brigade resumed their march with the goal of reaching Front Royal, there to occupy Manassas Gap to the east and to observe the broad valley south from Chester Gap, a few miles south of Front Royal. Hurrying out of Front Royal on the Culpeper Turnpike, the men found the Confederates waiting. Elements of Pickett's shattered division supported by a battery of six guns filled Chester's Gap. On the 21st, Union cavalry pushed Rebel pickets to within a mile of the summit. Dismounting, the men attacked and drove the Rebels to the very cusp of the opening. The fighting was severe as the Union troops tried to push the Confederates the final few yards over the top and into the broad valley beyond. In the uphill fight, the 3rd Indiana suffered several casualties. Maurice O'Connor of Company E was hit in the hand but continued to fight while Emsley Suits of Company D staggered to the ground with a bullet in his thigh.[25] In Company C, John Schroeder went down severely wounded.[26] The rebels held, and Gamble brigade was forced to pull back from the Gap's crest. The men had to be content with the capture of 100 horses and 800 head of cattle.[27]

On the 22nd, the men sniped at Rebels passing on the Culpeper Pike. Annoyed by the impertinence of a few hundred cavalry, the Rebels threw out a battle line and attacked the flank of Gamble's brigade. "We are stationed at Chester Gap to watch the rebbs we had a little scratch day before yesterday in which we done some of the cleanest gitting out of the way there has bin done for some time they brought in strong force of Infantry we had but afiew Cavalry but it did good running when ordered to evry man save him selfe," described one man of the ensuing action. They did "good running" to the east all the way to Barbee's Crossroads. Unfortunately, Peter Bright of Company C wasn't able to run fast enough, and was killed in the retreat.[28]

Now out of harm's way and with a force too small to effectively interfere with the Rebels' progress, the men were able to settle into camp for a couple of days. The infantry had come up but were too late to assist in the capture of Chester Gap. As the men awaited their next assignment, their attention was drawn to objectives of the more epicurean persuasion. In and around the nearby Blue Ridge Mountains grew an abundance of blackberries. Now in late July, these dark delicacies were ripening by the million, and the men spent most of those days collecting and feasting on these sweet fruits.[29]

Still duty needed to be conducted. Word had been received that a group of horses were held in the nearby mountains by a small Rebel force. Given the condition of their mounts, a squad of men decided to go after the herd. Eventually, 15 men under Lieutenant Abner Shannon set out on the morning of the 25th. Finding a hidden corral, the Union men achieved complete surprise and captured 17 horses and three Confederates, including a major.[30] The returned to camp and informed Colonel Chapman of their captures. Chapman now had a decision to make.

The men owned their horses. Because of this unusual arrangement, the horses did not carry the "U.S." brand like all other horses in the army. While expected to turn in all captured horses to the Quartermaster Corps to be branded government property, the men were never compensated for the loss of their privately owned mounts by injury, capture, or death. Realizing an opportunity when he saw one, Colonel Chapman allowed his men to exchange their own worn out mounts for the captured horses. When the lot was turned in, the 17 strong healthy horses that had been captured a few hours before had been transformed into a gaggle of lame, skinny, sore backed nags. When questioned by the quartermaster as well as brigade commander Gamble, Chapman "assured them that those horses were all he had to turn in and they had to be satisfied."[31]

A thunderstorm on the evening of July 25 brought welcome relief from the heat and humidity. The next morning, the fog burned off, and the men took in the beauty of the Blue Ridge Mountains. Marching did not seem so arduous on such a day, particularly when they turned their horses east, away from the mountains. Arriving at Rappahannock Station on the Orange and Alexandria Railroad the next day, the Hoosiers settled into camp for the next week. On the 28th, word was received that Morgan and his remaining raiders had been captured in southeast Ohio. That same day, mail came in, and the boys had some good laughs as they shared stories from home concerning Morgan's ride through Indiana.[32]

On August 1, the regiment prepared to cross the Rappahannock River at a familiar place—Beverly Ford, the site of their attack on Brandy Station less than two months before. General Meade wanted to know what was happening on the other side and called on Buford's men to find out. Unfortunately, the pontoon bridges needed to cross the rain swollen river were nowhere to be found, so the men trotted down to Kelly's Ford where pontoons had arrived and crossed around noon.[33] The day was turning hot, with temperatures reaching 100 degrees by mid-afternoon.

Turning up river, the command headed to Brandy Station where they forced a small Confederate contingent southwest toward Culpeper Court House. Pressing the gray cavalrymen, the men met stiffening resistance at a little village called Inlet Station. Finding that the Confederate cavalrymen had been falling back on their infantry support, the men retraced their steps to Brandy Station. "The tables turned," admitted Colonel Chapman later that night.[34] The fighting settled into a swirling, dusty, hot skirmish with men and horses on both sides succumbing to bullets and heat. Having found the rebels in strength in the area, the 1st Division pulled back toward Rappahannock Station. The 3rd Indiana saw little direct action in this fight, but casualties did occur. John Irby in Company C had his hand mangled by an artillery shell, leaving him only a thumb and forefinger.[35] In Company A, William Ferguson was killed, adding to the growing list of Hoosiers who had died in battle.[36]

Mercifully, this action was the last the 3rd Indiana would see for over a month. Except for picket duty, the regiment spent most of its time scouting along the Rappahannock River between Rappahannock Station and Fredericksburg, a distance of 20 miles. They settled into the routine of camp life. Drill was instituted. The men and horses began to recover from the past three months' campaigns. Men captured earlier in the summer had been exchanged and returned to the regiment. Others returned from the hospitals. Food, however, was still not regularly provided. Falling on the age old practice of foraging on the land, they found that two years of war had devastated the area. "We take sheep when we are so lucky as to find one so you see we live tolerable well in some places Old VA has almost played entirely out it look like a God forsaken country and I realy believe that God has given it up entirely to its sins," opined one Hoosier.[37] Movement in the area had to be done in small groups—scouting parties were in almost daily contact with guerrillas and bushwhackers in the area.[38]

The humdrum and boredom of camp life drove the men to find distractions. Some turned to a little free enterprise as the trade in horseflesh started up among the men. Extra horses had been acquired by some individuals by capture and were now being sold and traded among the regiment and others from surrounding units. Likewise, with revolvers and carbines collected on the battlefield. Sergeant John Wildman of Company F put it this way, "It is not considered wrong to take them [horses] after running the risk to get them." He himself had sold two horses and two revolvers over the past few months.[39]

On August 11, Governor Morton received an interesting letter from General Marsena Patrick, Provost General of the Army of the Potomac. The general requested that Sergeant Milton Cline be commissioned an officer, indicating that he had been attached to his office since early the previous winter. The endorsement on the outside of the letter was signed by General George Meade, commander of the Army of the Potomac, with this note, "Sgt. Cline has been the Leader of a band of Scouts for six months, and has been receiving the pay of a Captain of cavalry since February 24th ultimo. The service has been eminent and hazardous, though secret."[40] Despite such endorsements, Cline was never commissioned.

Colonel Chapman now commanded the brigade. Gamble had been ordered to Washington to help re-organize the Cavalry Bureau. With Chapman now at brigade headquarters, William McClure was again the regiment commander.[41] His able leadership of the regiment and brigade at Brandy Station gave the men confidence that he was up to the task. Unfortunately, McClure was unwell and asked for medical leave on August 21. Chapman was also laid up and in bed and later vented about the request, "He manifested some of his ill temper and stubbornness—to name it mild—and we had words. I am wrong in treating him with so much consideration, I suppose."[42] Compounding the situation was the absence of Major Patton, currently on 10-day picket duty. McClure had to be content with the arrival of Captain Benjamin Gresham of Company B, having recovered from his May 2 wound.[43] Battle tested leaders were always welcome with action imminent.

As they rested, traded, and lazed around camp, circumstances hundreds of miles away would have them crossing the Rappahannock once again. Major General William Rosecrans Army of the Cumberland had, through skillful maneuvering, pushed the Confederate forces under Braxton Bragg out of Tennessee into northern Georgia in a nearly bloodless campaign. Lee sent two divisions from his Army of Northern Virginia, beginning on September 8, to reinforce Bragg in an attempt to reverse the losses of territory. Union scouts learned of the movement, and Meade was determined to take advantage of Lee's shrunken army. First, however, he needed to determine the exact whereabouts of his adversary. The cavalry was ordered to move out.

The 3rd Indiana and the rest of the 1st Division was ordered to cross the Rappahannock on the morning of September 13 and to push rapidly to the Rapidan River, a distance of 15 miles. Crossing once again at Kelly's Ford, the men moved over the familiar terrain around Brandy Station. Meeting resistance near Brandy Station, the Union horsemen, with the 3rd Indiana in the vanguard, pushed the Confederates out of the way and continued toward Culpeper Court House.

The Rebel line at Culpeper forced McClure to deploy Company E as skirmishers. As the men advanced, the Confederate line was suddenly hit on its right by elements of Kilpatrick's division. The Rebel line dissolved and sent them reeling back toward the Rapidan with the 3rd Indiana close behind. A running battle ensued ending only after the rebels reached the banks of the Rapidan near Racoon Ford.[44] Pulling back about four miles, the roll was called. James Adams Company A had been killed as well as Simeon Banks of Company C. Isaiah Elston had been wounded in the arm, Bowman Jounker was suffering from a wounded shoulder, and G.A. Porter was hobbled by a wound, as well.[45] For a relatively small amount of fighting, the cost had been high.

The following morning, the regiment moved out toward the Rapidan and found the southern shore protected by entrenched Confederate troops and 11 pieces of Stuart's horse artillery. Dismounting, the 3rd Indiana and its comrades of the 1st Brigade took positions along the river and spent the day in a deadly exchange of gunfire across the stream. Between the artillery and the rifle fire, casualties were inevitable. Second Lieutenant Dennis Davis of Company B was hit in the thigh. Over in Company E, Robert Monfort was hit in the foot. William Kennedy and Isaac Lewis in Company C were also bleeding from wounds. Martin Heath, bright red blood and bubbles coming from a severe chest wound, also lay on the ground.[46] The two day toll of inconclusive fighting was 12 more men of the regiment killed or wounded.

Pulling back from the river, the men made their way toward Stevensburg and encamped until the 20th. Still determined to find a way around Lee, Meade ordered the 1st and 2nd Cavalry Divisions on a reconnaissance with nearly 7,000 horsemen. Their goal was to ascertain the conditions of roads south and west of Madison Court House as well as south of the Rapidan River. Madison Court House was a little crossroads located in the rolling hills of Madison County, about 18 miles southwest of Culpeper.[47]

On Monday morning, September 21, the two divisions moved out from Culpeper, crossing the Robertson River in early afternoon. About sundown, they arrived at Madison Court House. A small Confederate outpost of 15 men was stationed there, and they went scurrying off to the south to notify Stuart of the thousands of blue cavalrymen now in the area. The Union horsemen camped at the Court House, and the next morning awoke to a typical early fall day. Buford, in command of the expedition, ordered Kilpatrick to take the 2nd Division to the southwest and cross the Rapidan River. He was to turn southeast and follow the river to Liberty Mills. There he was to rendezvous with the 1st Division and Buford.

Chapter 9. July 2, 1863–September 9, 1863

Buford had only two of his three brigades advancing with him, having sent the 2nd Brigade under the able command of Thomas Devin to the southeast to Burnett's Ford. There, Devin was to cross the Rapidan, turn west and meet Buford and Kilpatrick at Liberty Mills. Chapman's brigade with the 3rd Indiana in the lead would ride straight south on the Gordonsville Road about 10 miles to Liberty Mills. All routes of march were within a few miles of each other, allowing mutual support. As expected from a veteran leader such as Buford, it was a sound plan.[48]

Chapman's 1st Brigade had the shortest route to Liberty Mills and Buford chose to accompany Chapman and his men. Chapman promptly ordered an advance guard thrown out and Major McClure sent companies A and B out ahead.[49] All went well until they neared a small crossroads of two or three houses. Called Jack's Shop, it was about five miles south of Madison Court House. Sporadic firing soon developed into a steady patter of gunfire as the two companies ran into Stuart's gray-clad horsemen. Stuart had re-organized the mounted forces of the Army of Northern Virginia into two divisions only 13 days earlier. Fitzhugh's division was camped fifteen miles away at Verdiersville. Hampton's division, minus three regiments, was positioned at Jack's Shop.[50] This would be Stuart's first opportunity to fight his command in this new configuration.

As the rest of the brigade spread out behind them, companies A and B started to give ground as large numbers of gray horsemen filled their front. Carbine fire crackled up and down the line as the firefight grew in size and intensity. Stuart continued to feed more men into his line. Chapman became concerned about his flanks and ordered Major McClure to secure his left. Captain George Thompson and companies E and F were ordered to ensure no threat from that sector.[51]

While Chapman was fighting his brigade, Buford ordered up his other brigade and sent word to Kilpatrick to hurry to Jack's Shop as soon as possible. Kilpatrick had already crossed the Rapidan when he received Buford's message. Kilpatrick hurried his command to the northeast on the Ruckersville Road. His path would bring his division into Stuart's rear, possibly cutting off Stuart's retreat to the Rapidan.[52] Meanwhile, Devin and his brigade were riding to the sound of guns from the east.

Kilpatrick pushed his men hard and arrived around noon. The fords across the Rapidan here were narrow, allowing only a few men at a time to cross, but he promptly attacked Stuart from behind. As soon as he heard Kilpatrick's men firing, Buford ordered Chapman to redouble his efforts to push Stuart's men south toward Kilpatrick. In the meantime, Thompson's squadron on the left had worked their way around the flank of the Rebel cavalry. Coming into the rear of the unsuspecting Confederates, Thompson threw out skirmishers and advanced. Realizing he was vastly outnumbered, Thompson decided to fire one volley and retreat. The volley threw the Rebels into disarray for a moment, and the gray-clad horsemen slowly began to give way to the pressure mounted by Chapman and the rest of the brigade.[53] This slackening of enemy fire was due in part to Chapman's attack and also to Stuart moving troops from in front of Chapman to meet Kilpatrick's slowly growing force.

Half of the Confederate Army of Northern Virginia cavalry was caught in a three way vise of Buford, Devin, and Kilpatrick.

Stuart's gamble paid off as his troops pushed Kilpatrick's vanguard back, giving them an escape route to the southeast and to the river. Stuart called his troops from the north, starting their retreat through the hamlet and toward safety.[54] Chapman promptly ordered his dismounted men to horse, and they dashed after the Confederates. The pursuit soon degenerated into a wild scramble to the Rapidan, gray horsemen bent over their mounts' necks urging them on, blue horsemen dashing after them with saber and pistol. As the Confederates raced out of Jack's Shop, they came under the cross fire of Devin's men, positioned on both sides of the road. Stuart was losing men, wounded and dead, and not a few were being captured.[55]

Upon reaching the banks of the Rapidan River, Rebel resistance stiffened, and the Union horsemen dismounted and took positions on the north shore. Upon seeing this, Chapman showed what leadership in combat was all about. Under fire, the diminutive bespectacled colonel nonchalantly rode over the river bank down to the river's edge, looked up and down the stream for a few moments and casually turned his horse back up the riverbank. Shamed by Chapman's daring behavior, the men mounted, splashed across the river, and continued the pursuit.[56]

They chased their broken enemy for a couple of miles before running into Rebel infantry at Liberty Mills and the gray cavalry of Fitzhugh Lee's division. Lee's command had ridden 15 miles to the succor of their comrades of Hampton's division. With Lee's arrival, the chase ended, and the Union troops pulled back to the north shore of the Rapidan, threw out pickets and set up camp.[57]

The fighting had lasted over eight hours. They had come within a whisker of handing Stuart and his command a devastating defeat. As it was, the Federal troops had killed at least 50 Rebels and captured 100 more. Exhausted men of the 3rd Indiana listened as the day's cost was tallied. Companies E and F had been most severely hurt by the fight. In Company E, Robert Marshall and George Meuser were under the surgeon's care. In Company F, it was worse. Benjamin Loder had been killed. Pollard Brown, Hezekiah Dailey, Fred Leffler, and Sergeant Louis Klussman had been wounded. John Keith of Company A had been hit in the hip in the early skirmishing.[58] The men, however, knew that they had "whupped" Stuart again, and they could feel the balance of power continuing to shift.

Chapter 10

September 23, 1863–February 27, 1864

The next day, the men recrossed the Robertson River, arriving on the evening of September 23. The following morning, in a show of gratitude to the regiment, General Buford issued 11 gallons of whisky to the Hoosiers as a reward for their gallant and spirited conduct.[1] The general in his report stated that Chapman's brigade "had the hardest fight, and behaved elegantly."[2] The men may also have used the spirits to soothe their anger for they found that the reconnaissance would be for naught.

Out in Tennessee, the Union general William S. Rosecrans' Army of the Cumberland had been caught strung out in the rugged terrain south of Chattanooga along the Chickamauga and had been soundly thrashed. This debacle was aided by the timely arrival on the battlefield of Confederate general James Longstreet's Corps, on loan from Lee's army. Travelling by train, the Confederates literally unloaded from rail cars and went directly into battle against the Union troops. Despite the debacle on the border of Georgia and Tennessee, Meade saw an opportunity to attack the weakened Lee, and Buford's expedition to Jack's Shop had been the first step in Meade's evolving plan. However, with Rosecrans' army surrounded in Chattanooga with only a tenuous "cracker line" for supply, Lincoln ordered Meade to send elements of the Army of Potomac to break the siege on Rosecrans. Meade dispatched 18,000 men to the southwest and hunkered down, all thoughts of attacking Lee gone. For the 3rd Indiana, this respite allowed wounds to heal and horses to recruit.

It was also time to say good bye to comrades. The war was now over two years long, and it did not have an end in sight. Indiana was raising additional troops, and the veterans of the 3rd Indiana saw opportunities for advancement in the new units. Colonel Chapman was kept busy writing recommendations for enlisted men for commissions in the new regiments and also for officers who hoped for higher rank in the new units.[3] During the months of September and October, nine men resigned their commissions or were discharged to accept commissions in new cavalry units being raised. Most notably, Major William McClure, the current commander of the regiment, would leave to assume the colonelcy of the 9th Indiana Cavalry.[4]

Although barely past their second anniversary as a unit, the question of re-enlistment started to take up a great deal of the men's time. At stake were bonus dollars and, more importantly, thirty days' furlough. For the men, the furlough meant as much as the bonus money. Going home, seeing family and recruiting the regiment back to full strength were the incentives the men weighed in their discussions. These were volunteers of the summer of 1861 and had gone to war to see an end to it. Remarkably, despite their hard service and exposure to harm, there had been virtually no desertion from within the regiment's ranks. On October 8, the regiment voted to "veteranize" and re-enlist. The men could now look forward to August when they could go home and draw their $402 veteran bonus.[5]

In the midst of this flurry of administrative action, Meade needed the men for real action. He needed to know more about the Rebel army's intentions—whether they were retreating, moving forward or still where they had been a few weeks ago. He ordered the cavalry and a corps of infantry to cross the Rapidan once more to find Lee. Around noon on October 10, the regiment splashed across the river at Germanna Ford. They were to move west and secure Morton's Ford for the infantry to cross.

Marching over the rough terrain on the south side of the river, the men surprised the Rebels' outer picket posts at Morton's ford. Pulling back slightly, the cavalry went into camp, posted pickets and set about guarding the crossing until the infantry arrived. The next morning, the infantry were nowhere in sight. A courier rode into camp with a troubling message for Buford. The Confederate army was not retreating. In fact, it was advancing. Lee had pulled a large part of this army out of line along the Rapidan and massed it on the Union left flank, in the vicinity of Madison Court House. At this moment, the Confederate army had already crossed Robertson's River. The message belatedly ordered Buford not to cross the Rapidan but return to the Rappahannock River. Realizing he was in peril of being cut off from the Union lines, Buford knew that time was now a factor if he was to save his command.

The blue horsemen immediately attacked the few rebels still remaining around Morton's Ford to clear a path back across the Rapidan. When the ford was reached, it was found to be unsuitable for the crossing of his artillery and wagons. Devin's 2nd Brigade was ordered to man rifle pits on the south shore of the river to protect from attack. Part of Chapman's First brigade traded carbines for shovels and went to work grading the approaches and cutting timber for a corduroy road. The other part of the brigade, including the 3rd Indiana, were sent to the north side of the river to protect work parties. Suspecting that there were Confederates nearby, the work crews bent to axes and shovels while the rest of the command scanned the horizon for signs of the enemy.[6]

It didn't take long. Devin's command on the south side became engaged. The Confederate cavalry of Fitzhugh Lee's division had arrived and were pressing the outnumbered Union horsemen back. It was apparent that Devin would not be able to hold for very long. On the north shore, Chapman's brigade prowled the road to Stevensburg and spotted a column of enemy cavalry and infantry trying to flank them. Word was sent to Buford, and he immediately ordered the men at the ford to drop their tools, grab their guns and report to Chapman. In addition, he was able to cross Williston's battery of horse artillery to join Chapman and the wagons to escape to

Chapter 10. September 23, 1863–February 27, 1864

the northern shore.[7] Lee had taken one of his brigades across the Rapidan at Racoon Ford and marched to cut off Buford's line of retreat. Accompanying him was a part of an infantry brigade. In essence, he was attempting to replicate the Union action at Jack's Shop. He had Buford in a vise and was about to squeeze the jaws.

Chapman saw infantry and knew that things were going from bad to worse. To buy time, he ordered a dismounted charge. The 3rd Indiana went forward in skirmish order, and the unexpected attack caused momentary confusion in the Confederate line. The charge eased the pressure on the Union forces, but it had been costly. Company D's James McConnell was shot in the thigh. He endured the rest of the day only to have his leg amputated in the evening.[8] Company A had Alexander Pollock and James Reed bleeding from various wounds, and James Long's leg was mangled by an exploding artillery shell. He, too, would undergo amputation that night.[9]

The charge and its effectiveness was short lived. Two Rebel cavalry regiments were working their way around the federal right flank. Fortunately, Devin's brigade had been ordered to cross at the ford and were able to thwart the attack. The way was still open to Stevensburg, and the two brigades started a leapfrogging retreat. First, one brigade disengaged and went up the road about a mile. There, they would establish a line. Then the other brigade would retreat through the line to set up a line about a mile closer to Stevensburg. In this way, the two brigades held the rebel forces at arm's length in a fighting retreat.[10]

Slowly, the two brigades made their way to Stevensburg and the expected presence of the Army of the Potomac. As they neared the village, they could see infantry retiring toward Kelly's Ford and across the Rappahannock River. Realizing he now needed to buy time for the vulnerable infantry to cross, Buford switched tactics. The landscape was made up of smooth, rolling ground, perfect for mounted operations. The order went out to draw sabers. At the order, the two brigades faced their pursuers and launched a charge. The classic ebb and flow of mounted attack now took place—"Grand charges," described one Hoosier.[11] Charge and countercharge surged across the Virginian countryside. Having bought enough time for the infantry to escape, the cavalry started a fighting retreat to the familiar surroundings of Brandy Station, four miles to the north.[12]

Their move to Brandy Station had been precipitated by a report that Kilpatrick's division was coming toward Beverly Ford from the north. Realizing he would have to stay on the south side of the Rappahannock to hold the ford until Kilpatrick arrived, Buford set up a defensive position with troops to the west of Brandy Station and also on Fleetwood Hill.[13] Artillery on the hill, supported by the 3rd Indiana, pounded the attacking Confederates as they rebels shifted their attention to Kilpatrick's approaching column. Cutting his way through the intervening gray line, Kilpatrick was able to reunite with Buford. There were now 8,000 Union cavalry in and around Brandy Station, but until they crossed the Rappahannock, they would still be vulnerable to Confederate infantry attack.

The two divisions resorted to the leapfrogging tactic used earlier by Buford.

In a fighting retreat, the men fought and marched three miles to a pontoon bridge to the east. Stuart had arrived on the battlefield and well knew the terrain. Rather than attack the Union forces directly, he attempted to outflank Buford and Kilpatrick but was repelled. Finally, at 8:00 p.m., the men and horses splashed across the river to obtain the safety of Union infantry.[14] The exhausted men had thought the day would never end. One Hoosier summarized in in Biblical terms, "The sun stood still in the midst of the heaven and hasted not to go down about a whole day," he wrote.[15]

Despite the labors of October 11, the men had not seen the last of Brandy Station. The next morning, they were ordered back across the river to determine if Lee's army was still advancing. Groaning and swearing, the tired men of the 3rd Indiana stretched their aching muscles and once more mounted to cross the Rappahannock River. Once across the pontoon bridge, the men dismounted and joined a skirmish line made up of the entire division. Behind them came two infantry corps as support. Advancing toward Fleetwood Hill, the Hoosiers met no resistance. Mounting once more, they proceeded up the road toward Culpeper with Captain Ephraim Martin's Company C leading the way.[16] As the men rode forward, they met enemy videttes who showed little stomach for a fight. Nearing Culpeper, resistance stiffened, and desultory fighting took place. Both forces had orders to screen their perspective infantry so neither were inclined to attack the other. Yet even in this inconsequential fighting, consequential things happened. Phillip Love of Company B took a bullet to the head and was just as dead as if he had fallen in the "grand charges" of the previous day.[17]

The crossing had yielded very little information. Buford broke off the action and returned to Brandy Station where the men were able to recover some of their seriously wounded comrades who had been left on the field the day before. The men also had the grisly task of burying the dead and found abundant evidence of the dire supply situation of the Confederacy. The Union dead had been stripped of weapons, boots, and clothing.[18]

There would be no rest; the Army of the Potomac was moving. As mentioned above, Lee had massed his army in an attempt to flank Meade's army and race toward Washington. Realizing Lee's intent, Meade started a retrograde movement to Centerville, fifty miles to the north. The 3rd Indiana and the 1st Division were now given the thankless duty of escorting the huge wagon train to the army's new base at Centerville. Starting October 14, the men rode alongside the plodding, slow moving wagons. The less than enthusiastic ardor of the quartermasters and teamsters in the train made the task difficult and frustrating. And, naturally, it began to rain.

As the wagons crossed Bull Run, it was safely on its way to Centerville. Unfortunately, the wagons took a wrong turn and recrossed the stream and toward Lee's pursuing army. Rushing to the head of the column, the 1st Division was able to fend off the attacks of Rebel cavalry and redirect the wagons back to the east side of Bull Run. The fighting, however, was not bloodless. Henry Reeve of Company F was disfigured by a bullet to the face, and Christopher Peelman of Company C hobbled across the stream with a bullet in his leg.[19]

The tired men and horses of the 3rd Indiana moved northeast to Fairfax Station and encamped—though "collapsed" might better describe their dismount. Finding a nice grove of pine trees, the men settled down to what was hoped to be a long period of rest.[20] They were surprised on the evening of the 16th by the arrival of nearly 40 new recruits from Indiana. These were welcomed additions to the regiment after the losses of the previous month. Any pleasure derived by this reinforcement was quickly tamped down when orders were received to be ready to move out the next day.

Meade had won the race to Centreville. Both he and Lee knew that the Confederate army could not stay long this far north from their main supply depots, especially with winter weather coming. Sullenly, the Confederate army started the long march back to the Rappahannock River defensive line. Meade needed to keep pressure on the Rebel army so that no more troops could be sent to Tennessee. He ordered the 1st Division out to look for Lee.

Changing their line of march to the west, the 3rd Indiana rode west through Thoroughfare Gap, turned south and trotted into Warrenton on October 20 around 10:00 p.m. Here they rested for two days.[21] On the evening of the 23rd, it began to rain and poured down for 36 hours. Miserable, the men had been ordered to prepare for the march the next day only to have it rescinded that afternoon. The morning of October 25 dawned with clearing skies, and the men marched to Bealeton Station on the Orange and Alexandria Railroad. As they approached the station, shots rang out.

Dismounting, the 3rd Indiana was ordered to proceed along the railroad toward the station. As the line advanced, Confederate infantry came up on the division's left flank causing the entire division to retreat. In the short engagement, three more men joined the casualty list of the regiment. Owen Reynolds cradled his wounded left arm, Henry Willman had been hit, and Thomas Smelley of Company C had taken a serious wound to his side.[22]

Eventually, the division reached the familiar environs of the Rappahannock River and settled in once again across from Brandy Station. For the next 10 days, the regiment would be able to rest and recover from the strenuous campaigning of the summer and fall. Surprisingly, the original members of the 3rd Indiana had held up well. It was the recruits of 1863 who were not as tough and less capable of the hard work required of them. In one company, 13 recruits had joined in May. By October 24, only three men were fit for duty. "If it was not for the old soldiers, the Army would soon play out in active service," grumbled Francis Bellamy in a letter to home.[23]

The condition of the horses was appalling. "Our poor horses are starving to death—having nothing to eat but the dry frostbitten grass they pick up from the fields."[24] Supplies began to come in two days later with food and forage for the horses and overcoats and blankets for the men.[25]

During the 10 days along the Rappahannock, the men were able to take up the rhythm of camp life. Except for picket duty, the men took advantage of this long period of inactivity to fatten themselves. Supplies came through in regular fashion, and the boys were unaccustomed to being so well provided. Almost out of habit, some of the men foraged in the countryside for a supplemental chicken or hog. Though the region had been crisscrossed by both armies for the past two years and foraging had devastated many farms, there were some possibilities still to be found, if one was good at foraging—and these Hoosiers had become experts at the art. Pete Gates, Sanford Faught, Charlie Robbins and William Watlington were able to find a calf to supplement their diet and feasted on it for two days.[26] Even in and around camp, however, the men had to be careful. On November 1, Cornelius Hollenbeck and Francis Livings of Company A were captured while on detached duty guarding the division cattle herd.[27]

The happy interlude came to an end, however, when they were ordered to cross at Sulphur Springs and proceeded to Culpeper. There they would cover the crossing of the army at Beverly Ford and Kelley's Ford. On November 8, the 3rd Indiana once again led the division across the Rappahannock. All went well until five miles from Culpeper. Major Patton ordered companies C and D to deploy as mounted skirmishers while companies E and B were formed dismounted in a small timber stand. As the men advanced, they came under heavy fire and found themselves outnumbered. "They whipped our little brigade in about fifteen minutes but the boys did not know it and we kept on fighting them all night," wrote one man.[28] The "little brigade" had indeed run into more than it could handle.

The regiment had been hit hard. Sergeant William "Ham" Stapp was hit in both thighs and fell, badly wounded. In Company B, William McFarland was also hit in the thigh but was in much worse shape.[29] James Jordan took a round in the hip. Also limping to the rear were Francis Minnot and Alexander Vanosdol. Grievously wounded in the thigh, Samuel Hall of Company F was to endure amputation later in the day.[30]

The regiment had run up against Rebel infantry who now threatened their right flank. Succor arrived in the form of an 8th Illinois attack who held off the infantry long enough for the Hoosiers to mount and ride away. About a half a mile to the east, the men dismounted once more and formed another skirmish line. Chapman himself placed an artillery piece to best take advantage of the terrain.[31] As shadows lengthened, the fighting tailed off, and the brigade was able to withdraw a short distance and bivouac. The next morning, the regiment mounted and rode back to Brandy Station. The following day, the men retraced their steps to Culpeper where they spent the next two weeks in camp and picketing the Rapidan River.[32]

The weather was now becoming noticeably colder, and the campaign of 1863 would soon be over. Over the next two weeks, the men continued to regain their heath and strength. "You can't imagine how good I feel now that I am rested," reflected one Hoosier.³³ Overcoats and blankets were issued, and the men anticipated the need to build winter quarters.

Dangers lurked around the camps, however. Partisan rangers called Mosby's men were nearby. How close was illustrated when Thomas Day and Samuel Bain of Company E were captured by the notorious partisan leader himself.³⁴ Carelessness also found its victims. Corporal Isaac Shutts of Company C was killed in camp by the accidental discharge of a carbine. A court martial was held and the shooting was ruled accidental. Three weeks later, William Perrin of Company F nearly lost his thumb as his pistol discharged prematurely.³⁵

The regiment was dealt a bitter blow as winter settled in. The earlier vote to re-enlist and "veteranize" had been disallowed, and the men were required to vote again. Even more devastating, there would be no furlough. The chance to go home and see their families meant more to them than anything. Having this opportunity taken away left the men feeling betrayed. They believed that they had voted in good faith and expected the government to hold up its end of the bargain. The second vote would be much harder to pass. Adding insult to injury, other regiments of the brigade were allowed to go home on veteran furlough, leaving the 3rd Indiana stuck in the mud and cold of Culpeper. "The boys have been humbugged so much that they do not pitch in very freely," admitted one angry man.³⁶

One man had taken his frustration a step too far, and a court martial was convened to deal with a long-standing issue. First Lieutenant Robert Porter had a drinking problem. In an army where imbibing spirits was common and considered a mark of manhood, Porter's excesses were even more glaring. After a particularly heavy bout of drinking, Porter said he would no longer tolerate taking orders from "that whorehouse pimp" Chapman.³⁷ Charged with "Drunkenness, conduct to the prejudice of good order and military discipline, conduct unbecoming an officer and a gentleman," Porter received his wish. Found guilty of all charges, he was dismissed from the army on December 20, 1863, never to receive an order from Chapman again.³⁸

Amid all of the above, the men had to deal with the death of a respected leader. General John Buford had been weakened by the incessant campaigning and was forced to take sick leave in mid–November. His condition worsened, and he died on December 16. The men had liked the quiet man with no tolerance for ceremony, and they loved him for his common sense and care for his men. He left an indelible mark on the men of the 1st Division of the Cavalry Corps. The loss was sharpened when the division came under the temporary command of General Wesley Merritt. An 1860 classmate of George Custer at West Point, the boyish commander had already made a name for himself as an iron disciplinarian. The 3rd Indiana now "had to put on more military style, brightening our arms and equipments and our ideas of military tactics, appearing in our best on Grand Reviews and dress parade [and] company inspection of arms … was no infrequent occurance [sic]," lamented one.³⁹ Inspection of arms should have been a little easier for the regiment had been recently rearmed with Sharps carbines. For the first time, the entire unit carried the same carbine of the same caliber.[40]

War-ravaged, the surrounding area could still supplement the rations the men drew. A quartet of men from Company E located a 300 pound hog in the area. As a precaution, the owner had the pig penned in a part of his house, and provost guards regularly patrolled the area to keep foragers from invading private dwellings. Undeterred, the men were able to make off with the giant hog. In the camp of the 3rd Indiana, a sumptuous feast of pork and ham had been prepared, and the remaining meat hidden under the floorboards of one of the cabins. Sure enough, the owner complained to regimental headquarters, and a search was made of each company's area. Nothing could be found, and the men of Company E were able to enjoy fresh meat for several days.[41]

As December came to an end, the men made do. Huts were built to keep out the winter chill, though some were better than others. One Hoosier described their domicile for three men: "We have a house here or something that we call one here it is 13 feet by 7 covered with shelter tents with a hole in one end for a chimney the consequence of which is that we are tolerable well smoked."[42]

The regiment greeted 1864 with groaning and moaning. They had been ordered back north to Bealeton Station for temporary picket duty in that sector. Leaving camp, the weather was moderate, but by noon, the temperature plummeted. The ground began to freeze, and the snow began to blow. By the time they reached the station, the men were nearly frozen. Halting for camp, the men scrambled about trying to find anything that would burn. They built roaring bonfires and fed them all night. For many of the men, this was the coldest night of their service.[43]

After three days at Bealeton Station, the regiment was ordered back to their camps on the Rapidan. Arriving there on January 5, they found their former camp picked clean of all lumber, which had been burned as fuel by nearby units. The huts so carefully made weeks before were nowhere to be found. Only the mud and stick chimneys marked their existence.[44]

The question of re-enlistment was coming to a head. Colonel Chapman came down to the regiment and made an impassioned speech, trying to convince the men that they should continue in the service. Chapman tried a different approach to Governor Morton. On January 16, he wrote to his Excellency and suggested that the regiment would re-enlist if they were "cut adrift" from the western wing and recruited up to a full strength of 12 companies. If Morton could assist in accomplishing this, Chapman was certain enough men would re-enlist to keep the regiment in the field.[45]

On January 20, the regiment voted once again on the question of "veteranizing." Only 57 men chose to re-enlist. "The veteran cause is creating some excitement here but this regiment will barely go now they use to be in but have bin [sic] fooled so often they conclude to dry the thing up," was how one man described it.[46] A dejected and melancholy Chapman informed the governor of the vote and also revealed the real reason for his proposal four days ago. "My command is so much reduced in numbers that I sometimes feel that I would like to be assigned to one of the new regiments so that I might at least have a Colonel's command…. I dislike to drop from the command of a brigade to that of six Companies. Especially as my recommendations for promotion have been such to foster a belief on my own mind that I am capable for a larger Command, but I prescience I shall have to 'grin and bear it' and 'watch and pray' for a salvation to my hopes."[47]

Chapman had shown his hand. The 8th Illinois would soon return from veterans' furlough. Their commander, Colonel William Gamble, had been released from his work with the Cavalry Bureau, and as the senior colonel of the brigade, would assume brigade command as soon as the Illinoisians returned. Chapman lamented the fact that the 3rd Indiana only had six companies, perhaps as a reminder of his suggestions in his January 16 missive. He also reminded the governor that Chapman's previous recommendations had been stellar. "I am capable for a Larger Command" could only mean one thing: he was asking Morton to use his considerable political clout to push for a Brigadier General's star for Chapman. Governors could commission officers up to the rank of colonel, but one could make general only with Congressional approval. Given Chapman's performance as a brigade commander during 1863, he had earned the right to believe that he deserved promotion. Unfortunately, only political clout could move the government to award the coveted star.

Even as he dwelled on his future, Chapman had to deal with officer vacancies within the regiment. Though not as pronounced as a year ago, military experience had highlighted the need for each company to have a full complement of officers. Consequently, after Porter's court martial and dismissal, Benjamin J. Gilbert was promoted to first lieutenant, and Thomas Lamson moved up from orderly sergeant to second lieutenant in Company A. Company C had gone through a couple of second lieutenants since spring of 1863. Both Ira Tinker and Isaac Gilbert had been discharged. To fill the vacancy once again, George Rogers was commissioned.[48]

Throughout the month of January, the regiment had been picketing the extreme right flank of the army near Cedar Mountain. The picketing became so routine that observant Confederate pickets were able to predict the changing of the pickets with ease. On January 27, Sergeant Henry Sparks led a group of 14 men to relieve a group of the 8th New York. Sparks had been enjoying the benefits of his recent promotion to sergeant and the additional freedom it afforded him. Only a few days before, he had taken time to go rabbit hunting. This morning, however, he and his squad were the hunted. Nearly 100 of the 4th Virginia waited patiently for the daily routine to take place. When the relief came into view, the ambush was sprung, capturing Sparks and 12 other men. Two others have fallen behind and galloped back to camp. They prisoners were taken by their captors at the gallop to Madison Court House where their horses and belongings were taken from them. They then began the long, cold walk to Richmond.[49]

This mini-invasion into the army's lines and the loss of 13 men could not go unpunished. On January 30, a reconnaissance force of 200 men left the Union lines headed for Madison Court House. After making a round trip of 50 miles, Chapman reported the capture of 12 rebels, 11 horses, and the killing of one enemy soldier. He also brought into Union lines the family of his guide. The fact that Chapman personally led the raid was an indication of how deeply he felt the loss of the men on the 26th.[50]

The month of February also saw activity of a much sweeter nature. Just like the previous winter, love had blossomed for a couple of men in the regiment. Pleasant D. Mulvaney of Company D married Susan Glass in Culpeper on February 1. Another man in Company B found love too much to resist. He deserted with his beloved and absconded to Lynchburg. The men were incensed. "If we ever come across him it won't be quite so romantic," seethed one man.[51]

As the weather started to hold promise of spring, the men knew that hard work lay ahead. Those who had re-enlisted would not get furlough because so few had signed up. Those who voted to not re-enlist knew that the coming spring and summer would be their last in the service. As each man contemplated what the future held, the seeds of the new campaign season was being sown in Washington, D.C., by General Judson Kilpatrick.

Chapter 11

February 28, 1864–May 6, 1864

Judson Kilpatrick was described by another officer as a "frothy braggart without brains and not overstocked with [the] desire to fall on the field."[1] A self-promoter, he was always on the lookout for opportunities to serve the needs of Judson Kilpatrick. Known as "Kill Cavalry" by the men for his injudicious use of speed on every occasion, Kilpatrick had concocted a plan that he was so convinced would work that he did not risk review from his superior officers. He went straight to the President.

His plan purposed a cavalry raid the likes of which had not been seen. With 5,000 cavalry and a battery of horse artillery, he would charge across the Virginian countryside to the very gates of Richmond, free the estimated 15,000 Union prisoners at Belle Island and Libby Prison, and escort them to safety to Benjamin Butler's small army on the Peninsula. On the way to Richmond, his raiders would wreak havoc, destroying bridges, telegraph lines, and railroad tracks. A smaller detachment of 500 men would travel west of the main column to widen the path of destruction as well as disrupt the Virginia Central Railroad. This column would be commanded by the one-legged, 21-year-old Colonel Ulric Dahlgren. Son of the Union admiral John Dahlgren, the young colonel had met Kilpatrick at a party in Washington and was invited by the impertinent general to come along on the raid.

As outlandish as it sounded, there was a small chance it could be successful. The suffering of the prisoners at Belle Island was widely known.[2] It was also known that beyond the front line, the defenses around Richmond were made up of old men and convalescents. If the column got cleanly through Lee's army, there was a chance it might just work. Lincoln was impressed with the audacity and purpose of the plan, and he signed off on the venture. Kilpatrick's chutzpah had paid off—now he had to pull it off.

As the plan evolved, the force was scaled back to 3,500 men. Added to the plan would be a diversionary raid to the far west of the army by the 3rd Division. Orders were sent out to the various cavalry commands for contingents of their best troops mounted on the best mounts available. Men from 15–18 regiments began to converge on Stevensburg. The 3rd Indiana's troops were led by Major William Patton. The men's arms were carefully inspected, and seven days' rations were issued.[3]

The forming of the column occurred amid an environment of speed, urgency, and chaos. Officers were placed in command of men they did not know. Men were

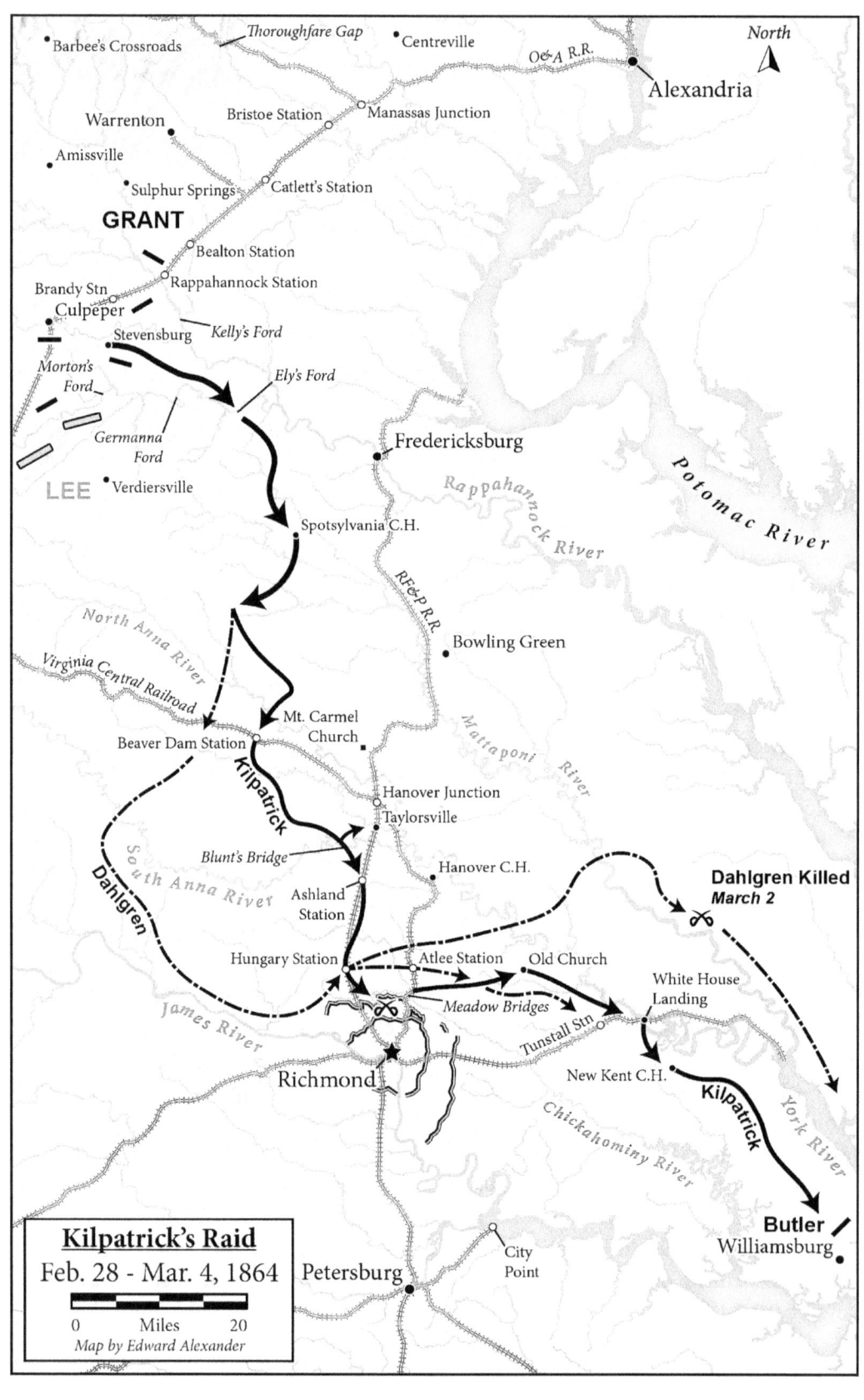

thrown together in formations with men from other regiments destroying unit integrity. Unfortunately, there was no time to instill the cohesiveness necessary for troops to perform well in combat. An operation of this size needed the utmost secrecy if it was to be successful. It was common knowledge, however, what the purpose of the raid was. And if the men knew, it was safe to guess the Confederates knew. At midnight of February 28, the men splashed across the cold waters of the Rapidan at Ely Ford and headed south.[4] Dahlgren's force of 500 men split from the main body and headed to the west.[5]

Early in the afternoon of the 29th, the main column crossed the North Anna River and rode into Beaver Dam Station of the Virginia Central Railroad, burning the depot, water tanks, railcars, and several storage facilities.[6] Remounting, the men rode steadily south through a pelting storm of rain and sleet, and made good progress despite the weather. They reached the midway point between Fredericksburg and Richmond without running into enemy troops. The real problem was the weather. Rain and sleet had continued throughout the day, and as the day turned to night, the road turned into a churned mass of mud. Once it was dark, the men had to rely on their sense of hearing and instinct to follow the man and horse in front of them. Men became lost; gaps developed in the column, and time was being lost.[7] At midnight, Kilpatrick detached 500 men to destroy the railroad near Taylorsville. Fifty men of the 3rd Indiana accompanied this column.

Kilpatrick, after sending off his raiding party to Taylorsville, continued with the main force of 2,500 troops toward Richmond. About 6:00 a.m., March 1, the column crossed the South Anna River at Blunt's Bridge one at a time as only one timber was left spanning the river.[8] Unknown to Kilpatrick, home guards had been watching the crossing, and word was headed toward Richmond 20 miles away of their approach and line of march. After a short halt where the grateful men brewed up coffee and fed their horses, the column pushed on toward Ashland Station where they tore up track and destroyed several small bridges. Only a few miles now separated the men and the Confederacy's capital. Kilpatrick arranged his forces for the final approach. The 3rd Indiana found itself the first to move out.[9]

As the vanguard moved cautiously forward, they passed through the unmanned outer defenses of the city, impressive in their sheer number and size. As they approached the inner works, the column's luck ran out. At 1:00 p.m., a cannon fired to their front, and a 32 pound cannon ball came bounding down the road, for all the world looking like a bowling ball bouncing down an alley.[10]

The horse artillery were brought up and went into battery, engaging the artillery of the city. Patton was ordered to deploy the 3rd Indiana and the 5th New York to the left of the road and to dismount as skirmishers. The men advanced to about 250 yards of the Confederate embankments and opened fire. Men were fed into the skirmish line. For two hours, the two lines banged away at each other. The Rebel defenders were not seasoned troops; they were clerks, old men, and convalescent soldiers. Most of their fire went high, doing little damage to the attacking Union troops. The

250 yard range was at the maximum of the cavalry carbines' range, doing little damage to the defenders.

Kilpatrick now had a decision to make. About 600 men were now actively engaged with the enemy. He still had not heard from Dahlgren's 500-man force, nor had he yet heard from the diversionary force sent to Taylorsville. Train whistles could be heard in the city announcing the possible arrival of enemy reinforcements. He was being held up by a force of indeterminate size protected by formidable defenses. He could either attempt an all-out attack, or he could withdraw. The glory he anticipated coming from the raid did not look likely. Faced with a tough decision, Kilpatrick blinked. He ordered a retreat.[11]

Patton and his force were recalled and remounted, with Henry Papst missing and Isaac Higgins nursing a wounded wrist.[12] Kilpatrick ordered the column to march east to the Chickahominy River and cross at Meadows Bridges. Here, the diversionary force finally caught up with the main body. After destroying the bridges, the men considered themselves safe, and the now 3,000-man column moved about a mile and made camp. Since leaving Stevensburg 72 hours ago, the men and horses had not slept. It was now March 2 and the men did not even bother to loosen their saddles, falling to the ground as if shot and soon asleep. After dark, the skies once more opened up with rain and sleet. Despite this, many of the men continued to sleep soundly.[13]

Meanwhile, Confederate general Wade Hampton had thrown together a small force of 300 men from the 1st and 2nd North Carolina Cavalry along with two artillery pieces. Anticipating the Union retreat to the east, he led his little army to Mt. Carmel Church, on the north side of the Chickahominy. Creeping up through the rain, sleet, and snow, Hampton moved his men into position near Atlee Station, only 150 yards from the sleeping Yankees. At 9:00 p.m., all hell broke loose. Placing 100 men on foot, Hampton announced his presence with artillery fire into the camp of

Judson Kilpatrick's unsuccessful raid failed to rescue Union prisoners in Richmond plus his high-handed approach to the president led to his removal from the Army of the Potomac in the fall of 1864 (Library of Congress).

Chapter 11. February 28, 1864–May 6, 1864

the 7th Michigan. The dismounted Rebels came running into camp followed by their mounted comrades—all raising the Rebel Yell. In the 3rd Indiana's bivouac, men tried to comprehend what was happening. "I had heard the firing for several minutes before I was fully awake," admitted one groggy Hoosier, "and after I had gotten to my feet, it was several more minutes before I could realize where we were and what was going on."[14]

The fighting and confusion lasted about 30 minutes before the Confederates disappeared. Hampton was good, but 300 against 3,000 was a mismatch no matter who commanded. The chaos and fear Hampton's attack produced did have the desired effect, however. Any lingering ideas Kilpatrick may have had about returning to Richmond and making another attempt to breach its defenses were now gone. Spooked by the attack, Kilpatrick ordered the column to resume its retreat to the east, stopping at 4:00 a.m. near Old Church.[15]

Men scoured the area for food for man and feed for horse. Many were surprised by the scarcity of food in the area. "A whole day's travel would not discover a single well stored barn, nor show a single stack of hay or wheat," wrote one to the folks back home. The rampant inflation and devalued Confederate currency was revealed when they learned that a pound of coffee was $14, and a barrel of flour fetched an astounding $300.[16]

Near Tunstall Station, the men were surprised to see the bedraggled survivors from Dahlgren's diversionary force coming up behind them. Their attempt to enter Richmond had been thwarted and the men had had their own harrowing escape to the east. Not with them were about 80 men, including Dahlgren, who had become separated from the column.[17]

The tired men built fires and brewed up coffee. Too soon, the column was ordered to move out toward White House Landing, arriving after dark. To ensure there would be no repeat of the surprise attack the previous night, pickets were posted, and the 3rd Indiana was one of the unlucky units selected. The next day, the column slowly, tiredly, ad painfully moved east and made contact with Benjamin Butler's Army of the James. Plodding through New Kent Court House, they continued to Williamsburg. That night, the horses were unsaddled for the first time since the start the raid. Roll was called, and the regiment recorded the cost of the raid. Henry Hayes of Company D had been killed. Isaac Higgins had been wounded, and several men were missing.[18]

On March 4, the regiment moved through Williamsburg and reached Yorktown at sundown. Camping behind an old house, the men were informed that the dwelling had been the site of Cornwallis' surrender to Washington over 80 years before. Given the historic nature of their campsite, a number of the men took advantage and toured the Yorktown battlefield the next day.[19]

The makeshift raiding party began its journey back to the Army of the Potomac to rejoin their various commands. The 3rd Indiana contingent boarded boats at Yorktown on March 11, and after a rough ride through the Chesapeake Bay and

Potomac River, arrived at Alexandria the next evening. Four days later they rejoined the rest of the regiment.[20] After the past three weeks, the returning men had to be a little jealous of the men left in camp. With too few men to mount regular picket duty, the truncated unit spent most of its time reading, sleeping and listening to lectures. In addition, convalescent soldiers returned to the unit so that by March 8, there had been over 100 men in camp.[21]

Even in the quiet of the small camp, Hoosier politics continued to brew. George Chapman, in command of the brigade and not on the raid, wrote Laz Noble with an idea. Chapman had heard that there were four new cavalry regiments in rendezvous in Indiana. Arguing that the army already had a Michigan brigade of cavalry, it seemed appropriate that army should have an Indiana one, as well. "I should think it would be desirable to form such a brigade which under the command of an experienced office would not fail to render good service." As to who the "experienced officer" should be, the colonel was discreetly silent.[22]

Promotions also came through but did little to build up the officer corps. Captain Benjamin Q.A. Gresham was back on detached duty with the Cavalry Bureau but was promoted to major.[23] While important to Gresham, this did little to improve the efficiency of the command structure of the regiment. In fact, his promotion created a vacancy as captain of Company B, one that would never be filled. On March 16, Major McClure finally left for Indiana and his new command. Major William Patton now led the regiment. Patton was 45 years old when he assumed command. A native of Ireland, he still carried the Irish brogue of his homeland. He had served with the regiment since formation and had already assumed temporary command of the regiment numerous times over the past several months.[24]

The easy life continued after the regiment had been reunited. Surgeon Elias Beck presented lectures on spiritualism. Others carved pipes out of the roots of the abundant laurel tree. Some of the more artistic carved rings and other memorials from bones found at the nearby Cedar Mountain battlefield. When a surprise snowfall dumped 12 inches of the white stuff on March 24, the regiment joined in a monumental snowball fight among the surrounding units that raged for hours.[25] After the snow melted, a nonstop game of "round ball" began and lasted for days.[26]

The long months of picketing and the recent raid had taken a toll on the men, horses, arms and equipment of the regiment. As had always been the way of "western men," they did not put much stock in military protocol and procedures, and the current life of leisure did nothing to rectify their unmilitary bearing. An inspector from Cavalry Corps headquarters found the camp of the 3rd Indiana in very poor condition and recommended that it be moved. In addition, "the arms of this regiment were in very bad order. Their equipments and clothing relieved the eye by their great variety. The ordinary uniform and horse equipments of the United States are ignored by this command, which cannot be excelled in efficiency in action and only fails to be as efficient in other respects on account of indifference of the officers to military appearance and requirements," complained the officer.[27]

Also instituted was carbine and pistol practice. On March 26, two hours were spent in carbine practice with the three best shots in each company recognized. Pistol and carbine practice continued over the next three days.[28] On March 29, the men were required to spruce up for a grand review. Major General George Meade, commander of the Army of the Potomac would be in attendance. There was to be one other general there. Lieutenant General Ulysses S. Grant, newly arrived from the western theater, would be in attendance. Upon seeing the new commander of all Union armies, the men were impressed by his plain dress and plain talk. "Liked his appearance [sic] verry [sic] much," remarked one.[29]

Three days before the review, the men found out

Philip Sheridan's supreme confidence in himself led to his defeating Stuart's Confederate cavalry at Yellow Tavern. He later commanded the forces in the Shenandoah Valley (Library of Congress).

that Grant meant to shake things up. Word spread that General Pleasanton, commanding the Cavalry Corps, had been ordered to St. Louis. His testimony against Meade in front of the Congressional Committee on the Conduct of the War had sealed his fate. Pleasanton's self-promotion and intrigues were not able to keep him from retribution. A few days later, April 4, the men found out who the new Corps commander would be.

Five foot five inch, 33-year-old Irishman Philip Sheridan made the rounds to introduce himself to his new command. An 1853 graduate of West Point, he had served on the western frontier throughout his prewar career. A short stint as colonel of the 2nd Michigan Cavalry was his only cavalry experience. As an infantry officer in the western theater, Sheridan had grown in the estimation of Grant. It was this relationship that led to the volatile Irishman being given command of the Cavalry Corps.

These changes in the higher level of leadership soon had a trickle-down effect on the 3rd Indiana. A West Point classmate of George Custer was about to become the Hoosiers' division commander. General James Wilson had been on Grant's staff in the West as an engineer until summoned to Washington to take over the Cavalry Bureau. With Grant's elevation, Wilson was now ordered to rejoin Grant in Virginia.

Kilpatrick's failed raid had made him a marked man, and he was relieved as commander of the 3rd Division.[30] Wilson was given command in his stead, creating an awkward situation. Wilson was, by date of commission, junior to all three of his brigade commanders. To alleviate the situation, Sheridan exchanged two of the brigades with those of other divisions and replaced the commander of the third. With a stroke of a pen and military courtesy observed, the 3rd Indiana and the rest of the 1st Brigade, 1st Division, became the 2nd Brigade, 3rd Division.

The change was a psychological blow. The 1st Brigade had been the first organized when the Cavalry Corps was in its infancy back in 1862. Proud of their record and still mourning the loss of Buford, the men were unhappy to find themselves suddenly under a division commander who, so far, had virtually no combat experience. Sergeant Matthews spoke for many, "I do not like it a bit, but it's no use to grumble." The regiment would start the new campaign season with a new army commander, new corps commander, and new division commander, and as a part of a different division. One consolation for the men was that Colonel Chapman would be in permanent command of the brigade now made up of the 3rd Indiana, 1st Vermont, and the 8th New York. It was the smallest brigade in the smallest division of the Cavalry Corps.[31] With Chapman permanently in command of the brigade, Major William Patton led the regiment. The morning of April 19, the men mounted and rode to join the 3rd Division. Midway, they passed General George Custer and the Michigan Brigade, their replacements in the 1st Division.[32]

The men found that their new West Point educated commander expected things done by the rules. Private William Watlington summed up the average Hoosier's opinion on this matter: "Our new command had some new ways, which we had not been much accustomed to, such as watering horses by Companies and the company drill on horseback. This latter regulation had never received much favor in the 3rd Ind. after going to the front. It seemed too much like the U.S. Regular style, better suited for dress parade and grand reviews than the skirmish line."[33]

What the men and horses needed more than anything was not drill and better uniforms but rest. That would be in short supply for Grant was anxious to have a go at Lee. His strategy for the 1864 campaign was simple. Lee's army was to be the target, and Grant intended to bleed the Confederate Army of Northern Virginia white through the use of superior weaponry, manpower, and a tenacious will to never give up. The opening action would be a "left hook" around Lee's army, crossing the

Chapter 11. February 28, 1864–May 6, 1864

Rappahannock at Ely and Germanna Fords. This would allow him to get between Lee and Richmond, forcing the Confederates to abandon their current position. The 3rd Division would lead the way.

This campaign would be Major William Patton's first as the commander of the 3rd Indiana. He confided his misgivings about the coming responsibility in a letter home. "I have to lead these men through dangers and perhaps death. I feel the awful responsibility heavy upon me, and pray god to give me the strength and judgement to perform it. I have been much incouraged by Col. Chapman who commands the brigade, he is a great friend of mine and compliments me highly for my bravery and efficiency. God knows I wish to do my duty to my adopted country. If I fail it will not be for want of the will. I trust in god & will not fail."[34]

Orders trickled down the command chain from Grant to Meade, from Meade to Sheridan, from Sheridan to Wilson, and Wilson to Chapman. Chapman's brigade was to lead the way, and without hesitation, the new brigade commander turned to his old regiment and ordered the 3rd Indiana to be the point of the spear. Early in the morning of May 4, the men and horses of the 3rd Indiana splashed across the river at Germanna Ford as the vanguard of the Army of Potomac. Routing Rebel pickets, Major Patton threw out a skirmish line, and by 4:00 a.m., engineers were placing pontoon bridges across the Rapidan. The Wilderness Campaign had begun.[35] As infantry started crossing the bridges, the cavalry reverted to protecting the crossing from prying Confederate counterparts. Moving south from Germanna Ford, Wilson's division was expected to screen the Union army as they moved through the tangled underbrush of the Wilderness.

Wilson was in his first combat action. An engineer, he had little experience leading men in battle at any level. Chapman, on the other hand, had plenty of experience and his command skills had been honed by nearly

William Patton was a native Irishman who began the war as first lieutenant of Company A. Promoted to captain and then to major by the end of May 1863, he commanded the regiment at the end of the original organization's term of service (Pickerill, *A History of the Third Indiana Cavalry*).

three years of constant service in the field. Leaving the Rapidan on the morning of May 5, Wilson crossed Robertson's Run and split the division, leaving a brigade at the Run and proceeding west with Chapman and his smaller 2nd Brigade.[36] Just west of a rundown building known as Craig's Meeting House, carbine fire broke out at the head of the column.

The 3rd Indiana was directed to the left of the small Union line and ordered to dismount. Firing in the area became heavier as more Confederate troops were fed into the fight. The Hoosiers' move to the left found their adversary near an old house and log stable. Part of the regiment were positioned in the open where Rebel riflemen could fire on them from the log structures. The rest of the unit was screened from the Confederates' view by jack oaks and bushes. The men in the open lay flat on the ground in an attempt to avoid the fire from the cabin and stable. Realizing that staying in this exposed position meant more casualties, the men rose up and charged the cabin and stable. The rest of the regiment joined in, and the Hoosiers were soon chasing the panicked Confederates. After a chase of half a mile, the men stopped near a small woods and formed a line to prepare for what would happen next. They didn't have to wait long.

Grey clad infantry and cavalry in large numbers were seen advancing toward the outnumbered regiment. It was now time for the Hoosiers to run for their lives. Racing helter-skelter through the woods, the men knew that they needed to reach their horses back at the Meeting House to secure their escape. Short of ammunition and chased by overwhelming numbers of the enemy, the 3rd Indiana faced a desperate situation.[37] Men were cut down by pursuing cavalry; others were captured. Those who made it back to the horses were so exhausted they were barely able to mount and ride away.[38]

The men raced back to Robertson's Run and the covering fire of the 1st Brigade. Wilson set up two batteries of artillery at a nearby farm to slow the Rebel pursuit. Wilson pleaded with the men to attack. A handful of Hoosier horsemen responded to the plea and surged at the advancing Confederates in a clash of horseflesh and steel. Wilson and his escort, led by Company C's first lieutenant William Long, dashed into the melee and finally blunted the pursuit.[39] The men and horses of the 2nd Brigade filed through the lines of the 1st Brigade and reformed. Over the next couple of hours the two brigades would resort to the leapfrogging tactics used the previous summer. In this way, the division was able to extract itself from a tight situation and retreated to Todd's Tavern. There they met the 2nd Division which covered the command. It was barely 3:00 p.m., yet the fight felt like it had lasted forever. The nerve-racking leapfrog action required strong nerves and precise timing. It was a testament to the experience and leadership of the two brigades and their commanders that they had pulled off the maneuver without losing a man.

Wilson had been caught off guard in his first action as a commander. Confederate forces had slipped behind his division and had nearly cut them off. His inexperience had also cost the 3rd Indiana. Several men had been captured in the run to the horses, and six were missing. Nine men had been wounded. The Brindley brothers in Company A had both been shot in the foot. Company B had George W. Beard with a wounded thigh, and Daniel Nathaniel had been hit in the left leg. Company D reported William Bromley with a painful ankle wound while Company E had Sandford Faught badly wounded in the thigh, and George Porter with a wound so bad that his foot was amputated. Company F had Ernest Fluher down with a wound to the thigh, and George Golden also wounded.[40]

After a few hours of rest, the division was ordered to Chancellorsville for resupply, arriving there in the early hours of May 6. On the 8th, the division was ordered east on the Fredericksburg Pike and proceeded to Spotsylvania Court House. It was understood that an infantry corps would follow them and reinforce their position.[41] Upon reaching the courthouse, the 3rd Indiana was sent out to the outskirts of the small village as pickets. All hunkered down to await the infantry.

The march had placed the division in the rear of Lee's army. Grant's plan called for an attack from the north and a corps of infantry along with the cavalry to the south creating a vise around the Confederate army. Unfortunately, the plan unraveled almost immediately. The attack from the north stalled, and the infantry support for the cavalry never arrived. Lee sent five brigades of infantry toward Wilson's undersized division, and for the second time in three days the men tucked tail and "skedaddled" back to Union lines.[42] Fortunately, no Hoosiers were injured in the coming or going. With Spotsylvania Court House firmly in Confederate hands, Grant would have to try and muscle his way through the village in bloody fighting. The cavalry, however, would have a different assignment and another exhausting ride ahead.

Chapter 12

May 7, 1864–June 15, 1864

The fiasco of May 8 in and around Spotsylvania Court House brought to a head a simmering situation between Philip Sheridan and General George Meade. Meade was the commander of the Army of the Potomac while Grant, as commander of all Union forces, chose to accompany this army in the field rather than stay in Washington. This made for an awkward situation for Meade. Sheridan had served with Grant for quite some time. While technically a subordinate of Meade's, Sheridan felt very comfortable in going to Grant whenever he so chose. Meade possessed a prickly temperament as exemplified by his nickname "Old Snapping Turtle." Sheridan was known to possess a hair trigger and a hot temper. It was inevitable that these two would come to loggerheads.

In midmorning of May 8, Sheridan stormed into Meade's tent, blaming the general for the predicament that nearly cost him Wilson's 3rd Division. Why hadn't the northern attack been successful? Why weren't the cavalrymen supported by infantry as planned? Sheridan climaxed the tirade with the statement that he could whip the Confederate cavalry under Stuart if Meade would only let him.[1]

Meade responded in kind. When Sheridan stalked out, Meade strode the few yards over to Grant's tent and related to his commanding officer this appalling act of insubordination by the short-legged, red-headed Irishman with the big mouth. If Meade expected Grant to reprimand Sheridan, he was in for quite a shock. When Meade got to the part where Sheridan boasted that he could whip Stuart if Meade would only let him, Grant perked up. Informing the stunned Meade that Sheridan generally knew what he was talking about, Grant suggested that Sheridan be unleashed on Stuart. The chagrined Meade wasted no time in getting the cavalry going. At 1:00 p.m., Sheridan was ordered to "proceed against the enemy's cavalry." A pique between generals set into motion a raid with one goal—the elimination of the Confederate cavalry.[2]

This would be different than the Kilpatrick raid. Their objective was not a place but the mounted arm of the Army of Northern Virginia under Stuart. The plan was to move south around Lee's army and threaten Richmond. The ruse, if it worked, would bring the Confederate cavalry out into the open for a grand climatic mounted battle. The 3rd Indiana knew something big was about to happen. One Hoosier remembered "every camp in the Cavalry Corps seemed to be in an unusual hurry,

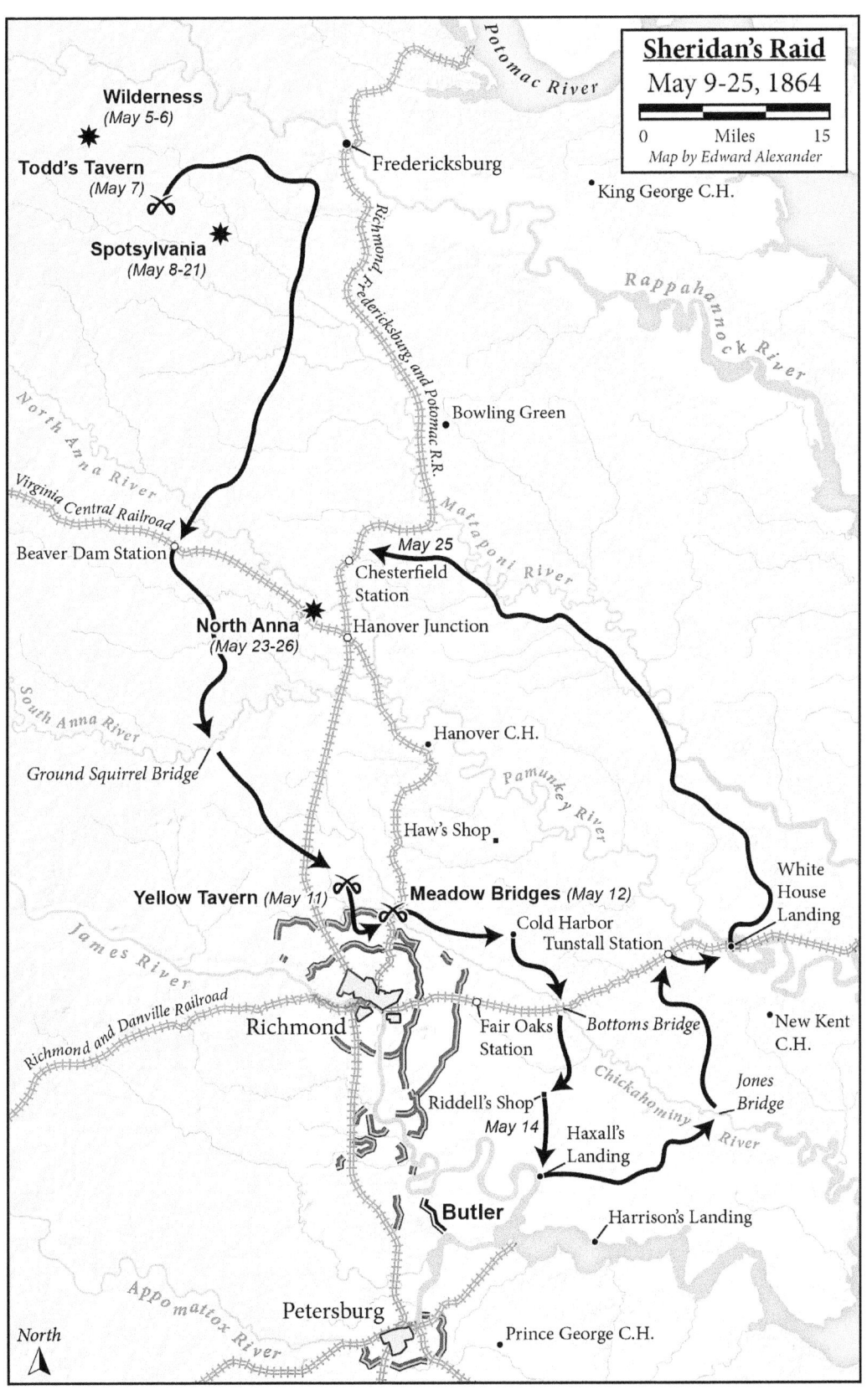

preparing for a march on short notice and of no small magnitude."[3] All wagons were to be left behind, and only a few pack animals were allowed per regiment.

Less than 24 hours since the dustup between Meade and Sheridan, 10,000 veterans of the Cavalry Corps moved out. Moving to the east and around the Confederate army's right, the column met little resistance. By 9:00 p.m. of May 9, they had reached Beaver Dam Station where they bivouacked for the night. The next morning, the corps continued their southern advance, tearing up railroad track and keeping a wary eye open for their pursuers. After crossing the South Anna River, they settled in for the evening. This was not the mad dash by Kilpatrick of two months ago; Sheridan meant to conserve his men and horses' strength for the coming battle. As they made camp, that evening, the men were amazed to receive orders to unsaddle their horses.[4]

As the Union cavalry moved south, the Confederate cavalry was hustling down the parallel Telegraph Road to the east. They finally got ahead of Sheridan and, on May 11, were forming lines of battle at a little crossroads called Yellow Tavern. Sheridan, seeing the gray clad horsemen ahead, had his fight with Jeb Stuart. He attacked immediately.

The 3rd Division was well back in the marching column when initial contact was made. As the Third Indiana came up, the battle had been raging for several hours. Chapman's brigade was ordered to the left of Custer's Michigan Brigade. Custer had formed astride the Telegraph Road and was facing the enemy. The plan was for Chapman to advance dismounted while Custer delivered a mounted charge. The order to proceed came at 4:00 p.m., and the men moved forward. As the Third Indiana fanned out in skirmish order, John Nichols was hit in the wrist, and John Keith went down. Joseph Adkinson was grievously wounded in both thighs, and George Little was struck in the chest.[5] Just as the regiment and the rest of the brigade came on the extreme right of the Confederate line, Custer unleashed his mounted attack. In the midst of the noise and swirl of combat came a violent thunderstorm, adding to the surreal landscape of battle.

Watching the attack unfold, Jeb Stuart had placed himself in the front lines when Custer's attack slammed into the Confederates. That choice proved his downfall for within minutes he fell, mortally wounded. The Rebels, seeing their charismatic leader down, began to fall away, and the retreat soon became a rout. "Our whole line moved rapidly forward … completely routing Stuart's forces and scattering them in many directions," remembered one Hoosier.[6] The battle of Yellow Tavern backed up Sheridan's boast to "whip Stuart's cavalry."

Yet the victory was still not finished; they were miles behind enemy lines with Confederate forces forming in their rear. It was now time for the return to the Army of the Potomac. Sheridan planned to ride east and south around Richmond by way of Fair Oaks and reach Ben Butler's Army of the James at Huxtall's Landing. The route was eerily familiar to many of the men—it was the same one taken by Kilpatrick just months before. In a driving rain, the Union soldiers tended to their wounded, buried the dead, and waited for nightfall.

At 11:00 p.m., the men were given an unusual order. There was to be no talking in the ranks, and they were to keep the column closed up. Inevitably, rumors began to fly that they were going to enter Richmond and kidnap Jefferson Davis. Given that Kilpatrick's raid had had similar goals, the men believed this was entirely possible.[7] The column proceeded cautiously down the roads in the inky darkness of the stormy night. Even in the dark, however, the men recognized that part of their route was taking them over the very road they had traveled with Kilpatrick. Vigilance was sharpened as they realized how close they were to the Richmond defenses.

Adding to the strain of the night was a new weapon deployed against them. "Torpedoes"—mines—had been planted in the road since their last visit. Throughout the night they would be startled by the explosions of these devices, killing horses and injuring others.[8] The nightmarish journey brought them to the point where, two months before, they had dodged a 32 pound cannon ball careening down the road. Here, they turned right and headed southeast.

A guide had been secured, and the column marched through the slumbering countryside. All was quiet except for the splash of horse hooves in puddles and the occasional rattle of a saber. The men, exhausted from the day's fighting and the night's marching, rode half-awake as they continued their movement around Richmond's defenses. Around dawn, they reached the Mechanicsville Pike and were jolted from their stupor by rifle and cannon fire. Confederate forces from the city had set up a barricade across the Pike and had damaged the Meadows Bridge across the Chickahominy River. Only 300 yards from the Richmond's defenses, the artillery there started firing. With the twin impediments to their march, the column halted, and the 3rd Indiana was ordered to dismount and deploy as skirmishers. On the far right of the Union line, the regiment faced infantry from the city.[9]

Pushing forward, the bridge was reached but found damaged and would need time to repair. The regiment now settled into a familiar task. They and the rest of the 3rd Division were to provide cover and protection until the bridge was ready. "We were encircled by a complete line of the enemy and they fired on us from all points of the compass," commented one member of the regiment.[10] The firing on the line was brisk, and G.W. Beard and Thomas Purcell were wounded.[11] The necessary time had been bought, however, and the column began crossing the Chickahominy. By mid-afternoon, the rearguard was called in and headed to the bridge.

The previous day and night's rain plus the passing of 10,000 horses had turned the approaches to the bridge into a quagmire. Diverting to a river ford nearby, the Third Indiana had to cut through a swamp before crossing. The horses had to "high step it" through the mud and muck up to their knees.[12] Even this route became a mess as some horses became mired and unable to move. To keep them from being captured, the men were ordered to shoot the unfortunate animals. Saddles were ordered destroyed as well. Those now left unmounted struggled forward on foot. "So terrible to see every time a poor horse would give out by sheer exhaustion—out with a pistol & shoot him—break up the saddle and walk on," reported Surgeon Beck.[13]

Safely across the Chickahominy and no longer in immediate danger, the men rested before moving out for Huxtall's Landing the next morning, arriving early on May 14. Their leisurely return was briefly interrupted by the fire of Union gunboats, mistaking them for Confederate cavalry. "Shells about the size of nail kegs" came crashing down around them but, fortunately, no one was injured.[14] Once safe under the protection—and not the fire—of the Union gunboats, the regiment drew much needed rations and forage. They had left Union lines almost a week before with just three days' rations and just two days of forage.

As the men ate and the horses grazed, the men could be proud of what they had accomplished. They had ridden around the Confederate army and bested the vaunted Rebel cavalry in open combat. They had inflicted heavy casualties on their enemy and had killed their leader in the process. The entire command had returned to Union lines in good shape after riding through enemy fortifications and having been surrounded. The men decided that Sheridan would do. They also realized something else. "The rebel cavalry are merely amusement for us. The time has been when we dreaded them, but that time is over," bragged one.[15] The 3rd Indiana left Huxtall's Landing on May 12, having rested along the James River for about a week. Their return to the Army of the Potomac took them slowly north to Chesterfield Station, arriving on May 25. Even such a trip well away from the front could be dangerous. Owen Reynolds of Company F accidentally shot himself in the foot with his pistol during the movement.[16]

George Gilchrist started out as the orderly sergeant of Company E. Promoted progressively through the ranks, he was commissioned captain in July 1864. A competent staff officer, he served on Buford's division staff until the general's death before joining Chapman's staff at brigade headquarters. He veteranized and served to war's end (U.S. Army Heritage and Education Center).

The 3rd Indiana was now a battle hardened regiment. Its men had become adept in the mounted and dismounted combat they were often called upon to perform. Now just three months shy of the end of their enlistment, they were led by a competent yet depleted officer corps. Colonel Chapman was in brigade command and had taken Adjutant Gamaliel Taylor and Captain George Gilchrist of Company B to brigade headquarters. Major Benjamin Q.A. Gresham had resigned and headed home to accept a commission as lieutenant colonel of the 10th Indiana Cavalry.[17] Commanded by Major William Patton, the regiment had no other field officer on duty. Partially compensating for this lack of leadership was the fact that the companies had their full complement of officers with the exception of Company E where First Lieutenant Abner L. Shannon was the only officer on duty. In a diary note on May 26, Major Patton noted the following company strengths: Moffitt's squadron (companies A and F), 98; Thompson's squadron (companies B and E), 100; Martin's squadron (companies C and D), 68. Also present for duty were six staff officers and seven men designated as Pioneers. In all, regimental strength was 279.[18]

Gresham's resignation had set off a fire storm of letter writing by Lieutenant Colonel Robert Klein, commander of the west wing of the regiment. Throughout the coming months, he lobbied the Indiana adjutant general for a major to be appointed to the West Wing. Orders were even issued by the War Department for an officer from the East Wing to be transferred to Tennessee, but were rescinded. When the dust settled in June, Klein got his way with Captain Alfred Gaddis of Company H promoted to major for the West Wing. At the same time, Captain George Thompson of Company E was promoted to major in the East Wing.[19]

Upon arriving in their old camp on May 25, the men expected a continuation of the easy life but that would not be the case. The next day, the men found themselves on the very roads they had traveled on their recent return to the army, but in reverse direction. Grant had decided to find his way around Lee's army and that required cavalry probes and reconnaissance. On May 30, the regiment encountered Confederate forces on the Pamunkey River near Hanover Court House. A lively but short-lived skirmish ensued. In an unusual departure from most of their recent combat, this fight was done mainly on horseback and the use of revolvers. Apparently their recent pistol practice had been for naught. Private William Watlington admitted, "This mode of warfare being unusual to our horses, that they became almost unmanageable, so much so that our navies, I presume, were not very effective."[20] The Confederate horses were apparently more accustomed to close gunfire for Rebel bullets hit Company E's John Nichols in the wrist as well as Keith Martin in Company A.[21]

This movement and fight were part of Grant's new strategy. His intent was to wear down the Confederate army with constant pressure. A man with a bulldog temperament, Grant had his teeth in the Army of Northern Virginia, and he had no intention of letting go. Frustrated by Lee's ability to thwart his attempts to flank the Confederate army, Grant envisioned another wheel to the left to try and get past Lee's dogged defense. At the same time, he wanted to attack the supply lines to Richmond. To do so required the cavalry to be in constant motion and action, switching back and forth between destroying railroads to screening the Union movement, to providing support for the infantry. Only veteran horsemen could do both—and sometimes at the same time.

The coming month of June would see some of the most intense combat duty the men had ever experienced. Anticipating this reality, Captain D.R. Spencer of Company D realized he was not up to another campaign and reported too sick for duty. First Lieutenant Daniel Calhoun was thrust into the company command on the eve of the campaign.[22] On June 1, the Hoosiers mounted up and moved to the Union left. Their target was the Virginia Central Railroad where they spent most of the day burning crossties and bending track. Another party was sent to burn the railroad bridges over the South Anna River. Occasional parties of Confederate cavalry would appear and disrupt the work, forcing the men to scramble to their weapons and defend themselves. It was during one of these attacks that Francis Moxley of Company A was wounded.[23] Tired and worn out, the men returned to Union lines.

After returning from this grueling task, the men were able to rest until 5:00 p.m. the next day. Having just operated some 15 miles north of the battle lines around Richmond, the men were now ordered to return to the Union right and prepare for action. Once more in the saddle, the regiment rode all night until stopping for food and coffee at daybreak of June 3.[24] Given a short rest, the men mounted once again around 10:00 a.m. and were ordered forward to drive Confederate cavalry from a small village named Haw's Shop. After driving out the enemy cavalry, the men were to attack rebel infantry from the rear as a general advance was made by the Union army. Only four days before, the larger 1st Division had tried this maneuver and met strong resistance. Now it was the 3rd Division's turn. It would turn out to be a long day for the men of the 3rd Indiana.

The advance made contact with the rebel lines around noon. The Confederates, entrenched in breastworks, were proving to be stubborn, and the Union horsemen were ordered to dismount and attack on foot. The attacking cavalry pushed through three sets of breastworks before being recalled. Having completed their first task, the Hoosiers and comrades of the 3rd Division were ordered to mount and cross the Totopotomoy Creek. Arriving at the stream, they found more Confederates entrenched on the far side. The horse artillery were brought up and placed. Dismounting the 3rd Indiana, Major William Patton coordinated with the 2nd New York and organized a charge that would be precipitated by the first roar of the cannon. At the boom, the Hoosiers and New Yorkers ran down the banks of the creek, waded across, and stormed up the opposite shore. A few scattered shots greeted them, and the defenders soon broke and fled. Now nearly dark, the men remounted and marched back toward Union lines.[25]

Losses for the regiment had been surprisingly light; only Silas Farrell in Company A had been wounded.[26] One member of the regiment delighted in the day's action. "I got a 7 shooter Spencer carbine from a Johnnie I took prisoner," wrote a pleased Francis Bellamy. His emphasis may have been prompted by the fact that he captured the sought after weapon from the enemy. Still armed with single shot Sharps carbines, they men envied those units who had been supplied this revolutionary firearm.[27] For the next five days, the men and horses were allowed to rest

Chapter 12. May 7, 1864–June 15, 1864

with the exception of routine scouts. Not aware of the bigger picture, the men made the most of this downtime.

On June 3, Grant had launched an ill-advised frontal attack at Cold Harbor with appalling loss of life. His attempts to flank Lee had been thwarted, once again. His losses were escalating with little to show for his men's sacrifice. He was still outside Richmond, and Lee's army was still a potent fighting force. What he needed, Grant decided, was a big enough diversion that would cut Lee's supply line and pull the Confederate cavalry away from his army. He ordered Sheridan to move well to the west and try and replicate Yellow Tavern. He was to draw the enemy cavalry with him and defeat it in another pitched battle. Grant also wanted to secure his flank with cavalry as he moved the Army of the Potomac across the Chickahominy and James Rivers in another left flank maneuver. Hoping the combined raid on the railroad and his simultaneous flank attack would force Lee out of Richmond, Grant ordered Sheridan to work out this twofold mission for the cavalry.

The solution was for Sheridan to take the 1st and 2nd Divisions west and leave the Wilson's 3rd Division—including the 3rd Indiana—with Grant. Wilson would be supported by the small cavalry division of Butler's Army of the James. On June 7, Sheridan left any dismounted men from the 1st and 2nd Divisions with Wilson and headed west. Grant was now ready to make his left flanking attack with his goal being Petersburg, a railroad hub 40 miles south of Richmond. Its capture would cut off supplies from the south to the capital city and to Lee's army. If Sheridan was successful to the west, the flow of men and supplies from Tennessee and the Shenandoah Valley would also be cut off.

Naturally, the cavalry would lead the attack, and naturally, the 3rd Indiana was once again the point of the spear. This time they were to cross the Chickahominy, drive in the pickets, and protect the army as it crossed the river. Moving from the right flank to the army's left, the men prepared to lead the way. On June 12, Chapman ordered the regiment to the Chickahominy and there meet a pontoon train and cross the pontoon bridge that had been constructed. Arriving at the crossing site late in the evening, they men expected to see a bridge. The only problem was the officer in charge of the pontoon train had made no attempt to deploy his equipment. Intimidated by the picket fire from the Confederates on the opposite side, the pontoon parts remained on the wagons. The infantry accompanying the train were ordered to follow the cavalry across and saw no reason to deviate from those orders. There matters stood until the cavalry arrived.

Exasperated by the lack of fight in the engineers and infantrymen, Chapman ordered Major Patton to dismount his men. They had been ordered to cross the river and cross it they would. They were not known as the "Horse Marines" for nothing. The 22nd New York was sent to look for a ford while the 3rd Indiana grabbed several of the pontoons and prepared for an improbable amphibious assault. The rest of the brigade deployed along the river to provide covering fire. At the crossing point, the river divided around a small island. The men would have to cross to the island, carry

Shown on its wheeled transport, pontoons such as this were used in the river crossing assault on June 12, 1864 (Library of Congress).

the pontoons across the island, re-launch the boats, and cross the second branch—all while under fire. With daylight fading fast, the attack had to go now.

Wooden and heavy, the pontoon boats were over 30 feet in length and cumbersome on land. Cursing the engineers' timidity, the men dashed down the banks of the river, floated the boats, and climbed aboard. Paddling furiously, the "Horse Marines" hit the opposite shore, grabbed the boats and dragged them across the 50 foot wide island and reboarded. Paddling like madmen, they hit the south shore of the Chickahominy and stormed up the riverbank. Almost simultaneously, the 22nd New York, having found a ford, hit the enemy flank. The Confederates broke and ran, leaving the crossing in the hands of the Union cavalry.[28]

The brigade pushed out about ¼ miles and established a picket line. The pontoons were sent back across so the bridge could finally be built, and the infantry sent across. By 1:00 a.m., the engineers had completed the structure, and the Hoosiers were recalled and reunited with their horses.[29] Exhausted by the day's march and fight, the men and horses were to receive no rest as they mounted and headed south. By daylight, they had reached a dismal area known as White Oak Swamp. The name described the area well. Wetlands with large oak trees rising out of the water were tangled with an undergrowth of smaller trees. Having been the site of the Seven

Chapter 12. May 7, 1864–June 15, 1864

Days battle in long ago 1862, the reminders of that fight could be seen in the form of skeletons and battle debris. On top of this, another hot, humid day was breaking. If the men entered the swamp with trepidation, it was with good cause.

Lee had detected Grant's movement and rushed to counter the Union shift to the southeast. Lee was able to move troops more rapidly and intercepted the Union troops before they even had a good start. By daylight of June 13, Lee had sent cavalry to retard Grant's movement while moving infantry in behind them. As the men of the 3rd Indiana advanced, they ran into resistance. The Confederates were fighting a delaying tactic as they slowly retreated toward Richmond—until they reached Riddle's Shop. Pronounced "Rye-dell" locally, the little shop stood at the intersection of the main road to Richmond and the Malvern Hill or Quaker road. Here, the rebel resistance stiffened and the Hoosiers were ordered to dismount. Suddenly, a disorienting lull came across the landscape.[30]

With the quiet came a fear of what would happen next. Experienced soldiers, the 2nd Brigade began to build rudimentary breastworks. Fence rails, logs, and rocks were appropriated for the task. For more than two hours, the men worked in the quiet of the afternoon to build and strengthen their little line.[31] On the 3rd Indiana's flanks were the 1st Vermont and the 8th New York. The line ran from the left of the Quaker Road to the right to well beyond the road to Bottom's Bridge. Behind them was a battery of horse artillery with the guns being supported by the brigade reserve of the 1st New Hampshire and 2nd New York.[32]

The lull was shattered by the appearance of several Confederate infantry regiments. Spreading out in line of battle, they charged down the Bottom's Bridge road directly at the 3rd Indiana. Men checked their Sharps and made sure percussion caps were properly seated. Throats were dry, and the knot in each man's belly grew bigger. Chapman had sent word they would need infantry support to maintain his position at this vital crossroads. It was Gettysburg all over again. The cavalrymen would have to hold until the infantry arrived.

The fighting developed rapidly as the Confederate battle lines approached the thin blue defenses. All along the regiment's front, men were hit, screaming in agony or silently died. The small breastworks they had constructed quickly showed its inadequacy. Chunks of rotten logs, used to build part of the rampart, proved little use in stopping minié balls, providing only a shower of rotten wood when hit.[33] The pressure of the attack was so great that Chapman slowly withdrew his men from the first line and fell back on the reserve and the artillery. This was a slugfest in comparison to the regiment's recent fighting, and the growing casualty list proved it. Finally, a brigade of blue infantry arrived to strengthen the line. Their appearance slowed the Confederate attack, and the attackers finally withdrew.

Company B had four men down—George Melton (chest wound), Hugh Stevenson and George Nelson (leg wound), John Wiseman (shoulder wound). In Company D Thomas Baker had been wounded while Company C had Henry Franklin. The word spread that Samuel Heath was dead. During the afternoon's skirmishing,

Heath was seen ahead of the line and spotted a "Johnnie" in like pursuit. The two men stalked each other, as if intending on hand to hand combat. At 30 yards, the men simultaneously brought their carbines up to firing positions just as an artillery shell from the horse battery came whizzing through the air. Neither man got off a shot as the shell decapitated Heath and cut off both legs of the "Johnnie."[34]

Company E had Alexander Monroe (wounded thigh), George Brinkman (wounded arm), and Bennett Land (broken shoulder). The brunt of the fighting, however, had been on Company F's front. Harvey Keegler was dead. James Gorman lay still and bleeding profusely from a wound to the abdomen. He would die before the day was over. Oliver Brenton, Frank Buchanan, William Hines, and Louis Klussman all bled from various wounds. In all, the regiment's butcher's toll was three dead and sixteen wounded.[35]

The uneven fight in the swamps and heat of tidewater Virginia was still not over. As sunset approached, enemy infantry returned and attacked, causing some of the Union infantry support to retreat. The regiment was forced to retreat further back where they moved toward Harrison's Landing, going into camp around 2:00 a.m. "Collapsing" into camp was a better description. The last 48 hours had seen the men and horses move from the right flank to the left flank of the Army of the Potomac, make a daring amphibious assault across a river under fire, protect the bridgehead while a pontoon bridge was constructed, advance on the enemy through a hostile landscape, capture a vital crossroads, build breastworks, withstand infantry attack, and retire in good order back to Union lines.

The men of the 3rd Indiana had not participated in the monumental cavalry battle at Trevilian Station far to the west, but their recent service brought pride to the men. While exaggerated, one man's letter home typified this sentiment: "On the 13th at Riddle's Shop, we had the severest cavl [sic] fight of the war. Our brigade whipped Lees Divis of Cav'l. and a Brigade of Infy and then held Lee's Army in check for 4 hours."[36] And while their counterparts of the 1st and 2nd Divisions were slowly returning to the east, the 3rd Division would be tested once again. For the 3rd Indiana, only two months from muster out, the most arduous and dangerous experience of their service career still awaited them.

Chapter 13

June 16, 1864–July 12, 1864

Grant's anticipated knockout blow to Lee's army had been thwarted once again. His movement by the left flank had been successful, and Federal troops had reached Petersburg ahead of Lee's men. A lack of aggressiveness by the Union commanders in the field let vital time slip away, and Confederate reinforcements poured into Petersburg. When the Union assault was finally launched on June 18, it was repulsed. The Army of the Potomac found itself on the east and south side of Petersburg and began preparations for a siege of this vital Confederate railroad hub.

The railroads. Grant still wanted to cut the rail supply lines that went through Petersburg to Richmond as well as supplying Lee's army. When word was received that Sheridan had been successful in cutting the Virginia Central Railroad out at Trevilian Station, Grant saw an opportunity to cripple Lee's supply line. In reality, Sheridan had fought Wade Hampton's Confederates to a draw and was slowly making his way back to the army, harassed all the way by Hampton.

All Grant knew was that Sheridan had cut the railroad to the west. He also knew that the Southside Railroad came into Petersburg from the west bringing the rich bounty of the Shenandoah Valley to Lee's army and Richmond. Another railroad, the Richmond and Danville, crossed the Southside line about 80 miles west of Petersburg. The Richmond and Danville ran directly to Richmond bringing foodstuffs and other supplies from southwestern Virginia, Tennessee, and North Carolina. With these two lines cut plus the destruction of the Virginia Central Railroad by Sheridan, reasoned Grant, Lee would be forced to come out of Petersburg or starve.

The big question was, whom to send? Sheridan and the 1st and 2nd Divisions had not yet reached the army. Waiting would only allow time for the Confederates to repair the damage to the Virginia Central. Grant wanted all three railroads out of commission immediately. On June 20, Grant ordered Meade to have the 3rd Division prepare for a long raid as soon as possible. Added to the raiding force were General August Kautz's 2,500 cavalrymen of the Army of the James.[1]

"As soon as possible" turned out to be 48 hours. Wilson's men had been resting from their heavy duty in the previous days since June 15. They were currently located around Prince Georges Courthouse on the eastside of Petersburg. The time in camp had allowed "solid comfort and rest" for the men and horses of the 3rd

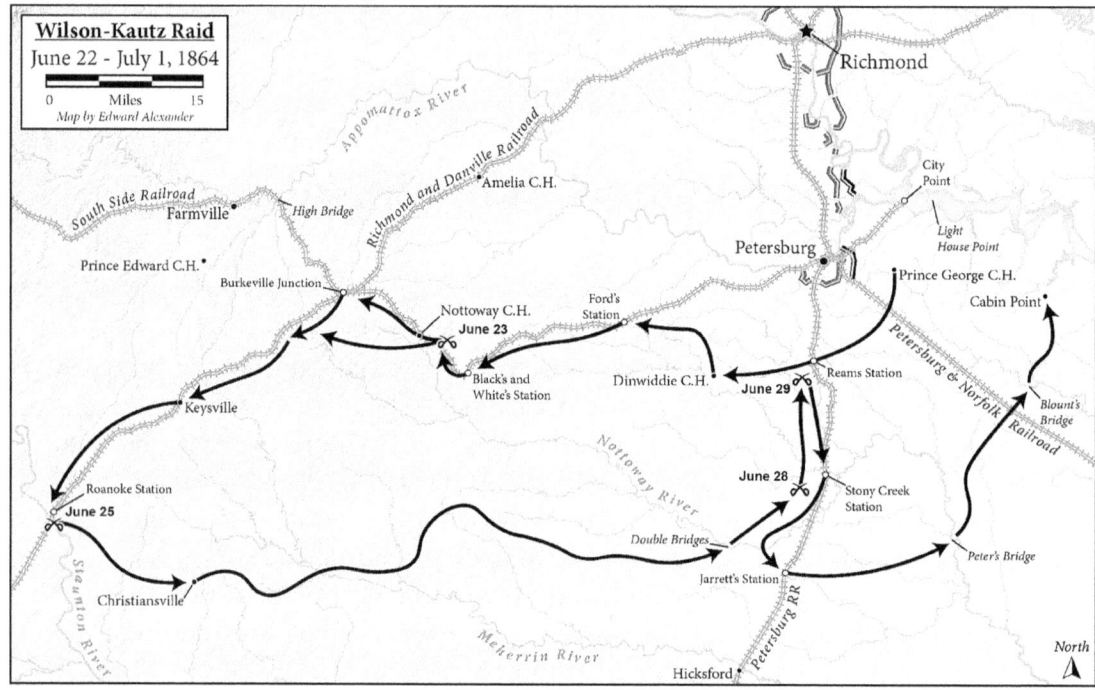

Indiana.[2] A semblance of normal camp life had already evolved, including company drill.[3] That rest would be needed in the coming days for the men received orders to prepare for departure at 2:00 a.m. on June 22. As the column moved out to the west, some men were in a playful, almost festive mood. One wrote about the coming raid in light-hearted terms: "the change of base which General Grant has now assumed opened up new fields for us cavalry, in which there were several railroads for us to inspect and put into [dis]repair for the [in]convenience of our confederate brethren."[4]

The men rode through Ream's Station to Dinwiddie Court House before turning north to Ford's Station on the Southside Railroad. Here they camped overnight. Their march so far had been shadowed by Confederate cavalry, but they did little to impede their progress.[5] Wilson didn't take any chances, however. All regiments were ordered into line and to leave their horses saddled and bridled. The men lay where they were, wrapped reins around their arms, and tried to sleep. At dawn of June 23, the men continued their march.

They also began the hot, dirty, wearying work of destroying track. Whole sections of rail would be overturned, cross ties and all, and thrown into bonfires. If there was enough time, the red hot rails would be twisted around trees to make them useless. The crossties, made out of pine, created a black smoke, and the column's progress could be traced by the dozens of fires and smoke columns.[6] Adding to the strain of the work was a hot oppressing sun that drove temperatures up to 100 degrees.[7] For 20 miles the cavalrymen tore up track, passing through Black's and White's station and approached Nottoway Court House, about 20 miles from the intersection of the Richmond and Danville and the Southside Railroads.

Here, the Confederate cavalry reappeared and started harassing the column. Exhausted, the men dismounted and formed line of battle behind the railroad berm and waited for the next development. The rebel cavalry accepted the challenge and attacked. The Union line, well protected by the berm, forced the enemy to retreat. Chapman was given the word to follow, and the 2nd Brigade swung into saddle and dashed after the retiring Confederates. In short order, they had captured three cannon but were unable to hold their position long enough for them to be removed to the Union line. As they retreated, the men did the next best thing; they spiked the guns, making them temporarily useless.[8]

Desultory fighting continued until evening as the rebel troops kept the Union raiders from proceeding. Finally, Wilson ordered the column to cut cross country, arriving in Keysville on the Richmond and Danville Railroad. Here, they camped for the evening and again slept on the ground in line of battle, horses saddled and bridled.[9]

The next morning, the men awoke to the prospects of another hot, grimy day. As they marched southwest toward Roanoke Station, they continued destroying track and kept a watchful eye out for the enemy. The work that day went somewhat easier as the rails were made of wood with iron straps covering the top. When placed in fire, the rail and crossties were consumed, and the iron straps warped from the heat, rendering them useless.[10] The work continued uninterrupted until sundown when Confederate cavalry once more made an appearance in the 2nd Brigade's rear. Chapman ordered the men into line and "had a little fight," Sergeant Joseph Matthews laconically wrote.[11]

The men stood in line until 2:00 a.m. when they moved further south toward Roanoke Station. As they plodded along, the direction of the march changed so that by daybreak they found themselves near Christiansville, nearly 20 miles east of Roanoke Station.[12] Exhausted by the previous day's labor and nighttime march, men fell asleep in the saddle, and horses gave out. Many of the men had already eaten their three days of rations and were hungry. Squads were detailed into the countryside to appropriate food and horses from local farms.[13]

As the 3rd Division burned rails and contended with harassing Confederate cavalry, Kautz and his men had reached Roanoke Station. There, they were to burn a long wooden trestle bridge spanning the Staunton River. He found the bridge strongly defended by 1,000 rebel infantry and home guards in forts. After two attempts to get to the bridge were repulsed, Kautz had to report to Wilson that it was not possible to destroy the structure. Having torn up over 70 miles of track, Wilson decided that enough had been accomplished and ordered both divisions back toward Union lines. Chapman was to cut cross country back to Christiansville where he was to form the raiders' advance.[14]

Upon reaching Christiansville, the 3rd Indiana was fortunate to find a large supply of corn and fed their horses. This had been a fortuitous discovery as the regiment had been without resupply since leaving the lines several days ago. Feeding the horses was of vital import as they were the means of escape back to friendly territory. They were even able to scoop up enough to feed their horses for the next two days.[15] Now fed, the men and horses still had to endure the heat and humidity. It was reported that the temperature that day reached 105 degrees.[16] In addition, every encounter with the harassing Confederate cavalry took valuable time and added to the casualty list. Long lines of confiscated wagons and carriages bearing the wounded now followed the column.[17]

The next day, June 27, the 3rd Indiana moved out as the lead unit of a column of nearly 4,500 cavalrymen. Its "tail" had grown significantly as hundreds of fleeing slaves attached themselves to the column. The men marveled as they marched through an area that had not been touched by war. Fields of wheat offered additional supplements to their diet. Food was currently not the problem. Time was. Hampton's return from Trevilian Station had significantly increased the number of Confederate cavalry coming after them. While just as exhausted as the Union men, the rebels had the advantage of regular rations and the chance to destroy or capture a large Union raiding party. With time and luck, Hampton hoped to cut the raiders off at Ream's Station.

At the same time, Confederate infantry had beaten back a Union attempt to occupy the station as a safeguard for the returning blue cavalry. When Hampton arrived he began consolidating his forces, many of whom had been occupied with small spoiling attacks from the south and east of the Union column. As the 3rd Indiana rode to Ream's, they rode toward a trap instead of safety. The southerly route toward Ream's Station had, so far, not encountered strong resistance. The terrible heat continued to punish man and beast. It was fervently hoped that another long day and 30-mile ride tomorrow would bring them back into Union lines.

A thunderstorm on the evening of June 27 brought some relief from the heat as well as the dust. Men were falling asleep while mounted, and those whose mounts had given out staggered on foot down the road, trying to keep up. Orders were sent to Chapman to push forward to Stony Creek Station and its ford. He sent word to Major Patton to take the 3rd Indiana and check out the crossing. As the men approached the ford, carbine and rifle fire zipped around their heads. The regiment pushed the Confederate pickets back across the creek and was met by a sheet of fire, wounding Lieutenant Abner Shannon and Oscar Trigg of Company E.[18] The regiment whirled around and recrossed the stream where Patton dismounted the men along the creekbank and sent word back to the main body that the crossing was blocked.

The 1st Brigade was sent to reinforce the regiment, and both commands stood in line all night. Sporadic fire along the creek kept the men on edge. Artillery had been brought up, and a blind fire commenced. After a long, sleepless night, the 3rd Indiana was ordered to rejoin their brigade, which had formed a line of battle 600 yards behind the 1st Brigade. The men began building breastworks as the 1st Brigade retired through their lines. Positioned on the face of a small stand of timber,

Chapman was ordered to hold the position for as long as possible or until he received word "the road was open."[19]

The road was decidedly not open. Kautz's division had moved around the left flank of the 3rd Division and moved up toward Ream's Station. Upon reaching the area near the station, he was confronted by a Confederate force of cavalry and infantry, blocking his movement. The presence of infantry was an ominous sign that troops from Petersburg were arriving.

Wilson was in a bind. To the east and south, Confederate cavalry continued to nip at Chapman's position near Stony Creek. To the north, the way was blocked by enemy cavalry and now infantry. A retreat to the west was open, but it would only carry him further away from Union lines and increase the likelihood of defeat or capture. Believing that Union troops possessed Ream's Station, Wilson decided to try and break through. On the night of June 28, he would attempt to bypass the intervening Confederate forces and reach what he thought would be the safety of Ream's Station. Chapman and his brigade would now form the rearguard for the division. The 3rd Indiana found itself responsible for holding the road open until the entire column had passed. They were isolated, and they knew it. One described it as they were "to be sacrificed."[20]

But Hampton had ideas of his own. The next morning, all hell broke loose around the dismounted 2nd Brigade. Chapman's men were hit in the flank and rear with overwhelming force as the rebel leader made a bold bid to wipe out the Union raiders.[21] The rigors of the raid plus being up all night led to a breakdown in discipline throughout the brigade. Men, fueled by adrenalin and the instinct for survival, raced back to their horses in an attempt to escape. In the 3rd Indiana camp, all was chaos. The attack from their rear had brought the Confederates within a few yards of the Hoosiers' held horses. Horse holders fought to control the animals as horses screamed in pain as bullets smacked into horseflesh. Some of the holders simply rode away to save their own lives. Men from the breastworks ran into this cauldron of panic and danger to grab a horse, any horse, with which to escape the onslaught of the rebel attack.[22] Chapman was barely able to grab a mount and galloped away. Eventually, he was able to gather about 300 men of his brigade and rode west then north toward the rest of the column, arriving around noon.[23]

Other men, running in panic, made their escape the best they could. Some followed in the wake of Chapman and were able to rejoin the brigade further north. Some went west and then south toward Double Bridges. One thing was certain: no one wanted to be captured. The horrors of Andersonville were well known, and no one wanted to end up there. In the confusion, Adjutant Gamaliel Taylor was captured and relieved of his pocketbook. Seeing Taylor, George Culver of Company F ran up to his Confederate captor and demanded *his* surrender. Once the rebel conceded, Taylor promptly demanded—and received—the return of his possession.[24]

The rest of the division with Wilson had been trying to break through to Ream's Station. Eventually, Kautz's division found a way west around the Confederates and made its way to Union lines. Wilson was now alone and decided to take his command back south to Double Bridges, re-cross Nottoway Creek, go to Jarrett's Station, turn east, and re-enter Union lines from the south.[25] Wilson looked at the hollow eyes of his men mounted on horses staggering with fatigue. Casualties were mounting with each passing moment. Horses pulling artillery and wagons full of wounded were too weak for their task. He faced heavy opposition in his front and had learned from Chapman's fugitives that rebel forces were in his rear and on his right flank. It would only be a matter of time before these forces hemmed him in on three sides.

Wilson made a decision. He ordered the artillery spiked, and the horses pulling them destroyed. All reserve ammunition was distributed to the men, and the rest was to be destroyed, along with the artillery rounds. All wagons and carriages were to be burned.

James Wilson had never commanded troops until taking command of the Third Division. Wilson's time in command included the disastrous Wilson-Kautz Raid. Upon the transfer of the 3rd Division to the Shenandoah Valley in late summer 1864, his performance continued to be sporadic. He was sent to Georgia when General William Sherman requested a cavalry leader (Library of Congress).

His next order illustrated the dire situation more than any other. All wounded too badly injured were to be abandoned to the enemy. Only able bodied men and horses would be allowed to make the attempted escape.

Men ran about stacking ammunition, shooting horses, and lighting wagons and carriages on fire. Firing continued to the north as cavalry and infantry attempted to overwhelm the vanguard. Confused and exhausted men from Chapman's brigade periodically entered Union lines, only to learn that this supposed haven was about to be overrun. Sporadic firing to the south and east indicated the approach of more rebels. Runaway slaves and their families, realizing their saviors were preparing to abandon them, were overcome with grief and panic. The 3rd Indiana's Charles

Cunningham, Elijah Brindley, George Umphries, and Christopher Vanosdol—too badly wounded to travel—were made as comfortable as possible even as they pleaded with their comrades to take them along.[26] If there was a hell on earth on June 29, 1864, it was located a few miles south of Ream's Station, Virginia.

The retreat south was to be to the west of the route taken that morning to avoid the forces who had attacked Chapman earlier. In a short time, the column moved out to the sound of exploding artillery shells and small arms ammunition. Mounting, the men grimly stared straight ahead as they rode through the maelstrom of abandoned wounded, dead horses, and screaming, scared runaways.

Using terms like "column" and "move out" implied that some military discipline was in force, and order had been restored. While the 3rd Indiana claimed to have some semblance of military order, most regiments mixed together, and unit cohesion for the most part had evaporated. The 2nd Brigade was once more tasked with leading the retreat, but it felt more like a rout. Just as the 3rd Indiana moved out, the rearguard gave way, and the Confederates charged after the rear of the fugitive mass. "We needed no flankers as the fugitives went pell-mell through the fields," reported one Hoosier.[27]

The Confederates hit the tail of the retreating force as the fugitives were crossing Stony Creek. Wholesale slaughter of the helpless runaways ensued. One man saw babies left by the side of the road as mothers fled for their own safety.[28] "The rebs fired into & with Saber Cut & slashed the poor Contrabands—women & children. Killing most inhumanly–& such shrieks was [sic] terrible," wrote Elias Beck. "At a small river [Stony Creek] with one bridge over hundreds jumped in & half never got out."[29] One man had seen a family of five in a small oxcart join the column on June 28. On June 30, he saw the man again, now on foot and carrying the baby having lost his other two children and his wife in the mass confusion of the march. That evening, the man placed the starving baby in some bushes, unable to watch the child die.[30]

"For many hours, the march was at a rapid pace—nearly a gallop," wrote one 3rd Indiana cavalryman.[31] Eight miles south of their start and having gained a little time, Chapman was compelled to halt briefly to reform his command. Men were grouped into makeshift companies. Arms and ammunition were redistributed. As more men caught up from the breakout, they were also reorganized into some semblance of military order. Still in enemy territory, the raiders had to be able to defend themselves if they were to survive. Moving out once again, the pace slackened considerably.

But the previous days' travel and the sudden burst of energy needed to achieve the breakout had taken their toll. Horses broke down and were shot on the spot. Dismounted men began to roam the countryside on both sides of their line of march in hopes of finding new mounts. A duo of 3rd Indiana men out looking for horses was surprised by a lone Confederate, but quickly reversed the situation by overpowering the would-be captor. Marching him back to the road, they presented their prisoner to General Wilson who personally interrogated the rebel. The grayback informed Wilson that Hampton was indeed on his left flank and was trying to get ahead of the Union cavalry to cut them off from the Nottaway Creek crossing at Double Bridges. Hearing this, Wilson ordered the impossible—an increase in speed to thwart Hampton's attempt.[32]

Beyond exhausted, men and horses staggered on throughout the night, reaching Double Bridges ahead of the pursuing Confederates at daylight of June 30. Crossing the Nottaway Creek, the men turned east. Two miles from Jarrett's Station, they stopped and were allowed to rest for a couple of hours. Men slept on their horses, sometimes rolling off their mounts' backs only to be jarred awake upon hitting the ground. Some ate. Others looked for friends. Others slid to the ground and sat in a stupor, too tired to sleep, eat, look or stand. All too soon, the order was given to continue the march.

Chapman's brigade continued to lead the march. The 3rd Indiana was headed for Peter's Bridge, another crossing of the Nottaway Creek. Starting at Jarrett's Station, the Nottaway made a huge arc to the north, then east, and back to the south. They needed to cross this eastern section of the Nottaway and then the Blackwater River before they could breathe easier. Arriving once again at the Nottaway at Peter's Bridge around 6:00 p.m., they found the bridge destroyed, but were able to ford the creek and continue east.[33] During the course of this march, Major Patton's horse stumbled and threw the Major, breaking two ribs and badly bruising his entire left arm. In intense pain, Patton yielded command of the regiment to the senior captain present, Thomas Moffitt of Company F.[34]

Heading east once again, their goal was Blount's Bridge over the Blackwater. Arriving there around midnight, the men found the bridge destroyed but unguarded. If they hurried, they could repair the bridge, cross the river and then destroy the bridge, denying its use to their pursuers. Wilson arrived and took in the surroundings. Written years later with a bit of poetic license, his description was apt: "It was a dark and dismal scene in the midst of a river bottom crowded with forest trees clad with festoons of black hanging moss and resounding with the hooting of distant owls and the baying of distant dogs."[35] His immediate need was to rebuild the bridge across a steep-banked, deep bottomed river in the dead of night.

The first attempt gave way and spilled several men and horses into the river below. A trained engineer, Wilson was in his element. He soon set the men to work repairing the span. Taking an active role in the construction, Wilson pitched in with gusto. One Hoosier observed that the general "handled rails and timber as though he had taken lessons in the art under the 'Old Rail Splitter' Father Abe."[36] Regardless of where he learned, the new attempt was much sturdier and the bulk of his command had crossed by daylight. Dismounted troops spread out along the river bank to cover any straggling members of the command. Finally, at 6:15 a.m., Wilson ordered the bridge to be burned; within the hour, the burning structure splashed into the river below. The hissing of hot timbers had barely stopped when a scout from Hampton's cavalry was seen advancing. The effective destruction of the bridge meant that Hampton could not cross. The men were finally safe.

Travelling slowly northeast, the men made camp at Cabin's Point, only 15 miles from their starting point for the raid 10 long days ago.[37] On July 2, the regiment moved to a camp near Light House Point on the James River and, finally, given time to recover from the past days' ordeal. Utterly exhausted physically, emotionally, and mentally, the regiment stayed in camp and tried to recover. July 3 was a Sunday and Sergeant John Matthews found time to attend worship service and give thanks for his escape. He was also thinking of home, "Oh how I would like to spend some of those quiet Sabbaths that I have spent in Ind."[38] Flavius Bellamy wrote home trying to explain the raid. He was so exhausted that his crisp handwriting slowly drifted to an almost undecipherable scrawl by the end of the letter.[39]

On the same day, Surgeon Elias Beck wrote a summary of the raid in a letter home. He undoubtedly spoke for many of the tired men around him: "We have just returned from the most terrible Raid on record. I have no time now to do more than to thank God I am safe from it & I have no language to Express the horrors & labors of these past 11 days…. O God what blood & horror. I am sick of such inhuman scenes & long for the day to come that I can quit."[40]

Men who had become separated during the chaotic retreat continued to return to Union lines for days after the raid. Individually and in groups, they told of evading Confederate patrols as well as vigilante groups of civilians bent on revenge. On July 5, A.J. Walk of Company C reported to the regiment, claiming to have seen Lieutenant Abner Shannon and 15 other men captured.[41]

Walk was fairly accurate. Lieutenant Abner Shannon had been captured with eight other 3rd Indiana men: John Farrell, David Haskall, and Francis Jackson of Company A along with John Glasscock, Jacob Grebe, William Staples, Oscar Trigg, and Augustus Weaver of Company E. All had been captured in the confusion of the fighting around Ream's Station on June 29.[42]

Also wounded but not abandoned were John W. Vanosdal of Company F with a badly wounded hand, John Halbert hit in the elbow, Welborn Holmes hit in the knee, and John Young nursing a wounded finger.[43] Two officers, Second Lieutenant Dennis Davis of Company B and Captain Thomas Moffitt, received slight hand wounds. Amazingly, only one man had been killed outright—Sergeant Benjamin Bledsoe of Company C.

In his report written on July 12, Chapman listed the 2nd Brigade's casualties as 30 killed, 230 wounded and 445 missing or captured for a total of 705.[44] As the days passed, men returned as mentioned above. Also, the few who had escaped with Kautz returned to the command. Others were still mixed up in the jumble of temporary units formed during the retreat. In the final report of the raid, Wilson reported revised casualties for the 2nd Brigade as 132 killed, 55 wounded, and 366 missing or captured for a total of 434. In the same report, the 3rd Indiana listed one man killed, nine wounded, and 14 captured. In all, Wilson's 3rd Division reported 795 men killed, wounded, captured or missing—approximately 30 percent of the force that had started the raid.[45]

In an unusually graphic and honest letter home, Major William Patton confided to his wife, "Among all the hard work the regiment has done, the last raid was the hardest. We were gone 11 days and the longest rest that man & horse had in any 24 hours, was 3 hours. We were continualy on the march, or tearing up rail road, burning depots and trains of cars or fighting. But the worst was when we undertook to come back we had creeks & little rivers to cross and only at bridges and we found these heavily guarded by any amount of Rebel Cavalry and infantry. The whole country was up in arms against us and for a day or two it was doubtful whether we could get out." After recounting the dangers of their retreat, he fervently stated, "I hope never again to go through such another raid."[46]

August 22, the last day of the regiment's enlistment, couldn't come soon enough.

Chapter 14

July 13, 1864–September 25, 1864

The Cavalry Corps of the Army of the Potomac was virtually incapable of duty in July 1864. The 1st and 2nd Divisions were recovering from the long ride to, fight at, and return from Trevilian Station. The 3rd Division had just gone through a grueling raid with high casualties. Even Kautz's "borrowed" division from the Army of the James was used up. The losses and weariness were not restricted to the men. Thousands of horses would be needed to replace the losses of raids. Those mounts that were serviceable needed time to recuperate and strengthen. On July 3, Sheridan reported that the horses of the Corps needed reshoeing and at least 12 days of rest before they could be used.[1] Exacerbating the situation were the severe heat and lack of rain. Creeks and streams were drying up, and the mere necessity for water for the large number of men and horses became a major concern.

For the men of the 3rd Indiana, all of this meant little work other than the occasional picket duty. For Ed Hollins of Company B, this proved to be hazardous duty. While out on picket, Hollins was attacked by six bushwhackers, shot twice, robbed of his pocketbook and horse, and left for dead. Amazingly, he survived the attack.[2] A little more than two weeks later, two men from Company F were captured while on picket duty.[3]

Once back in camp, Captain Moffitt relinquished command of the regiment to Major George Thompson, who had not accompanied the unit on the raid. With the capture of First Lieutenant Abner Shannon, Company E had no officers present. Orderly Sergeant Joseph Matthews found himself in command of the company. On July 13, the officers of the brigade presented Colonel Chapman a silver pitcher and goblets inscribed with the words "Yellow Tavern, Meadow's Bridge, Salem Church, Riddle's Shop," in commemoration of the brigade's service since April. No doubt ordered before the most recent raid, the pitcher could very well have had "Ream's Station" added to the list.[4]

There may have been additional impetus for the presentation. Many of the regiments had been formed for three years' service. For many, their time was near for separation from the military. Chapman had been in command of a brigade off and on for many months. Commanding a brigade entitled the leader to be promoted to Brigadier General, but promotion to that rank had not come through. If it did not, Colonel Chapman would muster out with his regiment. If the army wanted to keep

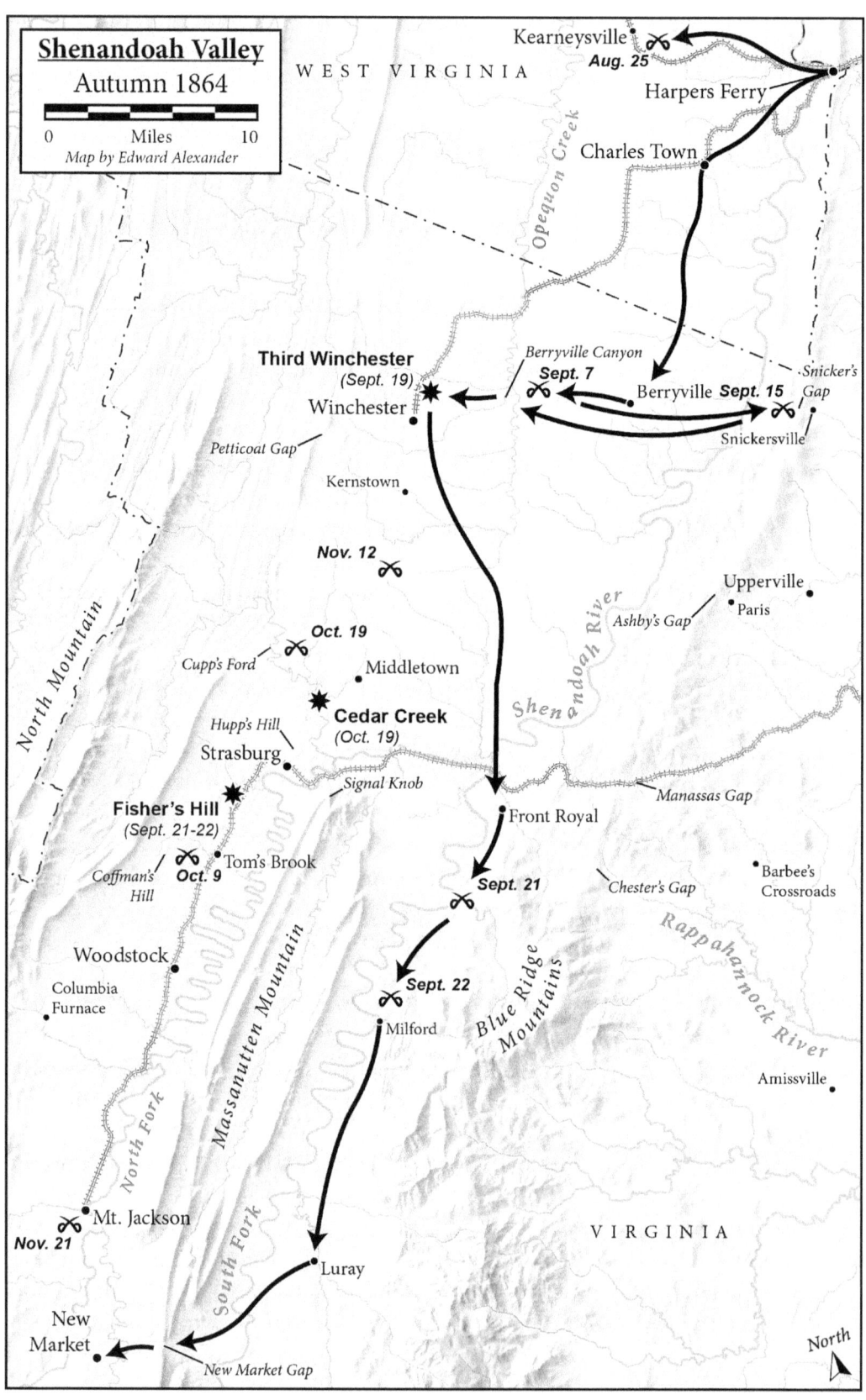

Colonel Chapman, a veteran and successful brigade commander, beyond August 22, promotion was a must.

As early as June 9, Major General George Meade, commander of the Army of the Potomac, had forwarded to the War Department the recommendation that Chapman be promoted to Brigadier General. In the dispatch, Meade noted that Chapman had been recommended for promotion at least once before.[5] A month later, on July 9, Charles A. Dana, Secretary of War Edwin Stanton's special agent with the army, wrote a note to the secretary. In it, he mentioned that General Grant had also requested the promotion of Chapman and Colonel J.B. McIntosh. "They have long commanded brigades and their regiments soon go out of service. They are officers of great value, and if refused cannot well be replaced."[6] On July 23, General Grant again wrote to Stanton and repeated his request for the promotion.[7] That did the trick. On July 26, Chapman tendered his resignation as colonel of the 3rd Indiana Cavalry to Governor Morton to accept a commission as a Brigadier General.[8] The short bespectacled former navy midshipman had come a long way.

On the same day Chapman wrote his letter to the governor, an order was issued that the 3rd Indiana Cavalry was to be withdrawn from the lines and sent to Washington for muster out.[9] Three days later, as part of the processing out, the men were required to sell their horses to the army. Most of the mounts brought $120–180, a price most considered fair.[10]

Not all of the men would be going home, however. Fifty-seven original members

Often identified as being taken in Petersburg in November 1864, this group photograph is more likely to have been taken much earlier as the Re-Organized 3rd Indiana Cavalry was in the Shenandoah Valley in November. Note two of the men wear "slouch hats," much preferred by the western men (Library of Congress).

of the regiment had veteranized, and there were a considerable number of recruits who still had time left on their three year enlistment. How to re-organize these men became a simple exercise; veterans and those who enlisted in 1863 and 1864 were formed into a re-organized Company A. Those who had enlisted between the original muster date and December 31, 1862, were assigned to a re-organized Company B.[11] Officers were assigned to the new organization as follows[12]:

	Company A	Company B
Captain	Charles W. Lee	Benjamin Gilbert
1st Lieutenant	Milton Wright	George W. Little
2nd Lieutenant	Eugene Myers	William Enos

Lee had been the captain of the original Company A while Gilbert had been his first lieutenant. Together the two companies mustered nearly 200 men and officers.[13]

As the men whose time was up prepared for home, they could reflect on the toll of their enlistment. Forty-one officers and men had been killed in battle. Forty others had died from disease. Over 230 had received wounds and 107 were missing or had been captured. An additional 178 men and officers had been discharged during the length of their service on account of disability.[14] Flavius Bellamy of Company A counted only 41 members present for duty of the 95 that had left Indiana three years ago.[15] It was a similar situation over in Company E. First Sergeant Matthews reported but 51 men on duty out of the 100 on the muster roll.[16]

On July 29, the men boarded the transport *Rebecca Bartow* for the trip to Washington. "Our friends came down to the wharf. Genl. Chapman gave us a farewell address. The parting was the saddest one I have ever witnessed, It was hard that any should be compelled to remain," lamented Sam Gilpin.[17] Veterans of over 50 battles and skirmishes, the six companies had been called upon to do the work of a full regiment of 12 companies. They had participated in the grand saber charges of Brandy Station, and fought stubbornly as dismounted troops at Gettysburg. They had been in dozens of nasty lesser known fights such as Middletown, Jack's Shop, Haw's Shop, and Ream's Station. They had served well and been a credit to the West in an army of Eastern men. Members of the regiment performed valuable duty as scouts and spies for the army of the Potomac. There were few other regiments in the Cavalry Corps which could boast of such a record.[18]

Disembarking in Washington, the men rested in Camp Stoneman, anticipating the final leg of the trip to Indiana. On August 8, they were shocked to see the two companies of the re-organized 3rd Indiana arrive in camp. "We did not expect to see them again when we left the Army of the Potomac, but the Surprise does not lessen the pleasure of the Meeting," wrote one homebound soldier.[19]

Why the sudden reunion? Just weeks before, Confederate general Jubal Early had been sent by Lee to the west, away from the Petersburg defenses. Lee hoped that a raid would force Grant to send troops north to try and contain Early. The

Confederate 2nd Corps under Early did more than Lee could have dared hoped for. Early turned north down the Shenandoah Valley, popping out near Winchester. Crossing the Potomac, Early swung east and threatened the depleted defenses of Washington, literally getting to the northern limits of the city before returning to the Winchester vicinity. His cavalry had gone all the way to Chambersburg, Pennsylvania, and burned the town in retribution for the burning of Staunton, Virginia, and the Virginia Military Institute buildings by Union troops earlier in the summer.[20]

The ineptitude of the Union commanders in the Shenandoah Valley ended Grant's patience with them. Grant sent Philip Sheridan to the Valley to assess the situation and to take command of all forces there. Sheridan realized he needed cavalry and asked for the 1st Division. Soon thereafter, the 3rd Division of the Cavalry Corps was also sent, traveling through Washington on the way. The impromptu reunion was a result of these changes.[21]

For the short timers, however, the next 10 days in camp were monotonous and tiresome. To kill time, the men visited other camps, saw the sights of Washington one last time, and discussed the endless rounds of rumors that inevitably cropped up when soldiers were idle. On August, 21, the men left the capital the same way they had arrived three years ago—loaded in dirty livestock rail cars bound for Baltimore. "A happy set of fellows, [even] if we do ride on hog cars," exclaimed one happy Hoosier.[22] The next day, August 22, the men left Baltimore around 4:00 p.m. Traveling throughout the night, they went through Pittsburgh at noon the next day before arriving in Indianapolis on August 24.[23]

The men and officers were met with great enthusiasm, and a reception was held on the statehouse grounds. Speeches were given and toasts made. Surgeon Elias Beck was called upon to answer for the regiment, and finally, the men were allowed to go home.[24]

Back in Virginia, men of the new squadron learned their role would be different from their previous service. Too small to serve as a cohesive combat unit within a brigade, the companies were to be used as headquarters escorts. Their jobs would vary from day to day. Carrying orders to the various commands would take up a large part of their time. In battle, they were to protect the commander and, if needed, be a ready reserve.

The men of Company B, the smaller of the two, were pleased to be assigned to the headquarters of none other than the newly minted Brigadier General George Chapman. Company A was on detached duty until August 27 when they were officially assigned as escort for Major General James Wilson, division commander.[25] They also received welcomed new armament. The men finally received the seven shot Spencer carbine.[26] Newly armed, reorganized, and with a new mission, the members of the squadron left Washington in the evening of August 12 and, after a leisurely ride, joined their new command around noon on August 17.[27]

Sheridan's arrival in the Shenandoah Valley plus the transfer of cavalry with him now gave the Union horsemen a greater than three to one advantage over the Confederate cavalry of Early. In addition, nearly all were armed with the superior Spencer carbine. Sheridan had three corps of infantry versus Early's lone division, though the Confederate commander had received some small reinforcement. The Union troops had every confidence that they were up to the task of eliminating Early's army. Man for man, Sheridan wielded a very potent weapon.

The Shenandoah Valley was a far cry from the humid, hot, and depressing landscape around the besieged city of Petersburg. The Valley was lush with fields of corn and other grains. The mountains of the Blue Ridge cooled the air at night, and the men and horses greatly appreciated the change of climate. Part of their re-acclimation to the Shenandoah Valley, however, was a heightened awareness of Confederate partisans and bushwhackers. Partisans were members of the Confederate army who were civilians by day and soldiers by night. Capture by them meant a trip to a Confederate prison camp. Bushwhackers were a law unto themselves with no military allegiance. There was no mercy asked for or given with them. Both groups were dangerous and deadly.

The best organized and disciplined partisan unit served under Confederate colonel John S. Mosby. His ability to materialize out of thin air in large force had the Union command being very cautious in sending messages between units. This was forcefully brought home to the Hoosiers when, on August 18, the entirety of Company A was sent to Martinsburg just to deliver a message.[28] Over the next two days, the company rode to Harpers Ferry via Williamsport and joined the division along the Winchester and Harpers Ferry Railroad about six miles past Charlestown. With little rest, the men encamped on the extreme left of the line where they skirmished with Rebels for about an hour the next morning. Two days later, the company was sent out on a scout to find the Confederate lines, meeting rebel pickets about two miles out. After a short fight, the men withdrew.[29]

The shift to the Valley and the strenuous nature of their recent service seemed to have strained the relationship between Chapman and Wilson. On August 22, Wilson ordered Chapman to send out small scouting parties. Apparently, the order was poorly written or Chapman took some exception to its meaning. As a newly promoted general, perhaps he felt the right to question the order. He replied to the division commander that he did not understand what was required of his brigade. Wilson icily replied, "I have just sent a staff officer to you with an order to send out three small scouting parties. This means of communication was taken to prevent delay. Instead of complying with the order you profess to misunderstand it, and ask for definite instructions. Such a course is not calculated to advance the interests of the service or to smooth matters in your command. You will, therefore, proceed at once to execute this order, ten to fifteen men in each party, directed to observe the movements of the enemy now advancing on the Charlestown pike. Acknowledge the receipt of this, time when received, and when the parties are started."[30] It is assumed Chapman followed the orders to the letter.

Chapter 14. July 13, 1864–September 25, 1864

On August 25, the 3rd Division moved out and attacked the Confederates at Kearneysville. Chapman's brigade advanced and dismounted as the rest of the division charged. The enemy gave way with the loss of 60 men. For the escorts, it had been a bloody day. Two veterans, William Vails and George Lee of Company A, had been wounded in the fighting.[31]

Four prisoners captured during the fighting claimed that Early was contemplating another crossing of the Potomac and threaten Washington once again. As a precaution, Sheridan ordered Wilson to take the 3rd Division across the river at Harpers Ferry and to proceed southeast to Sharpsburg. For the next three days, the men of the 3rd Division were engaged with watching the various river crossings. While the men were busy watching the river, General Wilson made an addition to his division staff. Captain Charles W. Lee was reassigned as the division Provost Marshal, leaving the command of Company A to First Lieutenant Milton Wright.[32]

On September 3, the men recrossed the Potomac and rode to Berryville where they began construction of breastworks. The 3rd Division spread out to protect the flanks of the new line, and the escorts rested in their respective camps until September 7 when the division was sent out on a scout toward Winchester. After making contact with Confederate pickets at Opequon Creek, the Union cavalry pushed the retreating rebels west until they reached the main line of infantry just two miles from Winchester. Returning to Berryville, the men went into camp for the next 10 days.[33] On September 15, General Chapman and 400 men from the 2nd Brigade made a scout to the east, hoping to capture Mosby. After splitting his force, Chapman took the main body to Paris where enemy horsemen began to show themselves. As the men marched, the rebels shadowed them at a safe distance. Upon reaching Snickersville, he sent a squadron to Snicker's Gap to rendezvous with the detached squadron. There, Mosby's men hit the isolated squadrons and disappeared as Chapman came up with the main force. All Chapman had for the scout was five men captured and 40 horses.[34]

For the men of the 3rd Indiana, it seemed inevitable that a lull in action produced a flurry of letters to Indiana. Captain Lee, as senior captain, wrote to the governor on September 12 about their plight. With only two companies and a total complement of 186 men, Lee asked Morton for permission to raise four more companies. No doubt remembering that Major George Chapman had become Colonel George Chapman while in command of six companies, Lee showed his hand by complaining to the governor that "the officers have little prospect of advancement" under the current situation.[35] In truth, Lee was overstating his strength. Company A had several original members of the regiment on their rolls who were in Confederate prisons, as did Company B. Also, as Lee well knew, the recruits of 1861 and 1862 would be mustered out as they reached the end of their three year enlistments, and the strength of the squadron would dwindle even further.[36]

Rest and camp came to an end as Sheridan made the decision to attack Early's forces in Winchester. He had received information that Early had split his forces.

In addition, Early had sent 3,000 men to reinforce Lee in Petersburg. If he moved quickly, he would be able to attack and defeat his enemy in detail. His battle plan was to bring the two divisions of cavalry from their northeastern encampments to hold one half of the Confederate army north of Winchester while Sheridan would take his infantry and attack Winchester and the other half of Early's army from the east. The 3rd Division was assigned to secure the crossings of the Opequon Creek until the infantry were across, then swing south and west with the goal of reaching the Valley Turnpike and cut off Early's retreat route.

At first light of September 19, the 3rd Division splashed across the wide Opequon Creek and drove in the Confederate pickets. The men dismounted and waited for the trailing infantry to arrive. Unfortunately, Sheridan's plan did not take into full consideration the road's route through a narrow defile called the Berryville Canyon. Infantry and artillery were packed into the canyon making rapid movement impossible. Sensing the danger, Early sent word for his troops to the north of Winchester to march rapidly back to the town to consolidate his forces. Finally, Union infantry came up, and Wilson's men remounted and moved south and west on the Milltown Pike. With luck, Wilson would be able to slip around the Confederate right and reach the Valley Pike. If they could accomplish this, they would in essence put the cork on the entrapment Sheridan had planned for Early, forcing the Confederate to surrender or have his army destroyed.

Fighting dismounted, the 3rd Division repeatedly tried to flank the Confederate army. George Chapman had ridden out to the firing line to ascertain the enemy position. Here his luck ran out. Company B members rushed toward a reeling Chapman when he was hit. Fortunately, Chapman had been hit on the belt buckle and badly bruised, enough to force him to cede command to Colonel William Wells.[37] In a great deal of pain, Chapman refused to leave the field, however.[38]

To the north, Early had committed his last reserves and by late afternoon the situation was grim for the Confederate commander. The initial fighting had gone well for the rebels, but the Union infantry kept coming. The final attack of the day did the trick. As the Union infantry made one final push to dislodge the Confederates, five brigades of blue clad cavalry formed boot to boot north of Winchester and unleashed a thunderous attack that broke the Confederate line. Rebel troops ran for their lives down the Valley Pike and through Winchester. Hearing the fighting crescendo, Wilson again tried to push through to the Pike and finally reached their objective but too late to materially change the outcome. Still, the rebel army was scattered, and the 3rd Division fell into pursuit. Wilson reported "with my staff and escort of Indiana troopers we were in the midst of it, firing and slashing right and left wherever we could see a rebel soldier."[39] At one point during the pursuit, a Union battery wheeled into position and Company A was ordered into support of the cannon until other troops could arrive. "It seemed that we were a target for several batteries" but their aim was too high and no one was hit in the barrage, remembered one Hoosier.[40]

Chapter 14. July 13, 1864–September 25, 1864

As the exhausted men of the escorts reported to headquarters that night, their duties were not done. Orders were sent out for the next day; men separated from their commands had to be sorted out and stragglers collected and returned to their regiments. A quick count, however, revealed losses in Company A. They had, indeed, been "in the midst of them" with Frederick Strouce wounded in the left leg, Edward English wounded, and Corporal Reuben Clements dead.[41]

Even as the men rested, Sheridan was devising a new plan to capture or destroy the enemy. He intended to pursue the decimated Rebel army and hammer it again. This might be a harder task than Winchester, however, as the unique geography of the Valley would play an important role. The Confederate retreat had stopped on the rugged heights of Fisher's Hill.

Twenty miles south of Winchester, the Massanutten Mountain splits the Shenandoah Valley north and south with the narrower Page Valley to the south. Overnight, Early's desperate men had retreated up the Valley Pike to Fisher's Hill, just south of Strasburg in the larger Shenandoah Valley. This geological oddity ran from the Massanutten on the south to North Mountain to the north, effectively blocking easy access to the Upper Valley. The formidable ridge was the only natural feature for fifty miles or more where a force could stop an attacker. As the Union troops moved south toward Fisher's Hill, the 3rd Division was ordered to Front Royal and the entrance to the Page Valley. Wilson was expected to prevent Early from slipping to his right and heading south up the smaller valley.

The men reached Front Royal after skirmishing with Confederate cavalry just north of the village, and Wilson was able to drive the rebels across the north branch of the Shenandoah River. At daybreak of September 21, Wilson attacked once again, behind a shroud of gray fog. Pushing the Confederates across the south branch of the Shenandoah, the men slowly pressed the attack until stalling at Gooney Creek, about six miles south of Front Royal.[42] Here the 3rd Division was reinforced by the 1st Division. The plan for the next day was for the 3rd Division to continue its attack up the Page Valley while the 1st Division would come up the north shore of the south fork, recross and come in on the Confederate left.

There was new urgency to this movement of the cavalry as Sheridan envisioned a crushing blow to the Confederates on Fisher's Hill. He needed his cavalry to push up the Page Valley, cross over the Massanutten via the New Market Gap, and try once again to bottle up Early's forces with cavalry to the west, North Mountain to the north, Massanutten Mountain to the south and Sheridan's army to the east. The cavalry was ordered to execute their part of the plan with all speed.

At daybreak of September 22, the Union cavalry began their advance on rebel forces at Gooney Run only to find them gone. The two divisions began an immediate pursuit, hopeful that they could reach Luray quickly and cut across the Massanutten. Several miles south, however, that hope was shattered when they found the Confederates in a strong position along a narrow gorge of the Overall Creek near the village of Milford.[43] Sitting behind stumps and logs, the rebels' flanks rested on the Blue Ridge Mountains and the south fork of the Shenandoah River. Wilson's 3rd Division, leading the march that day, immediately dismounted and began an assault on the position. Carbine and rifle fire snapped through the air as the two lines became engaged. Union artillery were swung into place to reply to Confederate cannon located on a knoll further beyond the rebel line. General Alfred Torbert had accompanied the 1st Division and was in overall command. After a few half-hearted attempts to dislodge the rebels, he turned back north toward Front Royal.[44] On September 23, they continued their retrograde movement to Front Royal where they heard of Sheridan's victory at Fisher's Hill.

Torbert and his men had been unaware of what was happening at Fisher's Hill. As the cavalry was pulling back from Overall Creek, over at Fisher's Hill, Sheridan had found a way around the Confederate left flank and launched a surprise attack that demoralized and unhinged the rebel line. The fleeing Confederates ran for miles as the Union infantry tried to catch them. Sheridan, anxious to hear of Torbert's arrival in New Market, kept pushing the pursuit. It was now vital for Torbert to about face, break through the bottleneck at Overall Creek to Luray, through the New Market Gap and block the way to the Upper Valley as rapidly as possible. Perhaps they could still crush Early's army once and for all.

The men returned to Overall Creek only to find the Confederates gone.[45] Torbert, realizing his need for speed, sent a message to Sheridan to let him know the way was now open for the cavalry to hurry south. Three men from the escort were detached to deliver the message—Robert Gray, a man named Ward, and William Watlington. After a hasty lunch, they set out at a brisk pace.[46]

Reaching Strasburg, they learned that the general was further up the Valley near Woodstock. Now on the smooth paved Valley Pike, they pushed their mounts hard. At the foot of Fisher's Hill, Gray and Watlington were forced to stop and rest their horses. Ward continued to Woodstock with the message. After resting, the men fell back slowly to Strasburg where they camped for the night with a squad of infantry and four members of their own division.[47]

Intent on returning to their units, the seven cavalrymen started out the next morning only to find that the division had moved. Now alone in enemy territory in a locale known to be crawling with Mosby's men as well as other less savory bands, the men continued riding up the Page Valley in hopes of overtaking the column. Pushing their horses to the limit, they reached an old encampment where several abandoned horses wondered about.

Watlington spotted one that appeared to be in better shape than his own and quickly switched his equipment to the new mount which promptly broke down within two miles. He encouraged the others to move on while he would follow on foot. Pulling his saddle off of the broken down horse, he carried all of his equipment to an old sinkhole and dropped everything in except his revolver and carbine. Up ahead, he heard shots. He later learned that Gray and the other cavalrymen had been captured by Confederates and were marched off to prison. After a

William Watlington did not join the regiment until mid-1863. He was an avid journaler, and his diaries formed the basis for numerous versions of his unpublished memoirs years later (Indiana State Library).

harrowing march both day and night, Watlington finally caught up to the division at Luray.⁴⁸

The division was already pulling out when Watlington arrived. Marching up the winding road through New Market Gap, the men arrived at New Market only to learn that their dawdling in the Page Valley had, once again, let Early slip away. His now tiny army was south and east at Brown's Gap in the Blue Ridge Mountains, 30 miles southeast of Charlottesville. There, he licked his wounds and gathered his far flung remnants of an army and awaited reinforcements.⁴⁹

For General George Chapman, the days following his injury had been uncomfortable. Upon arrival at New Market, Chapman took leave of the brigade and Company B for a medical leave. The extent of his injury could be questioned. The commander at Harpers Ferry reported Chapman's travel through the town to none other than Secretary of War Edwin Stanton. "General Chapman rode on horse-back ninety miles. His wound is not very serious." Perhaps the injury was an excuse to use his rank and take a break from fighting, Wilson, and the strain of command.⁵⁰ For whatever reason, Chapman took medical leave to "recuperate."

Early's retreat had been hasty and a great deal of supplies had been abandoned. On September 26, the 3rd Division marched to Staunton where a large Confederate supply depot was found. Food and other supplies were distributed to the troops, and what could not be carried was destroyed.⁵¹ Of particular interest to the men of the 3rd Indiana were supplies of a particularly unmilitary nature. As one gleeful Hoosier remarked, "Applejack and Tobacco—both of the best quality—were among the luxuries enjoyed by the boys."⁵² Not found, however, was forage for the horses, and the next day details were sent out to gather grain from the surrounding area. After returning to camp, they were attacked by Confederate forces, and a lively skirmish commenced. The nature of the fight was such that several men of the regiment had horses shot out from under them as they carried messages to and from division headquarters.⁵³

Sheridan viewed the campaign as complete. He had ended the threat to Washington that Early had posed, and it was now time to execute the rest of his orders—to eliminate the Shenandoah Valley as a source of supply for the Confederate army. Though Grant wanted him to march east to Petersburg and threaten Lee's rear, Sheridan convinced his commander to let him proceed with his original orders: "If the war is to last another year, we want the Shenandoah Valley to remain a barren waste."⁵⁴ With fall harvest just completed, he would move down the Valley to Winchester and destroy the capacity of the Valley to feed the rebel cause.

From Staunton, the cavalry spread across the Valley with the 3rd Division on the Back Road next to North Mountain and the 1st Division traveling on the Valley Pike, next to Massanutten Mountain. The 2nd Division was ordered to the Page Valley with the same orders. As Sheridan reported to Grant, "I will go on and clean out the Valley."⁵⁵ The Burning was about to commence.

Over the next 10 days, Sheridan, by his own count, burned over 2,000 barns filled with wheat, hay and farming implements. Seventy mills, similarly stocked with wheat and flour, were destroyed. Before his army were driven 4,000 head of stock and at least 3,000 sheep had been killed to feed his men. Horses and mules were confiscated. Down the Valley and across the Valley, it was the same thing. Cavalrymen rode up to a farm with torches in hand and set structures ablaze. After staying long enough to be sure the fire would consume everything, they would ride off and repeat the act once again. Thorough in their business, the Union troops left a broad path of destruction in their wake. Spreading out across the fifteen miles between the Allegheny Mountains to the north and the Massanutten Mountain ridge to the south, the entire Valley was smudged with the dirty dark smoke of the fires. Anything deemed of value to the Rebel cause went up in smoke.⁵⁶ In their wake families were left devastated, facing winter in just a few short weeks.

CHAPTER 15

September 26, 1864–December 31, 1864

Just before commencing The Burning, Sheridan had received orders on September 25 from Grant to recommend one of his cavalry commanders to take over leadership of General William Sherman's horsemen in Georgia. Sheridan had a decision to make. Grant had suggested Torbert or Wilson but left the decision to Sheridan. Sheridan could have sent Torbert, but he had no other officer ready to assume overall command of his cavalry. The 3rd Division's performance had been sporadic, at best, under Wilson's leadership. In his first engagement as division commander, he had maneuvered the unit into isolation and near disaster while his performance in the July raid had nearly destroyed the effectiveness of his command. His leadership thus far in the Valley had been creditable, but uninspired. Given the above, Sheridan considered Wilson the most expendable, and on October 1, Wilson left for Georgia.[1]

Sheridan now needed a new commander for the 3rd Division, one that could inspire confidence and be the kind of aggressive commander that Sheridan coveted. He did not have to look very far. As Wilson left, Brigadier General George A. Custer was named as his replacement. Currently, he was only temporarily in command of the 2nd Division.[2]

Quite a bit had happened to young George Custer since the 3rd Indiana met him 18 months before. At the time, he was a captain on the staff of the Cavalry Corps' commander. Just weeks after accompanying Company E on the secret mission to the Northern Neck, Custer had been promoted to Brigadier General over literally hundreds of other officers. Now barely 25 years old, this 1860 West Point graduate now commanded a division. His leadership of the 1st Brigade of the 1st Division—better known as the Michigan Brigade—had gained him many laurels. Much would be expected of him in his new role. For the men of the 3rd Indiana assigned to his headquarters, it was like welcoming an old friend. They knew and liked Custer, and he knew them. His reputation for aggressiveness and action would mean that the men could expect to be near where the fighting was the heaviest.

As the Union cavalry slowly moved north, they were shadowed by a new adversary. Thomas Rosser's Laurel Brigade of Confederate cavalry had arrived from Lee's army at Petersburg.[3] A classmate of Custer at West Point, Rosser was known as a man with swagger, and some wag began calling him the "Savior of the Valley"—a title he did not reject.[4] Many of his men came from the area and knew the families

151

living there. Their rage could only be imagined as they watched their beloved Valley literally go up in smoke.

Early's infantry were not able to stop the fast moving Union horsemen so he sent out his own cavalry to exact vengeance on the marauders. He now had about 2,200 cavalry and divided them into two small divisions, Rosser commanding the larger one. The wrath of the Virginians was released on any hapless northern soldier wherever found. In their rage, quarter was not asked for nor given. Throughout the Valley, deprivations and murder occurred regularly. Confederate soldiers left behind over the past several weeks had fled to the mountains, often joining bushwhacker gangs. Emboldened by the retreat of the boys in blue, they descended from the mountains to gobble up stragglers.[5]

George Armstrong Custer graduated last in his West Point class of 1860. Only 23 years old and a captain when the 3rd Indiana first met him, in June 1863, he was leapfrogged over hundreds of senior officers and appointed a brigadier general of volunteers. When Wilson was sent West in 1864, Custer assumed command of the 3rd Division (Library of Congress).

On October 7, Rosser had some initial success against the marauding blue horsemen. A wagon train was attacked, and Rosser boasted of capturing several wagons and forges, two of which belonged to the 3rd Division. The triumph may not have been as heroic as the Confederates wanted to believe. The attack had been made on the rear of the Union column through a mass of refugees travelling north. Many were Dunkards, German speaking men and women who eschewed warfare. Having seen their livestock and foodstuffs destroyed by the harsh orders of Sheridan, many hoped to travel to Pennsylvania to live through the winter with other members of the sect. One Hoosier sympathized with these unfortunates: "To these poor wretches the rebels seemed to show no mercy."[6]

Within this climate of chaos and danger, the men of the 3rd Indiana were kept

Chapter 15. September 26, 1864–December 31, 1864

busy delivering messages. By the evening of October 8, Custer and his escort had encamped south of Fisher's Hill along the north bank of Tumbling Run. Sheridan was furious with Torbert and the cavalry's seeming inability to deal with the harassing Confederate horsemen. The attack on the 7th was the last straw. Calling Torbert in for a proper dressing down, he ordered his cavalry commander to turn around and whip the Confederates or be whipped himself.[7] Sheridan also told Torbert that he would be personally observing the action from a nearby hill. Orders were sent to the 1st and 3rd Divisions. Be ready for action at 6:00 a.m. tomorrow.

Rosser's division of approximately 1,400 men had been following Custer on the Back Road, at the foot of North Mountain.[8] Custer, bright and early the next morning, retraced his steps to just north of Tom's Brook. Across the meandering creek he could see Rosser's division spread out over Coffman's Hill. Custer's division covered a broad plateau less than a mile north of the Confederate position. As the men of Company A stood by, their division commander was about to enact one of the most unusual events of the war.

Custer loved a spectacle and was a romantic at heart. As he examined his enemy across the way, he saw a group of enemy officers doing the same thing. Among them, he recognized the tall figure of his West Point classmate—Rosser. Moved by the moment, Custer cantered forward, removed his broad brimmed hat and made a wide sweeping bow to his foe. Rosser, seeing the gesture, rode forward and returned the tribute.[9] Having now saluted his adversary, Rosser was supposed to have said, "Do you see that man in front with the long hair? Well, that's Custer, and we must bust him up to-day."[10]

That would be a tall order for the Confederates. Custer had over 2,600 men scattered out below Coffman's Hill double Rosser's force.[11] In addition, Rosser had not selected this site for battle, but had merely bivouacked in anticipation of a continuing chase of the Union cavalry in the morning. His division was also separated from the tiny 800-man division over at the Valley Pike by two or three miles with only videttes connecting the two commands. The morning was shaping up as unlikely to have Custer "busted up."

Custer sent out his Hoosier messengers to the 1st Brigade with orders to begin the attack. At present, he kept the 2nd Brigade in reserve, ready to exploit any break in the rebel line. As skirmishers advanced, dismounted Confederates peppered them from the opposite bank of the creek. Custer rode back and forth across the face of the defending rebels, his headquarters flag streaming behind him, followed by his stalwart escorts of Company A. As the battle settled into desultory fighting across the creek, Custer was informed of a way around the left flank that would enable him to surprise the enemy. Ordering two regiments of Wells' 2nd Brigade to the left, he continued to distract Rosser with his riding back and forth. He also formed the remaining two regiments of Wells' brigade in column on the Back Road itself.[12] Meanwhile, Custer's artillery had been playing havoc with their counterparts, forcing them to withdraw further up Coffman's Hill. It would prove to be a pivotal move.

The flanking attack came in on the Confederate left flank, thundering up the western slope of Coffman's Hill, right at the recently re-positioned artillery. As the attack hit home, the rest of Custer's division began an assault. On the Confederate right, a brigade of the 1st Division had taken a right turn and was coming down on the opposite flank of the gray clad line. The two regiments on the Back Road galloped up the road and hit the Confederate line. Assaulted on both flanks, the rebel line disintegrated as men ran for their horses and their lives. Custer grabbed a battle flag and led his staff and Hoosier escorts into the fray.[13]

The saber wielding Union cavalrymen of the 3rd Division had the upper hand in this type of warfare. Most of their adversary had discarded their sabers long ago. Confronting literally thousands of blue horsemen swinging and slashing sabers was horrifying. The retreat became a rout as the running fight went on for miles all across the Valley. The Confederates finally stopped running at Columbia Furnace, 12 miles away. Only darkness and fatigue kept the Union horsemen from completely annihilating Rosser's command. Over on the Valley Pike, it had been worse. Confederate general Lunsford Lomax's tiny 800-man division was no match for the 1st Division. On better roads, Lomax's men were able to run 20 miles through Woodstock all the way to Early's army.[14]

By the end of the day, over 200 Confederates had been killed, wounded or captured.[15] A significant number never reported back. Tired of the war, worried about their homes and families, they simply "dropped out" of the Confederate army and headed home. Rosser and Lomax lost all of their artillery, wagons, supplies, ambulances, and spare ammunition. Both divisions had been scattered in every direction. To the supreme satisfaction of the men of the 3rd Division, the artillery captured on Coffman's Hill were the same six guns spiked and left by the division in the chaos of Ream's Station, nearly three months before.[16] Torbert's cavalry had indeed, whipped the rebels.

Custer's escort had been augmented by the arrival of Company B at division headquarters, and both companies were led into battle by First Lieutenant Benjamin F. Gilbert of Company B.[17] As prisoners were collected, Captain Charles Lee, division provost marshal, depended on the two companies to provide guards until the captives were marched north to prison. Finally able to return to camp, the men were treated to the scene of their diminutive commander wearing a clownishly large gray coat of a Confederate general, marching around headquarters to the merriment of all. Captured in the Confederate wagon train was Rosser's best dress uniform, and Custer could not resist the opportunity to parade his prize around camp.[18]

After resting from their "race" up and down the Valley, the Union withdrawal moved slowly up past Strasburg, reaching Cedar Creek the next day. The 3rd Indiana and the rest of the division established camp on the north bank of the stream. Even as the men marched during October 10, Sheridan's orders of destruction continued to be carried out. Sheridan was determined that nothing useful would be left

Chapter 15. September 26, 1864–December 31, 1864

to the Confederates, and the plumes of smoke marking his troops' progress affirmed this desire.

Now established near his supply line, Sheridan was convinced that Early presented no threat to his army, Washington or anywhere else. He allowed the army to camp haphazardly. The position at Cedar Creek left the army vulnerable to attack as divisions encamped on both sides of the waterway. The creek meandered through the area and hills and steep banks made it a bad defensive position. Several units did not bother to build breastworks.[19]

Early, however, had been reinforced from the dangerously thin lines of Petersburg—Kershaw's division once again entered the Valley. Still aware that his primary objective was to keep Sheridan from reinforcing Grant, Early had followed at a distance as the Union army moved north. His cavalry had been rallied, to an extent, and preceded him on his march. As he reoccupied Fisher's Hill, he was over 80 miles away from his supply base. The Burning had effectively removed any possibility that food could be secured between his army and the supplies far to the southwest. Early would have to attack soon or return to the Upper Valley for the winter.

The arrival at Cedar Creek began a period of relative calm for the 3rd Indiana. Regular camp life returned, and the men and horses could once more recover from a long period of campaigning. The fall chill reminded them that a cessation of fighting for the winter was not far off. Yet even in this inactivity there was danger as there was almost daily skirmishing with the bedraggled Confederate cavalry and the numerous guerrilla groups that infested the area.[20] On October 15, Sheridan left for Washington to confer with the army leadership as to his army's next assignment.[21]

Early was lurking, however, having moved up to Hupp's Hill where he could see the distribution of the Union camp. He sent a staff member to the top of Signal Knob on Massanutten Mountain for an even better view. What he saw was an army haphazardly camped with little signs of defensive works. Early made plans to attack, and a little before the chill dawn of October 19, his army sprang out of the early morning fog as if hell itself had loosed its denizens on earth. Screaming and swearing, the Confederates hit the Union left flank and started rolling the Union army up. The ominous sound of battle from the east brought the Union cavalry confirmation that a battle was underway. As the men hurriedly dressed and mounted, small units of rebel cavalry made spoiling attacks to try and hold the blue horsemen in their position.

Custer received orders to move to the army's center, and Hoosier messengers went galloping to the various units to inform them of the decision. They were to stabilize the line as well as throw out a skirmish line to collect demoralized infantry streaming away toward Winchester.[22] Arriving at his assigned post, he was ordered to leave three regiments and move the rest of his division to the right of the army where his men sat on their horses and endured artillery fire for over an hour.[23]

This shifting of Custer was precipitated by the continuing disintegration of the army. By 10:00 a.m., the Confederate army had occupied the Union camp. Men who had grimly marched through the devastation of The Burning came upon camps laden with supplies. Many of the Confederates had been marching and fighting for nearly 15 hours, and the temptation of this largess around them was too great. Hundreds of rebels fell out of the ranks and filled their empty bellies. Others found clothing to replace their own rags. Some lounged around the captured camp with the mistaken belief the battle had been won. The attack slowly ground to a halt, and an uneasy quiet settled across the landscape.

But the battle was decidedly not over. Sheridan had spent the night in Winchester and heard the artillery fire that morning. Realizing a battle was taking place, he put spurs to his horse and headed up the Valley Pike.[24] Almost immediately, he began meeting sullen, scared men who had been routed by the initial attack. Rallying his men, he gave them confidence to return. When he approached the battlefield, he was already formulating a counterattack.

As the infantry rallied and sorted into their units, Sheridan ordered Custer to move his division back to the extreme right flank of the army. As Early's men ate and lazed in the luxury of the Union camp, Sheridan reshuffled his lines and prepared for an attack of his own. By 4:00 p.m., Sheridan had performed a miracle. The demoralized and beaten army he met in the morning was now ready to deliver a decisive blow to their adversary. His plan was simple: he was going to attack the enemy in flank, roll up his lines and use the cavalry as shock troops to finish them off.

The attack hit the unprepared and somnolent Confederates in striking similarity to the morning attack they had used to such devastating effect on the Union troops. Winchester, Fisher's Hill, Tom's Brook—all had been the same: an attack on the flank and the rout of the Confederate army. Tired, ranks depleted, and sensing impending doom, the rebels broke. It was now the cavalry's moment to seal the victory.

On a level plain overlooking Cupp's Ford, Custer had arranged his division to support the attack of the infantry in the neighboring 19th Corps. As the 19th Corps' attack hit the Confederate line, it began to waver. Sensing the pivotal moment, Custer led his escort of Hoosiers to the head of the division and ordered the charge. To their right, the 1st Division joined in.

All military organization ceased to exist for the routed rebels. Escape was their only thought as they remembered those other battles in the past month and how they came out. As they ran, they heard the hoofbeats of Custer's men coming and heard the swish of sabers once more. For miles the Union horsemen pursued Early's broken army. "Our cavalry pushed on in tireless energy. Now and then a spirited charge through the ranks of the dismayed rebels and another battle flag would be added to the trophies of the day," remembered one exhilarated Hoosier.[25]

The breakdown of discipline and organization boggled the mind. More important militarily than the capture of flags was seizing military equipment. "Single horsemen were bringing in bands of stragglers, a rebel battery of several guns were trying to escape on a by-road was run down by one of the division escort, single

Chapter 15. September 26, 1864–December 31, 1864

handed, captured and brought back to the pike and sent to the rear," reported one Hoosier.[26] In his post action report, Custer claimed 45 pieces of artillery were captured by his division.[27] With the largess of prisoners and equipment, Captain Lee was organizing the captured troops into columns and starting them on their long march into captivity. The pursuit lasted into the night. When the men of the escort returned to their camp, they were bone tired. While constantly on the move and under fire, the Hoosiers had come through virtually unscathed. When the roll was called, Robert Terrell did not answer. His horse had been killed, and as he fell, he had broken his arm and injured his back before being taken prisoner.[28] The men slept, hoping that there was no movement contemplated for the morrow.

Sheridan had been embarrassed by the near debacle at Cedar Creek. That embarrassment turned into an intense desire to deal with Early and his troublesome rebels once and for all. At 11:00 a.m. the next morning, Custer led his division out on the Back Road to Fisher's Hill where several patrols were sent out. Their prey was graybacks, but for some men of the escort it was forage. At the foot of Little North Mountain, a supply of corn was discovered, and the Hoosiers filled their sacks, returning to headquarters around 9:00 p.m. The next day the men moved the headquarters camp a mile closer to the Valley Pike, just west of Middletown. Here they remained until November 9 when they moved back toward Kernstown and drew rations and clothing. Back in the saddle the next morning, the division moved once again, and Custer set up headquarters in the home of a Mr. Glass.[29]

This retrograde movement was made after determining Early and his shrunken army had retreated all the way up the Valley. Now 80 miles away, Early posed no threat to Sheridan. Still, Early was active. Mindful of his strategic objective of keeping Sheridan in the Valley, Early intended to keep track of his enemy. A small force of cavalry which had not been present at Cedar Creek traveled north to determine the disposition of the Union army. If they were found in an unfavorable location, Early might try to attack again.

When scouts reported the advance of this new threat, Custer sent units up both the Back Road and to the west on the Valley Pike. General George Chapman had recently rejoined the division and led the 2nd Brigade south on the Middle Road while Custer accompanied the 1st Brigade on the Back Road. The 1st Brigade pushed the gray cavalry for five miles, all the way back to Middletown and Cedar Creek. At that point, Custer sent out messengers to determine the progress of his smaller 2nd Brigade. Four men accompanied Lt. Benjamin Gilbert on a brisk two-mile ride to find Chapman, whose brigade was meeting stiff opposition. Custer recalled Chapman to the Back Road, and the division bivouacked for the night.[30]

The next morning, Custer again sent the 2nd Brigade to the Middle Road, and again, the 2nd Brigade met stout resistance. Around noon, the Confederates made a surprise flanking attack on Chapman's right, temporarily cutting off communications between the Middle Road and Custer. It may have been temporary, but for Isaac Romaine it was serious. Caught in the no man's land between Chapman and

Custer while delivering messages, he lost his horse and his hat and was nearly captured before entering friendly lines.[31]

Realizing that both brigades would be needed at the Middle Road, Custer rode to reinforce Chapman's attack, and the combined strength of the two brigades did the trick. Across the breadth of the Valley, the rebels had now been pushed back to beyond Cedar Creek. Assured that the Confederates would not follow, the men returned to their camp at the Glass residence. Given the time of year, all hoped that active campaigning would now draw to a close and winter quarters could be erected.

The Burning had done its work. Early was forced to curtail any attempt to close with his enemy and settled into his own winter quarters 100 miles south of Winchester, going so far as to disperse his artillery and cavalry so that they could find food. Only a small force was stationed at New Market on the off chance that Sheridan would undertake a winter campaign.[32] Now convinced that Early would not move, Sheridan sent most of his infantry to Grant and the siege lines around Petersburg. As the 3rd Indiana settled in and built winter quarters, they decided to do a little foraging. As old campaigners, they knew all the tricks and ruses. One group went out and was able to find "24 fat hogs" to supplement the rations drawn by the escort.[33]

But Early wasn't done. Even with his meager resources, he attempted to create enough concern in Sheridan's mind that he would not detach any further units to Grant. "Boots and saddles" blared through the division camp on November 21. Rumors were that they were to move back to the Army of the Potomac. Those ideas were quickly quashed when they were ordered back up the Valley. Early had sent a force of cavalry north to harass the army. The 2nd and 3rd Division was given the mission to intercept this force. The 2nd Division would lead the way up the Valley with Custer supporting the advance.

As the column reached Mt. Jackson, the 2nd Division was attacked as they crossed the turbulent and steep-banked Mill Creek. The attack included both cavalry and infantry, and the 2nd Division was forced to recross the waterway. Custer was ordered forward to cover the crossing. As the men dismounted they moved to the banks of Mill Creek to cover the returning 2nd Division. Suddenly, they were hit on the right flank by Confederates who had found a ford about a mile upstream. Custer was able to withstand this attack and, with the 2nd Division safely north of the creek, was now ready to withdraw.

William Watlington would remember this engagement vividly. The division adjutant, a Captain Seibert, had his horse killed as he crossed the creek. Not wanting to leave it for the rebels, he ordered Watlington to retrieve the equipment. Under fire, Watlington waded into the river, removed the saddle, remounted, and galloped north to catch up with the division. Now separated from the headquarters section, he rode several miles with the saddle draped uncomfortably across his lap. Finally catching up, he was able to deliver the saddle to the headquarters wagon that night in Woodstock.[34]

The blue clad horsemen continued their march north toward Winchester. At

Fisher's Hill, Custer sent a message ahead. The delivery had to be made across partisan and guerrilla infested territory. Members of the escort and a staff officer made a "flying trip and reached Winchester about noon having made a march of about 30 miles since morning."[35]

Returning to their camp around the Glass residence, the men continued to work on their winter quarters. Wagons went out to gather building supplies and hitching posts were erected. Thanksgiving came on November 24, and the men celebrated with a turkey dinner and hardtack. Campaigning for 1864 was finally at an end.[36]

Except it wasn't. On November 28, the men were jolted out of their warm cabins late in the day with orders to pack up camp and be ready to move at a moment's notice. Rosser and his grayback horsemen had slipped around the Union army to the north, traveling along the ridge of North Mountain, and attacked the Baltimore and Ohio Railroad. The enterprising rebels had torn up track and captured about 500 Union troops. With luck, Custer and his men would be able to intercept them near Moorfield.

Within a half hour, headquarters and staff were mounted and ready to ride. Moving out, the division marched rapidly up the Valley before beginning the long, cold, slippery climb up the mountain, reaching Moorfield on November 30. Scouts were sent out, but Rosser could not be found—he had made his escape southwest before their arrival. Disappointed and cold, the men marched back down the mountain, turned northeast and returned to their camps, arriving on December 2.[37]

As the weather turned colder, the war called once more. On the morning of December 19 the men were again in the saddle and again traveling back up the Valley on familiar roads. Near Fisher's Hill, the escort spotted two rebel scouts. Captain Lee and five members of Company A were ordered to capture the duo but were unable to close the gap, chasing them all the way to Woodstock. The division continued its march to Mt. Jackson where dispatches from Winchester caught up with Custer. After reading the messages, their boyish leader called for the men to huddle up and read them the news out loud. The first was about the total defeat of John B. Hood's Confederate army around Nashville, Tennessee. The second was a wild report that Jefferson Davis, President of the Confederacy, had made a second attempt to poison himself. "For this attempt three cheers were given to Jeff from the Third Division."[38]

Early the next morning, the men were shocked to hear the familiar, piercing Rebel Yell from their front and rushed to confront this surprise appearance by the Confederate cavalry. The attack pushed in the pickets, and a number of the division were captured. The blue clad horsemen promptly delivered their own charge and were able to recover a number of the short-lived captives. Having now determined the northern limit of the Confederate forces, Custer turned north and encamped at Woodstock.[39]

Guerrilla activity in this region was rampant. Messages sent to and from headquarters often required at least a company to ensure safe delivery. That evening, word was received from Union scouts that a rendezvous of 10–12 of these desperadoes was occurring that night. A squadron of cavalry along with William Watlington and Del Evans from the 3rd Indiana made an attempt to capture the band, but were only partially successful.[40] Two men were captured and the members of the 3rd Indiana delivered the duo to Captain Lee.[41]

Marching to Strasburg the next day, Custer thought it necessary to inform Sheridan of his imminent arrival. A staff officer and eight intrepid Hoosiers were detailed for the task. Again, the ride would be through the same dangerous territory as previous ones. "The message was one in haste, or at least we made it so, by arriving at Sheridan's headquarters in one hour and fifty minutes after leaving Strasburg, the distance being 18 miles." It took the smooth shod horses two weeks to recover from the racing ride over ice covered roads.[42]

The men once more settled into camp and the seemingly endless rounds of delivering messages and orders, collecting wood, and roll call. Christmas day brought a special gift for the 3rd Indiana. All members of the escort were issued a gill of whiskey in celebration of the holiday. Remembered one Hoosier, "He that did not want to drink, easily found someone to drink for him."[43]

By the end of December the supply of firewood became more severe. Woodcutting parties had to go further away to collect fuel. This was compounded by the need to provide guards to protect the woodcutters from guerrillas and partisans. Given this shortage, Custer decided to move the camp. Also, his beloved wife was expected soon, and the Glass residence just wouldn't meet her civilized standards of comfort and style.

On December 29, the men packed up and moved headquarters to the Ward residence, located two miles outside of Romney near Petticoat Gap. The house and outbuildings were more spacious and "for style, they were much superior to those left behind and the conveniences for both officers and men were much improved." Wood rails were plentiful and the location of the camp near Little North Mountain meant an ample supply of firewood.[44] The men turned once again to construction of winter quarters. To the men of the 3rd Indiana, they fervently hoped this would be the last winter camp they would have to build.

Chapter 16

January 1, 1865–April 7, 1865

January 1, 1865, found the 3rd Indiana scattered and the unit shrunken to a relative handful. Several members were still in Confederate hands in the prison camps at Andersonville and Belle Isle. Captain Charles Lee technically commanded the truncated unit with 85 men of Company A and approximately 35 men of Company B. Given Captain Lee's division staff duties as provost marshal, First Lieutenant Benjamin Gilbert ran the squadron.[1] Sometimes they were ordered to perform disagreeable duty.

On January 6, 1865, 12 men of the regiment were detailed to serve as Provost Guards for the execution of two deserters. The duo, from the 3rd New Jersey, had been captured by Union scouts outside of the lines. The scouts, in Confederate mufti, questioned the men who readily admitted that they were deserters, and even more damning, gave the ersatz Confederates a detailed description of Custer's camp. Brought in by the scouts, they underwent a swift court martial and were sentenced to death by firing squad.[2] The 12 men brushed their uniforms and cleaned their carbines in preparation for the onerous task of executioner. The sentence was to be carried out that morning of a cold, gray, blustery winter day.

The detail arrived at headquarters to learn that they would only serve as provost guards, not executioners. Men from the deserters' own regiment would be detailed to carry out the sentence. The relieved Hoosiers then loaded 12 carbines, six with blanks and six with live rounds. Once chambered, the man assigned the weapon would not know which type of round his carbine held. At 11:00 a.m., Custer, his staff, the escort, and the division band led the procession from camp. Behind them, a springboard wagon carried the condemned men along with their coffins. Six Hoosiers of the provost guard marched on each side of the wagon, carbines at the ready. Behind the wagon marched the 12 New Jersey men detailed as the execution squad. Finally, the entire 3rd New Jersey silently brought up the rear.[3]

About one half mile away, the rest of the division had been formed along two sides of a basin like field. As the procession filled the space between the two lines, the condemned men were led forward by the provost guard. The deserters were then seated on their coffins and blindfolded. About 12 paces away, the 12 New Jersey men took their position, backed by the 12 Hoosier provost guards, ready to complete the execution should the Jersey men waver. Behind them, Custer, his staff, and the rest of the 3rd Indiana escort took their place while the rest of the 3rd New Jersey formed behind them. When all were in their places, Captain Lee gave the command to fire. Carbines barked, and the two men fell into their coffins. The division marched back to their camps in silence.[4]

Death was also to touch the 3rd Indiana. Company B lieutenant George Rogers had been ill for some time and getting worse. His condition became so pronounced that he was no longer able to perform his duties and was discharged on January 16. Barely able to travel, he made his way home to Indiana only to die there two weeks later.[5]

Camp life continued, and the ubiquitous task of hauling wood continued as the men worked to create a more permanent appearance to the camp. A guard house was constructed as well as a photo gallery and stables for the horses. Morning roll call was never dispensed with, and the necessity of rolling out of a warm bunk to stand in ranks to answer "here" was a major irritant.[6]

Any length of time in camp also created the opportunity for another annoyance—the "Grand Review." On February 1, the men spruced up their uniforms, shined their boots, and cleaned their carbines for a review by General Sheridan. All three divisions participated. At 9:00 a.m., the men mounted and marched through Winchester to a review field on a part of the Winchester battlefield. For four hours, the men sat in their saddles, sabers at the shoulder in a cold raw wind waiting for their turn to pass in review. Finally, the order was given to move out. Feeling more like icicles than soldiers, the men passed the review and saluted. The only consolation for the entire affair was that their salute was returned by equally cold, nearly frozen officers.[7] After completing their pass by, the men of the 3rd Division regaled the decidedly Rebel citizens of Winchester with rousing choruses of "'Yankee Doodle' and 'John Brown's Body Lies A-mouldering in His Grave,'" much to the chagrin of the local population.[8]

Barely thawed out from the first one, the men had to endure another review on February 26. The weather had improved dramatically, and the veterans knew that a review at this time of year was a harbinger of a new campaign. The march by had a different problem from the frozen affair three weeks before. As the 3rd Division turned into line to follow their comrades of the 1st and 2nd Divisions, they found a mass of mud and mire churned up "into an extensive mortar bed" by the preceding horses. The men, horses, uniforms, saddle blankets, and arms were soon speckled with splattered mud.[9]

Returning to camp, the order was received to prepare to march. The men began to pack their gear and items were divided into "needed" and "not needed" piles as active campaigning was in the offing. Horses were brought up from the ambulance train, and the men of the 3rd Indiana—long known for their astute judgment of horseflesh—swapped out their horses as needed so that only the best remained with the escort. The rest were then sent to the unsuspecting dismounted men of the division.[10] Finally, each man drew 20 rounds of ammunition, and three days' rations consisting of hardtack and salt pork were distributed. As the men spent their last night in their comfortable bunks, all fervently hoped this campaign would be the last.[11]

The overall military situation in the East in late February 1865 had changed very little since the previous fall. Sheridan's successes in the Shenandoah Valley had eliminated a favorite invasion path for the Confederacy. More importantly, the region's capacity to supply the South had been gutted. Lee still clung tenaciously to Petersburg, but Grant had methodically spent the winter months extending his lines, forcing Lee to spread his dwindling army even thinner. Each casualty among the rebels could not be replaced. It seemed only a matter of time before Lee's thin lines and Grant's probing attacks would lead to a Union breakthrough. The end of the war in the East seemed tantalizingly close but, until Lee's army was defeated, the war would drag on.

Given the success of Sheridan's Army of the Shenandoah, Grant saw little reason for it to remain in the Valley, and orders were sent to proceed up the Valley to Charlottesville. The Virginia Central Railroad still functioned here, and food from farms to the west was still getting through. Destroying this vital supply line might force Lee out of Petersburg into the open countryside where Grant's superior numbers could deliver a final blow.[12]

For the men of the 3rd Indiana, it would be a bittersweet campaign. Brigadier General George Chapman would not be making the trip. A decision had been made to leave the 2nd Division, consisting of mostly dismounted men, in Winchester. Chapman's unenviable duty was to pacify Mosby and the several guerrilla bands still active in the Valley and to the east toward Washington.[13] In addition to saying goodbye to Chapman, Company B had seen 12 members of the unit discharged. These men had been some of the earliest recruits after the original muster, and their time was up. Receiving their pay, they settled accounts and headed to Indiana.[14]

Snow was falling on February 28 as the men mounted and started on their final trip up the Shenandoah Valley. The beautiful, lush farmland had been transformed into a wasteland. As they rode, they passed through familiar ground: Kernstown, Cedar Creek, Tom's Brook, Woodstock, and Mt. Jackson. The weather continued to be raw as previous days' rains and melting snow on the mountains swelled the numerous creeks they crossed. Passing through New Market and seven miles beyond to Lacey's Spring, the column stopped to make camp. As the halt was called, a party of Confederate cavalry dashed on the column. Responding quickly, a countercharge netted the Union horsemen several prisoners.

Confederate supply lines were so frayed that clothing rarely came through. Many of the captives wore parts of the Union uniform as a consequence. This did not sit well with the 3rd Indiana. They had heard the tales of Union prisoners ordered to strip off their uniforms and boots to clothe the poorly clad Confederates. They had also seen the dead and wounded stripped at Cedar Creek, and had, on more than one occasion, confused the blue uniforms worn by their enemy for friendly troops.

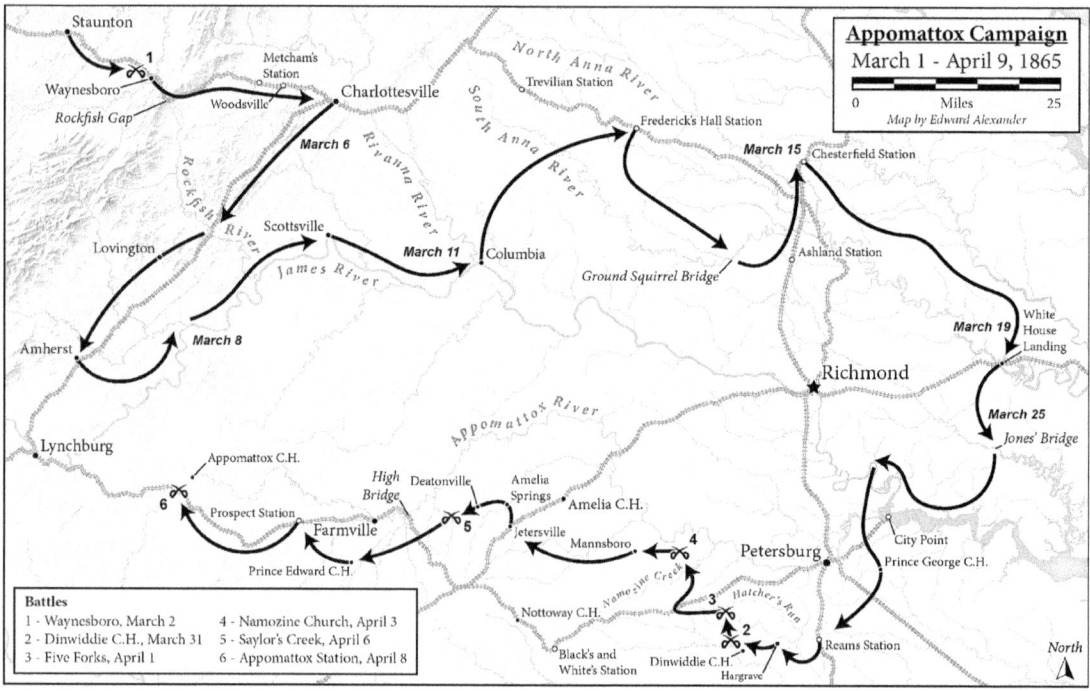

Custer was infuriated to see the captives in blue uniforms and ordered all prisoners to be "relieved" of any clothing that was Union blue. Stripped of their clothing, they marched away in the sleet of a late February evening, guarded by the escort.[15]

The following morning, the column ran into the remnants of Rosser's command. A sharp skirmish ensued, but the rebel horsemen were no match for the Union troops, no more than irritants to their march. The blue clad horsemen chased the rebels almost to Staunton. Content to let the Confederates go, the men made camp just short of town.

Early's army had spent the winter in and around Staunton. With a force barely numbering 1,500, Early had moved his men to the east to Waynesborough and awaited the arrival of Sheridan's army. On March 1, in a driving rain, Custer and his 1st Division led the column into Staunton. Upon their arrival around 10:00 a.m., the escort found no rebels and "nothing of consequent [sic] for us soldiers, except a few barrels of applejack, which our 'experts' had located after we had halted."[16]

Still raining, the division turned east and continued their search for Early's army. Contact was made near Waynesborough, and Custer immediately formed for the attack. Though he had been ordered not to bring on an engagement until the rest of the column came up, Custer knew his division alone outnumbered the Confederates. With nearly 10,000 cavalry in the entire command, he also knew that if his own 4,000 men couldn't handle it, many more were coming in from behind. Early had established himself in a good position, but his small numbers, low morale and weather did little to steel the miserable remnants of an army that had stormed to the very gates of Washington many months ago.

Custer took his time placing his command for the final attack. At 3:30 p.m., he dismounted two regiments on the left and massed the rest of the division mounted on Early's center. Upon a signal fired by the artillery, all would attack simultaneously. The gun boomed, and Custer's entire division charged pell-mell at the Confederates. Custer, with his Hoosiers close behind, led the mad dash and easily broke the enemy line. Now it was every rebel for himself, every Union man hell bent to capture the whole lot. It was reminiscent of Cedar Creek, Fisher's Hill, and Tom's Brook: "T'was exciting—the extreme—To the Blue, as they dashed here and there gathering battle flags, but to the Gray adding terror and dismay."[17]

Early's tiny army evaporated into the surrounding woods. Most were captured along with all of the army's supplies. Included in the spoils were two of Union general Crook's headquarter flags captured on the morning of Cedar Creek. In all, 17 Confederate battle flags were seized.[18] Collecting the wagons, artillery, caissons, captives, and arms, Custer moved through Rockfish Gap and camped on the east side of the Blue Ridge Mountains for the first time in many months.[19]

Early's army had been annihilated. What portion of it not captured was scattered to the point of irrelevance. Early had taken to the hills with a handful of men to elude capture, but little time was spent looking for him. In the big scheme of things, he represented little more than a common soldier.

Marching the next day to Charlottesville, their path resembled their summer raids of the previous year. Tracks were torn up and rendered useless. Supplies found at Metcham's Station and at Woodsville were destroyed, and the station houses burned. A railroad bridge over the Rivanna River was set ablaze. By 4:00 p.m., the men had arrived in Charlottesville and went into camp within sight of Thomas Jefferson's famous home, Monticello. For the next two days the army rested, and horses were shod for the long journey ahead of them.[20]

On March 6, 12 men from the escort joined a squad of 20 scouts as the lead element of Sheridan's advance. Moving southwest, they quickly reached Rockfish River and the bridge that spanned the waterway. A small group of rebel soldiers guarded the crossing but were quickly put to flight by the Union horsemen. After burning the structure, the detachment returned to headquarters. Here they found further evidence of the Hoosiers' prowess in foraging: "We found the boys well pleased with their camp as three barrels of applejack had been discovered not far off."[21]

No doubt awakening to swollen heads and dry mouths, the escort followed Custer through Lovington and proceeded to Amherst Court House. Now only 10 miles from Lynchburg, they anticipated moving south the next morning to engage in more railroad destruction. Foraging parties were sent out, and the Hoosiers scored again, discovering not only meat and flour, but shelled oats for the horses.[22]

They now faced the rain swollen James River and, after a search up and down its bank, could find no practicable way to cross. Two bridges had also been destroyed to slow the column's progress.[23] If Sheridan was to rejoin Grant at Petersburg, they would have to take Lynchburg and patiently wait for the river to recede. Once across, he still had 90 miles to cover before reaching Grant's lines. In typical daring fashion, the diminutive Irishman took a more aggressive approach. He would abandon the attack on Lynchburg and move north, paralleling the James River until the waterway made an easterly right turn near Lovington. From there, he would circle around Petersburg to rejoin Grant from the east. Sheridan sensed that the final act of the war was in play at Petersburg, and he did not intend to be left out sitting on a riverbank waiting for the water to recede.

Over the next several days the column retraced their steps to Lovington, then to Scottsville and finally turn east on March 11, arriving in Columbia. The rains of the past few days and bad road conditions forced Sheridan to stop and rest his troops and mounts. Only 40 miles from Richmond, the men and horses would need all of their stamina for the final dash to Grant.[24] Additional horses would be needed as the hard campaigning was taking a toll on the mounts. Squads of men were sent out to confiscate horses and mules.

A detail of the 3rd Indiana had had little luck in their hunt for horses as the countryside had been warned of the column's approach, and the animals and foodstuffs had been carefully hidden. Reining up in front of a commodious plantation home, the men had reason to be hopeful. A search of the barn revealed several of the stalls had been recently inhabited. Approaching the seemingly abandoned house, a couple of men walked through the front door. Thrown across the back of a chair was the gray uniform of a general officer—coat, pants, and vest. The men quickly retreated and called to the rest of the detail. Reinforced, the men re-entered the structure and found three women and a slave boy hiding in a back room.

The women taunted the blue-clad soldiers with dire predictions of what the hastily departed General would do to them and their comrades. A thorough search of the house turned up nothing, and the men had to be content with the uniform, if not the personage, of a rebel general as souvenirs.[25] As they left the house, the slave boy was questioned again, and he claimed to know nothing about horses or mules. Not satisfied with this answer, the men threw a halter over a limb and placed the other end around the youth's neck. Now faced with life or death, the boy admitted that there were several horses in a nearby ravine. The men returned to camp with a total of 12 mules and horses, one pair of pants, one coat, and one vest.[26]

The column was now 30 miles northwest of Richmond. It was time to turn east. Cutting southeast to Beaver Dam Station, the men found themselves on familiar ground. Crossing the South Anna River at Ground Squirrel Bridge, they realized that they had used this ford twice before—Kilpatrick's Raid and during Sheridan's Raid the previous summer.

At Frederick's Hall station a telegrapher with Custer's division intercepted a telegram. The message had been sent by Early to Lee informing the latter that he had assembled a force of 200 men and meant to attack Custer's division. Dispatches were sent out as the Hoosiers spread the news of Early's presence. It wasn't long before the Confederates were found and immediately attacked. Several were captured, and Early, with a small group of officers, again escaped and fled toward Richmond. Despite being pursued by the Union cavalry, Early made it to the Confederate capital.[27]

Scouts brought word that Confederate troops from Richmond were marching south to intercept the column. With this information, Sheridan elected to turn north once more and cross the North Anna River and then proceed to Chesterfield Station, arriving there on March 15.[28] Over the next three days, the army marched east, impeded only by the region's peculiar mud that, thoroughly churned by thousands of horses, created giant rolls of red clay as much as a foot in diameter. The horses had to "high step" the obstacles, tiring both man and beast. On March 19, the horsemen crossed the Pamunkey River and made contact with Union forces. They had arrived back in the east once again. They camped at White House Landing and drew rations for the first time since leaving Winchester three weeks before.[29] In between the men had lived off of the land and "at times some irregularities would happen, making a feast at the one and a fast at the other, but coming out about even in the end."[30]

Foraging habits were hard to break however, for on the same day as their arrival at White House Landing, a group of Hoosiers voluntarily joined a squad out looking for food and forage. Not familiar with the military situation of the area, the men were attacked by a squad of Confederates, and several were captured including two members of Company A and Andrew Siebenthal of Company B.[31]

For nearly a week the men and horses rested and recruited from the long ride. Messages had to be delivered and guard kept, but little of consequence occurred until March 24 when the men were mustered and paid for the six months ending January 1865. Flush with six months' pay, the men had little time to spend the largess as the column headed out the next day. They headed south as they continued their circumnavigation of the Richmond defenses. After crossing the Chickahominy River at Jones' Bridge, they made camp a few miles further along the banks of the James River. Continuing their march the next day, the marched across Bermuda Hundred to the Appomattox River, crossing at City Point.

One Hoosier came close to death by friendly fire as a nervous sentry mistook him for a Confederate cavalryman when he was out delivering a message. The shaken man remembered, "As the saying goes, 'a miss is as good as a mile,' but this orderly did not think so, else he would not have been so badly scared."[32] City Point was a busy supply terminal with boats coming and going constantly. Unexpectedly, the men saw President Lincoln on a dispatch boat passing by on his way to a meeting with General Grant. Now very close to the Confederate lines protecting Petersburg, the men received artillery fire, but no one was hit. Four miles later, the men camped along the Norfolk Railroad on the southeast side of Petersburg.[33]

March 27 was an important date for the 3rd Indiana, at least for eight members of Company B. Their time of enlistment was up, and they spent the day filling out muster rolls, receiving their discharge papers and their back pay. While most sensed that the war was nearly over, none wished to risk their lives to be a part of the ending. They took their papers and headed home.[34]

The rest of the shrinking regiment could almost see the end in sight. In their six months away from the Army of the Potomac, the lines had been extended a considerable distance west in an effort to overextend the Confederates. With the weather warming, all expected a renewed effort to break the rebel line, take Petersburg, and send Lee's army into flight. The signs were all there; the issuing of ammunition, rations distributed, and the general increase in activity told veterans that movement was eminent.[35]

Grant outlined his final plan in the conference at City Point with Lincoln. His plan was simple; he would extend his lines further west, stretching Lee's army even further. This was not new. What was new was the arrival of Sheridan's 10,000 cavalry. Grant intended for Sheridan to get around the right flank of the Lee's army and attack Petersburg from the rear. The cavalry was to first assist in the capture of Five Forks, a station along the Southside Railroad 13 miles west of Petersburg.

Lee was not unaware of Grant's plan; indeed the movement west had been a constant with Grant. Shifting men to his exposed far right flank, Confederate reinforcements arrived at Five Forks on March 30. Overall command of the 7,000 men was held by General George Pickett of Gettysburg fame. Included in the shift was the Confederate cavalry, now under the command of Fitzhugh Lee.[36]

One thing Grant could not control was the weather. The past several days' incessant rain had turned the roads into quagmires, and men and horses struggled to move in the miserable conditions. Custer and his division were assigned the unenviable task of guarding Sheridan's supply train. Custer waited impatiently at the head of his division as the rest of the cavalry struggled by in the mud and waited even more impatiently for the wagon train to catch up. He waited throughout March 29 and into the night. "We remained saddled during the night, amid a continuous rain, without protection from the decending [sic] torents [sic] soaked to the skin and sleepless. In all, it was one of the most disagreeable nights in our experience," wrote one Hoosier.[37] At noon of March 30, the wagons finally arrived, both drivers and teams exhausted from dragging themselves and the wagons through the muck. In celebration of their accomplishment, the skies open up even more and added to the misery of an already miserable scene.[38]

That night, the men were able to unsaddle their horses. Now located at Hargrave's Store, they were three miles east of Dinwiddie Court House. The rain continued but had diminished to a steady downpour. Exhausted men and horses tried to find an escape from the rain through sleep but were awakened by picket fire. The drowsy men saddled their horses and remained on the alert throughout another miserable night. By morning, the intermittent picket fire had grown into the sound of battle to the front and to the right. At noon, Custer was no longer able to wait; he led the division out of camp, leaving his Hoosier escort as the only protection for the wagon train.[39]

The battle was going badly for Sheridan's horsemen. The Confederates had been met two miles north of Dinwiddie Court House and were pushing back. The weather had now cleared, and the day turned sunny. Perhaps encouraged by this omen, Pickett and Fitzhugh Lee soon found that they had split Sheridan's command in half. Seizing the initiative, Pickett and Lee turned their attack south with hopes of defeating Sheridan's vaunted cavalry. Sheridan was in a fix and needed help. As his cavalry hurried south away from the pursuing rebels, he sent for Custer, who was already moving to his commander's support.

Custer was flamboyant, there was no doubt. The men of the 3rd Division loved him and readily followed him into every danger. Their admiration had grown so much that many let their hair grow long and wore long red scarves in emulation of the Boy General. The escort, having been relieved of their guard duty, hurried to catch up with the division. As Custer rode into Dinwiddie Court House, he was followed by his proud Hoosier escort carrying 17 captured Confederate battle flags. It was quite a scene.[40]

Sheridan met his young general and placed the 3rd Division in a defensive position north of the Court House. Dismounting, the men fell to building rudimentary breastworks in anticipation of the hot work about to descend upon them. Horse artillery, fighting the same thick mud the wagon train had dealt with, came up and bolstered the line. As men from Sheridan's other divisions appeared, they were fed into the line on Custer's left. The firing became louder, and the retreating men from the other commands more numerous. Finally, a mass of blue cavalrymen came running at them and passed through the waiting line.[41] At 5:00 p.m., the Confederates hit Custer's line.

Flushed with the fever of anticipated victory, they attacked the line of regrouped cavalrymen on the left flank. Moving right, they came into view of Custer's division. A ragged volley of carbine fire greeted them as the blue line worked the actions of their Spencers and sent a steady stream of lead into the Confederate attackers. Two times they charged; two times they were repulsed. Sheridan now saw an opportunity to turn the tables on his attackers. Custer was ordered to lead a mounted charge against the enemy, but it had to be done quickly; there would be little time to mount. Ordering his 1st Brigade to follow, Custer and the escort led the attack. Driving the enemy back, the rebels retreated into a woods where their fire halted the Union advance. Both sides, exhausted by the day's fighting, hunkered down for a needed rest. For the Hoosiers, there was one more dangerous duty to perform.

During the final attack, Custer's personal orderly had been wounded and left on the field. Custer was attached to the man, and four men of the 3rd Indiana decided to go out onto the battlefield and try and locate their comrade. Led by Isaac Romine, the quartet started out around 9:00 p.m. in search of the missing orderly. After leaving Union lines, they were drawn to faint cries that they believed came from their man. Inching their way closer to Confederate lines, the men resorted to their hands and knees until they reached the source of the cries. Incredibly, the call had come from the wounded orderly, lying only 30 paces from enemy lines. The men quickly seized the man and, as quietly as they could, laboriously carried him back to Union lines. Unfortunately, the man's wounds were mortal, and he died early the next morning. Custer, deeply affected by his death, mourned his passing.[42]

But, there was little time to mourn the dead. While Sheridan's cavalry had been roughly handled the day before, April 1 showed promise for a change of fortune. Pickett's men, in following Sheridan's retreat, had left the entrenchments at Five Forks empty. Union infantry were slowly working their way west toward the empty station. During the night, Grant gave Sheridan operational control of a Union infantry corps, and Sheridan now planned on his own attack. Meanwhile, Pickett realized his blunder, and early in the morning, he began a pullback to his lines at Five Forks. He built large bonfires along his lines, and the men made noise to give the impression that they were still in position in front of Custer. In contrast, Custer's men were not allowed fires and shivered through the long, chilly night. As daylight broke, the Union men were surprised to see not a gray soldier in sight.[43]

Sheridan had expected an entire infantry corps, but by daybreak, only one division had arrived. Easing his frustration over the missing infantry was the arrival of MacKenzie's small, two brigade division of cavalry from the Army of Virginia. Nettled but undeterred, Sheridan began his pursuit of Pickett with two of his own divisions plus MacKenzie's. Sheridan expected the rest of the infantry to be advancing on a line that would intercept Pickett's rebels on their retreat to Five Forks. He was bitterly disappointed as no Union foot soldiers appeared. He had to be content with Custer and his men harassing the retreating Confederates all the way to Five Forks where the enemy reoccupied the trenches around 2:00 p.m. Convinced that Sheridan would not attack, Pickett and Fitzhugh Lee blithely joined a shad bake along the banks of Hatcher's Run and, in so doing, left the Confederate troops leaderless.[44]

The rest of the infantry corps finally arrived, and Sheridan planned a general attack on the entrenched Confederates with Custer taking a portion of his division on a mounted attack on the extreme right of the enemy. The cavalry attack was meant as a diversion to the real attack by the infantry. Three attacks by dismounted cavalry against the enemy's center kept attention away from the slow moving infantry forming for their attack on the rebel left flank. Finally, at 5:00 p.m., the bugles sounded in the Union lines, and the blue-clad infantrymen smashed into the rebel line from the east.[45] On the west end of the federal line, Custer drew his saber and shouted, "Now boys, for your thirty day furlough!" and charged forward.[46]

The charging infantry and the rushing cavalry broke the rebel line. As the Confederates ran west, they encountered Sheridan's dismounted cavalry attacking the center of the line and, if fortunate enough to get through this trap, they ran into Custer's mounted men charging in from the west. "Hand to hand the struggle raged, but for a time only as the courage of the rebels wavered, they broke and a complete route [sic] was effected."[47] Leaderless and facing no other alternative, the

Chapter 16. January 1, 1865–April 7, 1865

Confederates surrendered in droves. Custer and his men pursued the shattered remnants of the rebel force into the night, breaking off the action around 9:00 p.m.

Pickett's entire command, except for the cavalry, was gone. A total of 6,000 men were killed, wounded, captured, or scattered in a few short hours. Six artillery pieces, eight thousand rifles and eighteen battle flags were collected. Adding this debacle to fighting around Petersburg's Fort Stedman, Lee's army had been shrunk by 11,000 in less than a week. The end wasn't just near—it was plainly in sight. Robert E. Lee, 13 miles away in Petersburg, tried to understand the loss and impact of Pickett's disaster. He realized he could no longer hold the city and protect Richmond. As if to drive this point home, Grant ordered an all-out attack on the Petersburg defenses early on April 2, finally breaching the Confederate defenses that had stymied him for the past eight months.

Lee had really only one option. First, move his army west to secure rations before turning south. Second, join with Joe Johnston's army in North Carolina. There he would still need to defeat the combined forces of Grant and Sherman. With the railroad now cut, Lee and his army had no other choice than to find food. Lee ordered Richmond abandoned and all Confederate forces there to head for Amelia Courthouse. Lee's plan was to pull his own Army of Northern Virginia out of the lines at Petersburg and head for a rendezvous with the Richmond forces. Food and forage was expected to be available when they reached the courthouse. It was race for survival now for the Confederates. Reach food and they could continue the fight. Without it, Lee would have to surrender.

For the 3rd Indiana, these facts were irrelevant. They had little time to enjoy the victory of Five Forks. Captain Lee and his provost marshals had to collect and assemble the captured rebels and move them to the Union rear. As the Hoosiers prodded the prisoners along the same churned roads that had stymied Union forces only days before, they began to sense it was nearly over.

But, the escort also knew that the next day would bring more fighting. The headquarters provision wagon had to be brought up so that General Custer and his staff could eat in the morning. Men were sent to retrieve the wagon only to have the vehicle break down a mile from camp. Repairs were made so the general was able to "break the fast" the following morning, courtesy of his faithful Hoosiers.[48]

April 2 dawned, and Sheridan had a hunch about Lee's next move. Anticipating the rebel retreat from Petersburg, Sheridan requested that he be allowed to take his cavalry and block the retreating Confederates as they moved west. Grant gave him permission to operate between the Appomattox River and the Southside Railroad. This was considered the most likely route for Lee to take. Custer took his division to Fords Inn on the Southside Railroad where they destroyed several miles of track. Finishing the work late in the day, they met slight resistance as they moved north. That evening, the men unsaddled their horses and slept through a night that was occasionally broken by sporadic bursts of rifle fire.[49]

Early on April 3, Custer's 3rd Division moved out as the advance of Sheridan's cavalry. While not meeting Confederate resistance as at first, there was still danger. Obstacles had been built to slow the Union advance, and some were deadly. Near the crossing at Namozine Creek, they encountered an abandoned artillery caisson filled with ammunition. Cunningly, a fuse had been lit by the retreating Confederates, and the explosion killed two officers of the 8th New York.[50] When the advance reached the crossing, shots rang out.

Posted on the opposite shore of the creek was a significant force of dismounted cavalry. Custer patiently waited for his entire command to come up and, with a shout, led his men across the Namozine River, sending the enemy into headlong flight. Pursuing the graybacks to Namozine Church, Custer's pursuing cavalry suddenly ran into a line of entrenchments. Momentarily checked, Custer reorganized his command, and a final charge carried the day for the Union. Pursuing the enemy for several miles, the men were finally ordered back, and the spoils of war collected.[51] Captain Lee had another 500 prisoners to escort to the rear, and the 3rd Indiana was pressed into duty as prison guards once again. They returned to the division at Mannsboro at nightfall.[52] Lee's Army of Northern Virginia was hemorrhaging men by the hour.

Lee's main force had arrived at Amelia Court House and found vast stores of ammunition and war materiel. But, the most important need—food—was nowhere to be seen. It was critical that the men be fed. After months of reduced rations during the siege in Petersburg and the past several days with no food for the men and little forage for the horses and mules, Lee's army literally was starving. Though he knew they had to keep going, Lee was forced to rest his men or he would have no army to lead.

It was a fatal decision. The time taken to rest also allowed the Union forces to catch up. Infantry were feverishly marching to catch up to the rebels; cavalry were desperately trying to get ahead of Lee's army to cut off its escape. In fact, the Union horsemen had outpaced their own supply trains and had resorted to living off of the land. That land, however, was some of the poorest in Virginia, and foodstuffs for man and beast—gray or blue—were virtually non-existent. The Union men did have one thing the Confederates did not—hope. They knew the end of the war was near, they just had to catch the rebel army. They just had to keep the rebel army from getting food. They just had to deliver a final death blow to the Confederacy. They just had to keep going.

By April 5, the dogged determination of the Union cavalry bore fruit as they finally got ahead of Lee. Sheridan reached Jetersville, a hamlet three miles west of Amelia Court House. Infantrymen were marching to the point of collapse to close the gap between them and Lee's army. Grant galloped after Sheridan, and they met to finalize the assault slated for the next day. All seemed in place for the decisive battle.

Except Robert E. Lee was not ready to be attacked. On the evening of April 5, Lee started moving his men on a night march due west to Farmville and rumored food. Lee's hungry, tired men were only able to go seven miles that night with the vanguard arriving at Amelia Springs at 8:00 a.m. Strung out behind them were perhaps 25,000 men of the shrinking Army of Northern Virginia.[53] Realizing that Lee had stolen a march on him, Sheridan ordered his cavalry to saddle before dawn on April 6.

His plan was simple. He would find Lee's army, attack it with one division, leapfrog the other two divisions and attack again and again until he could stop the rebels where the following infantry could come up and finish the job. The rear of Lee's column was barely out of Amelia Court House when the federal infantry began to hit them.

The cavalry began their day in the saddle. Custer's division was the second in line. Off to the north on a parallel road, a column of rebel wagons "as far as the eye could see" was spotted.[54] Though heavily guarded by both infantry and cavalry, Sheridan ordered an immediate attack near the ford of the Little Saylor's Creek at Deatonville. Repulsed, Sheridan ordered the men to disengage and move further west to find a better place to attack the column.

Custer ordered one brigade to attack a little further west from the initial attack. It was the perfect spot—a gap had developed and the charge netted 300 wagons and several pieces of artillery. The desperate Confederates behind the opening saw the attack. If the Union cavalry continued to pour into the gap, they would be cut off and captured. The resolute Rebels mounted a ferocious counterattack even as the lead elements of Lee's army were unaware of the disaster developing in their rear.

The cavalry had split the rebel army. As Custer's men blocked forward progress, Union infantry were now beginning to arrive from the east and the north. Even more cavalry were attacking from the south and southwest. Nearly half of the Rebel army was being encircled and mauled by the Union army. It became a free for all. Another gap appeared in the Confederate line, and more cavalry poured into the opening. Attacks were coming from every point of the compass. Sheridan believed that one more coordinated attack would bring the battle to an end. With dusk near, he lined up the entire Cavalry Corps of the Army of the Potomac plus MacKenzie's cavalry from the Army of Virginia. Infantry were massing for an attack from the east. In all, approximately 16,000 troops were poised to attack the entrapped rebels.[55]

The mounted attack would cover nearly 1,000 yards of open country. The charge was expected to deliver the knockout punch. Custer and his escort lined up at the head of his division, and he gave the order to advance. With nearly a half mile to cross, the charge started at the walk, then the trot, the canter and the last 200 yards, the gallop. Custer's men "charged their ranks in a body, bringing off the reminants [sic] of their regiments and brigades—in a body as prisoners, cutting off and capturing wagon tarins [sic] and batteries."[56]

Right behind Custer charged his stalwart Hoosiers. As they galloped, they expected a shock of contact and strong resistance. Instead, starving Confederate soldiers dressed in rags began to give up. Clusters of exhausted rebels surrendered.

As the attack continued down the wagon train, Private Cowan D. Evans plucked the battle flag of the 26th Virginia Infantry from its honor guard. William Holmes earned his 30 day furlough by capturing the flag of the 27th Virginia Infantry with Sergeant Absalom Jordan snatching another one.[57] William Shepherd rounded out the tally with one of his own.[58]

All over the battlefield, the same scenes were being acted out. In all, 9,000 Confederate troops surrendered. Perhaps another 2,000 escaped but were scattered in isolated groups. Some of the men simply quit and headed home. The combined Union forces captured nearly all of the Confederate army's artillery. Included in the day's haul were no fewer than six Confederate generals. Robert E. Lee, upon hearing of the debacle, exclaimed in anguish, "My God! Has the army been dissolved?"

Indeed, his army had nearly been "dissolved." Throughout the night of April 6, men of the 3rd Indiana collected prisoners and escorted them to the prison grounds. One member of the escort reported that the 3rd Division had captured 4,000 men, including four generals, 14 pieces of artillery, 30 battle flags, and several hundred wagons.[59] Captain Lee and a contingent of Hoosiers stayed in camp with four of the captured generals until they could be turned over to Cavalry Corps headquarters. The rest of the men traveled with Custer and the 3rd Division west once more.

Sheridan wanted his cavalry to keep up the pressure. Now behind the truncated Confederate army, he needed to head southwest to block any attempt by Lee to join Johnston in North Carolina. Other Union troops moved to harass the Confederates as they continued the march. Arriving at Prince Edward Court House, Sheridan received word that Lee had continued west. He determined that Lee was not headed to North Carolina, but Lynchburg. Hurrying his column back west, he camped for the night near Buffalo River. Less than four miles away to the northeast was Lee's Army of Northern Virginia.

Lee had reached Farmville and found some rations waiting for his men. Though not enough to sustain the men for long, it was enough for a good meal. For some of the men, it was their first real meal in nearly a week, but one meal would not be enough for the men and horses to recover. Lynchburg was now the goal for the tiny army. Food was their target. Lee telegraphed Lynchburg to have food waiting for him at Appomattox.

Sheridan's march to Buffalo River had once again gotten the cavalry ahead of Lee. They also had a shorter march to Appomattox. Sensing an opportunity, the men of Custer's division were up and moving before dawn. Scouts had brought word of two important developments. First, Lee was pushing his army hard for a third night of marching. Second, scouts had seen supply trains at Appomattox Station. Orders rang out, and within minutes, every Union cavalryman in Virginia was headed for those rail cars. If they got to those supplies before Lee, the war was over. Sheridan sent word to the following infantry to hurry to the front. He would need their firepower if they got to Appomattox Station first. The end of the war was 14 miles to the northwest.[60]

Chapter 17

April 8, 1865–Postwar

The ride to Appomattox was at a brisk pace. Sheridan accompanied Custer's division, and his own sense of urgency was felt by all the men of the unit. Food also occupied their minds. Supply wagons had still not caught up, and the prospect of food at Appomattox was felt almost as strongly among the Northerners as their Confederate counterparts.[1]

They reached the Lynchburg Railroad at Prospect Station and turned due west. Following the railroad for a few miles, the command cut south so as to approach the station from the southeast. If there were troops at Appomattox Station, they would be looking to the north on the Richmond-Lynchburg Stage Road for the approach of Lee's men. Better to approach from a less expected direction. The pace had slackened, and Sheridan chafed at the slowing speed of the advance. Turning to Custer, he ordered the young man to take one of his brigades to the station as fast as possible. Custer, grinning from ear to ear, ordered the men out at the trot.

Their advance was so rapid that the advance party and scouts leading the column had a hard time staying ahead of the general and his Hoosier escort. Even the horses seemed to sense the urgency of the moment, and straggling by man or beast was virtually non-existent during the mad dash to the station. Approaching the station about 2:00 p.m., four trains could be seen with few guards in sight. The brigade fanned out and approached the trains, capturing three and running off the guards. The men opened the cars and were astounded by the quantity of supplies inside—food, medicine, ammunition, it was all there. Captain Lee took charge of the captured supplies as more men arrived.[2] The reinforcements were sent west to tear up track so that it would be impossible for the trains to escape to Lynchburg and also make reinforcement impossible from the west.[3]

They had made it. Now what to do with the engines and cars? To leave them at the station would invite a major engagement with Lee's desperate army as it arrived, a fight the cavalry alone would find very difficult to win. A call for former train engineers went out to the command. Soon, volunteers were running the trains up and down the tracks, blowing the whistles and giggling like schoolboys. When Sheridan arrived, he ordered the engines and cars to the east toward the advancing Union infantry and away from the starving Confederate army.[4] Men and horses continued to arrive as the rest of the Cavalry Corps caught up with Custer's advance party.[5]

Unaware of what was transpiring, Lee's advance guard, consisting of his reserve artillery and wagon train, had camped two miles north of the station. Having just completed a grueling march through the cloying mud of Central Virginia, the exhausted rebels had settled in for a rest. Spying the resting Confederates, Custer ordered an immediate attack on the unsuspecting camp. Whooping and yelling, Custer and his men thundered down on the surprised artillerymen. Fortunately, the rebels had parked their cannon facing outward, and the gunners quickly overcame their surprise and manned their guns. As Custer's lead brigade dismounted to press the attack, the rest of the division began to arrive.

Throughout the rest of the day, Custer attempted to break through and capture the guns. One Hoosier remarked later about the noise of battle that day: "The enemy had brought their artillery into action, with their screeching shells plowing the tree tops, the hissing and whispering of bullets from carbine fire, filled the air. But, the clamor and din of battle was eclipsed by the incessant scream of whistles of the four locomotives at the station, creating pandemonium in full blast."[6] As darkness descended, fighting continued. Custer was everywhere and had at least one horse shot out from under him. As he and the escort rode back and forth around the battlefield, Confederate commanders recognized the flamboyant man in blue and ordered volleys fired at him.[7] Finally at 8:30 p.m., Custer's men broke the rebel line only to find most of the artillery gone, moving away to the north and out of reach. Despite this disappointment, Custer could claim the capture of 24 artillery and around 200 wagons.[8]

Throughout the night, elements of the Cavalry Corps kept arriving and ordered out along the Lynchburg-Richmond Stage Road in anticipation of Lee's main body arriving. The mood around the various headquarters was jubilant almost to the point of giddiness. The coming and going of couriers to the various commands spread a poorly kept secret. Grant had been in contact with Lee during the day about a possible cessation of fighting, but Lee was not ready to give up. Everyone knew that he would not surrender until he had exhausted every chance to escape.

Infantry who had marched for over 20 hours began to arrive in the early hours of April 9. Sheridan's and Custer's perilous grip on the station was strengthening by the hour. To the northeast, Grant with the rest of the army was pressing down on Lee's army from the east as a third Union column was approaching from the southeast. Enough reinforcements had arrived that Custer's men were moved into reserve and they were able to eat, feed their horses, and rest. At dawn they were ordered back to the front line and took up a position to the right of the infantry. Other cavalry divisions were harassing the advance of Lee's army, now just two miles from Appomattox Station. Every minute they slowed Lee's advance allowed more Union troops to arrive from west, east, and southeast. Finally, the Union cavalry broke contact and rode away. Confederate hopes soared as they marched toward the station and the promised food. That hope turned to utter despair with the appearance of a solid double line of Union infantry and artillery in the way to Appomattox.

Custer's red-scarved 3rd Division moved into position to support an attack by the infantry. As they reached the crest of Clover Hill, they beheld a fantastic sight. "We looked down upon—a portion—of Lee's army encamped around the Court House and then perhaps we would have dashed down upon the camps but, at our first appearance on the hill, a white flag was raised and Custer halted the command."[9] "His Hoosier escort watched silently as one of Lee's staff officers approached and requested the suspension of further hostilities, until a surrender could be affected with the proper officers. Custer at once dispatched one of his staff with the information to Sheridan, who likewise reported to Grant."[10]

Later that day, Grant met Lee at McLean House, and the surrender was formalized. The 3rd Indiana encamped where they were with only routine messenger duties the rest of the day. Pickets were not posted. For the first time in nearly four years, the Army of the Potomac and the Army of Northern Virginia truly rested. The Hoosiers "could lay down to sleep in comparative peace, to dream of home, instead of trials and tribulations of war."[11] The end of the war had finally come. An unreal quiet settled over Appomattox with its tens of thousands of men and horses going about the evening routine.

Home. The ink was barely dry on the surrender documents before the Hoosiers started dreaming and talking about going home. There was a problem, however. Lee had surrendered only the Army of Northern Virginia. Joe Johnston's army still was in the field in North Carolina, opposing Sherman. Until Johnston's army was captured or destroyed, the war would go on.

The men slept late on April 10 and hit the road around 10:00 a.m. They rode east, arriving at Prospect Station around 4:00 p.m. They were pleasantly surprised to find supply wagons waiting for them with all types of foodstuffs, including coffee and sugar. These were the first rations they had received since leaving Petersburg. As coffee brewed over campfires, the men settled down for the night. With coffee, sugar, and food, their day's travel had been leisurely. The euphoria of the surrender was still present, but would soon be replaced with the quiet relief that they had survived.

Over the next couple of days, the men rode east to Nottoway, arriving on April 13, and remained in camp for four days when they were ordered to Petersburg. Traveling through the desolation of the recently besieged city, the destruction was awe-inspiring. Sightseeing forays discovered the dugouts where troops and civilians had lived during the incessant bombardment of the city. Breastworks, rifle pits, and redoubts were all one could see for miles. Even in this other worldly landscape, there were signs of life and a new beginning. "Numerous sutlers had pitched their tents about the suberbs [sic] and a few grocer and notion stores had resumed business. Soldiers in gray thronged the streets and were at home from the war."[12]

The shocking news of the assassination of Abraham Lincoln on April 14 was met with outrage and grief. Revenge was on many of their minds. "I have never seen the simpathies of the soldiers so aroused as it is now. All the talk is revenge—for the death of the President. It would not be well for any Southern sympathies to pass through our camps now," threatened one Hoosier.[13]

Anxious for the war to end, home would have to wait for the Hoosiers of the 3rd Indiana. They had moved south along the Boynton Pike, and on April 24 received unwelcome orders. Custer's division was to go south to reinforce Sherman. Once they arrived, the men were to be detached from the Army of the Potomac and join their comrades of the 3rd Indiana, West Wing. The wings that had fought separately for four years were now causing great consternation among army bureaucrats. The biggest blow, however, was that they would cease to be the 3rd Indiana.

When the enlistments of the west wing had ended, recruits who had joined after the initial muster plus companies L and M were still obligated to complete their full three year enlistment. An even larger body of men than the re-organized East Wing, the West Wing was consolidated with the 8th Indiana Cavalry in January. Upon arrival in Sherman's army, the remaining men of the escort would be transferred to the 8th Indiana, and the 3rd Indiana Cavalry would cease to exist.[14]

Their fears were alleviated when word was received that Johnston had surrendered to Sherman. There now appeared no reason to march south and join Sherman's army and the ordered consolidation. Custer and his division marched back to Petersburg where they settled into camp. Their peace of mind received quite a jolt when Sherman's army started to arrive in Petersburg on May 5. Suddenly, the hated consolidation appeared once more as a real possibility.

Fortunately for them, Custer was not going to let that happen. He had known some of the men since his days in '63 as a mere captain on Pleasanton's staff. By May 10, Custer's division was ordered north, and he made sure the 3rd Indiana accompanied him. As the men rode along, they all sported new red neckties in honor and at the request of General Custer and his wife, who had recently joined the column.[15]

While the remnant of the 3rd Indiana, East Wing, rested easy and rode north with scarves and escorting women, men of the regiment had still been dying. William Kaney of Company C had been captured in January 1864 and sent to the infamous Andersonville prison camp. Twice wounded prior to capture, Kaney was a tough man who would survive the horrors of the camp. William Congers of Company B, Joseph Dillenhermer of Company E, and James Norman of Company F were freed from camp and moved to Vicksburg for a Mississippi riverboat ride home. In a hurry to get the men north, hundreds of emaciated, weakened men were crowded onto the riverboat *Sultana*. As many as 2,000 men may have been packed onto her decks. Overloaded and laboring against the current, the boat's boilers burst and sank near Memphis on April 27. Dillenhermer and Congers were pulled from the river and somehow survived. Tough Bill Kaney and Jim Norman were not so lucky. Both died in the cold swirling waters of the Mississippi days away from home. They were the last 3rd Indiana Cavalry, East Wing men who died in service.[16]

Back in Virginia, the men rode through the destroyed capital of the Confederacy and on toward Washington. Their ride took them over familiar territory: Yellow Tavern, South Anna River, Hanover Junction, Fredericksburg, and Manassas. On May 16, they arrived in Washington and set up camp on Arlington Heights until, on May 21, they were ordered to Bladensburg. It seemed fitting that their final campgrounds would be the same locale as their first camp in the capital city more than three and a half years before.[17]

The men spent the next two days cleaning equipment, washing clothes, and currying their horses. A grand parade by the victorious armies had been planned, and all brass was to be buffed to a bright shine; all leather polished until it shone like ebony. On May 23, the men proudly took their place behind the "Boy General" carrying his captured Confederate battle flags as Custer led his division down Pennsylvania Avenue. As bands played and horses pranced, the men straightened their lines and marched past the review stand filled with dignitaries. The formalities over, they returned to their camp at Bladensburg where they sat for three weeks.[18]

Company A had shrunk to 97 men by June 2. Lt. George Gilbert continued to command the company as Captain Lee was still detached as division provost marshal. Company B had but 22 men left with no officers present.[19] For the time being, the men contented themselves with routine camp life, the occasional sightseeing trip, and the filling out of muster rolls. Captain Lee had to contend with the drunkenness, petty theft, and general mischief endemic with garrison life—a far cry from six weeks before when he presided over the comforts of four Confederate generals.

Home was all the men could think about. The war was over. Jefferson Davis had been captured, and all hostilities had ceased. There were some rumors of them going to Texas to convince the opportunistic French to leave Mexico, but most of the men discounted those whispers with the sheer desire to go home trumping all other possibilities. One other possibility still concerned the men, however. The army bureaucracy could still order them to the 8th Indiana, even for a few weeks. Fortunately, much to their relief, orders arrived rendering that possibility moot. On June 10, the long-awaited orders finally came. They were ordered to Louisville, Kentucky—as in just across the river from Indiana and home.[20]

Taking rail cars to Pittsburgh before boarding a riverboat there, the men arrived in Cincinnati on June 15. Literally a handful of miles from many of the men's homes, the Hoosiers were not allowed to disembark. Instead, they suffered in high anxiety as they floated past Rising Sun, Vevay, Madison, and Hanover on the way to Louisville later in the day. As they disembarked, the revolver of Albert Bayze of Company A accidentally discharged and hit him in the foot. An original member of the regiment, he had gone through the entire war without a scratch. Now, he had the notoriety of being the last member of the 3rd Indiana Cavalry, East Wing to be injured in service.[21]

For two more weeks the men sat in camp before being ordered to Indianapolis for muster out. On August 8, 1865, the few remaining men of the regiment were feted in a ceremony and thanked for their service. They received their back pay and muster papers and left the city as civilians.[22] With one exception, the men were home. Captain Charles Lee was somewhere in Texas. Still a part of Custer's division staff, he had traveled with the general to the Rio Grande as part of the show of force to the

French. Lee would be brevetted to the rank of Major for his service. It was November before he was finally discharged as the last serving member of the regiment.[23]

The 3rd Indiana Cavalry, East Wing had participated in over 70 cavalry battles and skirmishes. During the course of its existence, nearly 750 officers and men had been on its muster rolls. Forty-one of them had paid the ultimate price in service to their country with an additional 232 wounded in combat, some multiple times. Officers and men debilitated by their service and discharged due to disability were 178. Those taken prisoner were 107 with 13 of the number dying in Southern prisons, including 11 at Andersonville.[24] Four members had been awarded the Medal of Honor for the capture of enemy battle flags.[25] Several had provided valuable and dangerous service as scouts for the Bureau of Military Information, including the Chief of Scouts. Quite a record for a half regiment of Hoosier farm boys, rivermen, and store clerks.

The men settled into civilian life as best they could. Among the commissioned officers, Scott Carter had returned to Vevay after his resignation and resumed his law practice, eventually being appointed a judge over four counties.[26] Jacob Buchanan also returned to Vevay and continued to suffer from ill health. In an attempt to improve his constitution, he moved to Arkansas where he managed a plantation for over two years. Returning to Indiana, he settled in Evansville and established a law firm which he later shared with his son.[27]

Major William Patton purchased the Vevay wharf boat and picked up right where he had left off.[28] In 1866, he was elected County Auditor and served for eight years. After his tiff with the governor over his commission in the 10th Indiana Cavalry, William McClure returned to Madison where he was appointed U.S. Government Store Keeper for Madison.[29]

Captain George Gilchrist moved to Iowa after the war and studied law. Upon entering the bar, he served in a variety of positions in Vinton and the surrounding county before being appointed a district judge. After he served his term, he returned to private practice.[30]

George Chapman never caught John S. Mosby but served honorably to the end. He was on a number of court martial boards before being mustered out on January 7, 1866, as a Brevet Major General. Back in Indianapolis, he resumed his law practice and served five years as a Marion County Criminal Court judge before being elected to the Indiana Senate where he served for a short time.[31]

William Pickerill, former adjutant of the regiment, chose a different path. Returning to Indiana after muster out, he moved to Indianapolis. Twenty years later, the Official Record of the War of the Rebellion began to be available. This 127 volume work was released over several years in the 1880s, and Pickerill began the laborious task of combing through each volume as they were released to reconstruct the service of the regiment. Published in 1906, Pickerill's history of the 3rd Indiana was written almost exclusively from his findings in the Official Record.[32]

Many of the enlisted men pursued former occupations of farming and store keeping upon their return from the war. George Beard of Company B, who veteranized and fought to the end, found farming not to his tastes when he returned. After a year of planting, he turned to journalism and became a newspaper editor in Bloomfield, Indiana.[33] Solon Tilford had seen enough death during the war that he sought a different path. He studied medicine and became a doctor in Frankfort, Indiana.[34] Lewis Wilson saw the need for a different kind of healing and pursued the ministry.[35]

James Jordan had spent the fall and spring of 1864–65 riding back and forth through his birthplace of Woodstock, Virginia. After the war, he studied law and passed the bar, setting up practice in Martinsville, Indiana. In 1894, he was elected to the Indiana Supreme Court where he served for 17 years.[36] Samuel Gilpin also turned to the law and was admitted to the bar in 1869 after moving to Winterset, Iowa.[37] Stephen Lee moved to Knox County, Indiana, after he returned to Madison and took a government job. The lure of the west soon attracted him, and he moved to Oregon where he served in the state legislature. He later became treasurer of the Oregon Rail and Navigation Company.[38]

Asa Hardman of Company F had been captured at Gettysburg on July 1 only to be released as the Confederates left the village three days later. The experience had a profound impact on his life as he returned to Gettysburg after muster out and married Carrie Sheads only 18 days after he left the army. After Carrie's death three years later, Asa returned to Indianapolis only to move to Leesburg, Florida, in 1882 where he became postmaster and a respected civic leader.[39]

Many had itchy feet after traveling so much in the service. Augustine Bardwell worked in a machine shop in Cincinnati for a few years and then set off on a grand adventure. His travels eventually led him to Panama. Here, he ran a dredge for a time during the building of the Panama Canal.[40] He traveled about Central America where he eventually operated a small coffee plantation in Guatemala.[41]

Milton Cline left his duties as Chief of Scouts of the Army of the Potomac to return to farming. He spent a couple of years in Illinois before drifting west. He filed a gold claim in Ouray, Colorado, and became the town's first mayor. Though never promoted, he often went by the honorary title of "Captain."[42] Gottlieb Anshutz of Company A wandered about the West as well before settling down in California working in the gold mines.[43]

Not all returned to civilian life unscarred. Both physical and mental wounds would follow many of the men for the rest of their lives. John Irby left the army with all but his thumb and forefinger of his left hand amputated. He recovered from his wound and spent the rest of his service detached to the Bureau of Military Information. When he got home, he moved to Vermillion County, Indiana, where he attempted to pursue farming. Unable to perform the tasks of farming with only part of a hand, Irby became despondent and took his own life.

Not all of the old veterans were human. Pollard Brown of Company F had somehow managed to get his wartime mount home. Brown moved to Kokomo, Indiana, where his horse lived out his days. "Old Bob" had been shot three times and had been under fire in over a hundred skirmishes and battles. Upon his death in 1887 at the age of 35, the old war horse was buried with full military honors.[44]

As time went on, the desire to reconnect with old comrades and to relive the adventures of their youth led to annual reunions. Those held in Madison, Connersville, and Vevay were expected venues. All were located in counties from which the east wing companies were recruited. But reunions were also held in Shelbyville, Muncie, and Indianapolis. Given the unique history of the entire 3rd Indiana, both East and West Wing members participated. Despite never serving together, the common experience of service and combat bonded the two wings together. Regardless of where the reunions were held, it became increasingly more difficult to gather the far flung ex-cavalrymen. No fewer than 24 states of residence for the East Wing members were listed in the 1904 roster of the reunion program.[45]

John Irby as a young man before three years of war and the loss of part of his hand left him despondent and depressed (U.S. Army Heritage and Education Center).

In 1913, the 50th anniversary of Gettysburg drew huge crowds of veterans, North and South. Over thirty members of the regiment, now in their 60s, 70s, and even 80s, made the trip to once again stand on McPherson's Ridge and remember the shot and shell of July 1, 1863. For most, it was also an opportunity to admire the marble obelisk erected by the state of Indiana in 1889 to commemorate their part of the great battle.[46]

Another memorial to the men of the East Wing had been proposed for a number of years by George Middleton of Company E. Middleton was the youngest son of a butcher in Madison, Indiana. In February 1862, though only 16 years old, he was finally allowed to join his older brother in the regiment. He had been a participant in

The state of Indiana dedicated this monument at Gettysburg in 1887. It is located on McPherson's Ridge near the railroad cut (author's collection).

the capture of the young Confederate artillery captain on the Northern Neck expedition in May 1863. He had fought at Gettysburg and was captured in August 1863. Sent to Belle Isle, he soon plied his father's trade in the cook house and later earned money from baking bread for the guards.⁴⁷

After being exchanged and mustered out, he returned to Madison and tried several business ventures. Growing tired of tame civilian life, he bought into a circus and found his life's calling. Over the next forty years, Middleton traveled all over the country with various shows. Eventually, he sailed overseas and visited Australia, New Zealand, Java, and South America. At one time he worked with Barnum and Bailey before moving on to the next phase of his career. Seeing opportunities in a new entertainment venue, he sold his shares of the circus and opened up a "dime museum" in Chicago. Here he brought

George Middleton joined the regiment in 1862 as a 16-year-old recruit. After being captured and spending time in a prisoner camp, he mustered out and returned to Indiana. He ended up paying for the monument in Jefferson County, Indiana, as a memorial to all Jefferson County veterans, but he made sure that his association with the regiment appeared prominently on a plaque affixed to the monument (Pickerill, *A History of the Third Indiana Cavalry*).

together all the wonders of the world under one roof. No longer tied to the weather and a travel season, people flocked to the venue to see the attractions for only a dime. Always on the lookout for new talent, he took a chance on a young magician named Harry Houdini and gave him his first job.⁴⁸

No matter where he was or what he was doing, he never forgot his comrades of the 3rd Indiana. He often credited his army life for providing the perfect training for his life in the circus and as a showman. He shared this with readers in the Madison, Indiana, newspaper and encouraged that a monument be erected in town to Jefferson County veterans. The idea took shape and on May 29, 1908, a monument was dedicated on the courthouse square. An inscription on the stone stated "They led and followed." Ever the showman, Middleton—who had put up a majority

Dedicated to all Jefferson County veterans, this monument sits on the grounds of the Jefferson County courthouse (author's collection).

of the money—also made sure that he was credited for the creation of the monument.[49]

The men aged, and slowly the march of time caught up with them. On May 6, 1941, the last member of the East Wing—John Nichols of Company E—passed away. In reporting his death the next day, the editors of the local newspaper saw fit to place his obituary on the sports page. On the same page was a story about Hank Greenberg, the highest paid player in baseball. With yet another war looming on the horizon, the Detroit Tiger slugger was reporting for the draft.[50] The story noted that Greenberg's new pay would be $21 a month, only $8 more than John Nichols received 79 years before.

Of course, Nichols got an extra $12 for his horse.

George Middleton, ever the promoter, made sure his name and affiliation were prominent on the memorial in Madison (author's collection).

Appendix:
Casualty List for Gettysburg

Name	Rank	Company	Injury	Died of Wounds
Charles Lemmon	Major	Staff	Head	July 2, 1863
John E. Weaver	Private	A	Left knee, amputated	August 8, 1863
John W Caughlin	Private	B	Right elbow	Survived
William Congers	Corporal	B	Unknown	Survived
Edward B. Douglass	Private	B	Left lung	Survived
James Hannah	Private	B	Unknown	Survived
John H. Leach	Corporal	B	Left arm and face	Survived
Augustus Lewallen	Private	B	Unknown	Survived
George W. Melton	Private	B	Unknown	Survived
Jesse T. Melton	Private	B	Right forearm	Survived
Henry C. Pavy	Private	B	Left arm, amputated	July 22, 1863
Thomas Purcell	Private	B	Left arm	Survived
Isaac E. Vibbert	Private	B	Killed in action	July 1, 1863
Morton D. Fugit	Blacksmith	C	Left knee	Survived
Samuel Lamb	QM Sergeant	C	Head	July 29, 1863
Martin Ephraim	Captain	C	Shoulder	Survived
Omar Howerton	Sergeant	D	Shoulder	Survived
George H. Porter	Sergeant	D	Unknown	Survived
Franklin Powers	Private	D	Left knee	Survived
Benjamin L Sellers	Corporal	D	Leg and side	Survived
Jesse Smith	Private	D	Body	July 1, 1863
William Tupper	Private	D	Right leg	Survived
August Wright	Corporal	D	Killed in action	July 1, 1863
James Boyd	QM Sergeant	E	Left side	Survived
William Park	Private	E	Right lung	July 10, 1863
William Storey	Corporal	E	Chest	July 10, 1863
Isaac Higgins	Private	F	Left thigh	Survived

Sources include NA Record Group 94 CMR; Indiana Adjutant General hospital records; *Aurora Commercial*, July 23, October 1, 1863; *Madison Daily Evening Courier*, July 17, 1863; *Vevay Reveille*, July 9, August 18, 1863.

Regimental Roster: Original and Re-Organized

The following is a roster of all of the men who served in the 3rd Indiana Cavalry, East Wing. The 1864 re-organized roster is at the end with no notes but notes for these individuals are included in the original roster. Many of the entries are updates to the original list in the Indiana Adjutant General Report and include much more depth of information. Multiple names listed indicate misspellings and other spellings used. Sources for information in the fifth column from the left are identified in the right column. Sources have been abbreviated for space considerations. The following is a key to those abbreviations.

CMR—Carded Medical Records
CWT—Connersville (IN) *Weekly Times*
Fishel—*The Secret War for the Union*
Hard—*History of the 8th Illinois Cavalry*
IAG Report—Indiana Adjutant General Report
IJ—Indianapolis (IN) *Journal*
IMHJ—*Indiana Military History Journal*
MDEC—Madison (IN) *Daily Evening Courier*
NA—National Archives
NT—National Tribune
OR—*Official Records of the Rebellion*
Pickerill—*History of the Third Indiana Cavalry* (1906)
Rummel—muster rolls from June 30, 1863
USAMHI—United States Army Military History Institute
VR—Vevay (IN) *Reveille*
Watlington—William Watlington's war reminiscence

Original

Third Indiana Cavalry (Rank at Date of Muster)

Carter	Scott	10/21/61	Col	Original Captain of Co.; resigned 3/11/63	IAG Report Vol. II
Chapman	George	9/21/61	Maj	Promoted Lt. Col, 10/25/62; promoted Colonel, 3/12/63; Promoted Brigadier General, 7/21/64; brevetted Major General	IAG Report Vol. II
Beck	Elias W. H.	10/21/61	Srgn	Mustered out	IAG Report Vol. II
Brosie	Luther	10/22/61	Asst Srgn	Resigned 11/29/62	IAG Report Vol. II
Knight	James H.	12/23/62	Asst Srgn	Mustered out	IAG Report Vol. II
COMPANY A					
Adams	James M.	8/22/61	Pvt	Killed at Madison Court House VA; 9/13/63; shot laterally through the abdomen	VR 10/8/63; IJ 9/25/63; NA Record Group 94 CMR
Adkinson	Joseph M.	3/10/62	Pvt	Wounded in both thighs at Yellow Tavern, VA, 5/11/64; Died at Point Lookout, VA, 6/8/64; wounds; buried at Pt. Lookout, MD	IAG Report Vol. V, VIII; Weaver; *MDEC* 5/25/64; *IMHJ*, May 1984
Adkinson (Addison, Atkinson)	Samuel	3/10/62	Pvt	Transferred to Company B, Residual Battalion; mustered out 8/7/65	IAG Report Vol. V
Anderson	James W.	3/10/62	Pvt	Transferred to Company B, Residual Battalion; mustered out 8/7/65	IAG Report Vol. V
Anshutz (Aushutz)	Gotlieb W.	8/22/61	Pvt	Listed as Corporal 6/30/63; Mustered out 9/7/64	Rummel; IAG Report Vol. V, VIII
Armstrong	George	8/22/61	Pvt	Discharged 10/62; accidental wounds	IAG Report Vol. V, VIII
Baird	George P.	1/24/63	Pvt	Transferred to Company B, Residual Battalion; discharged	IAG Report Vol. V

Baird	William P.	8/22/61	Pvt	Captured 5/29/64; sent to Andersonville Prison; Mustered out 12/14/64	Sparks Diary; IAG Report Vol. V, VIII
Banta	Henry D.	8/22/61	Sgt	Wounded at Poolesville, MD, 9/8/62; Mustered out 9/7/64; raised Co. E, 146th Indiana Volunteers and commissioned Captain	Weaver; IAG Report Vol. V, VIII, Switzerland Co. Biographies
Bardwell	Augustus	8/22/61	Pvt	Wounded at Barbee's Crossroads, VA, 11/5/62; Mustered out 9/7/64	Bardwell service record; IAG Report Vol. V, VIII
Baxter	Francis W.	8/22/61	Pvt	Discharged 11/26/62; disability	IAG Report Vol. V, VIII
Bellamy	Flavius J.	8/22/61	Pvt	Listed as Co. QM Sergeant, 6/30/63; Mustered out 9/7/64 as Sergeant	Rummel; IAG Report Vol. V, VIII
Brindley	Elijah	2/28/62	Pvt	Wounded in bowels during Wilson's Raid, 6/29/64; Captured 9/29/64; died in rebel prison, Richmond, VA; Transferred by roll to Company A, Residual Battalion	NA Record Group 94 CMR; *MDEC* 7/13/64; IAG Report Vol. V, VIII
Brindley	Henry J.	8/22/61	Pvt	Veteran; transferred to Co. A, Residual Battalion; mustered out 8/7/65	IAG Report Vol. V
Brindley	John D.	03/10/62	Pvt	Wounded in foot, 5/64; In Harewood Hospital, 5/64; Veteran; transferred to Co. A, Residual Battalion; mustered out 8/7/65	*IJ* 5/16/64; *IJ* 5/19/64; IAG Report Vol. V
Brindley	William G.	2/23/62	Pvt	Wounded in knee, 5/64; Transferred to Company B, Residual Battalion; mustered out 2/24/65	*IJ* 5/16/64; IAG Report Vol. V
Bristoe (Bristow)	Isaac W.	8/22/61	Pvt	Discharged 1/62; disability	IAG Report Vol. V, VIII
Brooks	Eli	3/10/63	Pvt	Wounded severely in left arm at Gettysburg, arm amputated. Discharged 12/19/63; wounds	*VR* 8/18/63; IAG Hospital Records; IAG Report Vol. V, VIII

Brown	Daniel	8/22/61	Pvt	Hospitalized for Bilious Fever; Discharged 9/62; disability	IAG Hospital Records; IAG Report Vol. V, VIII
Buchanan	Jacob S.	10/22/61	Captain	Promoted Lt. Colonel, 11/8/61; Resigned 10/24/62; served as Lt. Col. of 104th Indiana Volunteers (Minute Men), 7/11–18/63	IAG Report Vol. II & III
Bunchen	Dewitt W.	8/22/61	Pvt	Discharged 12/28/62; disability	IAG Report Vol. V, VIII
Burns	Barney	8/22/61	Pvt	Died 12/13/62; accidental wounds; Apparently shot by John Sauvin, court of inquiry found Sauvin not guilty	IAG Report Vol. V, VIII; NA Record Group 94 CMR
Clark	Charles R.	8/22/61	Pvt	Mustered out 9/7/64	IAG Report Vol. V, VIII
Cline	John C.	8/22/61	Pvt	Detailed to regimental hospital at Gettysburg; Mustered out 9/7/64	Rummel; IAG Report Vol. V, VIII
Cole	Benjamin	8/22/61	Pvt	Discharged 1/9/63; wounded in thigh at Mattaponi River, 8/14/62; was regimental butcher	Switzerland Co. history; OR; IAG Report Vol. V, VIII
Colton (Cotton)	Henry	8/22/61	Cpl	Mustered out 9/7/64 as Sergeant	IAG Report Vol. V, VIII
Cunningham	Charles S.	8/22/61	Pvt	Wounded in bowels during Wilson's Raid, 6/23/64; Died in Andersonville Prison	MDEC 7/13/64; IAG Report Vol. V, VIII
Currie	Marion	3/1/64	Pvt	Died of disease at Alexandria, VA, 5/26/64	Pickerill p. 186; IAG Report Vol. V, VIII
Dailey (Darley)	Josiah	8/22/61	Pvt	Wounded in knee, 7/11/63 near Hagerstown; Admitted to hospital with gunshot wound to right knee, 7/18/63; Mustered out 9/7/64	Bellamy Letters; NA Record Group 94 CMR; IAG Report Vol. V, VIII
Dailey (Darley)	Lorenzo D.	8/22/61	Pvt	In hospital for gonorrhea, 11/20/63–12/31/63; Mustered out 9/7/64; Appointed 1st Lieutenant, Co. I, 137th Indiana Volunteers	NA Record Group 94 CMR; IAG Report Vol. III, V, VIII

Dumont	Sidney M.	8/22/61	Cpl	Discharged 5/62; disability	IAG Report Vol. V, VIII
Dunn	William D.	8/22/61	Pvt	In hospital at Philadelphia, 6/63 for contusion; Transferred to Veterans Reserve Corps	IAG Hospital Records; IAG Report Vol. V, VIII
Dyer	David	8/22/61	Pvt	Discharged 12/61; broke leg while dismounting his horse	IAG Report Vol. V, VIII; Bellamy Letters
Eblin	John M.	8/22/61	Pvt	Wounded at Poolesville, MD 9/8/62; Discharged 1/3/63; wounds	VR 9/25/62; IAG Report Vol. V, VIII
Ellis	Enos	8/22/61	Pvt	In Mt. Pleasant Hospital 7/62; Discharged 1/13/63; disability	IJ 7/9/62; IAG Report Vol. V, VIII
English	Edward J.	8/22/61	Pvt	Wounded 9/5/64; Mustered out 9/7/64	NA Record Group 94; IAG Report Vol. V, VIII
Fallis	David	8/22/61	Sgt	Killed, Poolesville, MD; 9/8/62	VR 9/25/62; IAG Report Vol. V, VIII
Farrell	Hannibal	8/22/61	Pvt	Mustered out 9/7/64	IAG Report Vol. V, VIII
Farrell	John	8/22/61	Pvt	Captured at Gettysburg, PA; Captured at Cabin Point, VA; mustered out 6/6/65	VR 8/18/63; IAG Report Vol. V
Farrell	Silas	8/22/61	Pvt	Wounded in right arm along the Rapidan 6/3/64; Mustered out 9/7/64	NA Record Group 94 CMR; IAG Hospital Records; IAG Report Vol. V, VIII
Ferguson	William H.	8/22/61	Pvt	Killed at Brandy Station, VA; 8/1/63; NA says Culpeper Court House	VR 8/18/63; IAG Report Vol. V, VIII; NA Record Group 94
Gilbert	Benjamin F.	8/22/61	Orderly Sgt	Promoted 2nd Lieutenant, 5/31/63; promoted 1st Lieutenant 12/21/63; Promoted Captain of Company B, Residual Battalion	IAG Report Vol. V & II

Goodner	Jacob J.	9/24/63	Pvt	On Parole in Annapolis, 10/8/64; Transferred to Company A, Residual Battalion; mustered out 8/7/65	IAG Hospital Records; IAG Report Vol. V
Goodner	William S.	8/1/63	Pvt	Wounded in left wrist, 2/15/64; Discharged, 4/28/64; disability	NA Record Group 94 CMR; IAG Report Vol. V, VIII
Gordon	Harrison	8/22/61	Pvt	Mustered out 9/7/64	IAG Report Vol. V, VIII
Grimes	Stephen	3/27/64	Pvt	Transferred to Company A, Residual Battalion; mustered out 8/7/65	IAG Report Vol. V
Hart	Josiah A.	8/22/61	Cpl	Discharged 12/61; disability	IAG Report Vol. V, VIII
Harvey	Pruitt D.	9/10/62	Pvt	Discharged 9/25/63; disability	IAG Report Vol. VIII
Haskell	David M.	8/22/61	Sgt	Wounded in the leg at Upperville, VA, 6/21/63; Captured on Wilson's Raid, 6/29/64; mustered out 5/5/65	Bellamy Letters; *MDEC* 7/13/64; IAG Report Vol. V
Hatch	Lewis	8/22/61	Sgt	Mustered out 9/7/64	IAG Report Vol. V, VIII
Hays	Adam O.	8/22/61	Pvt	Mustered out 9/7/64	IAG Report Vol. V, VIII
Heath	Francis	8/22/61	Pvt	Mustered out 9/7/64	IAG Report Vol. V, VIII
Holingbuc (Hollenback)	Cornelius	8/22/61	Pvt	Captured at Catlett, VA, 11/1/63 while serving as divisional guard of cattle; Escaped 3/6/64, recaptured around 4/5/64; Died in Andersonville Prison, 10/25/64	NA Record Group 94 MR Box 790A; Hard, p. 343; IAG Report Vol. V, VIII
Hollenback	John	3/27/63	Pvt	Transferred to Company B, Residual Battalion	IAG Report Vol. VIII
Hourigaw (Harrigan) (Horrigan)	Michael	8/22/61	Pvt	Accidentally shot Samuel Posten by dropping revolver; Mustered out, no date	Bellamy Letters; IAG Report Vol. V
Hufferd (Hufford)	James L	8/22/61	Pvt	Discharged 12/29/62; disability	IAG Report Vol. V, VIII

Hulley	William H.	3/10/63	Pvt	Died of disease at Acquia Creek, VA, 5/8/63 before even joining regiment	Pickerill p. 186; IAG Report Vol. V, VIII; Bellamy Letters
Jackson	Francis	8/22/61	Pvt	Captured 11/62; Captured on Wilson's Raid, 6/29/64; Mustered out 9/7/64	VR 11/25/62; NA Record Group MR box 790A; IAG Report Vol. V, VIII
Johnston	William R.	8/22/61	Pvt	Mustered out 9/7/64	IAG Report Vol. V, VIII
Kassebaum (Hassbaum)	Frederick W.	8/22/61	Pvt	Wounded at Poolesville, MD 9/8/62; Discharged 12/3/62	VR 9/25/62; IAG Report Vol. V, VIII
Keith	John M.	8/22/61	Pvt	Wounded in hip at Jack's Shop, VA, 9/22/63; Wounded on the Rapidan 5/31/64; Mustered out 9/7/64	*IJ* 9/29/63; IAG Hospital Records; NA Record Group 94; IAG Report Vol. V, VIII
Kern (Kerns)	David C.	3/26/63	Pvt	Transferred to Company B, Residual Battalion; mustered out 8/7/65 as Sergeant	IAG Report Vol. VIII
Kern (Kerns)	Jacob C.	3/26/63	Pvt	Transferred to Company B, Residual Battalion; mustered out 8/7/65	IAG Report Vol. VIII
Kirkpatrick	David W.	8/22/61	Pvt	Wounded in wrist at Brandy Station, VA 6/9/63; Mustered out 9/7/64	VR 6/18/63; IAG Report Vol. V, VIII
Lamson (Lawson) (Lanson)	Rudolph M.	8/22/61	Pvt	Wounded at Poolesville, MD 9/8/62; Transferred to Company B, Residual Battalion as Sergeant; discharged	VR 9/25/62; IAG Report Vol. VIII
Lamson (Lampson)	Thomas D.	8/22/61	Co. QM Sgt	Promoted 2nd Lieutenant, 5/21/63; Captured during Wilson's Raid, 6/30/64; honorably discharged, 5/15/65	IAG Report Vol. V & II; *MDEC* 7/13/64
Lancaster	William W.	8/22/61	Pvt	Mustered out 9/7/64	IAG Report Vol. V, VIII
Lawrence	Theodore	8/22/61	Pvt	Discharged, 11/61; disability	IAG Report Vol. V, VIII

Lee	Charles W.	8/22/61	Pvt	Promoted to 2nd Lieutenant, 12/15/61; Wounded at Antietam, 9/17/62; Promoted Captain, 5/21/63; Transferred to Company A, Residual Battalion; Temporarily attached to Custer's staff at end of war as Division Provost Marshal; Brevetted Major; accompanied Custer to Texas; mustered out 12/65	IAG Report Vol. V; Weaver; NA Record Group 94 MR box 790A; IAG Correspondence
Little	George W.	2/24/62	Pvt	Wounded 5/11/64; Veteran; transferred to Company A, Residual Battalion, promoted Corporal; promoted 1st Lieutenant, Company B, Residual Battalion, 7/1/65; mustered out as QM Sergeant of Battalion	NA Record Group 94; IAG Report Vol. V
Livings	Francis	8/22/61	Pvt	Captured at Catlett, VA, 11/1/63 while serving as divisional guard of cattle; Mustered out 9/7/64	Hard, p. 343; IAG Report Vol. V, VIII
Long	James C. (Polk)	9/10/62	Pvt	Wounded in leg near Brandy Station, VA, 10/11/63; leg amputated; Discharged 4/6/64; wounds	NA Record Group 94 MR box 790A; *VR* 11/12/63; IAG Report Vol. VIII
Matthews	Elijah	8/22/61	Pvt	Mustered out 9/7/64	IAG Report Vol. V, VIII
McDonald (McConnell)	Frank	8/22/61	Wagoner	Mustered out 9/7/64	IAG Report Vol. V, VIII
McKay	Charles D.	8/22/61	Pvt	In Mt. Pleasant Hospital 7/62; Captured, 11/62; Mustered out 9/7/64	*IJ* 7/9/62; *VR* 11/25/62; IAG Report Vol. V, VIII
McKay	William M.	2/24/62	Pvt	On Hospital duty in Baltimore, 6/1/63–7/23/63; Transferred to Company B, Residual Battalion; mustered out 2/24/65	IAG Hospital Records; IAG Report Vol. V
Mead	William W.	8/22/61	Pvt	Mustered out 9/7/64	IAG Report Vol. V, VIII

Miller	James S.	8/22/61	Cpl	Wounded self while inserting pistol into holster, 12/28/61; Listed as QM Clerk, 6/30/63; Mustered out 9/7/64 as a private	Bellamy Letters; Rummel; IAG Report Vol. V, VIII
Miller	John I.	8/22/61	Pvt	Died 12/11/63; disease	IAG Report Vol. V, VIII
Mix	Lyman W.	8/22/61	Pvt	Discharged 8/12/64; disability	IAG Report Vol. V, VIII
Moore	John	8/22/61	Pvt	Mustered out 9/7/64	IAG Report Vol. V, VIII
Morton	Oliver H.	8/22/61	Bugler	Listed as Corporal on 6/30/63; In hospital with syphilis, 2/1 to 6/20/64; Mustered out 9/7/64	Rummel; NA Record Group 94 CMR; IAG Report Vol. V, VIII
Moxley	Francis J.	8/22/61	Pvt	Wounded on the Rapidan, 6/1/64; Mustered out 9/7/64 as a Corporal	NA Record Group 94; IAG Hospital Records; IAG Report Vol. V, VIII
Newkirk	Charles M.	8/22/61	Blksmth	Mustered out 8/31/64	IAG Report Vol. V, VIII
Pate	James W.	8/22/61	Blksmth	Discharged 11/26/62; disability	IAG Report Vol. V, VIII
Patton	William	8/22/61	1st Lt.	Promoted Captain, 12/15/61; promoted Major, 5/29/63; mustered out	IAG Report Vol. II
Pettit	William Q.	8/22/61	Bugler	Died of disease at Brandy Station, VA 1/11/64	Pickerill p. 187; IAG Report Vol. V, VIII
Phillips	James	8/22/61	Pvt	Mustered out 9/7/64	IAG Report Vol. V, VIII
Phillips	Theodore W.	8/22/61	Pvt	Discharged 10/62	IAG Report Vol. V, VIII
Pollock	Alexander	8/22/61	Pvt	In Alexandria, VA hospital as convalescent 7/62–8/62; Scalp wound received along the Rapidan, 10/13/63; Mustered out 9/7/64	IAG Hospital Records; NA Record Group 94 CMR; IAG Report Vol. V, VIII
Porter	Robert P.	8/22/61	2nd Lt.	Promoted 1st Lieutenant, 12/15/61; Dismissed for drunkenness 12/20/63	IAG Report Vol. II; *VR* 10/6/64

Name	First	Date	Rank	Notes	Source
Postin (Paston) (Posten)	Calvin R.	8/1/63	Pvt	Transferred to Company A, Residual Battalion as Musician; mustered out 8/18/65	IAG Report Vol. V
Postin (Poston) (Posten)	Sandford	2/22/64	Pvt	Accidentally wounded in back by discharge of revolver, 7/12/62; Listed as present at Gettysburg; Transferred to Company B, Residual Battalion; mustered out 2/24/65	Bellamy Letters; Rummel; IAG Report Vol. V
Quinn	James	8/22/61	Pvt	Wounded in hip at Hagerstown, MD 9/12/62; Died at Frederick City, MD 10/31/62; wounds	IAG Hospital Records; VR 9/25/62; IAG Report Vol. V, VIII
Quinn	James W.	2/24/62	Pvt	Wounded in leg 7/22/62 near Fredericksburg; On hospital duty in Baltimore, 7/23/63; Transferred to Company B, Residual Battalion; mustered out 2/24/65	IJ 7/28/62; IAG Hospital Records; IAG Report Vol. V
Quirk	John	8/22/61	Pvt	Mustered out 9/7/64	IAG Report Vol. V, VIII
Reed	James	8/22/61	Cpl	Fractured skull of Workman with ax during altercation in camp, 4/12/62; Captured, 11/62; Wounded in right foot along the Rapidan, 10/13/64; Mustered out 9/7/64 as a Sergeant	Bellamy Letters; VR 11/25/62; NA Record Group 94 CMR; IAG Report Vol. V, VIII
Roberts	Moses P.	8/22/61	Pvt	Mustered out 9/7/64	IAG Report Vol. V, VIII
Roberts	Robert W.	8/22/61	Pvt	Died of disease at Budd's Ferry, MD 3/31/62	Bellamy Letters
Rochat	Charles E.	8/22/61	Pvt	Mustered out 9/7/64	IAG Report Vol. V, VIII
Rogers	Henry	3/10/63	Pvt	Transferred to Company B, Residual Battalion; discharged 9/9/64, disability	IAG Report Vol. V
Sauvain (Sanbain)	William	9/10/62	Pvt	Transferred to Co. B, Residual Battalion	IAG Report Vol. VIII

Sedham	Levi	3/10/63	Pvt	Transferred to Company B, Residual Battalion; mustered out 8/7/65	IAG Report Vol. V
See	Robert	8/22/61	Pvt	Discharged 2/63; disability	IAG Report Vol. V, VIII
Seymore (Seymour)	William N.	8/22/61	Pvt	In Alexandra, VA hospital, 7/1/62; Mustered out 9/7/64 as a Corporal	IAG Hospital Records; IAG Report Vol. V, VIII
Sharp	William	8/22/61	Cpl	Listed as Sergeant on 6/30/63; Wounded at Antietam; Mustered out 9/7/64	Rummel; Weaver letter 2/22/1919; IAG Report Vol. V, VIII
Short	Robert B.	8/22/61	Pvt	Mustered out 9/7/64	IAG Report Vol. V, VIII
Siemantel (Siebenthal)	Andrew J.	8/22/61	Pvt	Transferred to Co. B, Residual Battalion; captured at White House, Va; mustered out 6/26/65	IAG Report Vol. VIII
Sprague	Daniel	8/22/61	Pvt	Wounded by knife in leg, 6/28/63; Mustered out 9/7/64	NA Record Group 94 CMR; IAG Report Vol. V, VIII
Stephens (Stevens)	William H.	8/22/61	Pvt	Incorrectly states in Vol. V promoted to Captain, Company I; correction in Vol V; Wounded at Poolesville, MD, 9/8/62; mustered out 9/7/64	VR 9/25/62; Weaver; IAG Report Vol. V, VIII
Stratford	Alfred	9/10/62	Pvt	Transferred to Company B, Residual Battalion; mustered out 2/24/65	IAG Report Vol. VIII
Stratford	Thomas W.	3/24/62	Pvt	Transferred to Company B, Residual Battalion; mustered out 2/24/65	IAG Report Vol. V
Sturman (Stotman) (Stepman)	James	8/22/61	Pvt	Accidentally shot self in knee while cleaning revolver, 9/62, leg amputated; Discharged, 4/22/63; wounds	VR 9/4/62; IAG Hospital Records; IAG Report Vol. V, VIII; NA Record Group 94 CMR
Thompson	James W.	8/22/61	Cpl	Mustered out 9/7/64	IAG Report Vol. V, VIII

Vanice	Jacob B.	8/22/61	Pvt	Discharged 12/6/62; disability	IAG Report Vol. V, VIII
Vanosdol (Vanarsodl)	Argus D.	8/22/61	Pvt	Promoted to Sergeant Major; Promoted to Captain, Company I; Wounded at Stone's River, 1/3/63; resigned 5/1/63; re-entered as 1st Lieutenant of 156th Indiana Volunteers	IAG Report Vol. V; *MDEC* 8/10/86
Vanosdol (Vanarsodl)	Christopher	8/22/61	Pvt	Wounded in right hand and thigh on Wilson's Raid, 6/23/64 and captured; Hand amputated; Died in Prison, Richmond, VA; no date	*MDEC* 7/13/64; NA Record Group 94 CMR; IAG Report Vol. V, VIII
Wallace	George	8/22/61	Pvt	Discharged 11/26/62; disability	IAG Report Vol. V, VIII
Walters	John	11/16/62	Pvt	Wounded in neck 6/9/63 at Brandy Station, VA; Transferred to Company B, Residual Battalion; mustered out 8/7/65	VR 6/18/63; IAG Report Vol. V
Weaver	Augustus C.	2/24/62	Pvt	Captured at Reams Station, VA during Wilson's Raid, 6/29/64; Spent 10 months in Andersonville Prison; Transferred to Company B, Residual Battalion; mustered out 5/5/65	NA Record Group MR box 790A; *MDEC* 7/13/64; Weaver; IAG Report Vol. V
Weaver	Henry B.	1/8/63	Pvt	Transferred to Company B, Residual Battalion; mustered out 8/7/65	IAG Report Vol. VIII
Weaver	John E.	2/24/62	Pvt	Wounded in left knee at Gettysburg; leg amputated; Died, 8/3/63; wounds	VR 7/9/63; *MDEC* 7/17/63; IAG Hospital Records; IAG Report Vol. V, VIII
Webb	William W.	8/22/61	Pvt	Treated for gonorrhea, 10/21/62; Discharged 12/11/62; disability	NA Record Group 94 CMR; IAG Report Vol. V, VIII
Whitton	Richard	3/10/63	Pvt	Unaccounted for	IAG Report Vol. V, VIII

Wolters	John	2/18/63	Pvt	Transferred to Co. B, Residual Battalion	IAG Report Vol. VIII
Wood	Fletcher	8/22/61	Pvt	Wounded in left wrist at Poolesville, MD 9/8/62; In hospital at Washington, 1/63; Transferred to VRC 7/1/63	NA Record Group 94 CMR; *VR* 9/25/62; *MDEC* 1/25/63; IAG Report Vol. V, VIII; *IJ* 8/3/63
Workman	Benjamin	8/22/61	Pvt	Fractured skull in altercation in camp by Ax to head; struck by J.R. Reed, 4/12/62; Wounded in chest and hand at Poolesville, MD, 9/8/62; Mustered out 9/7/64	Bellamy Letters; *VR* 9/25/62; IAG Hospital Records; IAG Report Vol. V, VIII
Wright	Edward	9/10/62	Pvt	Discharged 5/1/63; disability	IAG Report Vol. VIII
Wright	Ira M.	8/22/61	Pvt	Listed as Corporal, 6/30/63; Mustered out 9/7/64 as a Sergeant	Rummel; IAG Report Vol. V, VIII
Wright	James M.	8/22/61	Cpl	Died of typhoid fever at Baltimore, MD; 9/9/61	IAG Report Vol. V, VIII; *VR* 9/19/61
Yarnell	Edward B.	8/22/61	Saddler	Listed as Regimental Saddler, 6/30/63; Mustered out 9/7/64	Rummel; IAG Report Vol. V, VIII
COMPANY B					
Baley	William S.	8/22/61	Pvt	Unaccounted for	IAG Report Vol. V, VIII
Ballard	Richard H.	8/22/61	Pvt	Listed as Corporal, 6/30/63; Unaccounted for	Rummel; IAG Report Vol. V, VIII
Beam	Charles H.	8/22/61	Pvt	In hospital at Fort Ellsworth, MD for Typhoid Fever, 10/6/62; Unaccounted for	IAG Hospital Records; IAG Report Vol. V, VIII
Beard	George W.	8/22/61	Sgt	Listed as Co. Comm. Sergeant, 6/30/63; Wounded in thigh on the Rapidan, 5/3/64; Transferred to Co. B, Residual Battalion; discharged	Rummel; *MDEC* 5/25/64; IAG Hospital Records; IAG Report Vol. V

Beard	Perry C.	8/22/61	Pvt	In New Albany hospital with Measles, 4/3/65; Transferred to Co. B, Residual Battalion; mustered out 8/7/65	IAG Hospital Records; IAG Report Vol. V, VIII
Beard	William D.	8/22/61	Sgt	In hospital at Fort Ellsworth, MD for Typhoid Fever, 10/6/62; Discharged around 11/19/62	IAG Hospital Records; NA Record Group 94 MR box 790a
Beggerly	William M.	8/22/61	Pvt	Captured at Stony Creek, VA; mustered out 2/11/65	IAG Report Vol. V
Brock	Lafayette	8/22/61	Pvt	Unaccounted for	IAG Report Vol. V, VIII
Burtnister	Henry E.F.	8/22/61	Pvt	Unaccounted for; wounded in left leg at Bristoe Station, VA, 8/28/62 while serving as orderly for commander of 1st Brigade, Stevens' Division	IAG Report Vol. V, VIII; NA Record Group 94 CMR; OR
Calvin	James M.	8/1/63	Pvt	Transferred to Company A, Residual Battalion; mustered out 8/7/65	IAG Report Vol. V
Carr	Franklin	8/22/61	Pvt	Unaccounted for	IAG Report Vol. V, VIII
Cartwright	Charles	8/22/61	Bugler	Accidentally wounded in hand, 2/1/63; in hospital 2/9/63; Discharged 4/10/63	NA Record Group 94 MR box 790a
Caughlin	John W.	8/22/61	Cpl	Unaccounted for; Wounded in right elbow at Gettysburg, PA, 7/1/63	IAG Report Vol. V, VIII; NA Record Group 94 CMR
Charles	Jesse	8/22/61	Pvt	Unaccounted for	IAG Report Vol. V, VIII
Charles	William	8/22/61	Pvt	Discharged, 8/30/62	NA Record Group 94 MR box 790a
Congers (Conyers)	William	2/28/63	Pvt	Wounded at Gettysburg; Captured 6/29/64; Rescued from the sinking of the Sultana, 4/28/65; Transferred to Company B, Residual Battalion; mustered out 8/17/65	IAG Hospital Records; VR 8/18/63; NA Record Group 94; IAG Report Vol. V

Crabb	Henry C.	8/22/61	Pvt	Unaccounted for	IAG Report Vol. V, VIII
Crabb	William W.	2/20/65	Pvt	Mustered out 8/7/65	IAG Report Vol. V
Daniel	Nathaniel G.	3/10/62	Pvt	In hospital for epileptic fits, 2/64, 4/64, 10/64; wounded in left leg, 5/8/64; Transferred to Company B, Residual Battalion; discharged	NA Record Group 94 CMR; IAG Report Vol. V
Davis	Dennis	8/22/61	Orderly Sgt	In hospital for Typhoid Fever, 10/6/62; Promoted 2nd Lieutenant, 5/22/62; Wounded in thigh 9/14/63 at Madison Court House, VA; wounded in finger on Wilson's Raid, 6/23/64; mustered out 8/22/64	IAG Hospital Records; IAG Report Vol. V, VIII; VR 10/10/63; MDEC 7/13/64
Davis	Thomas C.	8/22/61	Pvt	In hospital in Philadelphia June 1862; Transferred to Veteran Reserve Corps	IAG Hospital Records; IAG Report Vol. V, VIII
Doll	Elias	8/22/61	Pvt	In Fort Ellsworth, MD hospital for Typhoid Fever; Unaccounted for	IAG Hospital Records; IAG Report Vol. V, VIII
Doll (Dole)	Frederick	8/22/61	Pvt	Listed as Sergeant, 6/30/63; In Annapolis Hospital, 7/63–8/63; Unaccounted for	Rummel; IAG Hospital Records; IAG Report Vol. V, VIII
Donelson	Emanuel	9/29/63	Pvt	Unaccounted for	IAG Report Vol. V, VIII
Douglass	Edward B.	2/2/63	Pvt	Wounded in left lung at Gettysburg; In hospitals 7/63–4/64; Transferred to Company A, Residual Battalion; discharged	IAG Hospital Records; VR 8/18/63; IAG Report Vol. V
Eaton	Benjamin S.	8/22/61	Pvt	Listed as Corporal, 6/30/63; Unaccounted for	Rummel; IAG Report Vol. V, VIII
Edmonson	James H.	8/22/61	Pvt	Unaccounted for	IAG Report Vol. V, VIII
Elliott	John T.	12/31/64	Pvt	Unaccounted for	IAG Report Vol. V, VIII

Evans	John H.	8/22/61	Cpl	Listed as Sergeant, 6/30/63; Killed at Rappahannock Station, 9/63; grave is said to be in the corner of the Rappahannock and A. & O. RR.	Rummel; Pickerill, p. 189; *IJ* 1/25/64
Fair	John	8/22/61	Pvt	Unaccounted for	IAG Report Vol. V, VIII
Flock	Abraham	8/22/61	Wagoner	Wounded along the Rappahannock, 8/25/62; Wounded in ankle, 10/6/62; Unaccounted for	NA Record Group 94 CMR; IAG Hospital Records; IAG Report Vol. V, VIII
Fullilove (Fullerton)	Martin V.	8/22/61	Blksmth	Unaccounted for	IAG Report Vol. V, VIII
Funk	Daniel	8/22/61	Pvt	Unaccounted for; Wounded while on picket at Dumfries, VA, 4/9/62; pinky finger of left hand amputated	IAG Report Vol. V, VIII; NA Record Group 94 CMR
Funk	Larpen	8/22/61	Pvt	Unaccounted for	IAG Report Vol. V, VIII
Gorden	James H.	8/22/61	Pvt	Listed as Corporal, 6/30/63; Wounded in left thigh, 11/63 as Sergeant; Unaccounted for	Rummel; NA Record Group 94 CMR; IAG Report Vol. V, VIII
Gossaman	John A.	8/22/61	Pvt	Discharged, 8/30/62	NA Record Group 94 MR box 790a
Grable (Grabble)	Joseph H.	8/22/61	Sgt	In hospital at Washington for Rheumatism; Transferred to *VRC*, 7/1/63	*MDEC* 1/25/63; IAG Hospital Records; *IJ* 8/3/63; IAG Report Vol. V, VIII
Green	Lorenzo H.	8/22/61	Blksmth	Unaccounted for	IAG Report Vol. V, VIII
Gresham	Benjamin Q. A.	8/22/61	1st Lt.	Promoted Captain, 5/22/62; severely wounded in scrotum and thigh near Chancellorsville 5/1/63; promoted Major, 3/5/64; promoted Lt. Colonel, 10th Indiana Cavalry	NA Record Group 94 CMR; IAG Report Vol. II; IAG Hospital Report

Grey	Jenkins H.	8/22/61	Pvt	Discharged 1/3/62	NA record Group 94, box 790A
Groartney (Gwartney) (Gordney)	John	1/28/62	Pvt	In hospital at Fort Ellsworth, MD, for Bilious Fever, 10/6/62; wounded in left arm, along the Rappahannock, 10/63; Transferred to Co. B, Residual Battalion; mustered out 1/28/65	IAG Hospital Records; NA Record Group 94; IAG Report Vol. V
Hanna	James	3/21/62	Pvt	Reported wounded at Gettysburg, 7/1/63; Transferred to Company B, Residual Battalion; discharged	NA Record Group 94; IAG Report Vol. V
Hanna	Thomas M.	2/24/62	Pvt	Transferred to Company B, Residual Battalion; mustered out 2/24/65	IAG Report Vol. V
Hanna	William A.	3/24/62	Pvt	Died at Frederick, MD, 9/30/62	IAG Report Vol. V, VIII; NA Record Group 94
Harris	George E.	8/22/61	Cpl	Unaccounted for	IAG Report Vol. V, VIII
Haskel	Hanibal	3/24/62	Pvt	Transferred to Company B, Residual Battalion; discharged	IAG Report Vol. V
Holland	Charles E.	3/18/63	Pvt	Wounded twice and left for dead while on picket 7/11/64; In hospital at Washington 10/64; Transferred to Company A, Residual Battalion; mustered out 8/7/65	IAG Hospital Records; *MDEC* 7/20/64; IAG Report Vol. V
Hunt (Hurst)	Oliver B.	8/22/61	Sgt	Unaccounted for; Wounded at Antietam, MD, 9/17/62	IAG Report Vol. V, VIII; NA Record Group 94
Hursh (Hurst)	Nimrod M.	8/22/61	Cpl	Unaccounted for	IAG Report Vol. V, VIII
Irvin	James D.	8/22/61	Captain	Resigned 5/21/62	IAG Report Vol. II
Jenkins	Benjamin F.	8/22/61	Cpl	Killed at Brandy Station 6/9/63	*IJ* 6/18/63
Jordan	James H.		Sgt	Wounded in left hip at Culpeper, VA, 11/8/63	NA Record Group 94 CMR

Kepley	Milroy	8/22/61	Pvt	In hospital at Baltimore, 8/63 with Phthisis; Unaccounted for	IAG Hospital Records; IAG Report Vol. V, VIII
King	Farron	8/22/61	Pvt	Unaccounted for	IAG Report Vol. V, VIII
Lahue	Marshall	8/22/61	2nd Lt.	Promoted 1st Lieutenant, 5/22/62; wounded at Poolesville, MD, 9/8/62; wounded in right side at Brandy Station, VA, 6/9/63; mustered out 8/22/64	IAG Report Vol. II; NA Record Group 94 CMR; VR 9/25/62
Leach	James M.	12/16/61	Pvt	In Mt. Pleasant Hospital 7/62; (Mistaken for John in some reports of Gettysburg) Transferred to Company B, Residual Battalion; mustered out 12/16/64	IJ 7/9/62; VR 8/18/63; NA Record Group 94; IAG Report Vol. V
Leach	John H.	12/16/61	Pvt	Listed as Corporal, 6/30/63; wounded in left arm and face at Gettysburg, PA, 7/1/63; Transferred to Company B, Residual Battalion as Corporal; discharged	Rummel; NA Record Group 94 CMR; IAG Report Vol. V
Lemay	Andrew J.	8/22/61	Pvt	In hospital at Fort Ellsworth, MD for diarrhea; discharged, sometime around 11/20/62	IAG Hospital Records; NA Record Group 94 MR box 790a
Lennel (Lemnell)	Michael	8/22/61	Pvt	In hospital at Washington, 1/63; Discharged 1/10/63	MDEC 1/25/63; IAG Hospital Records; NA Record Group 94 MR box 790a
Leslie	Philo G.	8/22/61	Bugler	Promoted to Regimental Commissary, 7/1/63; mustered out 8/22/64; re-entered as 1st Lieutenant, Co. D, 13th Indiana Cavalry	IAG Report Vol. III, V, VIII
Lewallen	Augustus	2/24/62	Pvt	Wounded at Gettysburg, PA, 7/1/63; Veteran; transferred to Company A, Residual Battalion; mustered out 8/7/65 as Corporal	VR 8/18/63; IAG Report Vol. V

Love	Philip P.	8/22/61	Pvt	Killed by shot to head Culpepper, VA, 10/15/63	NA Record Group 94 CMR; *VR* 11/12/63
Majors	John W.	8/22/61	Pvt	In hospital at Alexandria, VA, 7/62; Discharged 12/21/62	IAG Hospital Records; NA Record Group 94 MR box 790a
Marsh	James H.A.	1/30/62	Pvt	Transferred to Company B, Residual Battalion; captured 3/1/64; mustered out 1/21/65	IAG Report Vol. V
Marsh	William T.	8/22/61	Pvt	Listed as Corporal, 6/30/63; Unaccounted for	Rummel; IAG Report Vol. V, VIII
Martin	John	8/22/61	Pvt	Unaccounted for	IAG Report Vol. V, VIII
McCarty	James W.	8/22/61	Pvt	Unaccounted for	IAG Report Vol. V, VIII
McCloud	Martin H.	8/22/61	Pvt	Unaccounted for	IAG Report Vol. V, VIII
McFarland	William	8/22/61	Pvt	Mortally wounded in right thigh at Culpeper, VA, 11/8/63, Died 9 hours later	NA Record Group 94 CMR; *MDEC* 11/24/63
McNeel (McNeal) (McNeil)	David	2/24/62	Pvt	Died 5/17/62	NA Record Group 94 MR box 790a
McNeel (McNeal) (O'Neal) (Neal)	John	2/24/62	Pvt	In hospital at Mt. Pleasant, 7/62; Transferred to Company B, Residual Battalion; mustered out 2/24/65	IAG Hospital Records; IAG Report Vol. V
Melton	George W.	8/10/62	Pvt	Wounded at Gettysburg; Wounded in chest near Riddle's Shop, VA, 6/13/64; Transferred to Company B, Residual Battalion as Corporal; discharged	VR 8/18/63; *MDEC* 6/24/64; IAG Report Vol. V
Melton	Isaac J.	8/22/61	Pvt	Discharged 11/25/62; disability	NA Record Group 94 MR box 790a
Melton	Jesse T.	8/22/61	Pvt	Wounded in right forearm at Gettysburg, PA, 7/1/63; Unaccounted for	NA Record Group 94 CMR; IAG Report Vol. V, VIII

Miller	Matthias	8/22/61	Pvt	In hospital for syphilis, 6/28 to 8/14/62; Wounded in arm and side at Upperville, VA, 6/21/63; Unaccounted for	NA Record Group 94 CMR; IAG Report Vol. V, VIII
Molten (Mohler)	Martin V.	8/22/61	Pvt	Unaccounted for	IAG Report Vol. V, VIII
Mulvany (Mulvaney)	Pleasant D.	8/22/61	Pvt	Married Susan Glass of Culpepper County, VA, 1/12/64; deserted 1/29/64; Veteran	MDEC 2/5/64; Gilpin Diary; IAG Report Vol. V
Murphy	James T.	8/22/61	Pvt	Unaccounted for	IAG Report Vol. V, VIII
Nelson	George A.	8/22/61	Pvt	Wounded slightly in the leg at Riddle's Shop, VA, 6/13/64; Unaccounted for	MDEC 6/24/64; IAG Report Vol. V, VIII
Oldham	William H.	8/22/61	Pvt	Unaccounted for	IAG Report Vol. V, VIII
Olmstead	Charles W.	2/24/62	Pvt	Captured 6/29/64; Transferred to Company B, Residual Battalion; discharged	NA Record Group 94 IAG Report Vol. V
Ornick (Orwich)	Isaac	8/22/61	Pvt	Unaccounted for	IAG Report Vol. V, VIII
Page	Eugene	8/22/61	Pvt	Wounded in thigh 6/9/63 at Brandy Station, VA; Unaccounted for	VR 6/18/63; IAG Report Vol. V, VIII
Pavy (Pavey)	Henry C.	2/24/62	Pvt	Wounded at Gettysburg, PA, 7/1/63; left arm amputated; Died, 7/22/63	VR 8/18/63; IAG Report Vol. V, VIII; NA Record Group 94
Purcell	Isaac	2/26/65	Pvt	Mustered out 8/7/65	IAG Report Vol. V
Purcell	Thomas	10/1/62	Pvt	Wounded in left arm at Gettysburg, PA, 7/1/63; Wounded slightly along the Rapidan, 5/3/64; Transferred to Company B, Residual Battalion; mustered out 8/7/65	VR 8/18/63; MDEC 5/25/64; IAG Report Vol. V
Ragan (Reagan)	Irvin H.	8/22/61	Pvt	Unaccounted for	IAG Report Vol. V, VIII

Reagan	James H.	1/28/62	Pvt	Transferred to Company B, Residual Battalion; captured 3/1/64; mustered out 1/21/65	IAG Report Vol. V
Reed	James W.	2/24/62	Pvt	Transferred to Company B, Residual Battalion; mustered out 2/24/65	IAG Report Vol. V
Rintner	Peter M.	8/22/61	Saddler	Unaccounted for	IAG Report Vol. V, VIII
Rivers	Toleman	8/22/61	Pvt	Unaccounted for	IAG Report Vol. V, VIII
Rumbley	William P.	8/22/61	Cpl	Unaccounted for	IAG Report Vol. V, VIII
Ruth	Monroe	8/22/61	Pvt	Unaccounted for	IAG Report Vol. V, VIII
Sands	Martin V.	8/22/61	Pvt	Unaccounted for	IAG Report Vol. V, VIII
Senn (Sener)	Matthew	8/22/61	Pvt	In hospital at Alexandria, VA with broken leg, 7/62; listed as Bugler, 6/30/63; Unaccounted for	IAG Hospital Records; Rummel; IAG Report Vol. V, VIII
Shewmaker	David H.H.	8/22/61	Pvt	Wounded in right thigh at 6/9/63 at Brandy Station, VA; Unaccounted for	NA Record Group 94 CMR; *VR* 6/18/63; IAG Report Vol. V, VIII
Shuman	John B.	2/26/64	Pvt	Transferred to Co. A Residual Battalion	IAG Report Vol. V, VIII
Sibert	William W.	8/22/61	Pvt	Listed as present at Gettysburg, June 30, 1863; Family records claim he was wounded at Gettysburg and mustered out 8/64; Unaccounted for	Rummel; Daniel Harrison; IAG Report Vol. V, VIII
Smith	Charles	12/8/62	Pvt	Discharged 9/8/63; disability	IAG Report Vol. V, VIII
Spangler	John	3/10/62	Pvt	Transferred to Company B, Residual Battalion; discharged	IAG Report Vol. V
Stephens	Alanson	8/22/61	Cpl	Listed as Sergeant Major, 6/30/63; Unaccounted for	Rummel; IAG Report Vol. V, VIII

Sterman	James	8/22/61	Pvt	In hospital for Typhoid Fever, 10/6/62; Transferred to Company A	IAG Hospital Records; IAG Report Vol. V, VIII
Stevenson	Hugh	2/25/62	Pvt	Captured near Bowling Green, VA, 8/7/62; Wounded in right thigh near Riddle's Shop, VA, 6/13/64; Transferred to Company B, Residual Battalion; mustered out 2/24/65	Bellamy Letters; *MDEC* 8/11/62; *MDEC* 6/24/64; IAG Report Vol. V
Stoker	Adam	8/22/61	Pvt	Listed as Sergeant, 6/30/63; Unaccounted for	Rummel; IAG Report Vol. V, VIII
Stoker	Charles	8/22/61	Cpl	Unaccounted for	IAG Report Vol. V, VIII
Supp	Peter	8/22/61	Pvt	Unaccounted for	IAG Report Vol. V, VIII
Thompson	Walker	8/23/64	Pvt	Unaccounted for	IAG Report Vol. V, VIII
Trotter	John	8/22/61	Co. QM Sgt	Listed as Orderly Sergeant, 6/30/63	Rummel; IAG Report Vol. V
Trotter	Marcus L.	8/22/61	Pvt	Listed as Corporal, 6/30/63; Unaccounted for	Rummel; IAG Report Vol. V, VIII
Vibbert	Isaac E.	8/22/61	Pvt	Unaccounted for; killed at Gettysburg, 7/1/63	IAG Report Vol. V, VIII; Rummel, p. 11
Ward	William H.H.	2/25/62	Pvt	Veteran; transferred to Company A, Residual Battalion	IAG Report Vol. V
Wayne	Joshua	8/22/61	Pvt	In hospital at Washington, 1/63; discharged 2/7/63	*MDEC* 1/25/63; IAG Hospital Records; NA Record Group 94 MR box 790a
Wilson	Jesse	3/18/62	Pvt	Transferred to Company B, Residual Battalion; discharged	IAG Report Vol. V
Wiseman	Henry W.	2/22/62	Pvt	Died, 10/12/62	IAG Report Vol. V, VIII

Wiseman	John	2/24/62	Pvt	Wounded slightly in left shoulder at Riddle's Shop, VA, 6/13/64; Transferred to Company B, Residual Battalion; mustered out 2/24/65	MDEC 6/24/64; IAG Report Vol. V
Zimmerman	Elhanon W.	8/22/61	Pvt	Listed as Corporal, 6/30/63; Unaccounted for	Rummel; IAG Report Vol. V, VIII
COMPANY C					
Albro	James	8/22/61	Pvt	Listed as Corporal at muster out; Unaccounted for	Switzerland Co. Roll; IAG Report Vol. V, VIII
Allen	Charles W.	2/25/62	Pvt	Listed as Bugler, 6/30/63; Captured 11/8/63; Transferred to Company B, Residual Battalion as Musician; mustered out 3/4/65	Rummel; IAG Report Vol. V; Switzerland Co. Roll
Alley	Fuel	2/21/62	Pvt	Wounded in right leg, 4/5/63 while on picket near Dumfries, VA; Transferred to Company B, Residual Battalion; Appointed Sergeant and discharged	Bellamy Letters; NA Record Group 94 CMR; IAG Report Vol. V
Anderson	George	8/22/61	Pvt	Mustered out	IAG Report Vol. V, VIII
Banks	Charles	3/27/64	Pvt	Transferred to Company A, Residual Battalion; mustered out 8/7/65	IAG Report Vol. V
Banks	Simeon	8/22/61	Pvt	Killed at Madison Court House, VA, shot through head; 9/13/63	NA Record Group 94; IAG Report Vol. V, VIII; VR 10/8/63; IJ 9/25/63
Barkis	Francis A.	8/22/61	Pvt	mustered out	NA Record Group 94 MR box 790a
Bayze (Baze)	Albert	8/22/61	Pvt	Wounded accidentally in left foot, 6/15/65 at Louisville, KY; Veteran, transferred to Co. A, Residual Battalion; mustered out 8/7/65	NA Record Group 94 CMR; IAG Report Vol. V

Blackburn	James K.	8/22/61	Pvt	Shot "accidentally" 8/11/62 at Second Bull Run; Unaccounted for; in hospital for Syphilis, 10/24/62; deserted but returned for treatment 4/22/63	VR 8/21/62; IAG Report Vol. V, VIII; NA Record Group 94 CMR
Bledsoe	Benjamin	8/22/61	Pvt	Wounded in leg, 10/21/63 as Sergeant; Killed at White Oak Swamp on Wilson's Raid, 6/27/64	VR 11/12/63; *MDEC* 7/13/64; IAG Report Vol. V, VIII
Bosso	William	8/22/61	Pvt	Unaccounted for	IAG Report Vol. V, VIII
Bright	Osmar	8/22/61	Bugler	Discharged 5/22/63; disability	IAG Report Vol. V, VIII
Bright	Peter	2/28/62	Pvt	Killed at Williamsport, MD or Chester Gap, VA, 7/21/63	VR 8/18/63; *IJ* 8/5/63
Bucher (Butcher)	Charles	8/22/61	Pvt	Drowned in Rappahannock River, VA, 7/9/62; fell off of horse	IAG Report Vol. V, VIII; VR 7/24/62
Burton	Allen	8/22/61	Pvt	In hospital at Alexandria, VA for Fever, 8/62; promoted sergeant, 1/1/64; Unaccounted for	IAG Hospital Records; IAG Report Vol. V, VIII
Campfield	William	8/22/61	Pvt	Unaccounted for	IAG Report Vol. V, VIII
Clark	Paul	8/22/61	2nd Lt.	Promoted 1st Lieutenant, 12/15/61; resigned 6/21/62; re-entered as 1st Lieutenant, Co. D, 10th Indiana Cavalry	IAG Report Vol. III, V, VIII
Cline	Milton W.	8/22/61	Pvt	Became scout/spy for Army of Potomac; Mustered out with regiment as Co. Commissary Sgt.	Fishel; *MDEC* 12/3/63; NA Record Group 94 MR box 790
Courtney	Andrew	8/22/61	Pvt	Discharged, 3/11/62	IAG Report Vol. V, VIII
Coy	Joseph	8/22/61	Pvt	Transferred to Battery M, 2nd U.S. Artillery, 10/21/62	Switzerland Co. Roll; IAG Report Vol. V, VIII
Dailey (Darley)	Jesse V.	8/22/61	Pvt	Unaccounted for	IAG Report Vol. V, VIII
Danglade	Theophilus M.	8/22/61	Captain	Resigned, 12/15/61	IAG Report Vol. II

Demaree	Benjamin F.	4/2/63	Pvt	Transferred to Company A, Residual Battalion; mustered out 8/7/65	IAG Report Vol. V
Driver	Elliott	8/22/61	Pvt	Captured at Williamsport, MD, 7/22/63; Unaccounted for	VR 8/18/63; IAG Report Vol. V, VIII
Elston	Isaiah	3/10/63	Pvt	Wounded in arm 9/13/63 at Madison Court House, VA; In hospital at Washington for slight gunshot wound; Transferred to Company A, Residual Battalion; mustered out 8/7/65	VR 10/8/63; IAG Hospital Records; IAG Report Vol. V
Fagan	Marion	8/22/61	Sgt	Discharged, 11/27/62; disability	IAG Report Vol. V, VIII
Franklin	Henry	8/22/61	Pvt	Slightly wounded at Riddle's Shop, VA, 6/13/64; Mustered out, 2/14/65	MDEC 6/24/64; IAG Report Vol. V
Fugit (Fuget) (Faget)	Morton D.	8/22/61	Blksmth	Wounded at Gettysburg in left knee; captured 1/27/64	IAG Hospital Records; Switzerland Co. Roll
Fugit (Fuget) (Faget)	Walter	8/15/62	Pvt	Captured 1/27/64; died in Andersonville Prison, 7/20/64; Transferred by roll to Company B, Residual Battalion	NA Record Group 94 MR box 790A; Sparks Diary
Gailey	John	8/22/61	Pvt	Listed as blacksmith at muster out; Unaccounted for	Switzerland Co. Roll; IAG Report Vol. V, VIII
Gibbons	James W.	8/22/61	Pvt	Discharged 1/24/62; disability by epilepsy	IAG Report Vol. V, VIII
Goddin	Albert	8/22/61	Pvt	Captured 1/27/64 near James City, VA; mustered out 1/24/65	MDEC 2/5/64; IAG Report Vol. V
Greenwood	William W.	8/22/61	Pvt	In hospital at Philadelphia for fever, 12/62–1/63; Captured 1/27/64; Died in Andersonville Prison, 10/28/64	IAG Hospital Records; Sparks Diary; IAG Report Vol. V
Harris	Leander W.	8/22/61	Saddler	Severely wounded in abdomen near South Mt., MD, 9/13/62; Discharged, 4/4/63; wounds	MDEC 9/22/62; NA Record Group 94 CMR; IAG Report Vol. V, VIII

Heath	Martin	8/22/61	Pvt	In Washington Street Hospital, Alexandria 8/62; Wounded in left lung 9/14/63 Madison Court House; Died in Washington, D.C. 10/22/63; wounds	IAG Hospital Records; *VR* 10/8/63; *IJ* 8/5/62; IAG Report Vol. V, VIII
Heath	Samuel A.	8/22/61	Pvt	Married a Virginian woman from King Georges County, 2/22/63; Killed at White Oak Swamp near Riddle's Shop, 6/13/64	*MDEC* 4/18/63; Watlington p. 62; IAG Report Vol. V, VIII
Higgins	James	3/10/63	Pvt	Transferred to Company A, Residual Battalion; mustered out 8/7/65	IAG Report Vol. V
Higgins	John W.	2/23/62	Pvt	In hospital in New York, 12/63; captured 1/27/64; died in Andersonville Prison, 9/15/64; Veteran, transferred to Company B, Residual Battalion	IAG Hospital Records; *MDEC* 2/5/64; Switzerland Co. Roll; IAG Report Vol. V
Higgins	Martin M.	3/27/64	Pvt	Transferred to Company B, Residual Battalion	*MDEC* 2/5/64; Switzerland Co. Roll; Sparks Diary; IAG Report Vol. V
Hise	Granville	8/22/61	Pvt	Discharged, 1/10/63; disability	IAG Report Vol. V, VIII
Holmes	David W.	9/15/62	Pvt	Wounded in left knee on Wilson's Raid, 6/28/64; Transferred to Company B, Residual Battalion; discharged	NA Record Group 94 CMR; Switzerland Co. Roll; *MDEC* 7/13/64; *VR* 7/14/64; IAG Report Vol. V
Humphrey	Isaac	8/22/61	Pvt	Captured 1/27/64; Died in Andersonville Prison, 6/23/64	*MDEC* 2/5/64; Switzerland Co. Roll; Sparks Diary; IAG Report Vol. V
Hunt	Dudley	8/22/61	Pvt	Transferred to Battery M, 2nd U.S. Artillery, 10/12/62	Switzerland Co. Roll; IAG Report Vol. V, VIII

Irby	Charles W.	8/22/61	Pvt	Discharged, 4/20/62; disabilities	IAG Report Vol. V, VIII
Irby	John M.	8/22/61	Pvt	Listed as Corporal, 6/30/63; Severely wounded in left hand near Rappahannock River, 8/2/63, three fingers were amputated; mustered out; Unaccounted for	Rummel; VR 8/18/63; IAG Report Vol. V, VIII; NA Record Group 94 MR box 790
Johnson	Charles	8/22/61	Sgt	Wounded at Upperville, VA, 6/21/63 leg amputated on the field; Discharged, 3/7/64; wounds	VR 7/9/63; IAG Report Vol. V, VIII; NA Record Group 94
Joyce	James	3/23/62	Pvt	Died in Richmond prison, 11/12/63	Switzerland Co. Roll; IAG Report Vol. V, VIII
Kaney (Kana) (Kennedy)	William	8/22/61	Pvt	Wounded 9/8/62 in both hands at Poolesville, MD; Wounded in face at Madison Court House, 9/14/63; captured 1/27/64 and sent to Andersonville Prison; Lost on the *Sultana*, 4/27/65	Beck, 142; VR 10/10/63; Switzerland Co. Roll; *MDEC* 9/29/63; *MDEC* 2/5/64; IAG Report Vol. V
Kelso	Edward (Edmund)	8/22/61	Pvt	Captured near Bowling Green, 8/7/62; Captured 1/27/64; Died in Andersonville Prison, 6/13/64	VR 8/21/62; MEDC 8/11/62; Switzerland Co. Roll; Sparks Diary; IAG Report Vol. V
Kincaid	James C.	8/22/61	Wagoner	In hospital with small pox, 6/10/63; Mustered out	Switzerland Co. Roll; IAG Report Vol. V, VIII
Kincaid	John C.	8/22/61	Pvt	Wounded in foot, at hospital at Alexandria, VA, 8/62; Unaccounted for	IJ 8/8/62; IAG Hospital Records; IAG Report Vol. V, VIII
Kincaid	John W.	8/15/62	Pvt	Transferred to Company B, Residual Battalion as Corporal; discharged	IAG Report Vol. V
Kinnet	James W.	8/22/61	Pvt	Unaccounted for	IAG Report Vol. V, VIII

Kirkpatrick	Newton	8/22/61	Pvt	In hospital for deafness, 3/15/64; Died at Portsmouth Grove, RI; 7/20/64 of tuberculosis	NA Record Group 94 CMR; IAG Report Vol. V
Lamb	George W.	3/14/62	Pvt	Transferred to Company B, Residual Battalion; mustered out 2/14/65	IAG Report Vol. V
Lamb	Samuel	8/22/61	Cpl	Listed as Co. QM Sergeant 6/30/63; Compound fracture to head at Gettysburg; Died at York, PA 7/29/63; was engaged to be married to a young woman in Warren County, PA; Died, wounds	Rummel; IAG Hospital Records; VR 8/18/63; VR 8/13/63; IAG Report Vol. V, VIII
Lee	George W.	8/22/61	Pvt	Wounded in left thigh at Shepherdstown, VA, 8/25/64; Veteran, transferred to Co. A, Residual Battalion; mustered out 8/7/65	NA Record Group 94 CMR; Watlington p. 77; IAG Report Vol. V
Lee	John M.	4/2/63	Pvt	Captured 1/27/64; died at Andersonville Prison, 8/8/64; Transferred by roll to Company A, Residual Battalion	Sparks Diary; IAG Report Vol. V
Lemon (Lemmon)	Charles	8/22/61	1st Lt.	Promoted Captain, 12/15/61; promoted Major 3/12/63; died 7/2/63 of wounds received at Gettysburg; had premonition of death the morning of July 1; was mortally wounded at stone wall near Seminary later in day	IAG Report Vol. II; MDEC 7/17/63; VR 8/18/63; National Tribune-Day article; Indiana at Gettysburg
Lewis	Isaac	8/22/61	Pvt	Wounded in elbow 9/14/63 at Madison Court House, VA; Captured near James City, VA, 1/27/64 as Corporal; Died in Andersonville Prison, 7/7/64	IAG Hospital Records; VR 10/8/63; MDEC 2/5/64; Sparks Diary; IAG Report Vol. V
Long	John G.	8/15/62	Pvt	Transferred to Company B, Residual Battalion; discharged 4/6/64, wounds	IAG Report Vol. V

Long	William	8/22/61	Sgt	Captured 6/20/63 at Aldie, VA; Promoted 1st Lieutenant; returns to regiment after exchange 10/63	VR 8/18/63; IJ 6/27/63; IAG Report Vol. V, VIII; VR 11/12/63
Marsh	James	8/22/61	Pvt	Listed as Corporal at muster out; Unaccounted for	Switzerland Co. Roll; IAG Report Vol. V, VIII
Martin	Ephraim	8/22/61	Orderly Sgt	Promoted 2nd Lieutenant, 12/15/61; promoted 1st Lieutenant 6/22/62; promoted Captain, 6/22/63; Slightly wounded in shoulder at Gettysburg, PA, 7/1/63; mustered out 8/22/64	IAG Report Vol. V & II; VR 8/18/63
Martin	George W.	8/22/61	Pvt	Listed as Corporal, 6/30/63; Captured 1/27/64 near James City, VA as Sergeant; Died in Andersonville Prison, 5/31/64	Rummel; MDEC 2/5/64; Sparks Diary; IAG Report Vol. V
Martin	Joseph	8/22/61	Cpl	Discharged 2/12/62; disability	IAG Report Vol. V, VIII
McLeod	James S.	1/1/62	Pvt	Transferred to Company B, Residual Battalion; discharged	IAG Report Vol. V
McSparks	William	8/5/62	Pvt	Listed as Bugler, 6/30/63; Transferred to Company B, Residual Battalion as Musician; discharged	Rummel; IAG Report Vol. V
Miller	Benjamin C.	8/22/61	Blksmth	Discharged 3/11/62	IAG Report Vol. V, VIII
Minnot (Minnet)	Francis L.	8/22/61	Cpl	Unaccounted for; wounded below the knee at Sulphur Springs, VA, 11/8/63	IAG Report Vol. V, VIII; Switzerland Co. Roll; MDEC 11/24/63
Morris	Henry	8/22/61	Pvt	Veteran, transferred to Co. A, Residual Battalion mustered out 8/7/65	IAG Report Vol. V
Morris	John	8/22/61	Pvt	Unaccounted for	IAG Report Vol. V, VIII
Moxley	John	8/22/61	Pvt	In hospital at New York for Diarrhea and debility; Unaccounted for	IAG Hospital Records; IAG Report Vol. V, VIII

Myers	Abijah H.	3/24/62	Pvt	Veteran, transferred to Co. A, Residual Battalion, promoted to Corporal; mustered out as private, 8/7/65	IAG Report Vol. V
Myers	Eugene R.	8/22/61	Pvt	Listed as Sergeant, 6/30/63; Veteran, transferred to Co. A, Residual Battalion; promoted 2nd Lieutenant, 6/1/65; mustered out as Commissary Sergeant of Battalion	Rummel; IAG Report Vol. V
Myers	John M.	3/23/62	Pvt	Veteran, transferred to Co. A, Residual Battalion; In Washington Street Hospital, Alexandria 8/62	IAG Report Vol. V; *IJ* 8/5/62
Noah	Balser	8/22/61	Pvt	Unaccounted for	IAG Report Vol. V, VIII
Owens	Fletcher G.	8/22/61	Pvt	In hospital at Alexandria, VA, 8/62; In hospital for fever, 1/63; Discharged, 11/24/63; disability; re-entered service as Captain, Co. G, 123rd Indiana Volunteers	*MDEC* 1/25/63; IAG Hospital Records; IAG Report Vol. V, VIII
Pallman	William	8/22/61	Pvt	Discharged 1/20/62, disability	Switzerland Co. Muster Roll
Peabody	Ira	8/22/61	Pvt	Unaccounted for	IAG Report Vol. V, VIII
Pebler	David	8/22/61	Pvt	Reported missing at Gettysburg; Killed 9/11/63 at Brandy Station, VA	*VR* 8/18/63; Rummel; Pickerill p. 189; *VR* 11/12/63; IAG Report Vol. V, VIII
Peelman (Pellman)	Christopher C.	8/22/61	Pvt	Listed as Corporal, 6/30/63; Wounded in leg at Bristoe Station 10/15/63; Unaccounted for	Rummel; *VR* 11/12/63; *IJ* 10/19/63; IAG Report Vol. V, VIII
Peters	William D.	8/22/61	Pvt	Unaccounted for; promoted Sergeant, May 1863; Wounded in shoulder at Upperville, VA, 6/21/63	IAG Report Vol. V, VIII; Switzerland Co. Muster Roll; NA Record Group 94 CMR

Pickett	Alfred	8/22/61	Pvt	Died in hospital, 1/15/64	IAG Report Vol. V, VIII
Pickett	Theodore (Ed)	3/23/62	Pvt	In Grace Church hospital at Alexandria, VA for Fever 8/62; Discharged 4/6/63, disability	IAG Hospital Records; *IJ* 8/5/62; IAG Report Vol. VIII
Pittman	Hilliard	2/20/63	Pvt	Captured near Rappahannock River, 8/2/63; Transferred to Company A, Residual Battalion; mustered out 8/7/65	VR 8/18/63; IAG Report Vol. V
Plen (Plew) (Plue)	Abraham	8/22/61	Pvt	Died; AG says Discharged	Pickerill, p. 187; IAG Report Vol. V, VIII
Plen (Plew) (Plue)	David	8/22/61	Cpl	Scout/spy for the Army of the Potomac; Listed as detached and serving at an unknown location 6/30/63; Unaccounted for	Fishel; Rummel; IAG Report Vol. V, VIII
Powlesson	James R.	8/22/61	Pvt	Discharged 6/3/63	IAG Report Vol. V, VIII
Ricketts	Albert	8/22/61	Pvt	Mustered out	IAG Report Vol. V, VIII
Ricketts	George	8/22/61	Pvt	Discharged, 3/11/63, disability	Switzerland Co. Roll
Roberts	Daniel	8/22/61	Cpl	Discharged 11/12/61; disability	IAG Report Vol. V, VIII
Rogers	George	8/22/61	Cpl	Listed as Co. Comm. Sergeant, 6/30/63; Promoted 2nd Lieutenant, 11/3/63; captured 3/14/64; Transferred to Company B, Residual Battalion; mustered out, 1/14/65; Died 1/31/65	Rummel; IAG Report Vol. V & II; Pickerill, p. 137; *VR* 2/2/65
Rogers	James	8/22/61	Cpl	Listed as Blacksmith, 6/30/63; Unaccounted for	Rummel; IAG Report Vol. V, VIII
Rollinson	Calvin W.	8/22/61	Pvt	Mustered out	IAG Report Vol. V, VIII
Rothchilds	Max	9/23/62	Pvt	Deserted, 1/20/63	IAG Report Vol. VIII

Schroeder	John T.	8/22/61	Pvt	Severely wounded at Chester Gap, VA 7/22/63; Discharged, 7/26/64; wounds	NA Record Group 94; *VR* 8/18/63; IAG Report Vol. V, VIII
Shadday	Fogleman	3/10/63	Pvt	Discharged 7/12/64; disability	IAG Report Vol. V, VIII; Switzerland Co. Roll
Shadday	George	8/22/61	Pvt	Mustered out	IAG Report Vol. V, VIII
Sheets	William H.	8/22/61	Pvt	discharged, 11/29/62, disability	Switzerland Co. Roll
Shutts	Isaac H.	3/17/62	Pvt	Killed by accidental discharge of a carbine as Corporal 12/6/63	Switzerland Co. Roll; *MDEC* 12/17/63; IAG Report Vol. V, VIII
Smelley	Thomas	8/22/61	Pvt	Wounded in right side at Bealeton Station, VA, 10/25/63; Died 12/3/63	NA Record Group 94 CMR; Switzerland Co. Roll
Smith	William	8/22/61	Pvt	Mustered out	IAG Report Vol. V, VIII
Sparks	Henry	8/22/61	Sgt	Listed as Corporal 6/30/63; Captured 1/27/64; at Andersonville Prison until 11/9/64; Veteran, transferred to Company B, Residual Battalion as First Sergeant	Rummel; Sparks Diary; IAG Vol. V
Stepleton	Jesse O.	2/18/64	Pvt	Transferred to Company A, Residual Battalion; mustered out 8/7/65	IAG Report Vol. V
Stepleton	Wesley L.	10/23/62	Pvt	Discharged, 1/13/62; disability—elsewhere says he enlisted 2/29/64 in Co. A, Residual Battalion and was mustered out 8/7/65	IAG Report Vol. V, VIII
Stevenson	William	8/22/61	Pvt	Discharged 12/19/62, disability	Switzerland Co. Roll
Storm	George I.	6/1/63	Pvt	Transferred to Company A, Residual Battalion; mustered out 8/7/65	IAG Report Vol. V

Swango	Lewis	8/22/61	Pvt	Mustered out	IAG Report Vol. V, VIII
Taylor	Andrew	8/22/61	Pvt	Listed as Corporal, 6/30/63; promoted Sergeant, 7/1/64; Unaccounted for	IAG Report Vol. V, VIII; Rummel; Switzerland Co. Roll
Thomas	Frederick	8/22/61	Pvt	Mustered out	IAG Report Vol. V, VIII
Tinker	Ira B.	8/22/61	Co. QM Sgt	Promoted 2nd Lieutenant, 6/22/62; Honorably discharged 5/7/63; disability	IAG Report Vol. V & II NA Record Group 94 CMR
Tower	Oliver	10/27/62	Pvt	Transferred to Company B, Residual Battalion; mustered out 8/7/65	IAG Report Vol. V
Towers	John	8/22/61	Bugler	Listed as Saddler 6/30/63; Unaccounted for	Rummel; IAG Report Vol. V, VIII
Trowbridge	Enoch	8/22/61	Pvt	In hospital at Alexandria, 7/62 for lung disease; Died 10/12/62	IAG Hospital Records; IAG Report Vol. V, VIII
Vails (Vail, Vale)	William S.	8/22/61	Pvt	Wounded slightly 8/24/64; Veteran, transferred to Co. A, Residual Battalion; mustered out 8/7/65	NA Record Group 94; IAG Report Vol. V
Walks	Andrew	8/22/61	Pvt	Captured on Wilson's Raid, 6/28/64; Mustered out as Sergeant	NA Record Group 94 MR box 790a; IAG Report Vol. V, VIII
Walks	Martin V.	8/22/61	Pvt	In hospital and listed as wounded, 7/63; Slightly wounded in head 9/13/63 at Madison Court House, VA; Mustered out as Sergeant	IAG Hospital Records; NA Record Group 94 CMR; *VR* 10/8/63; IAG Report Vol. V, VIII
White	Charles N.	8/22/61	Pvt	Mustered out as Sergeant	IAG Report Vol. V, VIII
Wilcox	Charles	8/22/61	Cpl	Died 1/9/62 as Corporal at Budd's Ferry, MD	Switzerland Co. Roll; IAG Report Vol. V, VIII
Wiley	John R.	8/22/61	Pvt	Mustered out	IAG Report Vol. V, VIII

Williams	John	8/22/61	Pvt	Wounded at Philomont, VA, 11/1/62 as Corporal; discharged, no date; Unaccounted for	NA Record Group 94 Box 790A; Switzerland Co. Roll; IAG Report Vol. V, VIII
Wolf	John	8/22/61	Pvt	In hospital at Washington for wound to hand, 1/63; discharged	IAG Hospital Records; Switzerland Co. Roll; IAG Report Vol. V, VIII
Worstel	Matthew, Sr.	8/22/61	Sgt	Discharged 2/1/63; disability	IAG Report Vol. V, VIII
COMPANY D					
Abden	Armer	3/6/62	Pvt	In hospital at Washington for wound in hand 7/62; Unaccounted for	IAG Hospital Records; IAG Report Vol. V, VIII
Abdon	Benjamin	3/6/62	Pvt	Wounded in foot by pistol shot, 3/7/63; Veteran, transferred to Co. A Residual Battalion; mustered out 8/7/65	NA Record Group 94 CMR; IAG Report Vol. V
Armstrong	George W.	8/22/61	Pvt	In hospital for pain in chest, 7/62; Unaccounted for	IAG Hospital Records; IAG Report Vol. V, VIII
Baker	Thomas L.	8/22/61	Pvt	Wounded in left leg and arm, 6/13/64 at Riddle's Shop, VA; Discharged 9/10/64	History of D & O Counties, 1884; NA Record Group 94 CMR; Aurora Commercial 6/30/64; *MDEC* 6/24/64; IAG Report Vol. V, VIII
Barker	Elijah	8/22/61	Pvt	Died at Alexandria, VA 7/8/62 of typhoid fever; Buried at Alexandria National Cemetery	IAG Report Vol. V; IMH, June 1997, p. 131–34
Barrichlor	John S.	8/22/61	Pvt	Unaccounted for	IAG Report Vol. V, VIII
Barrington	John	8/22/61	Pvt	Unaccounted for	IAG Report Vol. V, VIII

Baskea (Basken)	Joseph	8/22/61	Pvt	Unaccounted for	IAG Report Vol. V, VIII
Beach	John R.	8/22/61	Pvt	Listed as Corporal, 6/30/63; Unaccounted for	Rummel; IAG Report Vol. V, VIII
Benson	David S.	8/22/61	Pvt	Captured near Front Royal, VA, 8/5/62; In hospital at New York 11/62–1/63 for scalp wound; Unaccounted for	*MDEC* 8/11/62; IAG Hospital Records; NA Record Group 94 CMR; IAG Report Vol. V, VIII
Biddell	Sanford W.	8/22/61	Pvt	Unaccounted for; later commissioned as 1st Lieutenant, Co. G, 146th Indiana Volunteers	IAG Report Vol. V, VIII; Vol. III
Bignel	Rozel	8/22/61	Bugler	Unaccounted for	IAG Report Vol. V, VIII
Boman (Bowman)	Eli	3/3/62	Pvt	Died in Aurora, IN before leaving to join regiment, 3/16/62	Aurora Commercial 3/20/62
Bromley	William	8/22/61	Pvt	Listed as Corporal, 6/30/63; Wounded in right ankle along the Rapidan, 5/5/64; Deserted, 10/22/64 from hospital in Philadelphia; Unaccounted for	Rummel; NA Record Group 94; IAG Hospital Records; IAG Report Vol. V, VIII
Bruce	Martin V.	3/10/63	Pvt	Transferred to Company B, Residual Battalion as Sergeant; discharged	IAG Report Vol. V
Bryan	Augustus S. (Arthur)	8/22/61	Pvt	Listed as Hospital Steward, 6/30/63; Unaccounted for;	Rummel; IAG Report Vol. V, VIII
Buchanan	Cornelius	8/22/61	Pvt	Unaccounted for	IAG Report Vol. V, VIII
Buchanan	Pleasant	8/22/61	Cpl	Died at Frederick City, MD, 11/1/62; Buried in Mt. Olivet Cemetery, Frederick, MD	IAG Report Vol. V, VIII
Bussell	James E.	8/22/61	Co. QM Sgt	Unaccounted for	IAG Report Vol. V, VIII
Calhoun	James	8/22/61	Cpl	Listed as First Sergeant, 6/30/63; Promoted 2nd Lieutenant 3/7/63; Mustered out 8/22/64	Rummel; IAG Report Vol. V

Carabaugh (Carnbaugh)	Andrew J.	2/8/63	Pvt	Transferred to Company B, Residual Battalion; mustered out 2/8/65	IAG Report Vol. V
Chance	Elisha	2/21/63	Pvt	Unaccounted for	IAG Report Vol. V, VIII
Chance	George W.	2/1/62	Pvt	Veteran, transferred to Co. A Residual Battalion; mustered out 8/7/65	IAG Report Vol. V
Clements	Joseph	8/22/61	Pvt	Unaccounted for	IAG Report Vol. V, VIII
Clements	Reuben	3/10/62	Pvt	Veteran, transferred to Co. A Residual Battalion, promoted Corporal; killed at Winchester, VA, 9/19/64	IAG Report Vol. V
Cole	Daniel R.	8/22/61	Sgt	Became a Scout/spy for Army of Potomac; Scouting 1/64; Still serving at muster out; Unaccounted for	Fishel; Aurora Commercial 1/14/64; NA Record Group 94 MR box 790; IAG Report Vol. V, VIII
Cole	Francis V.W.	8/1/63	Pvt	Transferred to Company A, Residual Battalion as Corporal; mustered out 8/7/65	IAG Report Vol. V
Connell	Thomas B.	8/22/61	Pvt	Unaccounted for	IAG Report Vol. V, VIII
Cooper	James M.	8/22/61	Pvt	Unaccounted for	IAG Report Vol. V, VIII
Craustre (Crauson)	Thomas	3/10/63	Pvt	Transferred to Company A, Residual Battalion; mustered out 8/7/65	IAG Report Vol. V, VIII
Cunningham	Samuel O.	3/25/62	Pvt	Sick with typhoid Fever in Washington, D.C., 5/62; Transferred to Company A, Residual Battalion; died in Andersonville Prison, 1864	Aurora Commercial 5/15/62; IAG Report Vol. V; Pickerill p. 190
Daniels	George R.	2/1/62	Pvt	Hurt by horse falling on him 5/64; In Harewood Hospital, 5/64; Veteran, transferred to Co. A Residual Battalion; mustered out 8/7/65	IAG Report Vol. V; *IJ* 5/16/64; *IJ* 5/19/64

Original and Re-Organized

Day	George	8/22/61	Pvt	Listed as Bugler, 6/30/63; Unaccounted for	Rummel; IAG Report Vol. V, VIII
Dorn (Dom)	Josiah	8/22/61	Pvt	Unaccounted for	IAG Report Vol. V, VIII
Duffy (Duffie)	George	12/29/63	Pvt	Transferred to Company A, Residual Battalion; deserted 8/64	IAG Report Vol. V
Foster	Lymen F.	8/1/63	Pvt	Transferred to Company A, Residual Battalion; mustered out 8/7/65	IAG Report Vol. V
Garrison	Henry	8/22/61	Pvt	Unaccounted for	IAG Report Vol. V, VIII
Golding	George A.	8/22/61	Cpl	Captured near Front Royal, VA 8/5/62 as Sergeant; listed as Co. Comm. Sergeant, 6/30/63; Unaccounted for	*MDEC* 8/11/62; Rummel; IAG Report Vol. V, VIII
Green	Marmaduke	8/22/61	Pvt	Died at Massaponax, VA, 8/6/62, shot through head while carrying dispatches from Gibbon to Hatch	IAG Report Vol. V, VIII; Pickerill, p. 189; *IJ* 8/14/62
Griffith	Henry	8/22/61	Pvt	Unaccounted for	IAG Report Vol. V, VIII
Harman	Michael	8/1/63	Pvt	Transferred to Company A, Residual Battalion; mustered out 8/7/65 as Corporal	IAG Report Vol. V
Hatten	James	8/22/61	Pvt	Veteran, transferred to Co. A Residual Battalion; mustered out 8/7/65	IAG Report Vol. V
Hayes	Henry C.	9/24/63	Pvt	Killed on Kilpatrick's Raid, 3/64 near Richmond, VA	Aurora Commercial, 3/17/64
Heck	Jacob	8/22/61	Bugler	On Parole at Annapolis, 10/8/64; Veteran, transferred to Co. A, Residual Battalion, promoted Musician; mustered out 8/7/65	IAG Hospital Records; IAG Report Vol. V, VIII
Hofstetter	John	8/22/61	Pvt	Unaccounted for	IAG Report Vol. V, VIII
House	James	8/22/61	Pvt	Unaccounted for	IAG Report Vol. V, VIII
Howard	Benjamin, Jr.	8/22/61	Pvt	Unaccounted for	IAG Report Vol. V, VIII

Howard	Benjamin, Sr.	8/22/61	Wagoner	Unaccounted for	IAG Report Vol. V, VIII
Howerton	Omar (Owen)	8/22/61	Pvt	Listed as Sergeant, 6/30/63; Wounded in shoulder at Gettysburg; In hospital at Baltimore for Dysentery, 7/63–8/63; Unaccounted for	Rummel; *VR* 8/18/63; *MDEC* 7/17/63; IAG Hospital Records; IAG Report Vol. V, VIII
Hubbard	Silas R.	8/22/61	Pvt	Unaccounted for	IAG Report Vol. V, VIII
Huffman	Aaron	8/22/61	Cpl	In hospital 1/63 for fever; Unaccounted for	*MDEC* 1/25/63; IAG Report Vol. V, VIII
Huffman (Hoffman)	Irvin (Irwin)	3/18/62	Pvt	Died at Falmouth VA of wounds received, 7/22/62	NA Record Group 94 MR box 790; *MDEC* 8/7/62
Jones	John	8/22/61	Pvt	Veteran, transferred to Co. A Residual Battalion; mustered out 8/7/65 as Sergeant	IAG Report Vol. V
Jones	John L.	1/1/64	Pvt	Transferred to Company A, Residual Battalion; mustered out 6/26/65	IAG Report Vol. V
Jounker (Younker)	Bowman H.	8/22/61	Cpl	wounded in left shoulder 9/13/63 at Madison Court House, VA; Unaccounted for	NA Record Group 94 CMR; *VR* 10/10/63; Aurora Commercial, 10/1/63; IAG Report Vol. V, VIII
Kalb	Sebastian	8/22/61	Pvt	Unaccounted for	IAG Report Vol. V, VIII
Keister	Daniel B.	8/22/61	Captain	Resigned 7/1/62	IAG Report Vol. II
Kelsey	James A.	8/22/61	Sgt	Promoted 2nd Lieutenant, 12/31/62; promoted 1st Lieutenant 3/7/63; mustered out 8/22/64	IAG Report Vol. V

Kennedy	George B.	8/22/61	Pvt	Discharged to receive commission, 11/13/62; promoted 1st Lt., Co. C, 7th Indiana Cavalry; mustered out as Captain	NA Record Group 94 MR box 790; Pickerill, p. 189; IAG Report Vol. III, V, VIII
Kern (Kerr)	Adam	2/24/64	Pvt	Transferred to Company A, Residual Battalion; mustered out 8/7/65 as Corporal	IAG Report Vol. V
Kerr	David D.	8/22/61	Pvt	Listed as Sergeant, 6/30/63; Unaccounted for	Rummel; IAG Report Vol. V, VIII
Kerr	William F.	3/24/62	Pvt	Transferred to Company B, Residual Battalion; discharged	IAG Report Vol. V
Kirsh (Kirth)	Philip	8/22/61	Pvt	Unaccounted for	IAG Report Vol. V, VIII
Kraus (Krouse) (Krause)	Jacob	8/22/61	Pvt	In hospital at Mt. Pleasant, 7/62; Unaccounted for	IAG Hospital Records; IAG Report Vol. V, VIII
Lamkin	Hudson	8/22/61	Pvt	Listed as Corporal, 6/30/63; Unaccounted for	Rummel; IAG Report Vol. V, VIII
Larue (Larew)	Abraham	8/1/63	Pvt	Transferred to Company A, Residual Battalion; mustered out 8/7/65	IAG Report Vol. V
Laycock	Charles F.	8/22/61	Pvt	Listed as Corporal, 6/30/63; Unaccounted for	Rummel; IAG Report Vol. V, VIII
Lynch	John B.	8/22/61	Pvt	Discharged to enlist in the regular army; on detached duty at the Military Telegraph in Washington 1862–63; Medal of Honor winner, 5/6/64 for carrying a message from the President to General Grant; award was later rescinded.	IAG Report Vol. V; NA Record Group 94 MR box 790; OR
Mason	Matthew B.	8/22/61	1st Lt.	In hospital for wound to abdomen 9/16/62 (VD?); Promoted Captain, 7/2/62; Discharged 10/3/62 as 1st Lieutenant	NA Record Group 94 CMR; IAG Report Vol. II

McConnell (O'Connell) (Connell)	James I.M.	8/22/61	Cpl	Captured near Fredericksburg 8/7/62; wounded in leg at Raccoon Ford, VA, 10/11/63, leg amputated; in hospital at Washington as Sergeant, 8/64; Discharged 9/5/64	*IJ* 8/14/62; NA Record Group 94 CMR; IAG Hospital Records
Meier	Valentine	8/22/61	Pvt	Captured near Front Royal, VA, 8/5/62; Unaccounted for	*MDEC* 8/11/62; IAG Report Vol. V, VIII
Menford	Robert H.		Pvt	Unaccounted for	IAG Report Vol. VIII
Mondary	George	2/3/62	Pvt	Unaccounted for	IAG Report Vol. V, VIII
Morgan	John W.	8/22/61	Pvt	Listed as Corporal, 6/30/63; Unaccounted for	Rummel; IAG Report Vol. V, VIII
Mundara (Mundary) (Mondary)	Joseph	8/22/61	Pvt	Veteran, transferred to Co. A Residual Battalion; mustered out 8/7/65	IAG Report Vol. V
Nye	Charles	10/17/63	Pvt	Transferred to Company A, Residual Battalion; mustered out 8/7/65	IAG Report Vol. V
Padgett	William H.H.	9/24/63	Pvt	Transferred to Company A, Residual Battalion; mustered out 8/7/65	IAG Report Vol. V
Parker	John	8/22/61	Orderly Sgt	Unaccounted for	IAG Report Vol. V, VIII
Parmer	John W.	8/22/61	Pvt	Unaccounted for	IAG Report Vol. V, VIII
Porter	Benjamin F.	8/22/61	Pvt	Listed as Corporal, 6/30/63; Unaccounted for	Rummel; IAG Report Vol. V, VIII
Porter	George H.	8/22/61	Cpl	Listed as Sergeant, 6/30/63; wounded at Gettysburg; Wounded in foot, 5/14/64 and had foot amputated; Died 6/4/64	Rummel; Aurora Commercial 10/1/63; IAG Hospital Records; Aurora Commercial 5/23/64; Aurora Commercial 2/23/65; NA Record Group 94 CMR

Porter	Gillett	8/22/61	Pvt	Killed at Raccoon Ford, VA, 6/9/64; muster roll says died of wounds received in action 6/1/64	GWL letter 9/9/64; IAG Report Vol. V, VIII; Aurora Commercial 6/30/64; NA Record Group 94
Powell	Eli H.	2/25/62	Pvt	Slightly wounded in foot by grape shot after it had passed through three horses, killing them all, at Snicker's Gap, VA, 10/26/62; Transferred to Company B, Residual Battalion; discharged	Indianapolis Sentinel, 11/10/62; IAG Report Vol. V
Powers	Franklin	8/22/61	Pvt	Wounded at Gettysburg in left knee, 7/1/63; Unaccounted for	IAG Hospital Records; *MDEC* 7/17/63; Aurora Commercial 7/23/63; IAG Report Vol. V, VIII
Rea	Robert W.	8/22/61	Blksmth	Unaccounted for	IAG Report Vol. V, VIII
Redding	James L.	8/22/61	Pvt	On detached duty as orderly to General Hooker at division headquarters; Unaccounted for	IAG Correspondence 2/13/63; IAG Report Vol. V, VIII
Sellers	Benjamin L.	3/5/62	Pvt	Slightly wounded in leg and side at Gettysburg as Corporal; Transferred to Company B, Residual Battalion as Corporal; mustered out 3/20/65	Rummel; *VR* 8/18/63; Aurora Commercial 7/23/63; IAG Report Vol. V
Senior	John W.	8/22/61	Sgt	Unaccounted for	IAG Report Vol. V, VIII
Shepeard	Samuel	3/4/62	Pvt	Captured near Front Royal, VA, 8/5/62; Transferred to Company B, Residual Battalion; discharged	*MDEC* 8/11/62; IAG Report Vol. V

Sheperd	William	12/2/63	Pvt	Captured near Front Royal, VA, 8/5/62; Transferred to Co. A Residual Battalion, promoted Sergeant; mustered out 8/7/65; Medal of Honor winner for capturing rebel flag at Saylor's Creek, VA, 4/6/65	*MDEC* 8/11/62; *IJ* 8/14/62; IAG Report Vol. V; USAMHI
Sherman	John B.	2/29/64	Pvt	Transferred to Company A, Residual Battalion; mustered out 8/7/65	IAG Report Vol. V
Siemantel (Siebenthal) (Siemandel)	George L.	2/1/62	Pvt	Veteran, transferred to Co. A Residual Battalion; mustered out 8/7/65	IAG Report Vol. V
Skirring (Skirving)	Andrew	8/22/61	Pvt	Listed as Blacksmith, 6/30/63; Unaccounted for	Rummel; IAG Report Vol. V, VIII
Smith	Charles	2/3/62	Pvt	In Mt. Pleasant Hospital 7/62; Transferred to Company B, Residual Battalion; mustered out 2/3/65	*IJ* 7/9/62; IAG Report Vol. V
Smith	Jesse	2/8/62	Pvt	Wounded at Gettysburg by artillery burst; Died at Gettysburg 7/1/63	VR 8/18/63; Aurora Commercial 7/23/63; IAG Report Vol. V, VIII
Soper (Sopers)	Orlando M. (Oramandel)	10/17/61	Pvt	Reported as Sergeant while on recruiting duty, 2/19/63; Transferred to Company B, Residual Battalion; mustered out 10/15/64	Aurora Commercial 2/19/63; IAG Report Vol. V
Spencer	John D.R.	8/22/61	Sgt	Promoted 2nd Lieutenant, 7/2/62; promoted 1st Lieutenant, 10/2/62; promoted Captain, 3/7/63; mustered out 8/22/64	IAG Report Vol. V
Stitt	John	2/6/62	Pvt	Unaccounted for	IAG Report Vol. V, VIII
Storm	Jonathan Y.	5/20/63	Pvt	Hospitalized for measles 4/14–7/6/64; Transferred to Company A, Residual Battalion; mustered out 8/7/65	NA Record Group 94 CMR; IAG Report Vol. V

Strouce (Strauce) (Strong)	Frederick	8/22/61	Pvt	Hospitalized for pneumonia, 4/29/63; 1/16/64 chronic diarrhea and cerebral inflammation; Veteran, transferred to Co. A Residual Battalion; wounded in left leg at Opequon Creek, VA, 9/5/64	IAG Hospital Records; IAG Report Vol. V; NA Record Group 94 CMR
Suits	Emsley	8/22/61	Blksmth	Wounded in left thigh at Chester's Gap, VA, 7/22/63; Unaccounted for	NA Record Group 94 CMR; IAG Report Vol. V, VIII
Swango	Abram	8/22/61	Pvt	Unaccounted for	IAG Report Vol. V, VIII
Taylor	William	8/22/61	Pvt	Unaccounted for	IAG Report Vol. V, VIII
Thompson	George W.	8/22/61	Pvt	Unaccounted for	IAG Report Vol. V, VIII
Trester	Oliver H.	8/22/61	Pvt	Mortally wounded at Hagerstown, MD, 9/13/62; Died, 9/14/62	*MDEC* 9/22/62; IAG Report Vol. V, VIII
Tufts	Louis	3/26/62	Pvt	Overcome by fear; went insane at Gettysburg; In hospital at Philadelphia, 6/63–7/63; Died 7/15/63	Aurora Commercial 7/30/63; IAG Hospital Records; IAG Report Vol. V, VIII
Tupper	William	8/22/61	Pvt	In hospital at Philadelphia 7/63 for contusion; Wounded in right leg by artillery shell (contusion) at Gettysburg, PA, 7/1/63; Transferred to Veteran Reserve Corps; Unaccounted for	IAG Hospital Records; NA Record Group 94 CMR: *VR* 8/18/63; Aurora Commercial 7/23/63; IAG Report Vol. V, VIII
Ward	Alonzo	8/22/61	Pvt	Veteran, transferred to Co. A Residual Battalion	IAG Report Vol. V
Ward	James	8/22/61	Pvt	Veteran, transferred to Co. A Residual Battalion	IAG Report Vol. V
Wheeler	Jackson	8/22/61	Pvt	In hospital with hemorrhoids, 11/2/62; Discharged 1/1/63	NA Record Group 94 MR box 790

Wheeler	Thomas D.	6/1/63	Pvt	Transferred to Company A, Residual Battalion; mustered out 8/7/65	IAG Report Vol. V
White	Enos	2/10/62	Pvt	Veteran, transferred to Co. A Residual Battalion; mustered out 8/7/65	IAG Report Vol. V
White	Henry	8/22/61	Pvt	Captured near Front Royal, VA, 8/5/62; Unaccounted for	*MDEC* 8/11/62; IAG Report Vol. V, VIII
Wiley	Hiram S.		Pvt	Listed as a private 6/30/63; promoted Co. Comm. Sgt	Rummel
Williamson	Andrew	1/4/64	Pvt	Transferred to Company A, Residual Battalion; mustered out 8/7/65	IAG Report Vol. V
Willman	Henry	2/26/62	Pvt	Slightly wounded at Bealeton Station, VA 10/25/63; Transferred to Company B, Residual Battalion; mustered out 2/24/65	Willman service records, NA; IAG Report Vol. V
Wright	Augustus	8/22/61	Cpl	Killed at Gettysburg 7/1/63	Aurora Commercial 7/23/63; IAG Hospital Records
Wright	Henry F.	8/22/61	2nd Lt.	Promoted 1st Lieutenant, 7/2/62; promoted Captain, 10/4/62; resigned 3/6/63; re-entered as Captain, 7th Indiana Cavalry; died at Memphis TN, 9/64	IAG Report Vol. II; Aurora Commercial 9/29/64
Wright	Milton	2/10/62	Pvt	Listed as Corporal, 6/30/63; Veteran, transferred to Co. A Residual Battalion; promoted Sergeant; promoted 1st Lieutenant, 6/1/65; mustered out as First Sergeant of Battalion	Rummel; IAG Report Vol. V
Wyley	Hiram S.	8/22/61	Pvt	Unaccounted for	IAG Report Vol. V, VIII
York	John	8/22/61	Saddler	Unaccounted for	IAG Report Vol. V, VIII

COMPANY E

Bain	Samuel	8/22/61	Pvt	Wounded at Brandy Station, 6/9/63; Captured, 12/1/63; Lost a foot at Belle Isle on 1/1/64 from freezing and later died; last heard of in Andersonville Prison	Gilchrist Lof C; *MDEC* 12/12/63; *MDEC* 9/8/85; IAG Report Vol. V, VIII
Barnes	William	8/22/61	Pvt	Wounded 7/26/62 near Orange Court House, VA; Discharged, ?/?/63; wounds; wounded 8/5/62 according to Gilpin	*MDEC* 8/11/62; IAG Report Vol. V, VIII; Gilpin diary
Boyd	James	8/22/61	Sgt	Listed as Com QM Sergeant, 6/30/63; Wounded at Gettysburg in left side; Promoted to 2nd Lieutenant	Rummel; IAG Hospital Records; IAG Report Vol. V
Branham	George	8/22/61	Pvt	NA says captured at Middleburg, VA, 6/21/63; Captured at Gettysburg; Promoted to 1st Lieutenant then Captain, Co. E of 10th Indiana Cavalry	NA Record Group 94 MR box 791; *MDEC* 7/17/63; IAG Report Vol. III, V, VIII
Branham	Oscar W.	8/22/61	Sgt	Died at Fredericksburg, VA, 8/24/62 of typhoid fever	*MDEC* 9/1/62; IAG Report Vol. V, VIII
Breuner (Bruning) (Brenner)	Francis	1/5/64	Pvt	Transferred to Company A, Residual Battalion; deserted 8/00/64	*MDEC* 6/24/64; IAG Report, Vol. V
Brinkworth	George	8/22/61	Pvt	Wounded in arm at Riddle's Shop, VA, 6/13/64; mustered out 9/8/64	*MDEC* 6/24/64; IAG Report Vol. V, VIII
Bromwell (Bramwell)	Edwin	8/22/61	Pvt	mustered out 9/8/64	IAG Report Vol. V, VIII
Brunning	Francis	1/5/64	Pvt	Deserted 8/64	IAG Report Vol. V
Cochran	David	8/22/61	Pvt	Captured along the Rappahannock, 4/14/63 as corporal; In hospital at Gettysburg with fever, 8/63; mustered out 9/8/64 as Corporal	Pickerill, p. 68; *CWT* 5/7/63; IAG Hospital Records; IAG Report Vol. V, VIII

Cox	William	8/22/61	Pvt	Unaccounted for	IAG Report Vol. V, VIII
Crane	Samuel A.	9/5/63	Pvt	Transferred to Company A, Residual Battalion; mustered out 8/7/65	IAG Report Vol. V
Cross	Samuel T.	8/22/61	Pvt	Wounded in lung at Hagerstown, MD 9/12/62; Discharged 1/22/63; wounds	VR 9/25/62; IAG Hospital Records; IAG Report Vol. V, VIII
Crow	Benjamin	8/22/61	Bugler	Discharged, 10/1/62; disability	IAG Report Vol. V, VIII
Crowfoot	Warren	8/22/61	Pvt	Discharged, 1/62; disability	IAG Report Vol. V, VIII
Day	Thomas G.	8/22/61	Pvt	Captured 12/1/63 near Stevensburg, VA; mustered out 1/21/65	NA Record Group 94; IAG Report Vol. V, VIII
Dickey	David	8/22/61	Pvt	Mustered out 9/8/64	IAG Report Vol. V, VIII
Dickey	John	8/22/61	Pvt	Discharged 2/17/63; disability	IAG Report Vol. V, VIII
Dickey	Philip	8/22/61	Pvt	Mustered out 9/8/64	IAG Report Vol. V, VIII
Dilenhermer (Dillender)	Joseph	8/22/61	Pvt	Captured 11/8/63; Veteran, transferred to Company A, Residual Battalion; rescued from *Sultana*, 4/28/65; mustered out 8/7/65	IAG Hospital Records; IAG Report Vol. V, VIII
Elliott	James H.	8/22/61	Pvt	Never mustered	IAG Report Vol. V, VIII
Evans	Cowan D.	2/24/64	Pvt	Transferred to Company A, Residual Battalion; mustered out 8/7/65; Medal of Honor winner for capture of the 26th Virginia's flag at Saylor's Creek, VA, 4/6/65	IAG Report Vol. V, USAMHI
Faught	Sandford	6/11/63	Pvt	Wounded in thigh along the Rapidan, 5/764; in hospital at New York, 7/64; Transferred to Company A, Residual Battalion; mustered out 8/7/65	NA Record Group 94; IAG Hospital Records; *MDEC* 5/25/64; IAG Report Vol. V
Flagg	John	8/22/61	Pvt	Never mustered	IAG Report Vol. V, VIII

Gasaway (Galaway)	John	8/22/61	Cpl	Mustered out 9/8/64 as Company Commissary Sergeant	IAG Report Vol. V, VIII
Gilbert	Isaac	8/22/61	Pvt	Promoted to 2nd Lieutenant, Company C, 3/12/63; mustered out 9/7/63 to accept commission; promoted to Captain, Co. M, 7th Indiana Cavalry but never mustered	IAG Report Vol. III, V, VIII; IAG Correspondence 9/63
Gilchrist	George M.	8/22/61	Sgt	Promoted Sergeant Major, 4/26/62; Promoted to 2nd Lieutenant, 7/2/63; promoted Captain, 7/1/64; Transferred to Company B, Residual Battalion, mustered out 1/16/65	NA Record Group 94, box 790A; IAG Report Vol. V
Gilpin	Samuel J.	8/22/61	Cpl	Listed as Sergeant, 6/30/63; Knocked down by shell explosion but unharmed at Falling Waters, 7/8/63; Mustered out 9/8/64 as Regimental Commissary Sergeant	Rummel; Reid Papers; IAG Report Vol. V, VIII
Glasscock	John R.B., Jr.	8/22/61	Pvt	Captured along the Rappahannock, 4/15/63; Captured during Wilson's Raid, 6/29/64; mustered out 4/28/65	Pickerill, p. 68; MDEC 7/13/64; IAG Report Vol. V, VIII
Glauber	Matthew (Matthias)	8/22/61	Pvt	Captured along the Rappahannock, 4/15/63; Released from Libby Prison and in parole camp waiting for exchange 3/10/64; In hospital at Annapolis wounded, 8/63; Mustered out 9/8/64	Pickerill, p. 68; IJ 3/16/64; IAG Hospital Records; IAG Report Vol. V, VIII
Graham	James	8/22/61	Pvt	Captured along the Rappahannock, 4/15/63 as corporal; injured in railroad accident, 2/64; Mustered out 9/8/64 as Corporal	Pickerill, p. 68; CWT 5/7/63; MDEC 3/4/64; IAG Report Vol. V, VIII
Gray (Grey)	Robert	2/27/64	Pvt	Transferred to Company A, Residual Battalion; mustered out 8/7/65	IAG Report Vol. V

Greiner	John	8/22/61	Pvt	Promoted to Regimental Commissary	IAG Report Vol. V, VIII
Grenba (Grebe) (Greble)	Jacob	8/22/61	Pvt	Captured during Wilson's Raid, 6/29/64; in hospital at Annapolis, 12/64; mustered out 5/24/65	MDEC 7/13/64; IAG Hospital Records; IAG Report Vol. V, VIII
Hall	Justice	8/22/61	Pvt	In hospital at Washington, 8/64; Mustered out 9/8/64	IAG Hospital Records; IAG Report Vol. V, VIII
Harris	John T.	8/22/61	Pvt	Discharged 2/5/62	IAG Report Vol. V, VIII
Higgins	Charles	1/1/62	Pvt	Transferred to Company B, Residual Battalion; mustered out 1/1/65	IAG Report Vol. V
Hoagland	John	8/22/61	Pvt	Helped capture boat, 12/61; Mustered out 9/8/64	MDEC 12/26/61; IAG Report Vol. V, VIII
Holmes	William T.	9/16/63	Pvt	Transferred to Company A, Residual Battalion; Medal of Honor winner for capturing the 27th Virginia's flag at Saylor's Creek, VA, 4/6/65; mustered out 8/7/65	USAMHI; IAG Report Vol. V
Howard	Allen J.	6/6/63	Pvt	Transferred to Company B, Residual Battalion; mustered out 8/7/65	IAG Report Vol. V
Huey	Norman R.	8/22/61	Pvt	In hospital at Gettysburg as Ward Master, 8/63; Mustered out 9/8/64	IAG Hospital Records; IAG Report Vol. V, VIII
Hughes	Hezekiah	2/10/64	Pvt	Transferred to Company A, Residual Battalion; mustered out 8/7/65	IAG Report Vol. V
Hutchinson	William	8/22/61	Pvt	Mustered out 9/8/64	IAG Report Vol. V, VIII
Jones	Jasper	8/22/61	Pvt	Discharged, no date	IAG Report Vol. V, VIII
Jordan	William	9/3/63	Pvt	Transferred to Company A, Residual Battalion; mustered out 8/7/65	IAG Report Vol. V

Jordon (Jordan)	Absalom	8/22/61	Pvt	Veteran, transferred to Co. A, Residual Battalion, promoted Corporal; Medal of Honor winner for capturing a Confederate flag at Saylor's Creek, VA, 4/6/65; mustered out 8/7/65 as Sergeant	USAMHI; IAG Report Vol. V, VIII
Kernan	John	8/22/61	Pvt	Mustered out 9/8/64	IAG Report Vol. V, VIII
Land	Bennett (Benjamin)	1/4/64	Pvt	Wounded in shoulder at Riddle's Shop, VA, 6/13/64; In hospital at Philadelphia, 6/64; Transferred to Company A, Residual Battalion; mustered out 8/7/65	MDEC 6/24/64; IAG Hospital Records; IAG Report Vol. V
Lansberry (Lansbury)	James H.	8/22/61	Pvt	Captured at Gettysburg and escaped; In hospital at Gettysburg on hospital duty; Mustered out 9/8/64	MDEC 7/2/13; IAG Hospital Records; IAG Report Vol. V, VIII
Large	Francis A.	4/23/63	Pvt	Transferred to Company A, Residual Battalion; mustered out 8/7/65	IAG Report Vol. V
Lee	Lindley W.	8/22/61	Pvt	Mustered out 9/8/64 as Corporal	IAG Report Vol. V, VIII
Lee	Stephen P.	8/22/61	Cpl	Captured near Bowling Green, 8/5/62; Mustered out 9/8/64	Gilpin diary; MDEC 8/11/62; IAG Report Vol. V, VIII
Lewis	George W.	8/22/61	Pvt	Captured along the Rappahannock, 4/15/63; Discharged and promoted to Regimental Quartermaster of 123rd Indiana Volunteers	Pickerill. P. 68; IAG Correspondence 9/63; IAG Report Vol. V, VIII
Lewis	Joseph	8/22/61	Cpl	Killed by pistol shot through heart at Hagerstown, MD, 9/12/62 as Sergeant; father of Geo. W. Lewis	NA Record Group 94 MR box 791; GAR souvenir, 1905; MDEC 9/20/62; IJ 9/25/62; VR 9/25/62; IAG Report Vol. V, VIII

Mallory	William	8/22/61	Pvt	Detailed as Regimental Veterinary, 9/63; Mustered out 9/8/64 as Blacksmith	McClure Papers; IAG Report Vol. V, VIII
Mann	Ebenezer	8/22/61	Pvt	Discharged ?/?/62	IAG Report Vol. V, VIII
Marshall	Robert	1/25/62	Pvt	Wounded at Madison Court House, 9/22/63; In hospital, 9/63 for wound; Transferred to Company B, Residual Battalion as Sergeant; discharged	*IJ* 9/29/63; IAG Hospital Records; IAG Report Vol. V
Matthews (Mattheus)	John P.	8/22/61	Co. QM Sgt	In hospital at Mt. Pleasant, 7/62; Captured along the Rappahannock, 4/14/63; Scalp injury on a Railroad accident near Brandy Station, VA, 3/14/64; Promoted to 2nd Lieutenant, 7/1/64; mustered out as a Sergeant 8/22/64	IAG Hospital Records; NA Record Group 94 CMR; Pickerill, p. 68; *CWT* 5/7/63; IAG Report Vol. V
McClain	James	8/22/61	Cpl	Captured at Rappahannock Station, VA, 8/31/63; last heard of in Andersonville Prison; froze to death at Belle Isle, 1/1/64	NA Record Group 94 MR box 791; Pickerill, p. 68; *CWT* 5/7/63; IAG Report Vol. V, VIII; *MDEC* 9/8/85
McClure	David D.	?/?/63	Pvt	Discharged to accept commission, 10/20/63; Appointed Captain Co. C, 13th Indiana Cavalry, never mustered	McClure Papers; IAG Report Vol. III & VIII
McClure	William S.	8/22/61	Captain	Promoted to Major, 10/25/62; Discharged to accept Colonelcy of 9th Indiana Cavalry, never mustered	IAG Report Vol. II; McClure Papers
McGreggor (McGregor)	Andrew C.	8/22/61	Pvt	Listed as Corporal, 6/30/63; Mustered out 9/8/64 as Sergeant	Rummel; IAG Report Vol. V, VIII
McLain	John	6/14/64	Pvt	Not in IAG Report; is found in Lt. John Matthews Company book, Virginia Matthews Collection	Matthews Company Book

McNeil	Thomas	8/22/61	Cpl	Listed as Sergeant, 6/30/63; Mustered out 9/8/64	Rummel; IAG Report Vol. V, VIII
McNeil	William	8/22/61	Pvt	Discharged 10/1/62	IAG Report Vol. V, VIII
Metcalf	Charles	8/22/61	Wagoner	Injured by horse falling on him, 11/14/62; In hospital at Washington, 1/63; Discharged ?/?/62	NA Record Group 94 CMR; *MDEC* 1/25/63; IAG Hospital Records; IAG Report Vol. V, VIII
Meyer (Mayer)	James A.	2/25/63	Pvt	Transferred to Company B, Residual Battalion	IAG Report Vol. V
Middleton	George	2/26/62	Pvt	Captured at Culpepper Courthouse, VA, 8/1/63 and held in Belle Isle 'til 3/7/64; brother of William; Transferred to Company B, Residual Battalion; Discharged	Personal service records; Day, *NT* 7/30/03; IAG Report Vol. V
Middleton	William	8/22/61	Pvt	Mustered out 9/8/64; brother of George E.	IAG Report Vol. V, VIII;
Millican (Milliken)	John	8/22/61	Pvt	Mustered out 9/8/64	IAG Report Vol. V, VIII
Mitchell	George	8/22/61	Pvt	Served as orderly for Iron Brigade commander at Gettysburg; Promoted to Captain of Co. H, 10th Indiana Cavalry; mustered out as Major, 6/21/65	IAG Correspondence; IAG Report Vol. III, V, VIII
Monfort	Robert H.	8/22/61	Cpl	In hospital at Washington for sickness, 8/63; wounded in foot at Raccoon Ford, VA, 9/14/63	IAG Hospital Records; *VR* 10/10/63; IAG Report Vol. V
Monroe (Munroe)	Alexander C.	12/7/63	Pvt	Wounded in left thigh at Riddle's Shop, VA 6/13/64; In hospital at Philadelphia, 6/64 for wound; Transferred to Company A, Residual Battalion; mustered out 8/7/65	*MDEC* 6/24/64; IAG Hospital Records; IAG Report Vol. V

Muser (Meuser) (Menser) (Miser)	George W.	3/5/63	Pvt	Wounded at Madison Court House, VA 9/22/63; Transferred to Company A, Residual Battalion; mustered out 8/7/65	*IJ* 9/29/63; IAG Hospital Records; IAG Report Vol. V
Naughton	John	8/22/61	Pvt	Captured along the Rappahannock, 4/15/63; Unaccounted for; sent to Libby Prison and exchanged. Was recaptured and sent to Florida for the rest of the war	Pickerill, p. 68; IAG Report Vol. V, VIII; *MDEC* 4/5/81
Nichols	Charles A.	8/22/61	Pvt	Listed as Bugler, 6/30/63; Unaccounted for	Rummel; IAG Report Vol. V, VIII
Nichols	John W.	2/26/63	Pvt	Wounded in wrist along the Rapidan, 5/30/64; Transferred to Company B, Residual Battalion; mustered out 8/7/65	*MDEC* 6/8/64; IAG Hospital Records; IAG Report Vol. V
O'Connor	Maurice	8/22/61	Blksmth	Wounded in left hand at Chester's Gap, VA, 7/22/63; Unaccounted for	NA Record Group 94 CMR; IAG Report Vol. V, VIII
Papst (Papse)	Henry	8/22/61	Pvt	Wounded in leg at Hagerstown 9/12/62; Captured at Brooks Farm, VA 3/14/64; mustered out 1/20/65	*VR* 9/25/62; IAG Hospital Records; Gilpin Diary; IAG Report Vol. V
Park	William J.	8/22/61	Pvt	In hospital at Washington with fever, 1/63; Discharged, 3/15/63	IAG Hospital Records; *MDEC* 1/25/63; IAG Report Vol. V, VIII
Park (Parker)	William	8/22/61	Pvt	Wounded at Gettysburg in right lung and captured; Died, 8/27/63; wounds	IAG Hospital Records; *MDEC* 7/17/63; Rummel; IAG Report Vol. V, VIII; NA Record Group 94 CMR
Patton	John R.	?/?/63	Pvt	Unaccounted for	IAG Report Vol. VIII

Peerson	Mathaniel B.	8/22/61	Pvt	Mustered out	IAG Report Vol. V, VIII
Phillips	Robert W.	8/1/63	Pvt	Transferred to Company A, Residual Battalion; mustered out 8/7/65	IAG Report Vol. V
Pierson (Pearson)	George W.	2/20/63	Pvt	Captured along the Rappahannock, 4/15/63; Transferred to Company A, Residual Battalion; mustered out 8/7/65	Pickerill, p. 68; IAG Report Vol. V
Prather	Jonathan	9/16/63	Pvt	Transferred to Company A, Residual Battalion; mustered out 8/7/65	IAG Report Vol. V
Prentiss	Nelmore	8/22/61	Pvt	Captured, 5/14/64; Died in Andersonville Prison, 1864	IJ 5/16/64; IAG Report Vol. V, VIII
Ramsey	Christopher	6/10/63	Pvt	Transferred to Company A, Residual Battalion; mustered out 8/7/65	IAG Report Vol. V
Rea	William	8/22/61	Pvt	Mustered out 9/8/64; Col. Chapman's orderly at Gettysburg	Day, NT 7/30/03; IAG Report Vol. V, VIII
Reed	Henry W.	3/21/62	Pvt	Transferred to Company B, Residual Battalion as Corporal; discharged	IAG Report Vol. V
Reid	Edward F.	8/22/61	Pvt	Promoted 2nd Lieutenant of Company C, 13th Indiana Cavalry	IAG Report Vol. V, VIII
Reid (Reagle)	William P.	8/22/61	Pvt	In hospital at Annapolis 7/8/63 for wounded thigh; Mustered out 9/8/64	IAG Hospital Record; IAG Report Vol. V, VIII
Rigg	Franklin	8/22/61	Pvt	Mustered out 9/8/64	IAG Report Vol. V, VIII
Ritchel (Ritchie)	Curtis C.	8/22/61	Pvt	Died of disease at Hope Landing, VA, 3/31/63	IAG Report Vol. V, VIII; Gilpin diary
Ritchel (Ritchie)	Silas T.	8/22/61	Pvt	Mustered out 9/8/64	IAG Report Vol. V, VIII

Robbins (Robinson)	Charles	8/22/61	Pvt	Mustered out 9/8/64; Ankle broken by shot while serving on detached duty as aide for General Stevens, 9/1/62	MDEC 9/9/62; IAG Report Vol. V, VIII; Gilpin Diary
Rogers	Samuel	8/22/61	Bugler	In hospital at Annapolis, 7/63; Mustered out 9/8/64	IAG Hospital Records; IAG Report Vol. V, VIII
Romine	Isaac F.	8/22/62	Pvt	Transferred to Company A, Residual Battalion; mustered out 8/7/65	IAG Report Vol. V
Romine	Smith L.	8/22/62	Pvt	Transferred to Company A, Residual Battalion; mustered out 8/7/65	IAG Report Vol. V
Rushton	David	8/22/61	Blksmth	Discharged 7/16/62; disability	IAG Report Vol. V, VIII
Seever	Smyrna W.	8/22/61	Pvt	Wounded at Middletown, MD, 9/12/62; died 9/14/62	IAG Report Vol. V, VIII
Shannon	Abner Lowry	8/22/61	2nd Lt.	Promoted to 1st Lieutenant, 7/2/62; Captured along the Rappahannock, 4/15/63; wounded and captured at Reams Station, VA during Wilson's Raid, 7/64; transferred to Company B, Residual Battalion	IAG Report Vol. II; Pickerill, p. 68; CWT 5/7/63; IAG Hospital Records; MDEC 7/13/64
Smith	John W.	8/22/61	Pvt	Mustered out 9/8/64 as Corporal	IAG Report Vol. V, VIII
Smith	William J.	8/22/61	Pvt	Captured and paroled at Gettysburg; Mustered out 9/8/64	MDEC 7/17/63; IAG Report Vol. V, VIII
Smock	David	8/22/61	Orderly Sgt	Died of typhoid fever at Fredericksburg, VA, 8/8/62	Gilpin Diary; IAG Report Vol. V, VIII
Snodgrass	Ansell	12/16/62	Pvt	Transferred from Co. L, 4/3/63; treated for syphilis, 8/2 to 9/25/63; 10/17/63; Transferred to Company B, Residual Battalion; mustered out 8/7/65	NA Record Group 94 MR box 791; NA Record Group 94; IAG Report Vol. V

Spivey	Isaiah	8/22/61	Pvt	Missing in action, 6/18/63; Treated for syphilis, 1/8/64; Mustered out 9/8/64	NA Record Group 94 MR box 791; NA Record Group 94; IAG Report Vol. V, VIII
Stanley	George E.	8/22/61	Saddler	Captured, exchanged 3/64; Listed as Sgt. when exchanged; Mustered out 9/8/64	*MDEC* 3/17/64; *IJ* 3/16/64; IAG Report Vol. V, VIII
Staples	William	2/25/64	Pvt	Captured during Wilson's Raid, 6/29/64; Transferred to Company A, Residual Battalion; mustered out 8/7/65	IAG Hospital Records; *MDEC* 7/13/64; IAG Report Vol. V
Stapp (Stopp)	William H.	8/22/61	Pvt	Helped capture boat, 12/61; Captured at Beverly Ford, VA, 4/29/63 and spent 7 days in Libby Prison before being paroled; Wounded in both thighs at Sulphur Springs, VA 11/8/63; Mustered out 9/8/64 as Sergeant	*MDEC* 12/24/61; *MDEC* 5/2/63; *MDEC* 11/24/63; IAG Report Vol. V, VIII
Stephens (Stevens)	Samuel J.		Pvt	Mustered out 9/8/64	IAG Report Vol. V, VIII
Story (Storey)	William	8/22/61	Pvt	Wounded at Gettysburg in Chest; Died 7/10/63; wounds. Corporal	*MDEC* 7/17/63; *VR* 8/18/63; IAG Hospital Records; IAG Report Vol. V, VIII
Tait	William	2/26/62	Pvt	Listed as Blacksmith, 6/30/63; Transferred to Company B, Residual Battalion as Blacksmith; discharged	Rummel; IAG Report Vol. V
Taylor	Ebenezer		Pvt	Discharged, 12/31/61; disability	NA Record Group 94 box 790A
Taylor	Gamaliel	8/22/61	Sgt	Promoted to Adjutant, 12/27/62; wounded in right leg at Brandy Station, VA, 6/9/63	IAG Report Vol. V, VIII; *VR* 6/18/63; NA Record Group 94 CMR

Thompson	George H.	8/22/61	1st Lt.	Promoted to Adjutant, 8/1/62; promoted Captain, 10/25/62; promoted Major, 6/24/64; Mustered out 9/8/64	IAG Report Vol. II
Tilford (Tolford)	Solon	8/22/61	Pvt	Wounded at Brandy Station, 6/9/63; Mustered out 9/8/64 as Corporal	Gilchrist L of C; IAG Report Vol. V, VIII
Townsend	Isaac C.	8/22/61	Cpl	Died of disease at Rockville, MD, 9/17/62	IAG Report Vol. V, VIII
Trigg	Oscar	8/22/61	Pvt	Helped capture boat, 12/61; Wounded in left shoulder on Wilson's Raid, 6/28/64; Mustered out 9/8/64	*MDEC* 12/26/61; *MDEC* 7/13/64; NA Record Group 94 CMR; IAG Hospital Records; IAG Report Vol. V, VIII
Tyrell	Robert	9/5/65	Pvt	Transferred to Company A, Residual Battalion; mustered out 8/7/65	IAG Report Vol. V
Watlington	William	6/11/63	Pvt	Transferred to Company A, Residual Battalion; mustered out 8/7/65 as Corporal	IAG Report Vol. V
Weible	John	8/22/61	Pvt	Wounded in upper part of left leg at Hagerstown, MD 9/12/62; Mustered out 9/8/64	NA Record Group 94 CMR; IAG Hospital Records; *VR* 9/25/62; IAG Report Vol. V & VII
Werner	Charles	8/22/61	Pvt	Treated for syphilis, 7/9/62; Mustered out 9/8/64	NA Record Group 94 CMR; IAG Report Vol. V, VIII
Wheadon	James T.	8/22/61	Pvt	Mustered out 9/8/64	IAG Report Vol. V, VIII
Whiteloch	William	8/22/61	Pvt	Discharged 6/1/63 as Sergeant	IAG Report Vol. V, VIII

Wildman (Wyman)	John F.	8/22/61	Pvt	In hospital at Philadelphia, 12/62 for wound in back; Listed as Corporal, 6/30/63; Promoted Sergeant 9/6/63; Discharged 10/63 and promoted to Adjutant of 130th I.V.; later major of 153rd Indiana Volunteers	IAG Hospital Records; Rummel; Wildman letter; IAG Correspondence 9/63; IAG Report Vol. V, VIII
Wills	Benjamin	8/22/61	Pvt	Mustered out 9/8/64	IAG Report Vol. V, VIII
Woodward	Thomas	8/22/61	Pvt	Mustered out 9/8/64	IAG Report Vol. V, VIII
Wooley	John	8/22/61	Pvt	Mustered out 9/8/64	IAG Report Vol. V, VIII
Wright	Henry T.	2/26/63	Pvt	Accidentally shot in left leg by pistol, 4/18/64; Transferred to Company A, Residual Battalion; mustered out 6/9/65	NA Record Group 94 CMR; IAG Report Vol. V
Wright	Jesse A.	8/22/61	Pvt	Mustered out 9/8/64	IAG Report Vol. V, VIII
Yates	Peter R.	8/9/63	Pvt	Transferred to Company A, Residual Battalion; mustered out 8/7/65	IAG Report Vol. V
Yost	William H.H.C.	2/23/63	Pvt	Transferred to Company A, Residual Battalion; mustered out 8/7/65	IAG Report Vol. V
COMPANY F					
Bailey	George M.	8/18/61	Pvt	Captured and exchanged 8/62; Discharged to accept commission, 4/24/63	IAG Report Vol. V, VIII; VR 8/21/62; McClure Papers
Beggs	Robert	3/12/63	Pvt	Transferred to Company B, Residual Battalion; mustered out 7/18/65	IAG Report Vol. V
Bennett	Jeremiah	3/23/63	Pvt	Transferred to Company B, Residual Battalion; mustered out 8/7/65	IAG Report Vol. V
Bond	Benjamin	8/18/61	Pvt	Died at Budd's Ferry, MD, 11/30/61	IAG Report Vol. V, VIII

Brenton	Oliver	9/18/63	Pvt	Slightly wounded in left leg at Riddle's Shop, VA, 6/13/64; Transferred to Company A, Residual Battalion; mustered out 8/7/65	*IJ* 6/24/64; IAG Report Vol. V
Britt	John	12/21/63	Pvt	Veteran; transferred to Company A, Residual Battalion; mustered out 8/7/65	IAG Report Vol. V
Brown	Pollard Jackson	8/18/61	Pvt	Listed as Corporal, 6/30/63; Hit in head by spent minié ball, cutting ear and giving him a headache, Falling Waters, 7/8/63; Wounded at Madison Court House, VA, 9/22/63; Mustered out 8/14/64; rode same horse entire enlistment	Rummel; Reid Papers; Pickerill, p. 96; IAG Report Vol. V, VIII; *MDEC* 10/23/86
Bruce	Isaac N.	3/21/63	Pvt	Discharged 1/23/63	IAG Report Vol. V, VIII
Bruce	John F.	3/21/62	Pvt	Served as orderly at Iron Brigade headquarters 8/62–2/64; Transferred to Company B, Residual Battalion; mustered out 3/21/65	NA Record Group 94, box 790A; IAG Report Vol. V
Buchanan	Frank	8/18/61	Pvt	In hospital at Annapolis, 7/63; Wounded in the stomach at Riddle's Shop, VA, 6/13/64; In hospital at Philadelphia wounded, 6/64; Mustered out 8/14/64	IAG Hospital Records; *MDEC* 6/24/64; IAG Report Vol. V, VIII
Carland	Patrick	8/22/61	Captain	Resigned 6/29/62; re-entered service as Captain in 9th Indiana Cavalry	IAG Report Vol. II
Childs	John A.	8/18/61	Pvt	Wounded in neck at Middletown, MD, 9/12/62; in hospital 10/62; Mustered out 8/14/64	*CWT* 10/2/62; IAG Hospital Records; IAG Report Vol. V, VIII
Collins	Mitchell	3/24/63	Pvt	In hospital at Fort Ellsworth, MD, 10/62; Transferred to Company B, Residual Battalion; discharged, no date	IAG Hospital Records; IAG Report Vol. V, VIII

Cotton	William	8/18/61	Sgt	Promoted 2nd Lieutenant, 7/29/62; mustered out 8/22/64; oldest man in eastern wing	IAG Report Vol. V; *MDEC* 10/15/85
Courtney	Hugh	8/18/61	Pvt	Mustered out 8/14/64	IAG Report Vol. V, VIII
Creekmore	James T.	8/18/61	Co. QM Sgt	Discharged 00/00/62; disability	IAG Report Vol. V, VIII
Cremens	William J.	2/25/63	Pvt	Transferred to Company B, Residual Battalion; mustered out 8/7/65	IAG Report Vol. V
Culver	George M.	8/18/61	Pvt	Mustered out 8/14/64	IAG Report Vol. V, VIII
Daily (Darley)	Hezekiah	8/18/61	Pvt	Wounded at Madison Court House 9/22/63; mustered out 8/14/64	IAG Hospital Records; *IJ* 9/29/63; IAG Report Vol. V, VIII
Dawson (Danson)	Charles N.	8/18/61	Pvt	Captured and paroled at Middletown, MD 9/12/62; Mustered out 8/14/64	*CWT* 10/2/62; Priest, p. 122; IAG Report Vol. V, VIII
Demarie (Demaree)	Cyrus	2/22/62	Pvt	Transferred to Company B, Residual Battalion as Sergeant; discharged	IAG Report Vol. V
Dennis	Isaac M.	9/25/63	Pvt	In hospital the majority of his time with fever and sprained back; Transferred to Company A, Residual Battalion; mustered out 8/7/65	NA Record Group 94 CMR; IAG Report Vol. V
Downey	William B.	8/18/61	Pvt	Captured along the Rappahannock, 4/15/63; Mustered out 8/14/64	Pickerill, p. 68; *CWT* 5/7/63; IAG Report Vol. V, VIII
Eagle	Michael	8/18/61	Blksmth	Discharged 2/27/62	IAG Report Vol. V, VIII
Ealy (Ely)	Dan J.	8/18/61	Pvt	Captured along the Rappahannock, 4/15/63; Mustered out 8/14/64	Pickerill, p. 68; *CWT* 5/7/63; IAG Report Vol. V, VIII

Eklor (Echler)	Daniel	3/24/62	Pvt	Captured along the Rappahannock, 4/15/63; Transferred to Company B, Residual Battalion	Pickerill, p. 68; *CWT* 5/7/63; IAG Report Vol. V
Enos	William M.	8/18/61	Pvt	In hospital for broken leg, 7/62; Veteran; transferred to Co. A, Residual Battalion, promoted Corporal; promoted to 2nd Lieutenant, Co. B, Residual Battalion, 7/1/65; mustered out as Sergeant	IAG Hospital Records; *CWT* 8/28/62; IAG Report Vol. V
Erle (Early)	Frederick	3/8/62	Pvt	Captured along the Rappahannock, 4/15/63; Transferred to Company B, Residual Battalion; discharged 5/16/65	Pickerill, p. 68; *CWT* 5/7/63; IAG Report Vol. V
Florce	John C.	8/18/61	Pvt	Mustered out 8/14/64 as Saddler	IAG Report Vol. V, VIII
Fluher	Ernest	8/18/61	Pvt	Wounded in thigh at Germanna Ford, VA, 5/3/64; Mustered out 8/14/64	IAG Hospital Records; *MDEC* 5/25/64; IAG Report Vol. V, VIII
Givin (Gwinn)	William	8/18/61	Sgt	Reported wounded and captured, 8/62; Discharged 10/19/62; wounds	*CWT* 8/28/62; IAG Report Vol. V, VIII
Golden	George S.	9/18/63	Pvt	Wounded along the Rapidan, 5/5/64; Transferred to Company A, Residual Battalion; mustered out 8/7/65	NA Record Group 94; IAG Report Vol. V; IAG Hospital Records
Goodpasture	Stephen		Pvt	Captured along the Rappahannock, 4/15/63; sent to hospital for measles; Transferred to Company A, Residual Battalion; mustered out 8/7/65	Pickerill, p. 68; *CWT* 5/7/63; NA Record Group 94 CMR; IAG Report Vol. V
Gorman	James D.	6/9/63	Pvt	Reported missing at Madison Court House, VA, 9/23/63; Killed at White Oak Swamp, VA, as a sergeant 6/13/64	*IJ* 10/6/63; Pickerill, p. 189; *MDEC* 6/24/64; IAG Report Vol. V, VIII

Gregg	Oscar H.	8/18/61	Pvt	Discharged 2/15/62	IAG Report Vol. V, VIII
Grubb (Grulb)	John	8/18/61	Pvt	Wounded at Middletown, MD, 9/12/62; In hospital at Baltimore for severe cut on scalp, 10/62; Veteran; transferred to Co. A, Residual Battalion; mustered out 8/7/65	*CWT* 10/2/62; IAG Hospital Records; IAG Report Vol. V
Halbert (Holbert)	John	3/23/63	Pvt	Wounded in left elbow during Wilson's Raid, 6/30/64; Transferred to Company A, Residual Battalion; mustered out 7/5/65	NA Record Group 94 CMR; *MDEC* 7/13/64; IAG Report Vol. V
Hall	Joseph	8/18/61	Pvt	In hospital at Washington, 8/62; wounded in right thigh, 7/15/63; In hospital at Annapolis, 7/63–8/63 for wound in right thigh; Veteran; transferred to Co. A, Residual Battalion; captured 4/7/65; mustered out 8/7/65	*CWT* 8/28/62; NA Record Group 94; IAG Hospital Records; IAG Report Vol. V;
Hall	Samuel O.		Pvt	Thigh broken at Sulphur Springs, 11/8/63; Wounded at Mud Run, VA; leg amputated; discharged 7/8/64	*MDEC* 11/24/63; IAG Report Vol. VIII; NA Record Group 94 CMR
Hannegan (Harrigan)	Cornelius	3/27/62	Pvt	Accidentally shot Samuel Posten by dropping revolver; Mustered out, no date	Bellamy Letters; IAG Report Vol. V, VIII
Harden	William H.	8/18/61	Pvt	Discharged, 00/00/61	IAG Report Vol. V, VIII
Hardman	Asa S.	8/18/61	Cpl	Captured and released at Gettysburg; Mustered out 8/14/64	*CWT* Vol. 6 No. 4; IAG Report Vol. V, VIII
Harney	Benjamin	8/18/61	Pvt	Mustered out 8/14/64	IAG Report Vol. V, VIII
Harrison (Heyden)	William H.		Pvt	In hospital at Washington for general debility, 7/62; Transferred to Company B, Residual Battalion; mustered out 8/7/65	IAG Hospital Records; IAG Report Vol. VIII
Hathaway	Ira	8/18/61	Pvt	Mustered out 8/14/64	IAG Report Vol. V, VIII

Higgins	Isaac	2/24/62	Pvt	Wounded at Gettysburg in left thigh, 7/1/63; Wounded 3/1/64; Transferred to Company B, Residual Battalion; discharged	IAG Hospital Records; NA Record Group 94 CMR; IAG Report Vol. V
Hines (Hinds)	William H.	8/18/61	Pvt	Slightly wounded in back at Middletown, MD 9/12/62; In hospital at Annapolis for fever, 7/63; wounded in left elbow at Riddle's Shop, VA, 6/13/64; Mustered out 8/14/64	IAG Hospital Records; *CWT* 10/2/62; *MDEC* 6/24/64; IAG Report Vol. V, VIII
Howell	Nathan P.	8/18/61	Pvt	Mustered out 8/14/64	IAG Report Vol. V, VIII
Hudson (Huttson)	John	8/18/61	Pvt	In hospital for Bilious Fever, 10/62; In hospital at Philadelphia for lung disease 3/63; Discharged 6/14/63	IAG Hospital Records; IAG Report Vol. V, VIII
Hyden	William H.	8/18/61	Pvt	Wounded in right foot at Upperville, VA, 6/21/63; Discharged 9/63 and promoted to Captain, 9th Indiana Cavalry	NA Record Group 94 CMR; IAG Correspondence 9/63; IAG Report Vol. V
Jones	Robert K.	8/18/61	Orderly Sgt	Discharged 5/24/63	IAG Report Vol. V, VIII
Jones	William F.	8/18/61	Pvt	Mustered out 8/14/64	IAG Report Vol. V, VIII
Jones	William J.	8/18/61	Pvt	Mustered out 8/14/64	IAG Report Vol. V, VIII
Keegler (Keeghler)	Harvey M. (Harry)	8/18/61	Pvt	Listed as Co. Comm. Sergeant, 6/30/63; Killed at White Oak Swamp, VA 6/13/64	Rummel; *IJ* 6/24/64; IAG Report Vol. V, VIII;
Kennedy	Walter O.	8/18/61	Pvt	Mortally wounded, 7/10/63 at Boonesborough as Corporal; died in hospital at Frederick, MD 8/10/63	Rummel; *IJ* 8/29/63

Klussman (Klousman)	Lewis (Louis)	8/18/61	Cpl	Wounded in left axilla 9/22/63 at Jack's Shop, VA; Wounded in foot at Riddle's Shop, VA, 6/13/64; Mustered out 8/14/64	NA Record Group 94; IAG Hospital Records; *IJ* 10/10/63; *MDEC* 6/24/64; IAG Report Vol. V, VIII
Leffler (Loffler)	Frederick G.	8/18/61	Pvt	Wounded in right arm at Jack's Shop, VA, 9/22/63; Mustered out 8/14/64	*IJ* 9/29/63; NA Record Group 94 CMR; IAG Hospital Records; IAG Report Vol. V, VIII
Little	Thomas M.	8/18/61	Pvt	Wounded in shoulder, captured and paroled, Middletown, MD, 9/12/62; Discharged 11/15/62; wounds	Fayette County History, p. 801; *CWT* 10/2/62; IAG Report Vol. V, VIII
Loder	Benjamin	3/28/62	Pvt	Captured 7/22/62; Killed at Madison Court House, VA, 9/22/63	*MDEC* 7/31/62; *VR* 10/8/63; NA Record Group 94; IAG Report Vol. V, VIII
Lynn	Payton S.	8/18/61	Pvt	Mustered out 8/14/64	IAG Report Vol. V, VIII
Martin	John O.	3/1/62	Pvt	Captured along the Rappahannock, 4/15/63; In hospital for syphilis, 4/29/64; Transferred to Company A, Residual Battalion; discharged	Pickerill, p. 68; *CWT* 5/7/63; NA Record Group 94 CMR; IAG Report Vol. V
McVey	John W.	8/18/61	Cpl	Listed as Regimental QM Sergeant, 6/30/63; Mustered out 8/14/64;	Rummel; IAG Report Vol. V, VIII
Mile (Meide) (Meade) (Mead)	Christian S.	8/18/61	Pvt	Mustered out 8/14/64	IAG Report Vol. V, VIII
Miller	Henry	3/6/62	Pvt	Transferred to Company B, Residual Battalion; mustered out 3/16/65	IAG Report Vol. V

Moffet (Moffitt)	Thomas W.	8/22/61	2nd Lt.	Captured and exchanged 8/62; Promoted Captain, 7/29/62; sick in divisional hospital 6/63; Wounded in finger on Wilson's Raid, 6/23/64	MDEC 7/31/62; IAG Report Vol. II; CWT 6/11/63; MDEC 7/13/64
Moore	William	8/18/61	Pvt	Mustered out 8/14/64/ Died in Andersonville prison, 1864	IAG Report Vol. V, VIII/ Pickerill p. 190
Mount	James	8/18/61	Cpl	Listed as Co. QM Sergeant, 6/30/63; Mustered out 8/14/64	Rummel; IAG Report Vol. V, VIII
Murphy	William F.	8/18/61	Pvt	Died in a Rebel Prison; no date	IAG Report Vol. V, VIII
Nash	William G.	8/18/61	Bugler	Mustered out 8/14/64	IAG Report Vol. V, VIII
Norman	James		Pvt	In hospital at Alexandria for Fever, 7/62; Wounded in thigh at Middletown, MD, 9/12/62; Lost on the steamer *Sultana*, 4/27/65	IAG Hospital Records; *IJ* 8/8/62; MDEC 9/22/62; IAG Report Vol. V, VIII
Nowland (Nolan)	Patrick	8/18/61	Cpl	Captured 7/21/62; Exchanged, 8/62; listed as Sergeant, 6/30/63	IAG Report Vol. V, VIII; MDEC 7/31/62; VR 8/21/62; Rummel
Offutt	Joseph E.	8/18/61	Saddler	In hospital at Washington, 8/62 for diseased heart; Discharged, 5/8/64	NA Record Group 94 CMR; CWT 8/28/62; IAG Report Vol. V, VIII
Oliphant	John W.	8/18/61	Blksmth	Discharged 2/28/63	IAG Report Vol. V, VIII
Payton	Presley Monroe	8/18/61	Pvt	Captured along the Rappahannock, 4/15/63; Mustered out 8/14/64	Pickerill, p. 68; CWT 5/7/63; IAG Report Vol. V, VIII
Perrin	William G.	3/6/62	Pvt	wounded in abdomen, 4/22/63; Wounded in thumb, 12/25/63; Transferred to Company B, Residual Battalion; mustered out 3/10/65	NA Record Group 94 CMR; IAG Report Vol. V

Peters	John W.	8/18/61	Pvt	Mustered out 8/14/64 as Bugler	IAG Report Vol. V, VIII
Pickerel	William N.	8/18/61	Pvt	Mustered out 8/14/64 as Corporal	IAG Report Vol. V, VIII
Powell	John	3/21/62	Pvt	Transferred to Company B, Residual Battalion; mustered out 3/23/65	IAG Report Vol. V
Powers	Oliver M.	8/22/61	1st Lt.	Resigned 7/28/62; re-commissioned as Captain of Company L; Transferred to 8th Indiana Cavalry as Captain, Company E	IAG Report Vol. II & V
Puckett	Samuel F.	8/18/61	Pvt	Accidentally wounded in knee by pistol shot, 4/12/63; Died 7/9/63 in Washington, D.C., 7/9/63 as Saddler	Pickerill p. 187; NA Record Group 94 CMR; IAG Report Vol. V
Reed	John H.	8/18/61	Pvt	Mustered out 8/14/64	IAG Report Vol. V, VIII
Reeve	Henry C.	8/18/61	Pvt	Wounded in face at Bristoe Station, VA, 10/15/63; Mustered out 8/14/64	IJ 10/19/63; NA Record Group 94 CMR; IAG Report Vol. V, VIII
Rench	Daniel W.	8/18/61	Pvt	Mustered out 8/14/64	IAG Report Vol. V, VIII
Reynolds	Owen	3/28/62	Pvt	Listed as Sergeant, 6/30/63; Wounded in left arm at Bealeton Station, VA, 10/25/63; Accidentally wounded in right foot by pistol, 5/24/64; Transferred to Company B, Residual Battalion as Sergeant; discharged	Rummel; NA Record Group 94 CMR; IAG Report Vol. V
Reynolds	William	3/7/62	Pvt	Discharged, no date	IAG Report Vol. V, VIII
Rodgers	Samuel D.	8/18/61	Pvt	Mustered out 8/14/64	IAG Report Vol. V, VIII
Saver	Philip	8/18/61	Wagoner	Mustered out 8/14/64	IAG Report Vol. V, VIII
Schievelbein (Sherberim)	Edward	3/20/62	Pvt	Wounded in head by saber blow at Hagerstown, MD, 9/12/62; Unaccounted for	VR 9/25/62; CWT 10/2/62; IAG Report Vol. V, VIII

Shoup (Shoap)	Samuel	8/18/61	Cpl	Transferred to Berdan's Sharpshooters; Entered Co. B, 2nd USSS as 2nd Lieutenant, 10/14/62; transferred to Co. F, 5th US Inf, 2/18/65; mustered out 7/5/65	IAG Report Vol. V, VIII; MI Vol. in Civil War
Smith	Carey W.	8/18/61	Bugler	Discharged 5/30/63	IAG Report Vol. V, VIII
Smith	Robert R.	8/18/61	Pvt	Discharged 7/6/63; disability	IAG Report Vol. V, VIII
South	David	3/18/62	Pvt	Veteran; transferred to Company A, Residual Battalion; mustered out 8/7/65 as Corporal	IAG Report Vol. V
Spahr	George W.	8/18/61	Cpl	Mustered out 8/64	IAG Report Vol. V
Spahr	John M.	8/18/61	Pvt	Discharged 00/00/62	IAG Report Vol. V, VIII
Spunger (Springer)	Moses C.	8/18/61	Pvt	Mustered out 8/14/64 as Corporal	IAG Report Vol. V, VIII
Steele (Steeth) (Street)	Fernandez	8/18/61	Pvt	Listed as First Sergeant, 6/30/63; Mustered out 8/14/64	Rummel; IAG Report Vol. V, VIII
Sterrett (Starrell) (Starrett)	John H.	8/18/61	Pvt	Listed as Corporal, 6/30/63; Veteran; transferred to Co. A, Residual Battalion, promoted to Sergeant; Captured at Mine Run, 5/5/64 and sent to Andersonville Prison; mustered out 6/28/65	Rummel; IAG Report Vol. V; NA Record Group 94 Pickerill, p. 193
Stewart	James F.	3/28/62	Pvt	Discharged, 3/24/63	IAG Report Vol. V, VIII
Sugden	Jonas	3/1/62	Pvt	Captured along the Rappahannock, 4/15/63; Transferred to Company B, Residual Battalion; discharged	Pickerill, p. 68; CWT 5/7/63; IAG Report Vol. V
Swift	George W.	8/18/61	Pvt	Captured and exchanged 8/62; In hospital at Washington 8/62; In hospital at Baltimore, MD for general debility, 10/62; Discharged 3/18/63	MDEC 7/31/62; CWT 8/28/62; IAG Hospital Records; IAG Report Vol. V, VIII
Thompson	John W.	8/18/61	Pvt	In Mt. Pleasant hospital 7/62; Died, Washington, D.C., 7/14/62	IJ 7/9/62; IAG Report Vol. V, VIII

Thornton	John F.	3/6/62	Pvt	Deserted, no date	IAG Report Vol. V, VIII
Tracey	Matthew J.	8/18/61	Sgt	Mustered out 8/14/64	IAG Report Vol. V, VIII
Umphries	George	8/18/61	Pvt	Wounded in head on Wilson Raid, 6/23/64; Captured at Petersburg; mustered out 9/25/65	NA Record Group 94 CMR; IAG Report Vol. V
Urmy	Samuel S.	8/18/61	Pvt	Discharged 9/21/63	IAG Report Vol. V, VIII
Vanosdol	Alexander	2/24/62	Pvt	Severely wounded in right ankle at Mine Run, VA, 11/10/63; Transferred to Company B, Residual Battalion; mustered out 5/30/65	NA Record Group 94; IAG Report Vol. VIII
Vanosdol (Vanosdal)	John W.	8/1/63	Pvt	Wounded on Wilson's Raid, 6/23/64; In hospital at New York for gunshot wound, 6/64; Transferred to Company A, Residual Battalion; mustered out 8/7/65	IAG Report Vol. V; IAG Hospital Records; *VR* 7/14/64
Webster	Daniel G.	8/18/61	Pvt	In hospital at Manassas, 8/62; Veteran; transferred to Co. A, Residual Battalion promoted Corporal; mustered out as Sergeant, 8/7/65	*CWT* 8/28/62; IAG Report Vol. V
Welch	Peter S.	8/18/61	Pvt	Wounded in left jaw by saber blow at Middletown, MD, 9/12/62; captured and paroled; In hospital at Baltimore for severe cut on chin, 10/62; Mustered out 8/14/64	NA Record Group 94 CMR; IAG Hospital Records; *CWT* 1/29/63; IAG Report Vol. V, VIII
Williamson	James W.	8/18/61	Cpl	Killed at Middletown, MD, 9/13/62 by saber blow to head	IAG Report Vol. V, VIII; *CWT* 10/2/62
Wilson	Lewis C.	8/18/61	Sgt	Captured and exchanged 8/62; Promoted 1st Lieutenant, 7/29/62; detailed as brigade QM 10/63–1/64; mustered out 8/22/64	*VR* 8/21/62; IAG Report Vol. V; *CWT* 10/22/63, 1/14/64

Winchell	William	8/18/61	Pvt	Died at Budd's Ferry, MD in hospital by overdose of morphine; 11/30/61	*CWT* 12/12/61; IAG Report Vol. V, VIII
Woldorf (Waldon)	Abner	3/10/62	Pvt	Discharged, 10/00/62	IAG Report Vol. V, VIII
Young	William	3/17/62	Pvt	Wounded in left index finger on Wilson's Raid, 6/30/64; In hospital at Philadelphia, 6/63–7/63; Transferred to Company B, Residual Battalion as Corporal; mustered out 3/10/65	NA Record Group 94 CMR; IAG Hospital Records; IAG Report Vol. V

Re-Organized*

COMPANY A

Abdon	Benjamin	Pvt.
Banks	Charles	Pvt.
Bayze (Baze)	Albert	Pvt.
Brenton	Oliver	Pvt.
Breuner (Bruning) (Brenner)	Francis	Pvt.
Brindley	Elijah	Pvt.
Brindley	Henry T.	Pvt.
Brindley	John D.	Pvt.
Britt	John	Pvt.
Buford	John W.	Pvt.
Calvin	James M.	Pvt.
Campbell	David	Pvt.
Chance	George W.	Pvt.
Clements	Reuben	Cpl.
Cole	Francis V.W.	Cpl.
Crane	Samuel A.	Pvt.
Craustre (Crauson)	Thomas	Pvt.
Cunningham	Samuel O.	Pvt.
Daniels	George R.	Pvt.
Demaree	Benjamin F.	Pvt.
Dennis	Isaac M.	Pvt.
Dilenhermer (Dillender)	Joseph	Pvt.

*Also called the Residual Battalion

Douglass	Edward B.	Pvt.
Duffy (Duffie)	George	Pvt.
Elston	Isaiah	Pvt.
Evans	Cowan D.	Pvt.
Faught	Sandford	Pvt.
Foster	Lymen F.	Pvt.
Golden	George S.	Pvt.
Goodner	Jacob J.	Pvt.
Gray (Grey)	Robert	Pvt.
Grimes	Stephen	Pvt.
Grubb (Grulb)	John	Pvt.
Halbert (Holbert)	John	Pvt.
Hall	Joseph	Pvt.
Harman	Michael	Pvt.
Hatten	James	Pvt.
Heck	Jacob	Bugler
Higgins	James	Pvt.
Higgins	John W.	Pvt.
Holland	Charles E.	Pvt.
Holmes	William T.	Pvt.
Hughes	Hezekiah	Pvt.
Huston (Houston)	Thomas M.	Pvt.
Jones	John	Pvt.
Jones	John L.	Pvt.
Jordan	William	Pvt.
Jordon (Jordan)	Absalom	Cpl.
Kern (Kerr)	Adam	Pvt.
Land	Bennett (Benjamin)	Pvt.
Large	Francis A.	Pvt.
Larue (Larew)	Abraham	Pvt.
Lee	Charles W.	Captain
Lee	John M.	Pvt.
Lewallen	Augustus	Pvt.
Martin	John O.	Pvt.
McClare (McLean) (McClain)	John W.	Pvt.
Monroe (Munroe)	Alexander C.	Pvt.
Morris	Henry	Pvt.
Mundara (Mundary) (Mondary)	Joseph	Pvt.
Muser (Meuser) (Menser) (Miser)	George W.	Pvt.
Myers	Abijah H.	Cpl.
Myers	Eugene R.	2nd Lt.
Myers	John M.	Cpl.
Nye	Charles	Pvt.
Padgett	William H.H.	Pvt.
Phillips	Robert W.	Pvt.
Pittman	Hilliard	Pvt.

Postin (Paston) (Posten)	Calvin R.	Bugler
Prather	Jonathan	Pvt.
Ramsey	Christopher	Pvt.
Romine	Isaac F.	Pvt.
Romine	Smith L.	Pvt.
Sheperd	William	Sgt.
Sherman	John B.	Pvt.
Siebenthal (Siemandel)	George L.	Pvt.
South	David	Pvt.
Staples	William	Pvt.
Stepleton	Jesse O.	Pvt.
Stepleton	Wesley L.	Pvt.
Sterrett (Starrell) (Starrett)	John H.	Sgt.
Storm	George I.	Pvt.
Storm	Jonathan Y.	Pvt.
Strouce (Strauce)	Frederick	Pvt.
Terrell	Robert	Pvt.
Tyrell	Robert	Pvt.
Vails (Vail, Vale)	William S.	Pvt.
Vanosdol (Vanosdal)	John W.	Pvt.
Ward	Alonzo	Pvt.
Ward	James	Pvt.
Ward	William H.H.	Pvt.
Watlington	William	Pvt.
Webster	Daniel G.	Cpl.
Wheeler	Thomas D.	Pvt.
White	Enos	Pvt.
Williamson	Andrew	Pvt.
Wright	Henry T.	Pvt.
Wright	Milton	1st Lt.
Yates	Peter R.	Pvt.
Yost	William H.H.C.	Pvt.

COMPANY B

Adkinson (Addison, Atkinson)	Samuel	Pvt.
Allen	Charles W.	Bugler
Alley	Fuel	Cpl.
Anderson	James W.	Pvt.
Baird	George P.	Pvt.
Beard	George W.	Pvt.
Beard	Perry C.	Pvt.
Beggs	Robert	Pvt.
Bennett	Jeremiah	Pvt.
Brindley	William G.	Pvt.

Bruce	John F.	Pvt.
Bruce	Martin	Sgt.
Carabaugh (Carnbaugh)	Andrew J.	Pvt.
Collins	Mitchell	Pvt.
Congers (Conyers)	William	Pvt.
Daniel	Nathaniel G.	Pvt.
Demarie (Demaree)	Cyrus	Sgt.
Eklor (Echler)	Daniel	Pvt.
Enos	William M.	2nd Lt.
Erle (Early)	Frederick	Pvt.
Fugit (Fuget) (Faget)	Morton D.	Pvt.
Gilbert	Benjamin F.	Pvt.
Gilchrist	George M.	Captain
Goodpasture	Stephen	Pvt.
Groartney (Gwartney) (Gordney)	John	Pvt.
Hanna	James	Pvt.
Hanna	Thomas M.	Pvt.
Harrison (Heyden)	William H.	Pvt.
Haskel	Hanibal	Pvt.
Higgins	Charles	Pvt.
Higgins	Isaac	Pvt.
Higgins	Martin M.	Pvt.
Hollenback	John	Pvt.
Holmes	David W.	Pvt.
Howard	Allen J.	Pvt.
Kern (Kerns)	David C.	Pvt.
Kern (Kerns)	Jacob C.	Pvt.
Kerr	William F.	Pvt.
Kincaid	John W.	Cpl.
Lamb	George W.	Pvt.
Lawson (Lanson)	Rudolph M.	Sgt.
Leach	James M.	Pvt.
Leach	John H.	Cpl.
Little	George W.	1st Lt.
Long	John G.	Pvt.
Marsh	James H.A.	Pvt.
Marshall	Robert	Sgt.
McKay	William M.	Pvt.
McLeod	James S.	Pvt.
McNeel (McNeal) (O'Neal) (Neal)	John	Pvt.
McSparks	William	Bugler
Melton	George W.	Cpl.
Meyer (Mayer)	James A.	Pvt.
Middleton	George	Pvt.
Miller	Henry	Pvt.
Nichols	John W.	Pvt.

Olmstead	Charles W.	Pvt.
Perrin	William G.	Pvt.
Pierson (Pearson)	George W.	Pvt.
Postin (Poston) (Posten)	Sandford	Pvt.
Powell	Eli H.	Pvt.
Powell	John	Pvt.
Purcell	Thomas	Pvt.
Quinn	James W.	Pvt.
Reagan	James H.	Pvt.
Reed	Henry W.	Cpl.
Reed	James W.	Pvt.
Reynolds	Owen	Sgt.
Rogers	George	Pvt.
Rogers	Henry	Pvt.
Sauvain (Sanbain)	William	Pvt.
Sedham	Levi	Pvt.
Sellers	Benjamin L.	Cpl.
Shepeard	Samuel	Pvt.
Siebenthal	Andrew J.	Pvt.
Smith	Charles	Pvt.
Snodgrass	Ansell	Pvt.
Soper (Sopers)	Orlando M. (Oramandel)	Pvt.
Spangler	John	Pvt.
Sparks	Henry	First Sgt.
Stevenson	Hugh	Pvt.
Stratford	Alfred	Pvt.
Stratford	Thomas W.	Pvt.
Sugden	Jonas	Pvt.
Tait	William	Blacksmith
Tower	Oliver	Pvt.
Vanosdol	Alexander	Pvt.
Walters	John	Pvt.
Weaver	Augustus C.	Pvt.
Weaver	Henry B.	Pvt.
Willman	Henry	Pvt.
Wilson	Jesse	Pvt.
Wiseman	John	Pvt.
Wolters	John	Pvt.
Young	William	Cpl.

Chapter Notes

Preface

1. *Official Records of the Rebellion* (Washington, D.C.: Government Printing Office, 1880), Series III, Vol. II, p. 617. Hereafter referred to as *OR*.
2. Stephen Z. Starr, *The Union Cavalry in the Civil War* (Baton Rouge: Louisiana State University Press, 1979), Vol. II, p. 58.
3. John S.D. Eisenhower, *Agent of Destiny: The Life and Times of General Winfield Scott* (Lawrence: University Press of Kansas, 2015), p. 209.

Chapter 1

1. *Corydon Democrat*, July 9, 1861.
2. *The Soldier of Indiana* (Indianapolis: Merrill and Company, 1866), p. 76. Earlier, a call had gone out to raise two companies of cavalry and they were sent East. These units eventually became companies I and K of the 1st Indiana Cavalry.
3. *Vevay Reveille*, May 5, 1861.
4. *History of Switzerland County, Indiana* (Chicago: Weakley and Co., 1885), p. 1198.
5. Adjutant General of Indiana Correspondence, 1st Indiana Cavalry file, July 19, 1861 (Indianapolis: Indiana State Library). Hereafter referred to as AGI Correspondence.
6. *Madison Daily Evening Courier*, July 6, 1861.
7. *Ibid.*, July 1, 1861.
8. *Corydon Democrat*, July 30, 1861.
9. AGI Correspondence, 1st Indiana file.
10. *Corydon Democrat*, July 19, 1861.
11. *Madison Daily Evening Courier*, July 6, 1861.
12. *Vevay Reveille*, June 20, 1861.
13. *Madison Daily Evening Courier*, August 1, 1861.
14. *Vevay Reveille*, August 15, 1861.
15. USS *Constitution* log, August, 1849.
16. *Indianapolis Journal*, June 17, 1882.
17. Indiana Adjutant General Report (Indianapolis: Indiana State Publishing Office, 1867), Vol. II, p. 448. Hereafter referred to as IAG Report.
18. *Vevay Reveille*, September 12, 1861. West Virginia was not a state until 1862, hence the site of their disembarkment being in Virginia.
19. *Ibid.*
20. William Pickerill, *History of the Third Indiana Cavalry* (Indianapolis: Aetna Printing, 1906), p. 11.
21. *Madison Daily Evening Courier*, September 9, 1861.
22. Pickerill, *History of the Third Indiana Cavalry*, p. 11.
23. *Indianapolis Journal*, September 19, 1861.
24. *Ibid.*
25. Flavius Bellamy Papers, Indiana State Library, Manuscript Division, Indianapolis, IN. Letter, September 6, 1861.
26. 1st Indiana Cavalry file, September 11, 1861.
27. *Vevay Reveille*, September 19, 1861.
28. Flavius Bellamy, letter, September 10, 1861.
29. Pickerill, *History of the Third Indiana Cavalry*, p. 12.
30. *Ibid.*, p. 13.
31. *Vevay Reveille*, October 17, 1889.
32. Flavius Bellamy, letter, October 1861.
33. Eloine Patton Chesnut and Scott Nelson Patton, *Major William Patton, Third Indiana Cavalry: His Civil War Diaries and Letters* (unpublished, 2016), p. 12.
34. Joseph Hooker Papers, Huntington Library, San Marino, CA. October 15, 1861. Hooker's division included the aforementioned brigades of Sickles and Cowdin.
35. The 1st Indiana Cavalry would go on and serve in the West throughout the war. Companies I and K mentioned earlier had been sent east early in the war and were organized into a squadron, serving as escorts for a succession of headquarters. In retrospect, the assignment of these two companies to the Third Indiana Cavalry would have made much more sense for both regiments.
36. The National Archives, National Archives and Records Administration, Record Group 94, Washington, D.C. Hereafter referred to as NA.
37. Lemmon's name was often spelled Lemon. "Lemmon" has been used throughout as this was the spelling used by his family in pension applications.
38. NA Record Group 94. Indiana had adopted a regimental numbering system that began with six, recognizing that five infantry regiments had been raised during the Mexican War. This ordinal numbering system gave cavalry units a state regiment number as well as an ordinal number as cavalry. Thus, the 3rd Indiana Cavalry was considered the third cavalry unit raised but also the 40th regiment raised overall. This incredibly clunky system

caused much confusion early in the war, and cavalry units were almost never referred to by their state ordinal number. Interestingly, artillery were numbered solely as artillery.

Chapter 2

1. Pickerill, p. 14.
2. Edwin C. Fishel, *The Secret War for the Union: The Untold Story of Military Intelligence in the Civil War* (New York: Houghton Mifflin, 1996), p. 72.
3. *OR*, Series II, Vol. I, p. 703.
4. Hooker Papers, Mason to Hooker, November 6, 1861.
5. IAG Correspondence, 3rd Indiana Cavalry file, November 2, 1861.
6. IAG Report, Vol. II, p. 440.
7. IAG Correspondence, 3rd Indiana Cavalry file, March 9, 1862.
8. Flavius Bellamy, letter, October 29, 1861.
9. There was no organization by this name at that time. This organization was a complete fabrication of Baker's.
10. Hooker Papers, Baker to Hooker, November 25, 1861.
11. *Ibid.*, Chapman to Hooker, various dates.
12. IAG Correspondence, 3rd Indiana Cavalry file.
13. *Special Agents, Pay Agents, et al., Visiting Troops, etc.* (Indianapolis: State Government Printing, 1863), p. 78.
14. *Ibid.*
15. *Connersville Weekly Times,* December 12, 1861.
16. Flavius Bellamy, letter, December 7, 1861. As the war progressed, getting discharged based on disability became much more difficult.
17. *Ibid.*, letter, December 21, 1861.
18. Vivian Zollinger, "'I take my pen in Hand': Letters from Owen County, Indiana Soldiers," *Indiana Magazine of History* (June 1997): 123. Private Barker of Company D died six months later of typhoid fever in Alexandria, Virginia. He never did get to see if they might "gro in that country."
19. IAG Report, Vol. II, p. 442.
20. *Aurora Commercial,* January 9, 1862.
21. Hooker Papers, Chapman to Hooker, December 15, 1861.
22. *OR*, Series I, Vol. V, p. 691.
23. *Madison Daily Evening Courier,* June 2, 1893.
24. Hooker Papers, Chapman to Hooker, December 29, 1861.
25. *Aurora Commercial,* January 9, 1862.
26. Flavius Bellamy, letter, January 4, 1862.
27. *Ibid.*, letter, December 28, 1861. This type of accident befell at least nine other 3rd Indiana cavalrymen during their time in service.
28. *Aurora Commercial,* March 20, 1862.
29. AGI Correspondence, 3rd Indiana Cavalry file. Companies G, H, I, and K would be assimilated into the Cavalry Corps of the Army of the Cumberland as the Third Battalion, Third Indiana Cavalry. In the fall of 1862, Cavalry regiments were authorized to add two more companies. Companies L and M were raised and kept in Indiana for almost a year where they performed provost marshal duty, enforced draft laws, help suppress threats of civil unrest from Knights of the Golden Circle, and chased Confederate general Morgan on his raid through Indiana and Ohio in July, 1863. They were eventually ordered to eastern Tennessee in late 1863 where they joined the western four companies to comprise the West Wing, Third Indiana Cavalry.
30. Hooker Papers, Chapman to Hooker, December 21, 1861.
31. *Ibid.*, Chapman to Hooker, January 9, 1862.
32. Flavius Bellamy, letter, January 18, 1862.
33. Hooker Papers, Chapman to Hooker, January 3, 1862.
34. Chesnut, *William Patton*, p. 25.
35. *Aurora Commercial*, March 1, 1862.
36. Flavius Bellamy, letter, May 13, 1862.
37. *St. Mary's Beacon* (MD), January 30, 1862.
38. Hooker Papers, Chapman to Hooker, January 14, 1862.
39. Chesnut, *William Patton*, p. 25.
40. *Madison Daily Evening Courier*, April 12, 1862.
41. NA Record Group 94, 3rd Indiana Cavalry file, Carded Medical Record.
42. NA Record Group 94, 3rd Indiana Cavalry file, March 27, 1862.
43. George Chapman diary, Indiana State Historical Society, Indianapolis, IN. April 7, 1862.
44. Flavius Bellamy, letter, April 16, 1862. Apparently Workman was a quick healer and thick skulled; Bellamy later reported on May 13 that Workman had recovered from his injury and rejoined the company while Reed had been released from arrest.
45. Chesnut, *William Patton*, p. 28. Patton was married with four young children. His wife was not among the group in "Womansville."
46. Flavius Bellamy, April 6, 1862.
47. *Vevay Reveille*, May 15, 1862.
48. NA Record Group 94, 3rd Indiana Cavalry file.
49. *Aurora Commercial*, June 5, 1862.
50. *Ibid.*, May 15, 1862.
51. Samuel J.V.B. Gilpin Papers, Library of Congress, Washington, D.C., May 17, 1862.
52. Chesnut, *William Patton*, p. 29.

Chapter 3

1. Chapman diary, May 22, 1862.
2. *OR*, Series I, Vol. XII, p. 295.
3. *Indianapolis Journal*, June 10, 1862.
4. *Madison Daily Evening Courier*, Gilpin speech, October 15, 1885.
5. *Ibid.*
6. *Indiana Journal*, June 16, 1862.
7. Chesnut, *William Patton*, p. 35. His use of "FFV" referred to First Families of Virginia.

8. Samuel V.B. Gilpin diary, June 13, 1862.
9. The unique geography of the Shenandoah Valley can create confusion. The Shenandoah River flows north; hence going up the river valley actually meant going south. Likewise, going down the valley meant going north.
10. *Indianapolis Journal*, June 6, 1862.
11. Chapman diary, June 29, 1862.
12. IAG Correspondence, 3rd Indiana Cavalry file. Carland would later raise a company for the 9th Indiana Cavalry and end the war as a major of that unit.
13. Clark would later re-enter service as 1st Lieutenant of Company D, 10th Indiana Cavalry.
14. IAG Report, Vol. II, pp. 442–44.
15. IAG Correspondence, 3rd Indiana Cavalry, July 2, 1862.
16. NA Record Group 94, 3rd Indiana Cavalry file. His letter carried an unusual note that the resignation be accepted "on the recommendation of his Colonel for the benefit of the public service." Powers had powerful friends, however, and when Company L was formed in October 1862, he was commissioned its captain. When the company was ordered south in November 1863 to join the West Wing, Powers arraigned to be placed on detached duty at a remount camp in Kentucky. He sat out the rest of the war in the comparative comfort and safety of this position.
17. IAG Correspondence, 3rd Indiana Cavalry file, July 11, 1862.
18. *Ibid.*
19. *Ibid.*, July 13, 1862.
20. Elias W.H. Beck Papers, Indiana State Library, Manuscript Division, Indianapolis, IN. Letter, July 2, 1862.
21. IAG Correspondence, 3rd Indiana Cavalry file, July 4, 1862.
22. IAG Report, Vol. II, p. 444.
23. IAG Correspondence, 3rd Indiana Cavalry file, July 9, 1862. White didn't get his commission but was a faithful correspondent to the *Madison Daily Evening Courier* with dozens of reports sent under his initials CNW.
24. *Indianapolis Journal*, July 17, 1862.
25. *Vevey Reveille*, July 24, 1862.
26. OR, Series I, Vol. XVI, p. 103.
27. Flavius Bellamy, letter, July 25, 1862.
28. *Indianapolis Journal*, July 28, 1862.
29. OR, Series I, Vol. XVI, p. 106.
30. IAG Correspondence, 3rd Indiana Cavalry file, August 1, 1862. The captured men were exchanged a month later.
31. IAG Report, Vol. II, p. 444.
32. IAG Correspondence, 3rd Indiana Cavalry file, August 1, 1862.
33. Samuel V.B. Gilpin diary, August 1, 1862.
34. Flavius Bellamy, letter, August 7, 1862.
35. *Madison Daily Evening Courier*, August 8, 1862.
36. OR, Series I, Vol. XVI, p. 123.
37. *Indianapolis Journal*, August 14, 1862.
38. *Aurora Commercial*, August 21, 1862.
39. Elias W.H. Beck, letter, August 8, 1862.
40. *Indianapolis Journal*, August 14, 1862.
41. *History of Switzerland County, Indiana* (Chicago: Weakley, Harraman & Co., 1885).
42. *Indianapolis Journal*, August 14, 1862.
43. Samuel V.B. Gilpin diary, August 8, 1862.
44. *Madison Daily Evening Courier*, August 11, 1862.

Chapter 4

1. IAG Correspondence, 3rd Indiana Cavalry file, August 13, 1862.
2. Flavius Bellamy, letter, August 12, 1862. Sturman would be discharged on April 22, 1863.
3. *Ibid.*
4. Samuel J.V.B. Gilpin diary, August 10, 1862.
5. Earl J. Coates and Dean S. Thomes, *An Introduction to Civil War Small Arms* (Gettysburg, PA: Thomas Publications, 1990). The Gallager carbine was also widely used by the regiment. Similar in weight and length to the Burnside, it was a .50 caliber weapon, complicating cartridge supply.
6. *Indianapolis Journal*, August 15, 1862.
7. IAG Correspondence, 3rd Indiana Cavalry file, August 22, 1862. Despite these glowing recommendations, Lemmon had to wait until March 1863 to receive his next promotion.
8. *Ibid.*, August 25, 1862.
9. NA Record Group 94, CMR.
10. Samuel J.V.B. Gilpin diary, September 4, 1862.
11. *Ibid.*, September 5, 1862.
12. *Ibid.*
13. *Ibid.*, September 6, 1862.
14. *Ibid.*
15. Abner Hard, *History of the 8th Illinois Cavalry Regiment of Volunteers* (Aurora, IL: privately published, 1868), pp. 170–71.
16. Robert E. Lester, "1919 Narrative of Augustus C. Weaver," *Civil War Unit Histories—Part 4*, Bethesda, MD: University Publications of America, microfilm, 1993.
17. *Ibid.* Banta would survive his wounds and serve his entire term of enlistment.
18. *Vevay Reveille*, September 25, 1862. Kassabaum, Eblin, and Wood were so incapacitated by their wounds that they were discharged.
19. Samuel J.V.B. Gilpin diary, September 8, 1862.
20. Elias W.H. Beck letter, September 11, 1862. Kennedy would be wounded again in September 1863 before being taken prisoner in January 1864. He survived Andersonville prison only to be tragically killed in the explosion of the steamboat *Sultana* on his way him from captivity.
21. Chesnut, *William Patton*, p. 42.
22. OR, Series I, Vol. XIX, p. 219.
23. Samuel J.V.B. Gilpin diary, September 9, 1862.
24. *Indianapolis Journal*, September 17, 1862.
25. *Ibid.*
26. *Ibid.*, September 25, 1862.

27. Samuel J.V.B. Gilpin diary, September 12, 1862.
28. Flavius Bellamy, letter, September 18, 1862. Bellamy gives the date as September 8, but the company was in Poolesville that day.
29. Pickerill, *History of the Third Indiana Cavalry*, p. 24.
30. *Ibid.*
31. *Vevay Reveille*, September 25, 1862. Quinn would linger for several weeks before succumbing to his wounds on October 31, 1862.
32. John M. Priest, *Before Antietam: The Battle of South Mountain* (Shippensburg, PA: White Mane, 1992) p. 115.
33. Timothy J. Reese, "The Cavalry Clash at Quebec Schoolhouse," *Blue and Gray* (February 1993): 24.
34. *Valley Register* (Middletown, MD), April 8, 1898. Interview with Pickerill.
35. *OR*, Series I, Vol. XIX, p. 824. It was erroneously reported that the attack was made by Cobb's Legion and three other regiments. In the only report of the action, Confederate general Wade Hampton reported only Cobb's six-company Legion participated.
36. *Connersville Weekly Times*, October 2, 1862; *Madison Daily Evening Courier*, September 22, 1862.
37. Samuel J.V.B. Gilpin diary, October 28, 1862. The diary entry identifies the man as "Bird," but there is no man by this name on the muster roll. It could have been a nickname. In his 1885 address at the reunion of the regiment, Gilpin chose not to identify the man by name.
38. *Vevay Reveille*, September 25, 1862.
39. *Valley Register* (Middletown, MD), September 22, 1899. Interview with Thomas Day.
40. Pickerill, *History of the Third Indiana Cavalry*, p. 26.
41. *Valley Register* (Middletown, MD), September 22, 1899. Day returned to Middletown in 1899, and when he told his story, a local man miraculously produced the Maynard carbine and gave it to Day. Apparently, the rebel officer neglected to pick up the carbine after attending to his other duties. The man collected the weapon and kept it until Day's visit. Day was so thrilled to have the weapon it became his constant companion at regimental reunions and GAR functions. He even took it with him when he visited Gettysburg in 1913 on the 50th anniversary of that battle.
42. *Ibid.*
43. Seever and Quinn would die of their wounds. No Union report was ever written about this fight. Division commander Pleasanton made no mention in his report of divisional activity during the Antietam campaign. The publicity conscious commander probably preferred not to mention a fight where his men got mauled. William Pickerill, regimental historian, never forgave Pleasanton for this omission and mentioned the slight in his 1906 history and in numerous other postwar writings.
44. *OR*, Series I, Vol. XIX, p. 824.
45. NA Record Group 94, 3rd Indiana Cavalry file, Carded Medical Record. After a long recovery, Harris was discharged on April 4, 1863, his wounds having proved debilitating.
46. This total reflects deaths by disease, drowning, killed in action and those wounded.
47. *Valley Register* (Middletown, MD). September 22, 1899 and April 8, 1898. Both Day and Pickerill commented on the valley's beauty.

Chapter 5

1. Samuel J.V.B. Gilpin diary, September 15, 1862.
2. *Madison Daily Evening Courier*, October 2, 1899.
3. Carded Medical Records, NA Record Group 94. A marker is located on the Antietam battlefield just west of Middle Bridge where the regiment served on the afternoon of September 17.
4. Samuel J.V.B. Gilpin diary, September 18, 1862.
5. Flavius Bellamy letter, September 19, 1862.
6. *Indianapolis Journal*, October 3, 1862.
7. *Ibid.*, October 6, 1862.
8. *Ibid.*, October 10, 1862.
9. Samuel J.V.B. Gilpin diary, October 3, 1862.
10. *Ibid.*, October 10, 1862.
11. *Ibid.*, October 13, 1862.
12. *Indianapolis Journal,* October 22, 1862.
13. *OR*, Series I, Vol. XIX, p. 40.
14. Gilpin speech, 1885.
15. *OR*, Series I, Vol. XIX p. 431.
16. Flavius Bellamy letter, October 26, 1862.
17. IAG Report, Vol. II, p. 440.
18. *Ibid.*
19. IAG Correspondence, 3rd Indiana Cavalry file, October 25, 1862.
20. William McClure papers, Indiana State Library, Manuscripts Division, Indianapolis, IN. October 25, 1862.
21. IAG Report, Vol. II, p. 440. In the convoluted world of the split wings of the regiment, William Klein of Company K was promoted to Major and command of the 3rd Indiana Cavalry, West Wing.
22. IAG Correspondence, 3rd Indiana Cavalry file, October 31, 1862.
23. William McClure papers, October 25, 1862.
24. Samuel J.V.B. Gilpin diary, *October 3, 1862.*
25. IAG Correspondence, 3rd Indiana Cavalry file, May 29, 1863. This letter was written after Wright had resigned, reconsidered and asked to be reinstated. Chapman had blocked Wright's request.
26. Flavius Bellamy letter, October 26, 1862.
27. William McClure diary, November 11, 1862.
28. IAG Report, Vol. II, p. 440 Chapman would have to wait until December to officially hear of his promotion. The commission dated from October 25, the day after Buchanan's resignation.
29. *Indianapolis Sentinel*, November 10, 1862.

30. NA Record Group 94 Box 790A.
31. Flavius Bellamy diary, November 2, 1862.
32. *Ibid.*, November 4, 1862.
33. Barbee's Crossroads is present-day Hume, Virginia.
34. Gilpin speech, 1885.
35. NA records, Bardwell, Augustine Service Record.
36. Gilpin speech, 1885.
37. Samuel Gilpin diary, November 23, 1862.
38. *Indianapolis Journal*, December 12, 1862.
39. Samuel Gilpin diary, December 19, 1862. There is little to be said about the cavalry's role in the debacle at Fredericksburg. Burnsides' unimaginative use of cavalry showed even less understanding for their role than his predecessor.
40. Starr, Vol. I, p. 331.
41. *Indianapolis Journal*, January 8, 1863.
42. Samuel V.B. Gilpin diary, December 21, 1862.
43. Joseph W. Dalrymple Papers, Indiana State Library, Manuscript Division, Indianapolis, IN.
44. *Indianapolis Journal*, April 16, 1863.
45. Congress had passed legislation to expand cavalry regiments to twelve companies. Companies L and M were raised in Indiana and mustered in October 23 and December 11, respectively.
46. Thomas F. Thiele, "The Evolution of Cavalry in the American Civil War; 1861–1863" (PhD diss., University of Michigan, 1951), p. 189.
47. George Chapman diary, December 2–4, 1862. The charges were passed on to brigade headquarters where the matter died. Wright assumed Chapman had not forwarded the charges.
48. NA Record Group 153, LL 261.
49. NA Record Group 94, 3rd Indiana Cavalry file. Sauvine was cleared of any criminal intent in a court of inquiry a month later.
50. *Ibid.*, Carded Medical Records.
51. *Aurora Commercial,* March 3, 1863.
52. Gilpin speech, 1885.
53. *Madison Daily Evening Courier*, April 27, 1863.
54. IAG Report, Vol. II, p. 441.
55. *Ibid.*, pp. 443–44. Many of these appointments were backdated, but the men did not receive notice until the winter.
56. *Ibid.*, p. 440. McClure was still getting used to his new rank. In the letter to the adjutant general endorsing Taylor's appointment, he started to sign as captain before scratching it out and writing major.
57. Chesnut, *William Patton*, p. 51.
58. IAG Correspondence, 3rd Indiana Cavalry file, January 11, 1863.
59. William Gray Papers, Indiana State Library, Manuscript Division, Indianapolis, IN. Frank Buchanan letter, March 21, 1863.
60. *OR*, Series I, Vol. XXV, p.51.
61. Edward Longacre, *The Cavalry at Gettysburg* (Lincoln: University of Nebraska Press, 1986), p. 46. At times his ailment would be so painful he was forced to travel by carriage.
62. Fishel, *The Secret War,* p. 292. The Bureau was established with 18 scouts, or spies. The trio of Hoosiers were later joined by John Irby, William Jones, and John Hatten. Cline was appointed chief of scouts and proved to be one of the most effective scouts for the army.
63. *OR*, Series I, Vol. XXV, p. 72.
64. Longacre, *Cavalry at Gettysburg*, p. 51.
65. NA Record Group 94, 3rd Indiana Cavalry file.
66. IAG Correspondence, 3rd Indiana Cavalry file.
67. *Ibid.* Wright did not suffer adversely from this distinction. He later re-entered service as a captain in the 7th Indiana Cavalry. He died of disease in Memphis, Tennessee, in September 1864.
68. *Ibid.*, May 13, 1863.
69. Fishel, *The Secret War*, pp. 306–10. Cline's remarkable scout is considered the longest and most daring scout of the war. His return to Union lines in the Northern Neck spelled trouble for Cole. Confederate suspicions in the area were aroused when Chapman fled to the Union lines and Cole was captured as he tried to enter Rebel lines in the same area.
70. George Chapman diary, March 13, 1863. There is no record of a flag for the regiment. Whether the flag was ever ordered and delivered is unknown.

Chapter 6

1. Chapman's and Lemmon's commissions for colonel and major, respectively, were dated from March 12, 1863. On the same date, Major Robert Klein of the West Wing was promoted to lieutenant colonel in command of the companies in Tennessee.
2. IAG Report, vol. II, p. 443. Isaac Gilbert had mustered as a member of Company E before his promotion to second lieutenant.
3. NA Record Group 94, 3rd Indiana Cavalry file, muster rolls.
4. *Madison Daily Evening Courier*, March 30, 1863.
5. NA Record Group 94, 3rd Indiana Cavalry file, muster rolls.
6. George Chapman diary, March 24, 1863.
7. Elias W.H. Beck letter, May 17, 1863.
8. *Indianapolis Journal*, March 27, 1863.
9. Joseph Adkinson Collection, Hanover College Archives, Hanover, IN. April 3, 1863.
10. Flavius Bellamy letters.
11. George Chapman diary, April 10, 1863.
12. *Ibid.*, April 11, 1863.
13. *OR*, Series I, Vol. XXV, pp. 1067–068.
14. Pickerill, *History of the Third Indiana Cavalry*, p. 187.
15. *Madison Daily Evening Courier*, May 2, 1863.
16. Samuel Gilpin diary, April 15, 1863.
17. *Madison Daily Evening Courier*, May 2, 1863.

18. Pickerill, *History of the Third Indiana Cavalry*, p. 69.
19. *Ibid.*
20. *Indianapolis Journal*, April 29, 1863. Their stays in rebel prison camp were short. By early June, all had been exchanged.
21. *Vevay Reveille*, June 4, 1863.
22. *OR*, Series I, Vol. XXV, p. 237.
23. *Indianapolis Journal*, April 29, 1863.
24. Samuel Gilpin diary, April 29, 1863.
25. *Ibid.*
26. *Ibid.*, May 1, 1863. Gresham's wounds would keep him from the regiment for many months. While still convalescing, he was ordered from his home to Indianapolis to serve as a horse inspector for the newly-created Cavalry Bureau. This bureau was responsible for the purchase of new horses and the rehabilitation of broken down mounts.
27. *Ibid.*, May 2, 1863.
28. *Ibid.*, May 3, 1863.
29. *Ibid.*, May 7, 1863.
30. George Chapman diary, May 11, 1863.
31. *OR*, Series I, Vol. XXV, p. 512.
32. *Richmond Whig* (VA), May 18, 1863.
33. NA Record Group 94, 3rd Indiana Cavalry file, regimental correspondence.
34. *OR*, Series I, Vol. XXV, p. 1116.
35. Hard, *History of the 8th Illinois*, pp. 238–39.
36. *Indianapolis Journal*, May 30, 1863.
37. *OR*, Series I, Vol. XXV, p. 1116.
38. Frederick Whittaker, *A Complete Life of Gen. George A. Custer, Major-General of Volunteers, Brevet Major-General U.S. Army, and Lieutenant-Colonel of the 7th U.S. Cavalry*, edited by Don Heinrich Tolzmann (Lincoln: Bison Press, 1983), p. 51.
39. *William B. Hardy Collection*, Virginia Military Institute Archives, Manuscript Collection, Virginia Military Institute, Lexington, VA. One of the privates in the capture party, George Middleton, would later cross paths with Hardy. After the war, Hardy relocated to California, eventually becoming the city attorney for San Jose. One day in 1910 while driving through San Jose, Middleton saw Hardy's office sign and, on a whim, knocked on Hardy's door. When the attorney answered, Middleton inquired if he was the same Captain Hardy of the Confederate artillery who had been captured on his porch reading Shakespeare. Astounded, Hardy affirmed that he was indeed that person. Middleton introduced himself as one of Hardy's captors, and the two former antagonists spent the rest of the afternoon visiting and reminiscing about a May day many years ago.
40. *OR*, Series I, Vol. XXV, p. 1116.
41. Jay Monoghan, *The Life of George Armstrong Custer* (New York: Toronto, 1959), p. 121.

Chapter 7

1. Samuel Gilpin diary, May 27–31, 1863.
2. Though never formally relieved of command, Stoneman would serve for a time as head of the Cavalry Bureau before heading west to serve as commander of the Army of the Cumberland's cavalry where, incidentally, he found the 3rd Indiana Cavalry, West Wing, under his command.
3. Edward Longacre, *General John Buford: A Military Biography* (Conshohocken, PA: Combined Publishing, 1995), pp. 87–88.
4. IAG Correspondence, 3rd Indiana Cavalry file.
5. IAG Report, Vol. II, p. 441–42.
6. Joseph W. McKinney, *Brandy Station, Virginia, June 9, 1863: The Largest Cavalry Battle of the Civil War* (Jefferson, NC: McFarland, 2006), p. 255. Five companies of the 9th New York and two companies of the 3rd West Virginia had been attached to the brigade prior to the battle.
7. *OR*, Series I, Vol. XXVII, p. 1048.
8. George Gilchrist letter, *Indianapolis Journal*, June 18, 1863 and *Vevay Reveille*, June 18, 1863. Pleasanton's report of the battle listed 22 wounded for the regiment.
9. Gilpin speech, 1885.
10. Samuel Gilpin diary, June 11, 1863.
11. Longacre, *The Cavalry at Gettysburg*. p. 91.
12. *Indianapolis Journal*, June 18, 1863.
13. Samuel Gilpin diary, June 16, 1863.
14. *Ibid.*, June 18, 1863.
15. Gilpin speech, 1885. One week later the 23-year-old Captain would be promoted over the heads of hundreds of other officers to Brigadier General command of his own brigade of cavalry.
16. Robert F. O'Neill, *The Cavalry Battles of Aldie, Middleburg, Upperville*. 2nd edition (Lynchburg, VA: H.E. Howard, 1993), p. 112.
17. *OR*, Series I, Vol. XXII, p. 921.
18. O'Neill, *The Cavalry Battles*, p. 134.
19. Samuel Gilpin diary, June 21, 1863.
20. *OR*, Series I, Vol. XXVII, p. 933. The 8th New York arrived on the field at the end of the coming action with little opportunity to impact its outcome.
21. O'Neill, *The Cavalry Battles*, p. 136.
22. *Ibid.*, p. 132.
23. *Ibid.*, p. 138.
24. *Ibid.*, p. 139.
25. Carded Medical Records, NA Group 94, 3rd Indiana Cavalry file.
26. O'Neill, *The Cavalry Battles*, p. 141.
27. *Ibid.*
28. Carded Medical Records, NA Record Group 94, 3rd Indiana Cavalry file.
29. O'Neill, *The Cavalry Battles*, p. 141.
30. NA Record Group 94, 3rd Indiana Cavalry file. Muster roll, June 30, 1863.
31. Flavius Bellamy letter, June 22, 1863. Johnson was discharged March 7, 1864.
32. *Aurora Commercial*, July 2, 1863.
33. Edward Reid Diary, Illinois State Historical Society, Springfield, IL. June 21, 1863.
34. Fishel, *The Secret War*, p. 471.

Chapter 8

1. NA Record Group 94, 3rd Indiana Cavalry file, muster roll, June 30, 1863.
2. The lack of uniformity in arms continued to plague the regiment. Since the Gallager and Sharps were different calibers from the Smith, supply of ammunition continued to be cumbersome.
3. *Ibid.*, ordinance report, June 30, 1863.
4. NA Record Group 94, 3rd Indiana Cavalry file, muster roll, June 30, 1863. Second Lieutenant George M. Gilchrist of Company E was on detached duty as an aide-de-camp on General Buford's divisional staff.
5. William Pickerill, *Indiana at the Fiftieth Anniversary of the Battle of Gettysburg* (1913), p. 42.
6. David G. Martin, *Gettysburg, July 1* (Conshohocken, PA: Combined Publishing, 1996), p. 74.
7. *National Tribune*, July 3, 1903.
8. Edward Reid diary, June 30, 1863.
9. *National Tribune*, July 3, 1903
10. *Ibid.*
11. Edward Reid diary, July 1, 1863.
12. *Ibid.*
13. There is some confusion as to the number of men on the skirmish line. Gamble, the brigade commander, stated that nearly 900 men were engaged. If true, over half of his command were deployed as skirmishers. Other sources believe it was closer to 700.
14. *National Tribune*, July 3, 1903, Thomas Day.
15. *Ibid.*
16. *Vevay Reveille*, August 18, 1863.
17. *Aurora Commercial*, July 23, 1863.
18. Hard, *History of 8th Illinois*, p. 257.
19. *OR*, Series I, Vol. XXVII, p. 927.
20. *National Tribune*, July 3, 1903. Glauber got his horse and rode him the rest of the war. Rea was not able to retrieve the saddle and pistols he had coveted.
21. *Aurora Commercial*, July 30, 1863. Removed to an insane asylum in Philadelphia, Tufts lingered nearly two weeks before dying July 14, 1863, as much a casualty of war as if he had been killed by a bullet.
22. This field would earn immortality in two days as the site of Pickett's Charge.
23. Flavius Bellamy diary, July 1, 1863.
24. *National Tribune*, July 3, 1903.
25. *OR*, Series I, Vol. XXVII, p. 1032.
26. *Madison Daily Evening Courier*, July 17, 1863. Weaver's leg would be amputated, but he died on August 3, 1863, from infection.
27. *Vevay Reveille*, August 18, 1863. Lamb's wound would prove mortal. He died on July 29, 1863.
28. *OR*, Series I, Vol. XXVII, p. 934. Lemmon died the next day.
29. Flavius Bellamy diary, July 1, 1863.
30. Edward Reid diary, July 1, 1863.
31. *Madison Daily Evening Courier*, May 24, 1888. Wildman would later receive a commission as adjutant of the 130th Indiana Infantry.
32. George Chapman diary, July 2, 1863.
33. Casualties were compiled from the OR, newspaper reports, Carded Medical Records, and the IAG Report.
34. *Ibid.*, p. 927.
35. Pickerill, *History of the Third Indiana Cavalry*, p. 82.

Chapter 9

1. George Chapman diary, July 2, 1863.
2. *Ibid.*, July 3, 1863.
3. Samuel J.V.B. Gilpin diary, July 3, 1863.
4. George Chapman diary, July 3, 1863. This was the famous Pickett's Charge.
5. Eric Wittenberg, *One Continuous Fight: The Retreat from Gettysburg and the Pursuit of Lee's Army of Northern Virginia, July 4-14, 1863* (El Dorado Hills, CA: Savas Beattie LLC, 2008), p. 96.
6. *Ibid.*
7. *Ibid.*, p. 124.
8. *OR*, Series I, Vol. XXVII, p. 934.
9. Samuel J.V.B. Gilpin diary, July 7, 1863.
10. *Ibid.*
11. *Ibid.*, July 8, 1863.
12. Edward Reid Papers.
13. Hard, *History of 8th Illinois*, p. 262.
14. *Madison Daily Evening Courier*, July 19, 1863.
15. Samuel J.V.B. Gilpin diary, July 8, 1863.
16. Flavius Bellamy letter, July 14, 1863.
17. *Indianapolis Journal*, August 29, 1863. Kennedy succumbed to his wound in a Frederick, Maryland, hospital on August 10, 1863.
18. Samuel J.V.B. Gilpin diary, July 10, 1863.
19. Joseph Adkinson letter, July 12, 1863.
20. *OR*, Series XLIII, Chapter 39, p. 936.
21. NA Record Group 94, box 790.
22. Today, Berlin is named Brunswick.
23. Samuel J.V.B. Gilpin diary, July 17, 1863. Gilpin mentions "Lieut. Cotton's force and Bill Mallory's corps coming up, reinforcing us hugely." Lieutenant Cotton was probably Second Lieutenant William Cotton of Company F. His group may have been men left in hospitals or recently remounted. The size of his contingent is not known. William Mallory was the veterinary surgeon for the regiment. In all probability, he was bringing a few men and horses left behind to convalesce.
24. Samuel J.V.B. Gilpin diary, July 18, 1863.
25. NA Record Group 94, CMR.
26. *Vevay Reveille*, August 18, 1863. Schroeder's wound was so severe that he was discharged on July 26, 1864.
27. Flavius Bellamy diary, July 21, 1863.
28. Joseph Adkinson letter, July 24, 1863.
29. Samuel J.V.B. Gilpin diary, July 25, 1863.
30. *Ibid.*, August 18, 1863.
31. *Ibid.*
32. *Ibid.*, July 29, 1863. Ironically, companies L and M were part of the forces chasing Morgan. Elements of the companies pursued the raiders all

the way to Buffington's Island, Ohio where Morgan and his men surrendered. Former captain of Company B, James Irvin, commanded a company of Home Guards at Corydon when Morgan attacked there. In addition, former lieutenant colonel Jacob Buchanan was named colonel of the 104th Indiana Infantry, a regiment of "minute men" formed to chase Morgan.

33. William D. Henderson, *The Road to Bristoe Station: Campaigning with Lee and Meade* (Lynchburg, VA: H.E. Howard, 1987), p. 18.

34. George Chapman diary, August 1, 1863.

35. Samuel F.M. Lamb Collection, Indiana Historical Society, Manuscript Division, Indianapolis, Indiana. August 6, 1863. Despite his wound, Irby would recover and serve six months in the Bureau of Military Information.

36. *Vevay Reveille*, August 18, 1863.

37. Joseph Adkinson letter, August 18, 1863.

38. *Indianapolis Journal*, September 9, 1863.

39. Wildman Family Collection, Jefferson County Historical Society, Manuscript Collection, Madison, IN. September 7, 1863.

40. AGI correspondence, 3rd Indiana Cavalry file.

41. William S. McClure papers, letter September 7, 1863.

42. George Chapman diary, August 21, 1863.

43. *Ibid.*, August 28, 1863.

44. *Vevay Reveille*, October 8, 1863.

45. *Ibid.* NA Records Group 94, CMR.

46. *Madison Daily Evening Courier*, September 29, 1863. Heath's wound would prove mortal. He died on October 22, 1863.

47. Henderson, *The Road to Bristoe Station*, p. 52.

48. *Ibid.*, p. 54.

49. *Vevay Reveille*, October 8, 1863.

50. Jack's Shop is present-day Rochelle, Virginia.

51. *Ibid.*

52. Henderson, *The Road to Bristoe Station*, p. 54.

53. *Vevay Reveille*, October 8, 1863.

54. Henderson, *The Road to Bristoe Station*, p. 60.

55. No full report can be found on the fight at Jack's Shop save a report of one of Kilpatrick's brigades. Buford wrote a short report the next morning but never submitted a full post action report. An article in the September 29, 1863, *Indianapolis Journal* issue, reported 50 Confederate dead. Most participants refer to the unusually large number of Confederate dead, wounded, and captured. Given that Stuart, while aware of Buford's advance, was unprepared for Kilpatrick's attack and the running nature of the fight for several miles, it seems reasonable to assume Stuart's losses were not trifling. This may account for no report from Stuart. He did not want to admit to being surprised and the extent of his losses.

56. Gilpin speech, 1885.

57. *Ibid.*

58. Casualty reports come from *Indianapolis Journal*, September 29 and October 10, 1863; Reid Papers; NA Record Group 94, CMR.

Chapter 10

1. Samuel J.V.B. Gilpin diary, September 24, 1863.

2. *OR*, Series I, Vol. XXVII, p. 141. Buford devoted only five sentences in his report to the fighting. Ever the professional, he devoted most of his report to information as to the intent of the expedition. He simply said, "The whole of Stuart's division opposed the reconnaissance, yet I am proud to say that he was whipped, his forces dispersed, and the reconnaissance made."

3. AGI correspondence, 3rd Indiana Cavalry file.

4. IAG Report, Vol. II. McClure arrived in Indiana only to find out that all officers for the 9th Indiana had already been appointed by the governor. Frustrated that he would have no say as to the leaders that would report to him, McClure resigned in a huff. Upon receiving his resignation, Adjutant General Noble decided that, since McClure had never been mustered in as a colonel, the governor should accept the resignation as a major of the 3rd Indiana. Despite this snub, McClure would be addressed by the honorary title "Colonel" for the rest of his life.

5. *Samuel J.V.B. Gilpin diary*, October 8, 1863.

6. Henderson, *The Road to Bristoe Station*, p. 89.

7. *Ibid.*

8. James McConnell Letters, Virginia Historical Society, Manuscript Division, Richmond, VA. January 20, 1865.

9. Casualty information came from *Vevay Reveille*, November 12, 1863; NA Record Group 94, CMR; Flavius Bellamy letters.

10. Henderson, *The Road to Bristoe Station*, p. 90.

11. Samuel J.V.B. Gilpin diary, October 11, 1863.

12. Longacre, *Buford*, p. 237.

13. Henderson, *The Road to Bristoe Station*, p. 99.

14. Longacre, *Buford*, p. 237.

15. Gilpin speech, 1885.

16. *Vevay Reveille*, November 12, 1863.

17. *Ibid.*

18. Longacre, *Buford*, p. 237.

19. *Indianapolis Journal*, October 19, 1863.

20. William Watlington, *Third Indiana Cavalry, Army of the Potomac: From Diary Notes of Wm Watlington, 1863–65*. Indiana State Library, Indianapolis, p. 19. (This typewritten journal has no page numbers. I have added page notes for clarity.)

21. *Ibid.*, p. 20.

22. NA Record Group 94, CMR and Willman Service Record. Smelley's wound would never heal. He died on December 3, 1863.

23. Flavius Bellamy letter, October 24, 1863.

24. Samuel J.V.B. Gilpin diary, October 28th, 1863.

25. *Ibid.*, October 31, 1863.
26. Watlington journal, October, 1863.
27. Hard, *History of 8th Illinois*, p. 343. Hollenbeck would die in Andersonville Prison on October 25, 1864. Livings was fortunate enough to be exchanged and survived his time at the infamous camp.
28. Samuel J.V.B. Gilpin diary, November 8, 1863.
29. *Madison Daily Evening Courier*, November 24, 1863. McFarland died of his wounds that evening.
30. *Ibid.*, November 24, 1863; *Vevay Reveille*, July 14, 1864; NA Record Group 94, CMR.
31. William Watlington. *Third Indiana Cavalry*, p. 20.
32. *Ibid.*
33. Joseph Adkinson letter, November 13, 1863.
34. *Madison Daily Evening Courier*, September 11, 1899. Mosby wrote to Madison in response to a letter from Thomas Day. Remarkably, both Day and Mosby recount having a pleasant meal after the cavalrymen's capture. Day and Bain had given their word of honor not to escape, and the three men ate the meal as if they were old acquaintances.
35. *Ibid.*, CMR.
36. *Vevay Reveille*, December 31, 1863.
37. NA Record Group 153, file 00–151.
38. IAG Report, Vol. II, p. 441.
39. William Watlington, *Third Indiana Cavalry*, p. 31.
40. Ordinance Report, January 1864.
41. Joseph Adkinson letter, December 30, 1863.
42. Samuel J.V.B. Gilpin diary, January 2, 1864.
43. *Ibid.*
44. William Watlington, *Third Indiana Cavalry*, p. 27.
45. IAG Correspondence, 3rd Indiana Cavalry file, January 16, 1864.
46. Joseph Adkinson letter, January 22, 1864.
47. IAG Correspondence, 3rd Indiana Cavalry file, January 20, 1864.
48. IAG Report, Vol. II, p. 442.
49. Henry B. Sparks Papers, Indiana State Library, Manuscripts Division, Indianapolis, IN. January 27, 1864. The men would eventually be sent to Andersonville. Only Sparks and two other men survived.
50. OR, Series I, Vol. XXXIII, p. 108.
51. Flavius Bellamy letter, April 4, 1864.

Chapter 11

1. Starr, Vol. II, p. 67.
2. Watlington, *Third Indiana Cavalry*, p. 32. At least seven members of the 3rd Indiana were known to be held there.
3. *Ibid.*
4. James Matthews diary, Matthews family private collection. February 28, 1864.
5. This force was led by Colonel Ulric Dahlgren and included Sergeant Milton Cline of the 3rd Indiana as chief scout.
6. Watlington, *Third Indiana Cavalry*, p. 33.
7. *Ibid.*
8. Bruce Venter, "The Kilpatrick-Dahlgren Raid on Richmond: February 28–March 4, 1864," *Blue & Gray*, Vol. XX, no. 3, p. 14.
9. Watlington, *Third Indiana Cavalry*, p. 34.
10. *Ibid.*
11. OR, Series I, Vol. XXXIII, p. 193.
12. Watlington journal, Indiana Historical Society, Manuscript Collection, Indianapolis, IN. Watlington wrote several versions of his history. This handwritten journal is unnumbered and describes several events not included in the typewritten version in the Indiana State Library. Hereafter it is referred to as Watlington journal.
13. Watlington, *Third Indiana Cavalry*, p. 35.
14. *Ibid.*
15. Venter, p. 45.
16. *Aurora Commercial*, March 17, 1864.
17. Duane Schultz, *The Dahlgren Affair* (New York: W.W. Norton, 1998), p. 134. Dahlgren was killed in an ambush, and an unsigned note was found on his body. It described the purpose of the raid as the assassination of Jefferson Davis, president of the Confederacy, and to burn down Richmond. This note soon became public and created a controversy that continues to the present day.
18. *Aurora Commercial*, March 17, 1864; NA Record Group 94, CMR.
19. Watlington, *Third Indiana Cavalry*, p. 37.
20. Joseph Matthews diary, March 8–15, 1864.
21. Samuel J.V.B. Gilpin diary, March 6, 1864.
22. AGI correspondence, 3rd Indiana Cavalry file, March 2, 1864.
23. IAG Report, Vol. II, p. 441. Gresham would later be discharged to accept the lieutenant colonelcy of the 10th Indiana Cavalry.
24. Chesnut, *William Patton*, pp. 1–2.
25. Samuel J.V.B. Gilpin diary, March 24, 1864.
26. *Ibid.*, March 31, 1864. Round ball was the predecessor of the modern game of baseball.
27. OR, Series I, Vol. XXXIII, p. 891.
28. Chesnut, *William Patton*, p. 96. Patton recorded several other instances of firearms practice over the coming months.
29. *Joseph Matthews diary*, March 29, 1864.
30. *Ibid.* Kilpatrick would eventually be sent West to command Sherman's cavalry on his March to the Sea. Ironically, the command would include the 3rd Indiana Cavalry, West Wing.
31. The total division strength reported by Wilson upon assuming command was 2692 mounted men. Chapman's 2nd Brigade numbered around 1,000. The 2nd Brigade's dubious distinction of being the smallest brigade was due to the 3rd Indiana having only six companies.
32. Joseph Matthews diary, April 19, 1864.
33. Watlington, *Third Indiana Cavalry*, p. 41.
34. Chesnut, *William Patton*, p. 93.
35. Watlington, *Third Indiana Cavalry*, p. 43.
36. Gordon Rhea, *The Battles for Spotsylvania Court House and the Road to Yellow Tavern* (Baton Rouge: Louisiana State University Press, 1997), p. 112.
37. *Ibid.*, p. 44.

38. *Ibid.*
39. *OR*, Series I, Volume XXXVI, p. 876.
40. *Indianapolis Journal*, May 16, 1864; *Madison Daily Evening Courier*, May 25, 1864; IAG Hospital Reports; NA Record Group 94, CMR. George Porter died on June 6, 1864.
41. Rhea, p. 49.
42. *Ibid.*

Chapter 12

1. Rhea, p. 68.
2. *Ibid.*, p. 69.
3. Watlington, *Third Indiana Cavalry*, p. 46.
4. Starr, Vol. III, p. 199.
5. Casualty reports from *Madison Daily Evening Courier*, May 25, 1864; NA Records Group 94; IAG Hospital Records. Adkinson would not survive his wounds, dying at Point Lookout, Maryland, June 8, 1864.
6. Watlington, *Third Indiana Cavalry*, p. 48.
7. *Ibid.*, p. 49.
8. Lester, Weaver narrative, p.4.
9. Watlington, *Third Indiana Cavalry*, p. 52.
10. Flavius Bellamy letter, May 15, 1864.
11. *Madison Daily Evening Courier*, May 25, 1864.
12. Watlington, *Third Indiana Cavalry*, p. 53.
13. Elias W.H. Beck letters.
14. Watlington, *Third Indiana Cavalry*, p. 54.
15. *Madison Daily Evening Courier*, June 2, 1864.
16. NA Record Group 94, CMR.
17. IAG Report, Vol. II, p. 441.
18. Chesnut, *William Patton*, p. 107. Pioneers had been ordered added to each regiment. They carried axes and additional rope and were tasked with removing barriers on the march. This total was less than half of the 579 men present for the regiment's first muster.
19. AGI correspondence, 3rd Indiana Cavalry file, May–June 1864. Thompson's commission was dated June 26, 1864.
20. Watlington, *Third Indiana Cavalry*, p. 58.
21. *Ibid.*
22. *Aurora Commercial*, June 30, 1864.
23. Flavius Bellamy diary, June 1, 1864.
24. Watlington, *Third Indiana Cavalry*, pp. 58–59.
25. *OR*, Series I, Vol. XXXVI, p. 883.
26. NA Record Group 94, CMR.
27. NA, Record Group 156, M1281 Ordinance returns.
28. Watlington, *Third Indiana Cavalry*, p. 60.
29. *Ibid.*, p. 61.
30. *OR*, Series I, Vol. XL, p. 644.
31. Watlington, *Third Indiana Cavalry*, p. 61.
32. *OR*, Series I, Vol. XL, p. 645.
33. Watlington, *Third Indiana Cavalry*, p. 61.
34. *Ibid.*, p. 62.
35. *Madison Daily Evening Courier*, June 24, 1864.
36. Flavius Bellamy letter, June 16, 1864.

Chapter 13

1. Starr, Vol. II, p. 178.
2. Watlington, *Third Indiana Cavalry*, p. 63.
3. Joseph Matthews journal, June 20, 1864.
4. *Ibid.*
5. *OR*, Series I, Vol. XL, p. 646.
6. Starr, Vol. II, p. 184.
7. *Ibid.*, p. 182.
8. A.B. Cummings, *The Wilson-Kautz Raid* (Blackstone, VA: Nottoway Publishing Company, 1961), p. 41.
9. *OR*, Series I, Vol. XL, p, 646.
10. Watlington, *Third Indiana Cavalry*, p. 64.
11. Joseph Matthews diary, June 25, 1864.
12. *OR*, Series, I, Vol. XL, p. 646.
13. Starr, Vol. II, p. 182.
14. *Ibid.*
15. Watlington, *Third Indiana Cavalry*, p. 66.
16. Cummings, p. 94.
17. *Ibid.*, p. 95.
18. Watlington, *Third Indiana Cavalry*, p. 67.
19. *OR*, Series I, Vol. XL, p. 646.
20. Samuel J.V.B. Gilpin diary, June 29, 1864.
21. Cummings, p. 127.
22. *Connersville Weekly Times*, July 27, 1864.
23. *OR*, Series I, Vol. XL, p. 646.
24. *Madison Daily Evening Courier*, July 13, 1864. Both were captured. Cunningham died in Andersonville Prison while Vanosdol had his hand amputated and died in a Richmond, Virginia, prison.
25. In retrospect, this should have been the original return route given that it was much further away from Petersburg and rebel forces. It has been suggested by some that Wilson, tired and worried about the whereabouts of Hampton's Confederate cavalry, hoped to return by the most direct route under the belief, now nearly a week old, that Union forces had taken Ream's Station.
26. Elias W.H. Beck letter, July 3, 1864. Serving as brigade surgeon, Beck reported 140 wounded left behind by the 2nd Brigade alone.
27. *Madison Daily Evening Courier*, July 17, 1864.
28. Watlington, *Third Indiana Cavalry*, p. 68.
29. Elias W.H. Beck letter, July 3, 1864.
30. Samuel J.V.B. Gilpin diary, June 30, 1864.
31. *Madison Daily Evening Courier*, July 13, 1864.
32. *Connersville Weekly Times*, July 22, 1864.
33. *OR*, Series I, Vol. XL, p. 647.
34. *Connersville Weekly Times*, July 22, 1864. Moffitt later wrote in his official report that after June 29 "nothing of importance occurred on our part during the raid." Odd words, all things considered.
35. James H. Wilson, *Under the Old Flag* (New York: D. Appleton, 1912), p. 474.
36. *Connersville Weekly Times*, July 22, 1864.
37. Joseph Matthews diary, June 29, 1864.
38. *Ibid.*, July 3, 1864.
39. Flavius Bellamy letter, July 3, 1864.

40. Elias W.H. Beck letter, July 3, 1864.
41. *Connersville Weekly Times*, July 22, 1864.
42. Joseph Matthews diary, June 29, 1864.
43. *Vevay Reveille*, July 4, 1864, and *MDEC*, July 14, 1864.
44. *OR*, Series I, Vol. XL, p. 647.
45. *Ibid.*, p. 233.
46. Chesnut, *William Patton*, p. 114.

Chapter 14

1. *OR*, Series I, Vol. XL, p. 675.
2. *Madison Daily Evening Courier*, July 20, 1864.
3. Joseph Matthews diary, July 22, 1864.
4. *Ibid.*
5. *OR*, Series I, Vol. XXXVI, p. 712.
6. *OR*, Series I, Vol. XL, p. 93.
7. *Ibid.*, p. 408.
8. IAG Correspondence, 3rd Indiana Cavalry file, July 26, 1864.
9. *OR*, Series I, Vol. XL, p. 483.
10. Watlington, *Third Indiana Cavalry*, p. 73. The Army's chronic shortage of horses prompted this action.
11. IAG Report, Vol. V, p. 451.
12. IAG Report, Vol. II, p. 441. Apparently, the lieutenants were never formally commissioned until June and July 1865. The IAG Report shows all four mustered out as sergeants.
13. IAG Report, Vol. V, p. 451. Included in the muster rolls were original members of the regiment who were in hospitals or prison camps. The likely size of the two companies would have been closer to 150.
14. IAG Report, Vol. II, p. 451. This is an aggregate count. Many had been wounded or captured more than once.
15. Flavius Bellamy letter, July 20, 1864.
16. *Joseph Matthews Company Detail Book*, unnumbered.
17. Samuel J.V.B. Gilpin diary, July 29, 1864.
18. The four men who had been detached to the Bureau of Military Information, Chief of Scouts Milton Cline, Daniel Cole, Daniel Plew, and James Irby, were mustered out with the regiment. One of Cline's last scouts pinpointed the location of Confederate general Jubal Early's forces north of Washington.
19. Flavius Bellamy letter, August 11, 1864.
20. Starr, Vol. II, p. 235.
21. *Ibid.*, p. 250.
22. Joseph Matthews diary, August 21, 1864.
23. *Ibid.*, August 24, 1864.
24. *Vevay Reveille*, September 1, 1864.
25. Watlington, *Third Indiana Cavalry*, p. 76. The company had been serving in this capacity, but official assignment was not made until August 27, 1864.
26. Ordinance report, September, 1864.
27. Watlington, *Third Indiana Cavalry*, p. 76.
28. *Ibid.*
29. *Ibid.*, p. 77.
30. *OR*, Series I, Vol. XLIII, p. 886.
31. Watlington, *Third Indiana Cavalry*, p. 77.
32. *OR*, Series I, Vol. XLIII, p. 520. Lee served in this capacity for the rest of the war.
33. Watlington, *Third Indiana Cavalry*, p. 81.
34. *OR*, Series I, Vol. XLIII, p. 543.
35. IAG Correspondence, 3rd Indiana Cavalry file. No action was taken upon the request and the 3rd Indiana Cavalry, East Wing, would consist of two companies for the rest of the war.
36. IAG Report, Vol. V, p. 410. Company B would have but 22 men on the rolls by war's end.
37. *OR*, Series I, Vol. XLIII, p. 518.
38. Scott Patchan, *The Last Battle of Winchester: Phil Sheridan, Jubal Early, and the Shenandoah Valley Campaign, August 7-September 19, 1864* (El Dorado Hills, CA: Savas Beatie, 2013), p. 421.
39. Wilson, p. 552.
40. Watlington, *Third Indiana Cavalry*, p. 85.
41. NA Record Group 94, CMR.
42. Jeffery Wert, *From Winchester to Cedar Creek: The Shenandoah Valley Campaign of 1864* (Carlisle, PA: South Mountain Press, 1987), p. 113.
43. *Ibid.*, p. 131. Milford is now called Overall.
44. *Ibid.*
45. Wert, p. 132.
46. Watlington, *Third Indiana Cavalry*, p. 86. There were three men named Ward in the company; however, Watlington did not identify which one was part of the party.
47. *Ibid.*, p. 87. In all probability, the four horsemen they joined had experienced similar problems with their own tired and worn out mounts.
48. *Ibid.*, p. 99. Watlington devoted 12 typewritten pages of his narrative to this harrowing event.
49. Starr, Vol. II, 290.
50. *OR*, Series I, Vol. XLIII, p. 183.
51. *Ibid.*, p. 520.
52. Watlington, *Third Indiana Cavalry*, p. 101.
53. *Ibid.*
54. *OR*, Series I, Vol. XLIII, p. 916.
55. *Ibid.*, p. 29.
56. John L. Heatwole, *The Burning: Sheridan's Devastation of the Shenandoah Valley* (Charlottesville: Rockbridge Publishing, 1998), p. 77.

Chapter 15

1. Starr, Vol. II, p. 293.
2. Custer replaced General John McIntosh who had been wounded at Winchester.
3. In addition, Kershaw's infantry division had been sent to reinforce Early's depleted army.
4. Miller, p. 55.
5. Heatwole, pp. 125–30.
6. Watlington, *Third Indiana Cavalry*, p. 103.
7. Miller, p. 105.
8. Rosser's strength had been weakened by men of the Laurel Brigade leaving the ranks to check on their families as they rode through The Burning. Many accounts claim Rosser had over 2,000 men but that is extremely unlikely and probably based on muster records rather than reality.

9. William J. Miller, *Decision at Tom's Brook: George Custer, Thomas Rosser, and the Joy of the Fight* (El Dorado Hills, CA: Savas Beatie, 2016), p. 123.
10. *Ibid.*, p. 124.
11. Again, accounts of the battle give varying strengths for Custer. Returns from September are used here as the best guess.
12. Miller, p. 131.
13. *Ibid.*, p. 133.
14. Miller, p. 162. Thus the action also being known as the "Woodstock Races."
15. *Ibid.*, pp. 226–33.
16. Watlington, *Third Indiana Cavalry*, p. 103.
17. OR, Series I, Vol. XLIII, p. 528.
18. Miller, p. 163. The coat was donated to the United States Military Academy after Custer's death at Little Big Horn.
19. Wert, p. 171.
20. Watlington, *Third Indiana Cavalry*, p.104.
21. Starr, Vol. II. P. 305.
22. OR, Series I, Vol. XLIII, p. 522.
23. *Ibid.*
24. This became known in history as "Sheridan's Ride."
25. Watlington, *Third Indiana Cavalry*, p. 108. After Winchester, Custer offered a 30-day furlough for every Confederate flag captured. With this type of incentive, the competition to bring one of the prizes was keen.
26. *Ibid.*, p. 109.
27. OR, Series I, Vol. XLIII, p. 526.
28. *Past and Present of Vermillion County, IL* (Chicago: S.J. Clarke, 1903), p. 756.
29. Watlington, *Third Indiana Cavalry*, p. 111.
30. *Ibid.*
31. *Ibid.*
32. Edward Longacre, *Sheridan in the Valley* (Harrisonburg, PA: Stackpole Books, 1992), p. 366.
33. Watlington, *Third Indiana Cavalry*, p. 115.
34. *Ibid.*
35. *Ibid.*
36. *Ibid.*, p. 116.
37. *Ibid.*
38. *Ibid.*, p. 120.
39. *Ibid.*
40. *Ibid.*, p. 121.
41. *Ibid.*
42. *Ibid.*, p. 122.
43. *Ibid.*
44. *Ibid.*, p. 123.

Chapter 16

1. AGI Report, Vol. II, p. 442.
2. Watlington, *Third Indiana Cavalry*, p. 125. Watlington was one of the 12 selected for this duty.
3. *Ibid.*
4. Peter T. Lubrecht, *New Jersey Butterfly Boys in the Civil War* (Charleston, SC: The History Press, 2011), p. 95.
5. *Vevay Reveille*, February 2, 1865.
6. Watlington, *Third Indiana Cavalry*, p. 126.
7. *Ibid.*
8. Watlington journal.
9. Watlington, *Third Indiana Cavalry*, p. 127.
10. *Ibid.*
11. *Ibid.*, p. 129.
12. Wert, p. 250.
13. Edward Longacre, *The Cavalry at Appomattox* (Mechanicsburg, PA: Stackpole Books, 2003), p. 31.
14. IAG Report, Vol. V, p. 411.
15. Watlington, *Third Indiana Cavalry*, p. 132.
16. *Ibid.*, p. 133.
17. *Ibid.*, p. 135.
18. *Ibid.*
19. Wert, p. 251.
20. Watlington, *Third Indiana Cavalry*, p. 136.
21. *Ibid.*, p. 138.
22. *Ibid.*, p. 139.
23. Starr, Vol. II, p. 381.
24. Watlington, *Third Indiana Cavalry*, p. 140.
25. *Ibid.*, p. 142.
26. Watlington journal.
27. Starr, Vol. II, p. 383.
28. *Ibid.*, 384.
29. Watlington, *Third Indiana Cavalry*, p. 146.
30. *Ibid.*, p. 147.
31. *Ibid.*, p. 148.
32. *Ibid.*
33. *Ibid.*
34. *Ibid.*, p. 149.
35. Longacre, *Appomattox*, p. 49.
36. *Ibid.* Fitzhugh Lee had recently been promoted to command of the Army of Northern Virginia's cavalry. Hampton had returned to his native North Carolina to defend the state against the advance of General William Tecumseh Sherman's Union army marching north out of Georgia.
37. Watlington, *Third Indiana Cavalry*, p. 150.
38. *Ibid.*
39. *Ibid.*
40. Starr, Vol. II, p. 440.
41. *Ibid.*, p. 151.
42. Watlington, *Third Indiana Cavalry*, p. 153. There is no record of the orderly being a member of the 3rd Indiana.
43. Star, Vol. II, p. 445.
44. Longacre, *Appomattox*, p. 88. None at the meal heard the ensuing sounds of battle just a few short miles away. An acoustical phenomenon in which the atmosphere masks sound was blamed for this improbable event.
45. Starr, Vol. II, p. 448.
46. Watlington, *Third Indiana Cavalry*, p. 153. At Winchester, Custer had promised 30 day furloughs for every man who captured a Confederate battle flag.
47. *Ibid.*, p. 154.
48. *Ibid.*, p. 155.
49. *Ibid.*
50. *Ibid.*, p. 156.
51. Longacre, *Appomattox*, p. 119.
52. Watlington, *Third Indiana Cavalry*, p. 157.
53. Derek Smith, *Lee's Last Stand: Sailor's*

Creek, Virginia, 1863 (Shippensburg, PA: White Mane, 2002), p. 55.
54. Starr, Vol. II, p. 468.
55. *Ibid.*, p. 471.
56. Watlington, *Third Indiana Cavalry*, p. 161.
57. IAG Report, Vol. V, 442. All three men were awarded the Medal of Honor for their exploits. There is no evidence that they received any furlough.
58. *Madison Daily Evening Journal*, June 25, 1887. Shepherd's capture was recognized in a U.S. Congress resolution to present Medals of Honor to those who had captured flags. In the list, Absalom Jordan is incorrectly listed as being a member of the 8th Indiana Cavalry.
59. Watlington, *Third Indiana Cavalry*, p. 161.
60. Longacre, *Appomattox*, p. 169.

Chapter 17

1. Watlington, *Third Indiana Cavalry,* p. 162. He reported that they had not seen supply wagons since April 1.
2. Longacre, *Appomattox*, p. 171.
3. *Ibid.* One engine with one or two cars attached did escape back to Lynchburg before the track destruction began.
4. *Ibid.*, p. 172.
5. *Ibid.*
6. Watlington, *Third Indiana Cavalry,* p. 164.
7. Longacre, *Appomattox*, p. 174.
8. *Ibid.*, p. 175. Watlington reported the capture of 35 artillery, 1,000 prisoners and over 100 wagons.
9. Watlington, *Third Indiana Cavalry,* p. 166.
10. *Ibid.*
11. *Ibid.*, p. 167.
12. *Ibid.*, p. 169.
13. Samuel Atkinson Letter, April 15, 1865.
14. IAG Correspondence, 3rd Indiana Cavalry file, April 24, 1865.
15. Watlington, *Third Indiana Cavalry,* p. 173.
16. *Report of the Adjutant General of the State of Indiana* (Indianapolis: Samuel M. Douglass, State Printer, 1866), Vol. V and VIII. Kany was also referred to as Kennedy in some sources. Likewise, Congers was also referred to as Conyers.
17. Watlington, *Third Indiana Cavalry,* p. 175.
18. *Ibid.*, p. 177.
19. IAG Correspondence, 3rd Indiana Cavalry file, June 2, 1865.
20. Watlington, *Third Indiana Cavalry,* p. 181.
21. NA Record Group 94, CMR.
22. *Vevay Reveille*, August 12, 1865.
23. IAG Correspondence, 3rd Indiana Cavalry file, November 8, 1865.
24. *Indiana at Antietam: Report of the Antietam Monument Commission* (Indianapolis: Aetna Printing, 1911), p. 153.
25. *Madison Daily Journal*, June, 25, 1887.
26. *History of Switzerland County, Indiana* (Chicago: Weakley, Harraman & Company, 1885).
27. *History of Vanderburgh County, Indiana* (Madison, WI: Brant and Fuller, 1889).
28. *Vevay Reveille*, October 23, 1864.
29. *Madison Evening Courier*, January 12, 1900.
30. James H. Wilson, "George M. Gilchrist," *The Annals of Iowa* (July 1912), pp. 392–93.
31. *Indianapolis Journal*, June 18, 1882.
32. Pickerill added a few anecdotes from his service and some limited correspondence with former members of the regiment. It does not appear that he made any effort to correspond with members of the West Wing as no other reference to their service is included other than what could be found in the Official Record.
33. J.H. Binford, *History of Greene and Sullivan Counties, state of Indiana: from the earliest time to the present, together with interesting biographical sketches, reminiscences, notes, etc.* (Chicago: Goodspeed Bros. & Co., 1884), p. 336.
34. *Hanover College Bulletin*, 1912–13.
35. *Portrait and Biographical Album, Washington County, Iowa* (Chicago: Acme Publishing and Engraving Company, 1887), p. 490.
36. Linda Gugan and James E. St. Clair, ed., *Justices of the Indiana Supreme Court* (Indianapolis: Indiana Historical Society, 2010), pp. 179–81.
37. *Hanover College Bulletin*, Alumni Record, 1829–1912.
38. *Ibid.*
39. Asa Sleath Hardman, "As a Union Prisoner Saw the Battle of Gettysburg," *Civil War Times Illustrated* (July 1962), p. 47.
40. David McCullough, *The Path Between the Seas: The Creation of the Panama Canal, 1870–1914* (New York: Simon & Schuster, 1978), p. 157.
41. Correspondence with Robert Wilcox, Bardwell's great grandson
42. Marvin Gregory and P. David Smith, *Mountain Mysteries* (Ridgway, CO: Wayfinder Press, 1992), p. 57.
43. *Madison Daily Courier,* February 17, 1878.
44. *Ibid.*, August 16, 1887.
45. Roster, 3rd Indiana Cavalry Reunion, 1904.
46. William Pickerill, *Gettysburg Anniversary Commission*. Another much smaller marker had been dedicated at Antietam in 1890 near their position in support of artillery on September 17, 1862.
47. George Middleton, *Circus Memoirs: Reminiscences of George Middleton as Told to and Written by His Wife* (Los Angeles: G. Rice & Sons, Printers, 1913) unnumbered.
48. *Ibid.*
49. *Madison Daily Journal,* May 20, 1908.
50. *Ibid.*, May 7, 1941.

Bibliography

Newspapers

American Tribune, Indianapolis, Indiana
Aurora Commercial, Aurora, Indiana
Connersville Weekly Times, Connersville, Indiana
Corydon Democrat, Corydon, Indiana
Indianapolis Journal, Indianapolis, Indiana
Madison Daily Evening Courier, Madison, Indiana
National Tribune, Washington, D.C.
Richmond Whig, Richmond, Virginia
St. Mary's Beacon, St. Mary's, Maryland
Valley Register, Middletown, Maryland
Vevay Reveille, Vevay, Indiana

Unpublished Memoirs, Letters and Diaries

Hanover College Archives, Hanover, IN:
    Joseph Adkinson Collection
Huntington Library Archives, San Marino, CA:
    Joseph Hooker Papers
Illinois State Historical Society Archives, Springfield, IL:
    Edward C. Reid Diary
Indiana State Historical Society Archives, Indianapolis, IN:
    George H. Chapman Diary
    William Watlington Journal
Indiana State Library, Manuscript Division, Indianapolis, IN:
    E.W.H. Beck Papers
    Flavius J. Bellamy Papers
    Joseph W. Dalrymple Papers
    William H. Gray Papers
    William S. McClure Papers
    Henry B. Sparks Papers
    William Watlington Papers
Jefferson County Historical Society, Manuscript Collection, Madison, IN:
    Sidney Dumont Collection
    Wildman Family Collection
Library of Congress, Manuscript Division, Washington, D.C.:
    Samuel J.V.B. Gilpin Papers
Matthews family private collection, Madison, IN:
    James Matthews diary
United States Army Military History Institute, Manuscript Collection, Carlisle, PA:
    Lowry Hinch Papers
Virginia Historical Society, Manuscript Division, Richmond, VA:
    James McConnell Letters
Virginia Military Institute Archives, Manuscript Collection, Lexington, VA:
    William B. Hardy Collection

Government Records

Adjutant General of Indiana, Correspondence file, unnumbered. (Indiana)
Adjutant General of Indiana, 1st Indiana Cavalry file (Indiana)
Adjutant General of Indiana, Hospital Records (Indiana)
Adjutant General of Indiana, 3rd Indiana Cavalry file (Indiana)
Governor Oliver Morton Correspondence (Indiana)
National Archives and Record Administration (Washington, D.C.)
Record Group 94, 3rd Indiana Cavalry file
Record Group 94, 3rd Indiana Cavalry file, Carded Medical Records
Record Group 156, MF 1261, Ordinance Reports
Record Group 153, Courts Martial

Journal Articles

Reese, Timothy J. "The Cavalry Clash at Quebec Schoolhouse." *Blue & Gray Magazine*, February 1993.
Venter, Bruce, "The Kilpatrick-Dahlgren Raid on Richmond, February 28–March 4, 1864." *Blue & Gray Magazine*, Winter 2003.
Zollinger, Vivian. "'I take my pen in Hand': Letters from Owen County, Indiana Soldiers." *Indiana Magazine of History*, June 1997.

Published Sources

Binford, J. H. *History of Greene and Sullivan Counties, state of Indiana: from the earliest time to the present, together with interesting biographical sketches, reminiscences, notes, etc.* Chicago: Goodspeed Bros. & Co., 1884.
Chesnut, Eloine Patton, and Scott Nelson Patton. *Major William Patton, Third Indiana Cavalry:*

His Civil War Diaries and Letters. Privately published, 2016.

Hard, Abner. *History of the 8th Cavalry Regiment of Illinois Volunteers.* Aurora, IL: Privately published, 1868.

Hardman, Asa Sleath. "As a Union Prisoner Saw the Battle of Gettysburg." *Civil War Times Illustrated,* July 1962.

Indiana Antietam Monument Commission. *Report of the Indiana Antietam Monument Commission.* Indianapolis: Aetna Printing, 1911.

Lester, Robert E., ed. "1919 Narrative of Augustus C. Weaver." *University Publications of America, Civil War Unit Histories—Part 4.* Microfilm, 1993.

Merrill & Company. *Soldiers of Indiana.* Indianapolis: Douglas and Conner, 1866.

Middleton, George. *Circus Memoirs: Reminiscences of George Middleton as Told to and Written by His Wife.* Los Angeles: G. Rice and Sons, Printers, 1913.

National Tribune. Letter from A.C. Weaver. March 7, 1907.

_____. Letter from Thomas Day. February 2, 1899.

Pickerill, William N. *History of the Third Indiana Cavalry.* Indianapolis: Aetna Printing, 1906.

Pickerill, William N. *Indiana at the Fiftieth Anniversary of the Battle of Gettysburg: Report; W. Rosters of the Army of the Potomac and the Army of Northern Virginia, and a Brief Hist. of Each of the Regiments from Indiana.* 1913.

State of Indiana. *Adjutant General of Indiana Report.* 8 vols. Indianapolis: Indiana State Printing Office, 1867.

State of Indiana. *Special Agents, Pay Agents, et al., Visiting Troops, etc.* Indianapolis: State Government Printing, 1863.

Wilson, James H. "George M. Gilchrist." *The Annals of Iowa,* July 1912.

_____. *Hanover College Bulletin, 1907.* Hanover IN: Hanover College, 1907.

_____. *History of Dearborn, Ohio, and Switzerland Counties, Indiana.* Chicago: Weakley, Harraman & Co., 1885.

_____. *History of Switzerland County, Indiana.* Chicago: Weakley, Harraman & Co., 1885.

_____. *History of Vanderburgh County, Indiana.* Madison, WI: Brant and Fuller, 1889.

_____. *Indiana at Antietam: The Report of the Indiana Antietam Monument Commission.* Indianapolis: Aetna Printing, 1911.

_____. *Past and Present Vermillion County, IL.* Chicago: S.J. Clarke, 1903.

_____. *Portrait and Biographical Album of Washington County, Iowa.* Chicago: Acme, 1887.

_____. *The Soldier of Indiana in the War for the Union.* Indianapolis: Merrill, 1866.

_____. *Under the Old Flag.* New York: D. Appleton, 1912.

Secondary Sources

Cleaves, Freeman. *Meade of Gettysburg.* Norman: University of Oklahoma Press, 1960.

Coates, Earl J., and Dean S. Thomas. *An Introduction to Civil War Small Arms.* Gettysburg, PA: Thomas Publications, 1990.

Cummings, A.B. *The Wilson-Kautz Raid.* Blackstone, VA: Nottoway Publishing Company, 1961.

Davis, Daniel T. *The Most Desperate Acts of Gallantry: George A. Custer in the Civil War.* El Dorado Hills, CA: Savas Beattie, 2019.

Davis, Daniel T., and Phillip S. Greenwalt. *Bloody Autumn: The Shenandoah Valley Campaign of 1864.* El Dorado Hills, CA: Savas Beattie, 2013.

Eanes, Greg. *Black Day of the Army, April 6, 1865: The Battles of Sailor's Creek.* Burkeville, VA: E&H Publishing, 2001.

_____. *Destroy the Junction: The Wilson-Kautz Raid & the Battle for the Staunton River Bridge.* Lynchburg, VA, H.E. Howard Inc.: 1999.

Eisenhower, John S.D. *Agent of Destiny: The Life and Times of General Winfield Scott.* Lawrence: University Press of Kansas, 2015.

Fishel, Edwin C. *The Secret War for the Union: The Untold Story of Military Intelligence in the Civil War.* New York: Houghton Mifflin, 1996.

Fordney, Ben F. *Stoneman at Chancellorsville: The Coming of Age of the Union Cavalry.* Shippensburg, PA: White Mane, 1998.

Gregory, Marvin, and P. David Smith. *Mountain Mysteries.* Ridgway, CO: Wayfinder Press, 1992.

Gugan, Linda C., and James E. St. Clair, ed. *Justices of the Indiana Supreme Court.* Indianapolis: Indiana Historical Society Press, 2010.

Hatch, Thom. *Glorious War: The Civil War Adventures of George Armstrong Custer.* New York: St. Martin's Press, 2013.

Heatwole, John L. *The Burning: Sheridan's Devastation of the Shenandoah Valley.* Charlottesville: Rockbridge Publishing, 1998.

Hebert, Walter H. *Fighting Joe Hooker.* Lincoln: University of Nebraska Press, 1999.

Henderson, William D. *Road to Bristoe Station: Campaigning with Lee and Meade.* Lynchburg, VA: H.E. Howard, 1987.

Krick, Robert K. *Conquering the Valley: Stonewall Jackson at Port Republic.* New York: William Morrow, 1996.

Longacre, Edward G. *The Cavalry at Appomattox.* Mechanicsburg, PA: Stackpole Books, 2003.

_____. *The Cavalry at Gettysburg.* Lincoln: University of Nebraska Press, 1986.

_____. *General John Buford: A Military Biography.* Conshohocken, PA: Combined Publishing, 1995.

_____. *Sheridan in the Shenandoah.* 2nd ed. Harrisonburg, PA: Stackpole Books: 1992.

Lubrecht, Peter T. *New Jersey Butterfly Boys in the Civil War.* Charleston, SC: The History Press, 2011.

Martin, David G. *Gettysburg July 1.* Rev. ed. Conshohocken, PA: Combined Publishing, 1996.

McCullough, David. *The Path Between the Seas: The Creation of the Panama Canal, 1870–1914.* New York: Simon & Schuster, 1978.

McKinney, Joseph W. *Brandy Station, Virginia, June 9, 1863: The Largest Cavalry Battle of the Civil War.* Jefferson, NC: McFarland, 2006.

Miller, William J. *Decision at Tom's Brook: George Custer, Thomas Rosser, and the Joy of the Fight*. El Dorado Hills, CA: Savas Beatie, 2016.

Monaghan, Jay. *Custer: The Life of General George Armstrong Custer*. New York: Toronto, 1959.

Mountcastle, Clay. *Punitive War: Confederate Guerillas and Union Reprisals*. Lawrence: University Press of Kansas, 2009.

Nugent, Michael, J. David Petruzzi, and Eric J. Wittenberg. *One Continuous Fight: The Retreat from Gettysburg and the Pursuit of Lee's Army of Northern Virginia July 4–14, 1863*. El Dorado Hills, CA: Savas Beatie, 2008.

O'Neill, Robert F. *The Cavalry Battles of Aldie, Middleburg, and Upperville*. Lynchburg, VA: H.E. Howard, 1993

Patchan, Scott. *The Last Battle of Winchester: Phil Sheridan, Jubal Early, and the Shenandoah valley Campaign, August 7-September 19, 1864*. El Dorado Hills, CA: Savas Beatie, 2013.

Patchan, Scott. *Shenandoah Summer: The 1864 Valley Campaign*. Lincoln: University of Nebraska Press, 2007.

Priest, John Michael. *Before Antietam: The Battle of South Mountain*. Shippensburg, PA: White Mane, 1992.

Rhea, Gordon C. *The Battle of the Wilderness*. Baton Rouge: Louisiana State University Press, 2004.

_____. *The Battles for Spotsylvania Court House and the Road to Yellow Tavern*. Baton Rouge: Louisiana State University Press, 1997.

_____. *To the North Anna: Grant and Lee, May 13–25, 1864*. Baton Rouge: Louisiana State University Press, 2000.

Schultz, Duane. *The Dahlgren Affair*. New York: W.W. Norton, 1998.

Shue, Richard S. *Morning at Willoughby Run: July 1, 1863*. Gettysburg, PA: Thomas Publications, 1995.

Smith, Derek. *Lee's Last Stand: Sailor's Creek, Virginia, 1865*. Shippensburg, PA: White Mane, 2002.

Sodergren, Steven E. *The Army of the Potomac in the Overland and Petersburg Campaigns*. Baton Rouge: Louisiana State University Press, 2017.

Stackpole, Edward J. *Sheridan in the Shenandoah*. 2nd ed. Harrisburg, PA: Stackpole Books, 1993.

Starr, Stephen Z. *The Union Cavalry in the Civil War*. 3 vols. Baton Rouge: Louisiana State University Press, 1979.

Trout, Robert J. *After Gettysburg: Cavalry Operations in the Eastern Theater July 14, 1863 to December 31, 1863*. Hamilton, MT: Eagle Editions, 2011.

Tsouras, Peter G. *Major General George H. Sharpe and the Creation of American Military Intelligence in the Civil War*, Havertown, PA: Casemate, 2018.

Urwin, Gregory J.W. *Custer Victorious: The Civil War Battles of General George Armstrong Custer*. Newark: Fairleigh Dickinson University Press, 1983.

Wert, Jeffrey D. *From Winchester to Cedar Creek: The Shenandoah Valley Campaign of 1864*. Carlisle, PA: South Mountain Press, 1987.

_____. *Mosby's Rangers: The True Adventures of the Most Famous Command of the Civil War*. New York: Simon & Schuster, 1990.

Whittaker, Frederick, *Custer: Complete Life of General George A. Custer, Major General of Volunteers, Brevet Major U.S. Army and Lieutenant-Colonel Seventh U.S. Cavalry*. Edited by Don Heinrich Tolzmann. Bowie, MD: Heritage Books1993.

Wittenberg, Eric J. *The Battle of Brandy Station: North America's Largest Cavalry Battle*. Charleston, SC: The History Press, 2010.

_____. *The Devil's to Pay: John Buford at Gettysburg*. El Dorado Hills, CA: Savas Beatie, 2014.

_____. *Six Days of Awful Fighting: Cavalry Operations on the Road to Cold Harbor*. Burlington, NC: Fox Run Publishing, 2020.

_____. *The Union Cavalry Comes of Age: Hartwood Church to Brandy Station, June 9, 1863*. Washington, D.C.: Brassey's, 2003.

Wittenberg, Eric J., J. David Petruzzi, and Michael F. Nugent. *One Continuous Fight: The Retreat from Gettysburg and the Pursuit of Lee's Army of Northern Virginia, July 4–14, 1863*. El Dorado Hills, CA: Savas Beatie, 2008.

Young, Alfred C., III. *Lee's Army During the Overland Campaign: A Numerical Study*. Baton Rouge: Louisiana State University Press, 2013.

Unpublished Thesis

Thiele, Thomas F. "The Evolution of Cavalry in the American Civil War; 1861–1863." PhD diss., University of Michigan, 1951.

Index

Numbers in **bold** indicate pages with illustrations

Abden, Benjamin: wounded 52
Abrell, John B. 21
Acquia Creek 35, 64, 66
Adams, James: killed 94
Adkinson, Joseph: death of 270*n*5; wounded 120
Aldie, Virginia 72, 76, 79
Allen's Fresh, Maryland 13
Alley, Fuel: wounded 59
Amissville, Virginia 50
Anshutz, Gottlieb 181
Antietam Creek 44, 48, 88–89; marker at Antietam battlefield 264*n*3
Applejack 150, 164, 165
Armstrong, George 9
Army of the James 111, 120, 125, 129, 139
Army of the Potomac 1–2, 17, 20, 22, 27, 35, 39, 50, 54–55, 57, 63, 76–78, 80–81, 90, 93, 99–100, 111, 113, 118, 120, 122, 125, 128–129, 139, 141–142, 158, 168, 173, 177–178, 181
Army of Virginia 26
Ashby's Gap 25, 73–74
Ashland Station, Virginia 109
attitude of regiment: dislike for Regular Army ways 20, 59, 112, 114, **141**; fondness for Buford 67, 112; fondness for Hooker 17, 77; happy to have a western brigade commander 71

Bailey, George: captured 30
Bain, Samuel: captured 103; wounded 71
Baker, Conrad (colonel of 1st Indiana Cavalry) 7
Baker, Lafayette C. 16, 18
Baker, Thomas: death of 262*n*18; wounded 127
Banks, Simeon: killed 94
Baltimore and Ohio Railroad 159
Banta, Henry 263*n*17; wounded 38
Barbee's Crossroads, Virginia 26, 49–50, 91, 265*n*33
Bardwell, Augustine 18; wounded 50

Barnesville, Maryland 37–38
Bealeton Station, Virginia 50, 63, 101, 104
Beard, George W. 181; wounded 117, 121
Beaver Dam Station, Virginia 109, 120, 166
Beck, Elias W.H. **28,** 58, 122, 135, 137, 143; opinion of Pleasanton 59, 76; spiritualism lectures 12, 112
Bellamy, Flavius 19, **47,** 49, 101, 124, 137, 142
Berlin, Maryland 90
Berryville, Virginia 26, 145
Beverly's Ford 59–60, 68, 71, 92, 99, 102
Black's and White's Station, Virginia 130
Bledsoe, Benjamin: killed 137
Boonesborough, Maryland 87–88
Bowman, Eli: died 19
Boyd, Benjamin: died 16
Boyd, James: wounded 81
Brandy Station, Virginia 62, 68, 70, 72, 79, 92–94, 99–102, 142
Brenton, Oliver: wounded 128
Bright, Peter: killed 91
Brindley, Elijah: wounded 117, 135
Brinkman, George: wounded 128
Bristoe Station, Virginia 26, 72
Bromley, William: wounded 117
Brown, Pollard 181; wounded 88, 96
Brusie, Luther 48
Buchanan, Frank: wounded 128
Buchanan, Jacob 7, 12, 27, 28, 37, 38, 180; promotion to lieutenant colonel 15; resignation 48
Budd's Ford, Maryland 13, 16, 20–21, 23, 64
Buford, John **67–**68, 72–74, 76, 88, 89–90, 92; death of 103, 114; at Gettysburg 78, 80–81, 84–86; at Jack's Shop 94–100
Bureau of Military Information **54–57,** 64, 180–181

Burkittsville, Maryland 40
"The Burning" 150–151, 155–156, 158
Burns, Barney: killed 52; wounded 31
Burns, William 31
Burnside, Ambrose 35, 50, 54
Burtnister, Henry: wounded 35
Bushwhackers 93, 139, 144, 152; definition of 51
Butcher, Charles: drowned 29
Butler, Ben 107, 111, 122, 125

Calhoun, Daniel 124
Carland, Patrick 12, 20–21; Methodist minister 9; opinion of Colonel Carter 26; organized company 5; resignation 27; served in 9th Indiana Cavalry 263*n*12
Carmel Church, Virginia 29
Carter, Scott 9, 11, 15, 19–20, 22, 25–28, 31–33, 35–36, 47–49, 180; commissioned colonel of the 3rd Indiana Cavalry 12; commissioned lieutenant colonel of 1st Indiana Cavalry 7; organized company 5; placed under arrest 37; resigned commission 56
Cartwright, Charles: wounded 52
Catoctin Mountain 39, 42–43, 47
Caughlin, John 52
Cavalry Corps, 1st Division 57, 67–68, 72–73, 76, 81, 87, 89, 92, 94, 100–101, 103, 114, 124–125, 128, 143, 147–148, 150–151, 154, 156, 162, 164: 1st Division, 1st Brigade 55, 59–60, 76, 84, 94–95, 114, 151, 1st Division, 2nd Brigade 95, 98
Cavalry Corps, 2nd Division 62, 64, 71–74, 94, 116, 128, 150–151, 156, 158, 163
Cavalry Corps, 3rd Division 107, 114–115, 118, 120–121, 124–125, 128–129, 131, 133, 137, 139, 143, 145–152, 154, 158, 162, 169, 171, 174, 177; 1st Brigade 116, 153, 157;

279

Index

2nd Brigade 114, 116, 127, 131, 133, 135, 145, 153
Cedar Creek 154–155, 157–158, 163, 165
Cedar Mountain 62, 105, 112
Centerville, Virginia 100
Chancellorsville, Virginia 63, 67–68, 117
Chapman, George H. **8**, 12–13, 15–18, 20–23, 27–29, 33, 35, 37, 39, 52–54, 59, 64, 71, 77, 84, 86, 91–93, 95–99, 102, 104–106, 112, 120, 122, 126–127, 131–133, 135, 137, 139, 142–145, 149, 157, 163, 180; brigade command 114–116; joined regiment as major 7; promotion to colonel 56–57; promotion to lieutenant colonel 48–49; resigned as colonel of Third Indiana Cavalry and promoted brigadier general 141; wounded at Third Winchester 146
Chaptico Creek, Maryland 13
Charlestown, West Virginia 144
Chester Gap 90–91
Childs, Jon: wounded 41
Chowning's Ferry 65
Christiansville, Virginia 131
Clark, Paul 12, **18–19**; promoted to first lieutenant 17; resigned commission 27; service in 10th Indiana Cavalry 263n13
Clements, Reuben: killed 147
Cline, Milton **55–56**, 76, 93, 181; Chief of Scouts 265n62
Cole, Benjamin: wounded 32
Cole, Daniel **55–56**, 57
Colt Army revolver 77
Colt Navy revolver 10, 16, 33, 77
Companies L and M 53, 178; chased Morgan 267n32; explanation of service 262n29
Confederate Hoosiers: captured 8, 38
Confederate troops: Chambliss' Brigade 74; Chew's Battery 37–38, 74–75; Cobb's Legion 40–42, 51, 70; Hampton's Legion 51; Jeff Davis Legion 70; Jones' Brigade 74; Laurel Brigade 151; Perrin's Brigade 83
Congers, William 178
Cotton, Henry 44, 58; promoted to second lieutenant 53
Court martial 52, 103, 105, 161, 180
Craig's Meeting House, Virginia 116
Crampton's Gap 40, 44
Culpeper Courthouse, Virginia 35, 62, 68, 92, 94, 100, 102–103, 106
Culver, George 133
Cunningham, Charles: death in prison 270n24; wounded 135
Custer, George A. 64–66, 70, 72–73, 105, 114, 120, 151–**152**,

153–161, 164–165, 168–173, 175–179

Dahlgren, Ulric 107, 111; controversy surrounding his death 269n17
Daily, Hezekiah: wounded 96
Daily, Jonathon 9
Daily, Josiah: wounded 89
Dana, Charles A. 141
Danglade, Theophilus 12; organized company 5; resigned commission 17
Darnestown, Maryland 36–37
Davis, Benjamin F. "Grimes" 55, 58, 59, 60, 62; at Brandy Station 68; death of 70
Davis, Dennis 77; wounded 94, 137
Day, Thomas: captured 103; captured by John S. Mosby 269n34; post war visit to Middletown 264n41; wounded 41, 80
Dearborn County, Indiana 5
destroying track 31, 107, 109, 120, 124, 130–131, 159, 165, 171, 175
Devin, Thomas 76, 78, 95–96, 98–99
Dillenhermer, Joseph 178
Double Bridges 133–134, 136
Doubleday, Abner 23
Dragoon: definition of 67, 85
Dragoon Pistol, Model 1842 **10**; see also horse pistol
Dunn, William 9
Dyer, David 16

Early, Jubal 142–147, 149–150, 155, 157–158, 164–167
Eblin, John: discharged 263n18; wounded 38
Elston, Isaiah: wounded 94
Ely's Ford 63, 109, 115
English, Edward: wounded 147
Enos, William: promoted to second lieutenant 142
Evans, Cowan D.: captured Confederate battle flag 147
Evans, Del 160
executions: 3rd New Jersey 161

Fairfax Station, Virginia 25, 101
Falling Waters, Maryland 89
Fallis, David: killed 38
Farnsworth, John 37
Farrell, Joh 137
Farrell, Silas: wounded 124
Faught, Sanford 102; wounded 117
Fayette County, Indiana 5, 7
fighting dismounted 61, 71–75, 81, 83, 88, 96, 99–100, 102, 120, 131–133, 137, 145–146, 148, 158, 165, 170, 176
Fluher, Ernest: wounded 117
foraging 25, 86, 92, 102, 114, 158, 165, 167

Franklin, Henry: wounded 127
Frederick, Maryland 39, 46, 76, 86, 147
Fredericksburg, Virginia 28–30, 32, 35, 50–51, 54, 63–64, 92, 109, 117, 178
Freeman's Ford 59–60
Front Royal, Virginia 25–26, 90, 147–148
Funk, Daniel: wounded 22
Funkstown, Maryland 89

Gaddis, Alfred 123
Gainesville, Virginia 25
Gallager carbine 77, 89, 263n5
Gates, Pete 102
Geary, Jonathan 25–26
George Waters (steamer) 35
Germanna Ford 98, 115
Gettysburg, Pennsylvania 76–79, 82–87, 89, 90, 127, 142, 168, 181–182, 187; monument **183–184**
Gibbon, John 30–32, 35
Gilbert, Benjamin 142, 154, 157, 161, 179; promoted to first lieutenant 105; promoted to second lieutenant 68
Gilbert, Isaac 58, 105
Gilchrist, George M. 58, 180; moved to brigade staff **122**; promoted to second lieutenant 53
Gilpin, Samuel 23, 39, 41, 44–45, 48, 53, 60, 62, 86, 88, 142, 181
Glasscock, John: captured 137
Glauber, Mathew 80–82
Golden, George: wounded 117
Gorman, James: mortally wounded 128
Grand Review 48, 59, 104, 113–114, 162
Grant, Ulysses S. 113–115, 117–118, 123, 125, 129–130, 141–143, 150–151, 155, 158, 163, 165–168, 170, 172, 176–177
Gray, Robert 148
Grebe, Jacob: captured 137
Green, Marmaduke: killed 32
Greiner, Jacob: appointed regimental commissary 48
Gresham, Q.A. 12, 27, 93; appointed captain 58; promoted major and assigned to the Cavalry Bureau 112; resigned commission to accept Lieutenant Colonelcy of 10th Indiana Cavalry 122; wounded 63
Grubb, John: wounded 41
Gwinn, William: wounded 30

Hagerstown, Maryland 45–46, 83, 88
Halbert, John: wounded 137
Hall, Joseph: wounded 90
Hall, Samuel: wounded 102
Hampton, Wade 110–111, 129, 132–133, 136–137

Index

Hardman, Asa 181
Hardy, William 65; post war visit from George Middleton 266n39
Harpers Ferry, West Virginia 47, 49, 144, 149
Haskell, David 75
Hatch, John 32
Hayes, Henry: killed 111
Heath, Martin: death of 268n46; wounded 94
Heath, Samuel 53
Higgins, Isaac 60; wounded 110–111
Hinds, James: wounded 41
Hines, William: wounded 128
Hoagland, Jack 17
Hollenbeck, Cornelius: captured 102
Hollins, Ed: wounded 139
Holmes, Welborn: wounded 137
Holmes, William: captured Confederate battle flag 174
Home guard 22, 32, 79–80
Hooker, Joseph 11, 13, 15–18, 20–22, **54–55**, 59–60, 63, 67–68, 72; replaced by Meade 77
Horse Marines 17, 66, 125–126
horse pistol 10, **19**; *see also* Dragoon Pistol
horses: condition of 36, 46–47, 50, 61–64, 76, 86, 88, 90–92, 101, 110, 112, 114, 121, 129, 131, 134, 139, 160, 162, 167–168; expense of cavalry 3; requisitioning of 91, 93, 131, 135, 150, 166; trading and selling of 16, 93; training and care for 10, 19, 29
Hyden, William: wounded 75

Illinois Troops: 8th Illinois Cavalry 37–40, 42, 46–47, 55, 64–65, 68, 70–73, 81, 83, 102, 105; 12th Illinois Cavalry 73, 77–78, 83–84
Indiana troops: 1st Indiana Cavalry 7, 11, 261n35; 8th Indiana Cavalry 178–179; explanation of regiment numbering 261n38; 20th Indiana Infantry 9; 27th Indiana Infantry 39; 45th Indiana Volunteers 12
Indianapolis, Indiana 7, 28, 56, 143, 180–182; mustered out 179
Irby, John **55**, 181–**182**; service in Bureau of Military Information 268n35; wounded 92
Irwin, James D.: formed a company 5, 12; resigned commission 27

Jack's Shop, Virginia 95–97, 99, 142
Jackson, Francis: captured 137
Jackson, Thomas "Stonewall" 23, 26
Jefferson County, Indiana 28, 32

Jenkins, Benjamin F.: killed 71
Johnson, Charles: wounded 75–76
Jones, Joseph: wounded 41
Jones, Robert K. (Universalist preacher) 9
Jordan, Absalom: captured Confederate battle flag 174
Jordan, James 181; wounded 102
Jounker, Bowman: wounded 94

Kassebaum, Frederick: discharged 263n18; wounded 38
Kautz, August 129, 131, 133, 137, 139
Keegler, Harvey: killed 128
Keister, Daniel: raised a company 5, 12; resigned commission 27
Keith, John: wounded 96, 120, 123
Kelly's Ford 62, 68, 70, 90, 92, 94, 99
Kelsey, James L. 58; commissioned second lieutenant 53
Kelso, Ed 21; captured 31
Kennedy, Walter: death of 267n17; wounded 89
Kennedy, William: drowned in *Sultana* sinking 178; wounded 38, 94
Kilpatrick, Judson 29, 89–90, 94–96, 99–100, 106–107, 109, **110**–111, 118, 120–121
Kincaid, John: wounded 32
King, Rufus 28, 35
King George's Courthouse, Virginia 51
Kirkpatrick, William: wounded 71
Klein, Robert 55; lieutenant colonel and commander of the West Wing 123, 265n1
Klussman, Louis: wounded 96
Knight, James H. 53, 58

Lahue, Marshall 58; wounded 71
Lamb, Samuel: death of 267n27; mortally wounded 84
Lamson, Rudolph: wounded 38
Lamson, Thomas: promoted to second lieutenant 105
Land, Bennett: wounded 128
Lee, Charles W. 142, 154, 161, 179; assigned as division provost marshal 145; promoted to captain 68; promoted to second lieutenant 15; wounded 44
Lee, Fitzhugh 168–170
Lee, George: wounded 145
Lee, Stephen C.: captured 31
Leffler, Fred: wounded 96
Lemmon, Charles 30, 35, 70, 77, **79–**80; mortally wounded 84; name explanation 261n37; promoted to captain 17; promoted to major 58

Leonardtown, Maryland 13
Lewis, Isaac: wounded 94
Lewis, Joseph: killed 41
Liberty Mills, Virginia 94–96
Little, George: wounded 120
Little, Thomas: wounded 41
Little Wicomico River 65
Livings, Francis: captured 102
Loder, Benjamin: captured 30; killed 96
Lomax, Lunsford 154
Long, James: wounded 99
Loudon Valley 72
Love, Phillip: killed 100
Luray, Virginia 26, 147–148
Lynchburg Railroad 175

Madison, Indiana 5, 7, 8, 28, 58, 77, 179–185; monument at **185–186**
Madison Courthouse, Virginia 94–95, 98, 105–106
Manassas Junction, Virginia 25–26, 72, 178
Manhattan (steamer) 64
Marshall, Robert: wounded 96
Martin, Ephraim 77; commissioned second lieutenant 17; promoted to captain 58; promoted to first lieutenant 27; wounded 81
Martin, Keith: wounded 123
Martinsburg, West Virginia 45, 144
Mason, Matthew 12, 27, 48
Massachusetts troops: 1st Massachusetts Cavalry 39
Mathews, Joseph 131, 139
McClellan, George B. 4, 13, 20, 37–39, 44–45; petition to 22–23; replaced as commander 50
McClure, David 48
McClure, William 12, 31, 49, 56, 58, 68, 77, 79, 93–95, 97, 180; Brandy Station and brigade command 70–**71**; promoted to major 53; raised a company 5; reason for resignation as colonel of 9th Indiana Cavalry 268n4; resigned commission to accept colonelcy of 9th Indiana Cavalry 112
McConnell, James: captured 32; wounded 99
McDowell, Irwin 3
McFarland, William: death of 269n29; wounded 102
McGregor, Thomas B.: captured Confederate from Indiana 8
McIntosh, J.B. 141
McNeal, David: died of illness 23
Meade, George 55, 89, 92, 97–98, 100–101, 113, 115, 118, 120, 129; endorsement of Milton Cline for a commission 93–94; promoted to command of the Army of the Potomac 77–78; recommendation of George

Chapman to brigadier general 141
Mechanicstown, Maryland 46
Medal of Honor 180
Melton, George: wounded 127
Merritt, Wesley 103
Meuser, Robert: wounded 96
Michigan troops: Michigan Brigade 112, 114, 120, 151; 2nd Michigan Cavalry 113; 7th Michigan Cavalry 111
Middleburg, Virginia 72–73, 79
Middleton, George 182, **184**; monument plaque **186**; post war visit with William Hardy 266n39
Middletown, Maryland 40, 42, 51, 87, 89, 142
Middletown, Virginia 157
Middletown Valley 40, 43
Milford, Virginia 148; now known as Overall 271n43
Millburn, Joseph B. 20
Miller, Benjamin 22
Miller, James S.: wounded 19
Miller, Matthias: wounded 75
Millstone Landing, Maryland 13, 18
Millville, Virginia 73
Minnot, Francis: wounded 102
Moffitt, Thomas 12, 27, 58, 136, 139; captured 30–33; promoted to captain 35; wounded 137
Monfort, William: wounded 9
Monroe, Alexander: wounded 128
Morton, Oliver P. 5, 9, 11, **15**, 19–20, 22, 27, 31, 35, 53, 93, 104–105, 141, 145
Morton's Ford 98
Mosby, John S. 144–145, 163, 180; capture of Thomas Day 269n34
Mount, James: wounded 41
mounted charges by regiment 32, 37, 75, 99, 156, 159, 169, 172–173
Moxley, Francis: wounded 124
Mulvaney, Pleasant 106
Myers, Eugene 142

Nathaniel, Daniel: wounded 117
Nelson, George: wounded 127
New Hampshire troops: 1st New Hampshire Cavalry 127
New Kent Courthouse, Virginia 111
New York Troops: 2nd New York Cavalry (Harris Light Cavalry) 29, 124, 127; 5th New York Cavalry 109; 8th New York Cavalry 46–47, 50, 52, 55, 60, 68, 70, 73, 83, 105. 114, 127, 172; 9th New York Cavalry 70; 22nd New York Cavalry 125–126
Nichols, Guy 17
Nichols, John 186; wounded 120, 123
Noble, Lazarus 27, 33, 35, 48, 56, 112

Nolan, Patrick: captured 30
Nolan's Ferry, Maryland 36–37, 39, 46–47
Norfolk Railroad 167
Norman, Jim: drowned in *Sultana* sinking 178; wounded 41
Norris, William 20
North Anna River 29, 62, 109, 167
North Carolina Troops: 1st North Carolina Cavalry 39, 42, 70; 2nd North Carolina Cavalry 74–75, 110
Northern Neck 64–66, 72, 151, 184
Nottoway Courthouse, Virginia 130, 177

Ohio County, Indiana 5
"Old Bob" 182
Oldham, William 52
Orange and Alexandria Railroad 62, 92, 101
Orange Courthouse, Virginia 30

Page, Eugene: wounded 71
Papst, Henry 110; wounded 41
Park, William: wounded 81
Patton, John 58
Patton, William 11–12, 21, 23, 37, 53, 58, 64, 70, 77, 93, 102, 107, 109–110, 114–**115**, 123–125, 132, 136, 138, 180; promoted to captain 15; promoted to major 68; took command of the regiment 112
Peelman, Christopher: wounded 101
Pennsylvania Troops: 8th Pennsylvania Cavalry 46–47, 50
Perrin, William: wounded 103
Peters, William: wounded 75
Petersville, Maryland 47, 90
Philomont, Virginia 49
picket duty 35, 50–52, 63, 92–93, 102, 104–105, 112, 139
Pinkerton, Allen 13, 16
Pittsburgh, Pennsylvania 8–9, 143, 179
Pleasanton, Alfred **36**, 53, 59, 66–67, 71, 113
Plew, Daniel **55**
Point Lookout, Maryland 13
Pollock, Alexander: wounded 99
pontoons 89–90, 92, 100, 115. 125–**126**, 128
Poolesville, Maryland 36–39
Port Conway, Virginia 51
Port Republic, Virginia 26
Port Tobacco, Maryland 13, 64
Porter, G.A.: wounded 94
Porter, George: death of 270n40; wounded 117
Porter, Robert P. 12, 20–21, 31, 58, 68, 102; court martialed and dismissed from service 103; promoted to first lieutenant 15

Potomac River 13, 16, 20–22, 24, 36, 45–47, 64–65, 76, 86–90, 112, 143, 145
Powers, Oliver M. 12; captain of Company L 53; explanation of resignation and wartime experience 263n16; resigned commission 27, 30–31
Purcell, Thomas: wounded 121
Purcellville, Virginia 49

Quinn, James: death of 264n43; wounded 29, 40–41

Rapidan River 62–63, 94–96, 98–99, 102, 104, 109, 115–116
Rappahannock River 28–29, 51, 59–60, 62–65, 68, 92–94, 98–102, 115–116
Rea, William 81–82
Ream's Station, Virginia 132–133, 135, 137, 139, 142, 154
Rectorville, Virginia 73
Red scarves 169
Redmond, R. Jackson 20
Reed, James 99
Reed, J.R. 22
re-enlistment 97, 104; *see also* veteranize
Reeve, Harry: wounded 100
Reid, Edward C. 80
Reynolds, Owen: wounded 101, 122
Richmond and Danville Railroad 129, 131
Richmond and Potomac Railroad 29
Robbins, Charles 102
Rogers, George: commissioned second lieutenant 105, 162
Romine, Isaac 157, 169
Rosser, Thomas 151–154, 159

Salem, Virginia 26
Sauvine, John 52
Savage pistol 10, **19**
Schievelbein, Ed: wounded 41
Schroeder, John: discharged 267n26; wounded 91
Scott, Winfield 7
Seever, Smyrna: death of 264n43; mortally wounded 41–42
serenading 82, 87
Shannon, Abner 12, 53, 58, 65, 91, 123, 139; captured 60–**61**, 137; wounded 132
Sharp, Will 9
Sharps carbine 77, 104, 124, 127
Shenandoah Valley 23, 25–26, 68, 72, 90, 125, 129, 141, 143–144, 147, 150, 163
Shepard, Samuel: captured 31
Shepard, William: captured 31; captured Confederate battle flag 174
Sheperdstown, West Virginia 45
Sheridan, Philip **113**–115, 118,

Index

120, 122, 125, 129, 139, 143–148, 150–158, 160, 162, 164–175, 177
Shields, James 26
shortage of officers 27, 31, 33, 77, 105, 139, 179
Shutts, Isaac: killed 103
Sickles, Daniel 11, 20
Siebenthal, Andrew: captured 167
Smelley, Thomas: death of 268n22; wounded 101
Smith, Jesse: killed 81–82, 84
Smith, Johnny 42
Smith carbine 77, 89
Snicker's Gap 49, 72, 145
South Anna River 109, 120, 124, 166, 178
South Carolina troops: 1st South Carolina Cavalry 70; 12th South Carolina Infantry 83; 13th South Carolina Infantry 83
South Mountain 40, 43–44, 87
Southside Railroad 129–130, 168, 171
Sparks, Henry 78; captured 105
Spencer, John D. R. 77, 124; promoted to captain 58; promoted to first lieutenant 53; promoted second lieutenant 27
Spencer carbine 124, 143–144, 169
Spotsylvania Courthouse, Virginia 117–118
Stafford Courthouse, Virginia 64
Staples, William: captured 137
Stapp, Willis H. "Ham" 17; captured 60; wounded 102
Stevens, William: wounded 38
Stevensburg, Virginia 94, 98–99, 107, 110
Stevenson, Hugh: captured 31–32; wounded 127
Stoneman, George 54–55, 60–63, 67
Stuart, J.E.B. 68, 72, 79, 94–96, 100, 118; death of 120
Sturman, James: wounded 33
Sugar Loaf Mountain 38–39
Suits, Emsley: wounded 91
Swift, George: captured 30
Switzerland County, Indiana 5

Tallaca (steamer) 64
Taylor, Gamaliel: appointed adjutant 53, 58; moved to brigade headquarters 122, 133; wounded 71

Terrell, Robert: captured 157
Thompson, George H. 12, 58, 64–66, 84, 95, 139; promoted captain 53; promoted major 123; temporary adjutant 27
Tilford, Solon 181; wounded 71
Tinker, Ira B. 58, 105
tobacco 50–51, 150
Torbert, Alfred 148, 151, 153
torpedoes 121
Trester, Oliver: killed 40
Trigg, Oscar 17; captured 137; wounded 132
Tufts, Louis: death of 267n21; goes insane 82, 84
Tunstall Station, Virginia 111
Turner's Gap 42

Umphries, George: wounded 135
Unison, Virginia 49
United States troops: Calef's Battery 78, 81, 83; Excelsior Brigade 20; Iron Brigade 44, 81–83; Pennington's Battery 46; 2nd U.S. Artillery 37; 2nd U.S. Sharpshooters Regiment 30; 6th U.S. Cavalry 47; Williston's Battery 98
Upperville, Virginia 25, 73, 76, 79
Urbanna, Virginia 64–65

Vails, William: wounded 145
Vanosdol, Alexander: wounded 102
Vanosdol, Christopher: death in prison 270n24; wounded 135
Verdiersville, Virginia 95
Vermont troops: 1st Vermont Cavalry 114, 127
veteranized 142, 181; *see also* re-enlistment
Vevay, Indiana 5, 8, 17, 179–180, 182
Vibbert, Isaac: killed 84
Victory of Baltimore (sloop): capture of 17
Virginia Central Railroad 31, 107, 109, 124, 129, 163
Virginia troops: 4th Virginia Cavalry 105; 6th Virginia Cavalry 75; 7th Virginia Cavalry 37, 70; 9th Virginia Cavalry 60; 10th Virginia Cavalry 74–75; 11th Virginia Cavalry 75; 12th Virginia Cavalry 37, 73, 75; 26th Virginia Infantry 174; 27th Virginia Infantry 174

Walk, A.J. 137
Walters, John: wounded 71
Warrenton, Virginia 26, 50, 101
Watlington, William 102, 114, 123, 148–**149**, 158, 160
Weaver, Augustus: captured 137
Weaver, John: death of 267n26; wounded 83
Weible, John: wounded 41
Welch, Peter: wounded 41
Wells, William 146, 153
White, Charles N. 28, 32
White House Landing, Virginia 111, 167
White's Ford 46
Wildman, John 84, 93; wounded 41
Williams, John: wounded 49
Williamsburg, Virginia 111
Williamson, Harvey: wounded 41–42
Williamsport, Maryland 46, 87–88, 144
Willman, Henry: wounded 101
Wilson, James 114–116, 125, 130–131, 133–**134**, 136–137, 143–147, 149, 151–152
Wilson, Lewis C. 58, 181; captured 30; promoted to first lieutenant 53
Winchell, William: died 16
Winchester, Virginia 25–26, 143–147, 150, 155–156, 158–159, 162–163, 167
Winchester and Harpers Ferry Railroad 144
Wiseman, John: wounded 127
Wood, Fletcher: discharged 263n18; wounded 38
Workman, Benjamin 22; wounded 38
Wright, Augustus: killed 83–84
Wright, Henry 12, 48, 52; death of 265n67; promoted to captain 53; promoted to first lieutenant 28; resigned commission 56; service in 7th Indiana Cavalry 265n67
Wright, James M. died 10
Wright, Milton 142, 145

Yorktown, Virginia 111
Young, John: wounded 137

www.ingramcontent.com/pod-product-compliance
Lightning Source LLC
Chambersburg PA
CBHW060337010526
44117CB00017B/2862